D1391752

THE DISADVANTAGED: CHALLENGE TO EDUCATION

Exploration Series in Education

Under the Advisory Editorship
of John Guy Fowlkes

Leipzig, Ford Foundation

WHO AM I?

MARIO D. FANTINI
The Ford Foundation

GERALD WEINSTEIN
Teachers College
Columbia University

THE DISADVANTAGED

CHALLENGE TO EDUCATION

HARPER & ROW, PUBLISHERS
New York, Evanston, and London

THE DISADVANTAGED: CHALLENGE TO EDUCATION

Library of Congress Catalog Card Number: 68–11131

CONTENTS

FOREWORD

No administrator, no teacher, no school-board member in the United States will be able to ignore this book. For Fantini and Weinstein have not only written the most important book on the disadvantaged child, but they have perhaps also written one of the most significant books about the education of all children.

Although the book represents an important new phase in the education of the disadvantaged, the authors' major thesis is that, through understanding the problems of the educationally deprived, we may come to an understanding of the educational problems confronting *all* children in America—because the problems of the disadvantaged sections of our population represent the problems of all Americans, only in more magnified fashion.

Conant, Deutsch, Sexton, and others opened the doors to the educationally disadvantaged by pointing to the problems of the "slum child." Fantini and Weinstein ably present these problems as a challenge to educators, but they also offer ways out with highly specific suggestions and strategies. Their book does not simply present analysis and diagnosis—although it does present both very well—it also offers treatment, recommendations, and the beginnings of a new science of pedagogy. It unites policy with technology, cognition with emotion, strategy with tactics.

John Dewey's functional curriculum has been brought up to date by the authors, as they propose that the curriculum move from the remote to the immediate, from the academic to the participatory, from the what to the why, and from the antiseptic to the real. The book also develops many new concepts which are already beginning to take root throughout the land. The Contact Curriculum, the Clinical Professor, Teacher Planning, the Career Oriented Educational Process, Change Agent Teaming, the Hidden Curriculum—these are just a few among the many emerging concepts explored. No one will be able to question that the authors have been there—in the classroom, in the school, in the community, on the firing line, and in the foundations—for these are concepts that the authors themselves have applied, Weinstein in using the hip language as a contacter of pupils; both authors in utilizing specific strategies of change that are carefully discussed in the case study presented in Chapter 8.

Fantini and Weinstein also raise serious questions about many of the shibboleths of modern education. A powerful critique of the compensatory theory is offered in Chapter 6 and an alternative approach is outlined. Chapter 9 raises questions concerning whether the most effective teacher for the disadvantaged is necessarily the more experienced teacher. The authors are not afraid to talk about power in the schools and how power can be reorganized to produce change consonant with the needs of our times and the needs of our children. Chapter 8 is especially valuable in illustrating the role of the administrative change agent and the instructional change agent in the school system, in a highly imaginative, double-teaming approach.

There are points on which to disagree. The authors appear to believe that the parent is the key agent of extraschool experience for the disadvantaged child. One might suggest that the sibling and the peer are perhaps more significant extraschool teaching agents for this child. Further, the phrase "phoney school" rings badly to these ears, and there is a bit too much concern with the development of "atmospheres" and process. The authors' recommendations might be well developed in our schools without the necessary accountability in terms of the actual improvement in learning of the children. The latter must be the ultimate aim, and the community must be constantly assisted to demand it. This learning, of course, cannot simply be measured by grades and achievement scores. New indices are required which relate to learning-how-to-learn and to understanding concepts and structure. A school system which makes pupils, parents, teachers, and administrators happy will not be sufficient unless a higher order of learning actually takes place.

Finally, although the science of education which begins to emerge from the book is heavily built upon the significance of contacting the student and relating his interests and style to the subject matter at hand, more attention is needed to stages of learning which go beyond contact. While the book points to some of these, it does not elaborate in as much detail beyond the contact stage.

But these are relatively minor criticisms in a book that should revolutionize education in America by revolutionizing it for the poor. It is only through the application and implementation of the authors' methods that we will be able to produce a genuine leap in the education of the poor so that they will not simply come up to old, disappearing grade levels, but will genuinely become equal partners in American society. This requires a moonshot in education, not a compensatory approach. The book is the leader of this "leap" phase and it is because of this that it may become a classic in American education.

FRANK RIESSMAN

Professor of Educational Sociology
New York University

INTRODUCTION

This is a book about the disadvantaged which goes far beyond the population envisaged in Title I of the Elementary and Secondary Education Act. For Fantini and Weinstein, the "disadvantaged" includes most of the population found in our elementary and secondary schools today. In fact, any child or youth for whom the curriculum is out-dated, inadequate, or irrelevant can be included in this category. Thus, while the authors think first of the impoverished and the racial or ethnic minorities, they worry too about the middle-class suburbanites who are leaving schools unknowingly shortchanged in terms of the values, attitudes, and commitments which are necessary in today's society. For this widened "target population" and its environment, Fantini and Weinstein present a view of what education should do and be for today's children and youth.

The authors have given a name to the vast and complex set of learnings which the child acquires before he enters the formal classroom: "the hidden curriculum." As a significant aspect of what and how the child learns, the hidden curriculum sets a foundation for the learner's progress in the organized school setting. Here the parent—consciously or unconsciously—provides both cognitive and affective content which current research respects as being influential in further learning.

Against this hidden curriculum, the authors present a criticism of the "Phoney School" curriculum, the unreal or artificial formal curriculum which may fall into one or more of four categories.

These are: antiseptic, semiantiseptic, nonessential, and remote. The authors are critical of what we are presenting not only to the inner-city slum child, but also to his middle-class peer, who is more ready to play the education game according to the rules. The sharp discrepancies between our stated purposes and the products of our schools call for processes and programs which diverge clearly from those presently available.

It is to these changes that the authors address themselves, skillfully blending research findings with theoretical considerations and practical designs and proposals. Their focus is upon a "relevant curriculum," which they describe fully and with enough illustration to be persuasive. When they couple such a design with suggested strategies for achieving change, the consequence is an important proposal which merits thoughtful reading on the part of educators and others who are concerned with adequate education for all. The relevant curriculum is a highly personalized and individualized curriculum. Its strategies for content selection and classroom methods call for individual pupil diagnosis and for building on the strengths of the individual child. If followed, it would put us a long way forward in meeting the needs of individual children.

Finally, Fantini and Weinstein have acted on the axiom that our concern with the disadvantaged could transform the quality of education being provided all learners. Both of these authors have spent a good deal of time on the firing line; they are obviously at home in a classroom and working with disadvantaged children. Their proposals in this book center on the disadvantaged but they are equally relevant to educators of all children. Hopefully, the readers will interact with these ideas in the broad framework intended.

A. Harry Passow

Professor of Education
Chairman, Committee on Urban Education
Teachers College
Columbia University

PREFACE

Although many books have been and will continue to be written on the education of the disadvantaged poor, the present authors have felt the sore lack of one which presented the problems connected with these groups within the larger context of the educational establishment as a whole. Most writings to date have treated the disadvantaged poor in our population as though they comprised an isolated educational problem, one that is disconnected from the standard educational approaches for its solution. In our opinion, such a limited attitude is not only ineffective in achieving its expressed aims, but also harmful to education generally and to the whole society served by education.

It is our opinion that the so-called "disadvantaged" segments of our society do not represent a unique and specialized problem in American education, but rather, that they reflect a far more pervasive problem which inheres in the standard educational process itself. In other words, our standard system of educating children is inadequate for *all* children, and its obvious failures with the poor are actually the symptoms of a much more sweeping, if less obvious, fault.

By regarding the education of the lower socioeconomic groups in the light of the total educational process, we may come to see this larger problem, and perhaps, too, some of the ways in which it can be met for the more successful education of all the nation's children. Accordingly, throughout the present book, the disadvantaged poor serve as the focus for reeaxamining and re-evaluating traditional modes of education, and for creating the beginnings of a new revitalized, and more nearly adequate process.

This book, then, is written for anyone who is involved with education, be he teacher, school administrator, project director, teacher trainer, or parent; and for anyone else who is in any way interested in education in our public schools.

In structuring the book, the authors have attempted to present a balance between diagnosis and prescription, between theory and practice, between abstractness and concreteness. In the first half of the book, the current educational processes and their problems are described, analyzed, and diagnosed with respect to the cultural norms of several disadvantaged subcultures, including our mainstream, middle-class disadvantaged; the current educational process is also reexamined with respect to the purposes for which it exists and the products it actually delivers to society. The second half of the book is devoted primarily to treatment; that is, to ways in which we might more efficiently meet current educational problems and to suggested alterations in accustomed procedures which can reshape American education into a more efficient, more effective, and self-renewing institution.

To present our thesis meaningfully was no easy task; to put it briefly, it is quite futile to deal with any one area of the educational establishment without dealing also with the many other areas with which it must interact. Thus, to accomplish our aims in this book, it became necessary to diagnose and prescribe—to some extent, at least—for all of the many areas and decision-making levels in the multifaceted educational establishment: the teacher-training institution, the Federal and state governments, the local school board, the superintendent and central office, and so forth.

Because of the enormity and complexity of this task, some limits had to be established, and we realize that, in keeping ourselves within these limits, we skimmed many aspects related to educating the disadvantaged, as well as many aspects connected with educational reform on a broad scale. For example, we only started to touch the important questions of desegregation and integration, and we have dealt only briefly with decentralization of schools, community involvement, and other important topics. Also, we have not described in sufficient detail a model school system as it might be streamlined to deal with human diversity most efficiently. The reader will, no doubt, be critical of many other omissions. We are acutely aware of such problems, but to have dealt with these areas in any depth would have led us into a second volume. Indeed, had it not been for the insistence of our publishers, we might still be writing this book.

That the book was written at all is due in large measure to the many people who have encouraged and inspired us. We are indebted to all the teachers, administrators, students, and university personnel connected with the Madison Area Project and the Urban Teacher Preparation Program in Syracuse, New York for their cooperation and willingness to strike out in new directions, and for the valuable insights with which they provided us. We are particularly grateful to Basil Bernstein, Frank Riessman, and Harry Passow, who not only lent their time and attention throughout the many dialogues that went on between each of them and the present authors, but who also enlarged our prospective by sharing with us their own professional viewpoints. This book also owes much to Marvin Weisbord for his comments and suggestions on the first chapter, and to Marvin Feldman for expanding the notion of career roles in vocational education as described in Chapter 12. The present authors are most appreciative of Frank Bowles, Edward Meade, the Fund for the Advancement of Education, and the Ford Foundation generally for providing us with the flexibility to complete the manuscript, and for their continuing encouragement. Unfortunately, space does not permit specific acknowledgement of the many others on whose ideas much of this book is based, although footnoted references are given wherever appropriate. Special thanks are due to those who helped with the difficult job of preparing the manuscript, however: Diane Bertine for transforming much of our rough notes and endless dialogues into legible copy; Charlene Davis and Virginia La Vaute for their dedicated assistance in typing the manuscript; and Susan Burstein, without whose magnificent effort in every phase of this book's development the manuscript would never have reached the printer. Finally, singular thanks are extended to our wives, who lent neither eye nor ear to the development of this publication, yet whose charm and wit inspired us nevertheless.

MARIO D. FANTINI
GERALD WEINSTEIN

December, 1967
New York, N.Y.

THE DISADVANTAGED: CHALLENGE TO EDUCATION

CHAPTER 1

WHO ARE THE DISADVANTAGED?

Henry Monroe

WHO ARE THE DISADVANTAGED?

Who are the disadvantaged?

Most of us.

This may be difficult to believe, but consider for a minute what *disadvantaged* has come to mean. "The slum child," writes Bernard Asbell in *The New Improved American,*

> . . . is a child of another world, our laws do not bind him, our standard middle-class ambitions do not inspire him. . . . Teachers in first to third grades feel the child slipping away. By the fourth grade he has fallen behind. By the eighth grade he may be as many as three years back, his mind closed, his behavior rebellious. By high school age he is more than likely a dropout, headed for chronic unemployment, disdaining the 'outside' middle-class world that already disdains him, secretly contemptuous of himself, a waste of a human being. A failure.[1]

[1]B. Asbell, *The New Improved American,* New York, McGraw-Hill, 1965, pp. 82–83.

Schlack, Monkmeyer

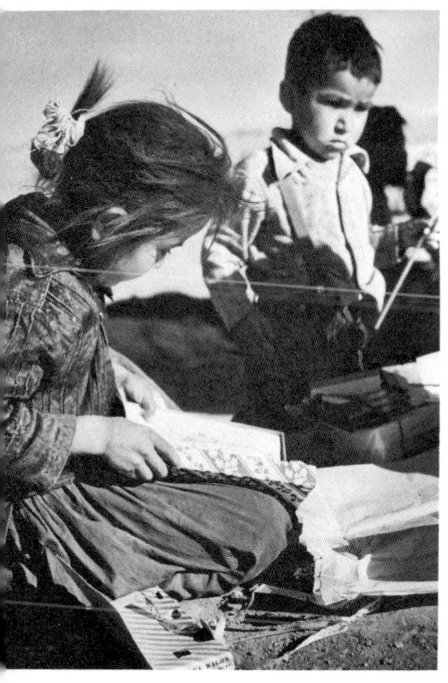

Wunder, Monkmeyer

Russel, Monkmeyer

This is a vivid description of the pupils teachers confront in poor, depressed neighborhoods. But are these the only "disadvantaged" pupils? If they are, then we should be able to call all other children "advantaged," and the reverse of Asbell's comments should be true of them, for, as children of the cultural mainstream, presumably they observe our laws, score well on our IQ tests, and are easily reached by teachers. The general assumption is that these children progress well in the first three grades, move rapidly by the fourth, and, by the eighth, are working at full potential, are clear-thinking, open-minded, and exemplary in behavior. By high school, many are honor students, headed for college, accepting roles in a middle-class world which accepts them. In short, we are accustomed to viewing these people as developed, successful members of society.

But are they? At the very least, the answer to this question must take into account the disturbing incidence of juvenile crime among the middle and upper classes, the numbers of mainstream-oriented dropouts from the educational process at the high-school and college levels, the extent of bigotry and dogmatism that exists among our so-called "advantaged" segments of society, and a host of other factors. But, in addition, answering this question properly requires a fresh examination of the very standards by which we evaluate "advantage" and "disadvantage."

The tendency to consider middle-class values as positive and lower-class values as negative suggests that, if the poor could only become middle class, they would no longer be deprived. But we are talking about more than poverty and low social status—the usual criteria for "disadvantaged" and mainly an economic definition. The meaning of *disadvantaged* must be broadened to include all those who are blocked in any way from fulfilling their human potential. This blocking can take place anywhere: in a slum, or in an affluent suburb where children also may be neglected, overprotected, ruled by iron-handed parents, or guided by no rules at all. Middle-class children may be compelled to study what does not interest them or allowed to forego true learning in favor of achieving marks.

The schools have failed the middle-class child as they have

the child from low-income families. The affluent child, who comes to school prepared to succeed in a mediocre, outdated educational process is also being shortchanged, and thus too, is disadvantaged. Simply because he does his homework, gets passing grades, and eventually graduates is not necessarily a sign of advantage. Although this book concerns mainly the poor, we intend to show that their problems no more than reflect the specter which stalks the affluent suburb, too. Disadvantage is a matter of degree. The poor suffer so greatly because they are on the bottom rung of an educational ladder which, even at the very top, is inadequate.

Thus, the answer to the question Who are the disadvantaged? is more complicated than it seems. The disadvantaged cannot be defined by race, residence, jobs, or behavior alone. Although we tend to think first of such districts as Harlem, the disadvantaged are to be found also in small towns, in the rural slums of backwoods Appalachia, in the Spanish barrios of El Paso, on American Indian reservations—or on the fashionable streets of Scarsdale. They are black, white, red, and yellow; with or without parents; hungry or overfed; they are the children of the jobless, the migrant workers, or the employed. The only thing they have in common is that all are left out of a process which purports to carry all humankind, regardless of background, towards the same basic goals: physical comfort and survival, and feelings of potency, self-worth, connection with others, and concern for the common good. *Anyone* deprived of the means to reach any of these human goals is disadvantaged, for it is the purpose of our democratic social institutions to advance the development of these human goals for *all* people. Failure in human goal attainment is therefore a reflection of institutional failure and, until our social institutions in general, and the schools in particular, are equipped to satisfy these goals, full human development is thwarted. Until then we are all disadvantaged. Our focus will, of necessity, be on the most obvious institutional casualties, but the implications for all should be recognized.

The tendency to view the disadvantaged as just that segment of the population at the negative extremity of the social continuum is illustrated in the very labels employed by professionals. Riessman explains also that the terms *culturally deprived, educationally deprived, deprived, underprivileged, disadvantaged, lower class,* and *lower socioeconomic group* are synonymous.[2] There are others: *culturally different, working class, slum culture, inner-city dwellers, culturally impoverished, experientially deprived, culturally handicapped, educationally disadvantaged, children of the poor, poverts,* and many more.

It is not surprising, then, that cartoons such as that shown in Fig. 1.1 have appeared in the daily newspapers. This cartoon is more ironic than humorous, since it suggests a rather serious indictment of intervention programs with low-income individuals.

If a child is poor and also a Negro, Puerto Rican, Mexican, or Indian, the barrier of culture to self-worth and dignity is very high. Yet these groups, far from being "culturally deprived," may have rich and complex cultures of their own—which only serve to set them further apart from middle-class American life. "Along with the customs and traditions," writes Frank Riessman, "culture consists of the institutions, the structures, and the methods of organization of the people involved."[3] Culture is neither good nor bad, and, as Riessman points out, the slum church, trade union, fraternal lodge, large family, and local club or gang are each a part of some culture.

When one subculture—which includes a certain structure of clubs, schools, and churches—becomes dominant, it sets the standards for everybody. Then the word *culture* takes on a positive connotation—as long as it refers to the dominant structure. Even the schools tend to see things this way, and members of cultural minorities tend to become *the* disadvantaged, instead of only the disadvantaged poor. Consequently, they tend to be blocked from participating in the dominant culture, and as members of minority groups, their feelings of disconnectedness—of being out of it—are reinforced in the school, which is a reflector of society.

[2]F. Riessman, *The Culturally Deprived Child,* New York, Harper & Row, 1962, p. 6.
[3]*Ibid.,* p. 1.

Fig. 1.1. Recent attention to the so-called "disadvantaged" has fallen far short of its purpose, as Feiffer so cogently points out. (© 1965 JULES FEIFFER. Permission granted by The Hall Syndicate, Inc.)

The tendency to view the dominant culture as positive and the lower class as negative hypothesizes that, by transforming the latter into the former, the whole problem of the disadvantaged will disappear. The implications of this notion can be dramatized by reversing the roles: Suppose that members of the mainstream culture (now considered to be "advantaged" were forced to adjust to the norms, values, and environmental conditions of the subculture we now label "disadvantaged." Prepared by background and training in middle-class standards, they would find themselves ill-equipped for survival and success in such a society, and a good many of the current labels now glibly tossed at the lower classes would be painfully applicable. As McKendall says so well: "Cultural disadvantage is an all-purpose phrase, and a somewhat self-conscious one. It refers of course to the variety of social, economic, and ethnic-interracial factors which impede full freedom of choice and which destroy an individual's right to maximum opportunity."[4]

[4]B. McKendall Jr., "Breaking the Barriers of Cultural Disadvantage and Curriculum Imbalance," *Phi Delta Kappan*, **46**:5 (1965), 307.

To limit definitions of the disadvantaged to low socioeconomic groups is to ignore another major aspect of the problem. If the various concerns associated with the disadvantaged pose threats to the good of society as a whole, they must be dealt with in terms of society as a whole. As Miller says:

> A way of classifying a population is a way of thinking about them. A frequent practice is to classify that large number of people who are members of households where the breadwinner is not involved in some kind of white collar (i.e., middle class) occupation as "lower class." This category is then considered to have high homogeneity and is treated as though it constituted a group with great centrality of attitudinal and behavioral patterns.[5]

Thus, traditional definitions, dichotomizing the nation into the middle-class and lower-class or "disadvantaged" groups frequently serve to encourage the dominant middle-class culture to view the subcultures and their problems as things apart from, and irrelevant to, its own existence. Such a view invites stereotyping, and, at best, reinforces a segregated rather than an integrated view of society—even among those who would engage themselves in corrective efforts. Clearly, the ultimate consequences of this view could seriously obstruct sustained inquiry into the very problems we seek to remedy.

Of course, there are the extreme disadvantaged, whose poverty and socially discriminated position severely limit their human potential. If the American society is to deal effectively with these problems, it must start here, and as educators the present authors must start here. But, if we must focus on the extreme needs, we must also bear in mind that this is just a beginning. There are significant segments of the population that lie both without and within most current definitions of the disadvantaged and which are not adequately described by them. Moreover, there are a host of causative factors—and, perhaps even more important, a host of potentially corrective resources—which such des-

[5]S. M. Miller, "The American Lower Class: A Typological Approach," *Social Research*, 31:1, 1964, 2.

scriptions tend to obscure. As Miller has warned, sweeping descriptive generalizations are unsuitable for effective intervention.[6] The more specifically we can define differences, the greater the likelihood there is of introducing ameliorative measures.

An expanded concept of the disadvantaged

The terms *cultural* and *experiential* are frequently used to modify the descriptive labels we apply to the disadvantaged. Riessman raises the question "culturally deprived or educationally deprived?"[7] By "educationally" Riessman is referring, of course, to the formal process through which we send our children, for the culture to which a child is exposed also provides him with an education, and with experiences. Every child learns his culture; if he happens to belong to a subculture, this is what he learns, that is what he experiences. Any child's experiences are many and varied, but they are not necessarily those experiences which the formal educational process recognizes, or which are valued by the dominant culture. In fact, many experiences of even an "advantaged" child would be considered inappropriate —perhaps shocking—by the mainstream society. One should bear in mind that disadvantaged children do have experiences, and that these experiences arise from a very real culture, though they may be of quite a different order than those respected and valued by the dominant society and its formal educational structure. It should be noted that the very notions of cultural and experiential deprivation have arisen from our conventional educational process, and, today in education, it has become almost fashionable to look at the problem of educating the disadvantaged as a problem quite apart from the education of children generally. Indeed, many disadvantaged children can be considered culturally or experientially "deprived" only by the standards set by this dominant society.

Sometimes experience itself can be severely restricted, how-

[6] *Ibid.*, p. 3.
[7] F. Riessman, *op. cit.*, p. 3.

ever, as it is with some hard-core cases. Such deprivation can have significant psychological consequences to personality development and intellectual ability. In summarizing the research and theory available on this subject, Hunt establishes the importance of preverbal experience to later cognitive (intellectual) development:

> First of all, cultural deprivation may be seen as a failure to provide an opportunity for infants and young children to have the experience required for adequate development of those semi-autonomous central processes demanded for acquiring skill in the use of linguistic and mathematical symbols and for the analysis of causal relationships.
>
> One can readily conceive the function of early experience to be one of "programming" these intrinsic portions of the cerebrum so that they can later function effectively in learning and problem solving.[8]

Although some studies have pointed to a tentative relationship among low social status, early experiential deprivation, and inadequate cognitive development, there are too many factors at work to conclude definitely that low socioeconomic status itself deprives the child of experience, or that it provides for inadequate intellectual growth. Failure to provide the newly born or infant child with proper sensory stimulation, for example, can have serious results on later cognitive functioning under any socioeconomic conditions, and such failure occurs also in prosperous middle-class families. But the problem is much more visible with the lower classes, as the very prosperity which surrounds the middle class tends to camouflage the nature, extent, and severity of such preverbal deprivation. Thus, only certain lower-class children, who may not have received the proper "programing" during their early formative years, become a part of what the school calls "culturally deprived."

Inadequate preparation for school—whether it arises from "inappropriate" experience or from actual deprivation of experience

[8]J. M. Hunt, "The Psychological Basis for Using Pre-School Enrichment as an Antidote for Cultural Deprivation," *Merrill-Palmer Quarterly of Behavior and Development*, **10**:3, 1964, 236.

—often results in traits that are labeled by educators as "verbally restricted," "antiintellectual," "unmotivated," or "alienated." Such assessments tend to overlook the more positive traits that may and probably have accrued to the lower-class child. Riessman points out that most attempts at classifying the disadvantaged have focused on what is "wrong" or "weak" about this group, and that not enough attention has been paid to its strengths.[9]

Thus, in attempting to answer too quickly the broad question Who are the disadvantaged? one can develop, even unconsciously, a negative and restricted notion of the lower socioeconomic groups. To continue to emphasize the pathology of the so-called "culturally deprived" is to attribute a basic inferiority to this sector of the population. By so doing, we are not only attributing unwarranted properties to each group, but we are also overlooking many "contact measures" for dealing effectively with the disadvantaged. We may also be clouding our perception of various fundamental forms of disadvantage and deprivation that exist in middle-class society.

Cultural or experiential deprivation, then, is not limited to the economically poor or to people of minority cultures, nor are all the poor or minority-group children culturally or experientially deprived. The child whose major experience is ignored or undermined by his school and dominant culture is disadvantaged indeed, as is the child whose perhaps less *apparent* faulty development is left to find its own way behind a screen of unexamined middle-class standards. With Mayer, we would define the disadvantaged in terms of *life chance* which includes "everything from the chance to stay alive during the first year after birth to the chance to view fine arts, the chance to remain healthy and grow tall, and if sick to get well again quickly, the chance to avoid becoming a juvenile delinquent—and very crucially, the chance to complete an intermediary or higher educational grade."[10] Thus, *disadvantaged* applies in some way to most children—to most adults as well—and traditional definitions of the

[9]F. Riessman, *op. cit.*, p. 3.
[10]K. Mayer, *Class and Society*, New York, Random House, 1955, p. 23.

term, restricted to people from low socioeconomic groups, must be enlarged to encompass most of the school population.

The disadvantaged groups

With the understanding that *disadvantaged* does not refer merely to the lower socioeconomic extremes of the social continuum, but cuts in various ways across all segments of society, let us proceed to examine in some depth those to whom we might appropriately—if broadly—apply the term. Certainly economic status, skin pigmentation, cultural and experiential background, and family stability are all forces which help to shape the extent of one's advantage or disadvantage; thus, the disadvantaged can be viewed from economic, environmental, cultural, and psychological perspectives. Though we shall partition our discussion of disadvantaged groups into roughly similar segments—the economically disadvantaged, the urban *vs.* rural disadvantaged, the culturally different, and the middle-class disadvantaged—such segmentation is obviously artificial. As we have already pointed out, there are many forces at work—some of which are as yet unknown—which overlap one another under an infinite variety of conditions. We cannot emphasize too strongly the salient fact that, when any two or more of these forces are at work on an individual, the effects on that individual far exceed the sum of the parts.

THE ECONOMICALLY DISADVANTAGED

Even according to an expanded concept of disadvantage, one condition is fairly constant: low income. Economic hardship constitutes a basic disadvantage for many of the 77 million Americans who are considered "deprived."

Economic disadvantage, according to Harrington's criteria as presented in *The Other America*, constitutes the basic disadvantage for from 40 to 50 million of Americans.[11] These

[11]M. Harrington, *The Other America*, Baltimore, Penguin Books, 1962, p. 9.

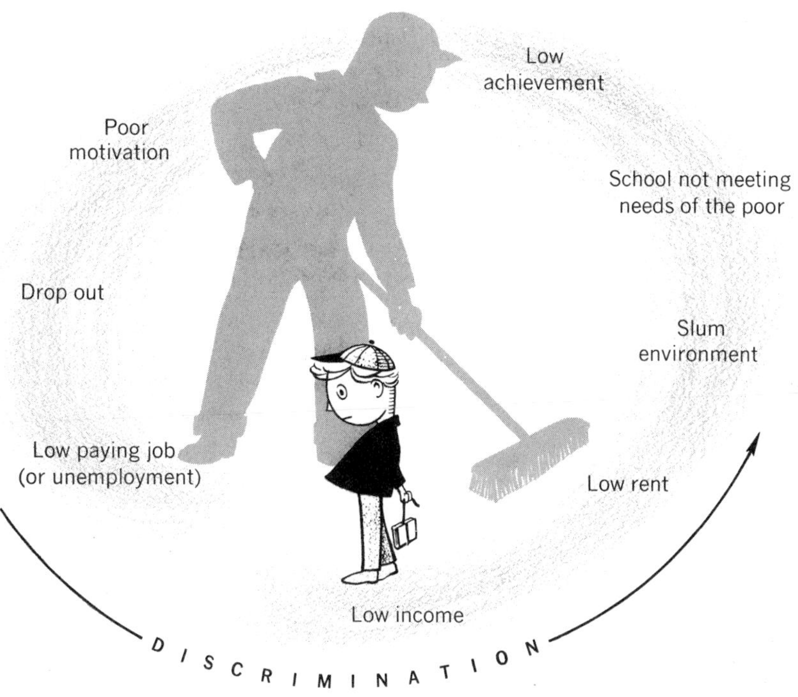

Fig. 1.2. The cycle of despair

people lack money to buy adequate food, shelter, or clothing. Minimal physical comfort and security are denied them. Most poor children live meanly, in tenements, shacks, ramshackle apartments, or in single homes with peeling paint on unpaved streets. No matter where they live, they tend to lack the simplest public services—such as adequate garbage collection, a guaranteed water supply, or functioning sewers. One or the other parent is often absent from the home, alcoholic, or unemployed. At best, both parents work, leaving no one at home to supervise the children. Such is the physical world of the disadvantaged poor and this physical world comprises the obvious, external effects of poverty.

But poverty has a more subtle, crushing dimension. To be poor is to be stigmatized by our society. A man's worth is determined by how much money he has, the car he drives, his address, his clothes, and his ability to spend. Lacking financial worth, he lacks personal worth. Moreover, he is all too willing to accept society's value definitions and consider himself a failure. He feels impotent; he believes there is little he can do about his destiny.

To some extent he is right. Money can buy lawyers, housing, time to find better work, police protection—any number of things which people who are better off financially use to reinforce their sense of personal worth. Lack of money places the economically disadvantaged in a very dependent position. Finally, this lack segregates him from others, especially from the well-off who set the norms for society. His disconnection from this society is obvious: Not only is he hard to reach and to help—even by conventional welfare—he is in no position to help himself or other people, which he must do if he is to feel worthy and involved.

Poverty and poor education, as Patricia Sexton shows in *Education and Income*, go hand in hand.[12] While the affluent disadvantaged get the best that an inadequate educational system can offer, the poor get the very worst. Not only are the disadvantaged poor not ready for the schools, but the schools, by and large, are not ready for them. When the child enters school, he moves into a different world, one which mirrors the society from which he is cut off, and which evaluates him in the same degrading terms he has come to accept as his lot. Poverty is a stigma that the school often unwittingly takes as a sign of personal unworthiness. The cycle of despair which imprisons so many people from the lower socioeconomic strata is generalized in Fig. 1.2.

Low income forces a family to seek residence in low-rent areas where housing is bereft of the more comfortable aspects of American living and where landlords are not motivated to keep their buildings in good repair. In some cases, even the municipality bypasses these areas in regular maintenance pro-

[12]Patricia Cayo Sexton, *Education and Income*, New York, Viking, 1961.

grams, largely because middle-class taxpayers keep maintenance departments busy with pressure on the city to attend to details in their own "finer" neighborhoods. Consequently, the whole area becomes more and more run down, garbage piles up, sewage drains clog, and rats and vermin move in with the tenants. The depressing, oppressive appearance of the slum neighborhood, along with general economic hardship, eats away at the aspirations and motivations of its inhabitants. The parents of children born into this environment may be away from home day and night trying to eke out a meager wage, or, unable to cope financially or emotionally, one or the other of the parents (especially the father) may flee home and neighborhood. Escapes are also available for those who remain: alcohol, frequent card or dice games on streets or in taverns, drugs, gossip, sex—to all of which the children are exposed at an early age as a natural part of their environment and as the accustomed way of adult living.

The severity of such conditions is well known and, in some communities, efforts at "slum clearance" have been made. However, the implicit, middle-class attitudes which underlie these remedial efforts have done little to improve the outlook and self-image of those for whom better housing conditions have been provided. In order to be accepted into a low-income housing project, applicants must answer—to the satisfaction of the housing authorities—a battery of personal questions that go far beyond the typical credit-rating information asked of middle-class applicants to privately sponsored housing. Moreover, once accepted, tenants must continue to meet the rules and regulations set up by the authorities. For example, if a family gains or loses a member, it is required to uproot itself—at its own expense—to move into a larger or smaller apartment, perhaps one which is in a distant and unfamiliar neighborhood. Imagine a middle-class family being required to pack up all of its belongings and move to another dwelling unit—one that they themselves have not chosen, and merely because a son or daughter has married and moved out of the household!

The plight of the housing-project dweller becomes cogently

clear when seen through the eyes of one 17-year-old resident, Juan Gonzales, as reported in *Two Blocks Apart:*

> Man, I hate where I live, the projects. I've been living in a project for the past few years and I can't stand it. First of all, no pets. I've been offered so many times dogs and cats and I can't have them because of the Housing. Then there's a watch out for the walls. Don't staple anything to the walls because then you have to pay for it. Don't hang a picture. There's a fine. And they come and they check to make sure.
>
> Don't make too much noise. The people upstairs and the people downstairs and the people on the side of you can hear every word and they've got to get some sleep. In the project grounds you can't play ball. In the project grounds you can't stay out late. About ten o'clock they tell you to go in or get out. Then . . . there's trouble because they don't want you to hang around in the lobby. . . .
>
> I guess in some ways the projects are better. Like when we used to live here before the projects, there were rats and holes and the building was falling apart. It was condemned so many times, and so many times the landlords fought and won. The building wasn't torn down until finally it was the last building standing. And you know what that is, the last building. . . . There's no place for those rats to go, or those bugs, or no place for the bums to sleep at night except in the one building still standing. It was terrible. The junkies and the drunks would all sleep in the halls at night and my mother was real scared. That was the same time she was out of work and it didn't look to us like anything was ever going to get better.[13]

Too often, when the child enters school, neither the system nor the teachers seem to care about or to comprehend the only world he knows; indeed, they seem to shun both him and it as ugly, sinful, and worthless. The activities required of the child by the school are meaningless and incomprehensible to him. The only society that accepts him is that of his equally frustrated peers, and this peer culture offers the child the only

[13]Charlotte Leon Mayerson (Ed.), *Two Blocks Apart: Juan Gonzales and Peter Quinn*, New York, Holt, Rinehart and Winston, 1965, pp. 39–40.

realistic escape from his increasingly negative image of himself. Finally, he gives up school altogether, perhaps with the dim hope that he may find employment, and thus freedom through financial independence. But he has no marketable skills, and the only jobs open to him are those which offer little security.

Unable to satisfy his physiological and psychological needs, an individual trapped in this cycle becomes frustrated and reacts by withdrawing or "acting out." The summer riots of 1967 in urban ghettos were symptomatic of the consequences of sustained imprisonment of human beings in this cycle. Such crimes against the "decent citizenry" come to the daily attention of the middle class through the mass media, and the stereotyped image of "criminal" slum people is reinforced in the minds of these middle-class citizens—and, indeed, in the minds of the slum people themselves. Employers become more and more suspicious and untrusting of such poverty-bound, chronically uneducated, chronically unemployed populations, and job opportunities become scarcer, dirtier, lower paid, and more exploitative. With no job and no money, the individual is forced to remain in the slum, where his children will most likely follow in his footsteps.

Although in this illustration we have started with the low-income factor, the cycle can begin at any point shown in Fig. 1.2; there are many variations. Many Negroes are, by the American tradition of racial prejudice, confined to slum ghettoes whether they have education and good jobs or not, and their children are raised and acculturated in the same filthy, run-down, oppressive surroundings. Mass immigration waves and the accompanying cheap-labor wages have forced many a self-respecting European family into this cycle, and it is often not until the third or fourth generation that many are able to break out—if indeed they are able to break out at all. Even middle-class families have, through hardship, fallen into this cycle which, like a whirlpool, has the effect of dragging its victims further and further down.

Children from these lower-income levels do not benefit sufficiently from our present educational system. Sociological studies by Lloyd Warner, Allison Davis, August Hollingshead, Robert

Havighurst, and Patricia Sexton have offered substantial data indicating that correlations exist between socioeconomic level and educational success.[14] Yet, low income and discrimination alone do not necessarily produce educationally disadvantaged children. Many school principals and teachers can point to numerous poor children who are succeeding.

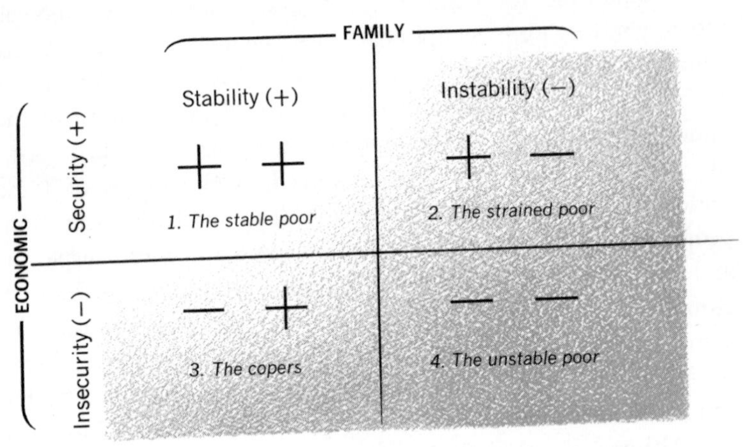

Fig. 1.3. This cross-classification of familial and economic influences on people reveals the positive and negative forces at work on individuals outside the school. (Adapted from S. M. Miller, "The American Lower Class: A Typological Approach," Social Research, **13**:1, 1964, 2.)

As important as economic deprivation is, there are other important factors that intervene, and these must be considered. Miller, for example, analyzed the combined effect of economic

[14]See W. L. Warner et al., Social Class in America, Chicago, Science Research Associates, 1949; A. Davis, Social Class Influences Upon Learning, Cambridge, Mass., Harvard Univ. Press, 1948; A. B. Holingshead and F. C. Redlich, Social Class and Mental Illness, New York, Wiley, 1958; R. Havighurst and Bernice L. Neugarten, Society and Education (2nd ed.), Boston, Allyn and Bacon, 1962; and Patricia Cayo Sexton, Education and Income, New York, Viking, 1961.

and familial influences by cross-classifying degree of economic security with level of family stability (Fig. 1.3).[15] Cell 1 indicates the *stable poor;* cell 2 the *strained poor;* cell 3, the *copers;* and cell 4, the *unstable.*

According to Miller, the *stable poor* are characterized by both familial and economic security. These are the regularly employed, low-skill families whose adult members have adapted relatively successfully to their status, to their environment, and to one another. Miller suggests that this group may be comprised largely of the nonurban poor and of the upper rungs of Negro society, as well as of individuals who, for one reason or another, were better off earlier in their lives or in the previous generation. Though Miller is careful to point out that many factors are at work on people in each of these cell groupings, he indicates that, with the exception of the aged, cell 1 families are the most likely to be upwardly mobile: "The children of cell 1 families are of all the children of the poor those most likely to be educationally and occupationally mobile. Cell 1 might be considered the "take-off" cell, representing the phase necessary before many can really make a big advance."[16]

The *strained poor* (cell 2) also are regularly employed at low-skill jobs, but the adults of the family tend to be maladapted to their life situation. Prolonged difficulty in coping with conditions associated with low income or other personal and family problems can lead to overall familial instability despite a relative security in financial matters. Such instability can have a serious adverse effect upon the offspring of these families and can result in "skidding."

The *copers* (cell 3), on the other hand, are generally those suffering economic insecurity, yet who manage to hold together as a reasonably harmonious family. During periods of great unemployment, this group increases in size and thus, like cell 1, is likely to contain a large proportion of people who have recently fallen from a more advantaged economic status. Such people are more likely to retain an emotionally stable life, and

[15]S. M. Miller, *op. cit.*, p. 8.
[16]*Ibid.*, p. 8.

children from recently impoverished but otherwise stable families are more likely to lift themselves than those from families who have been exposed to lifelong poverty and its miseries. Though precise data are lacking, it does not seem unreasonable to suppose that children from economically insecure families will generally have greater chance for upward mobility if their family life has been fairly stable.

The *unstable* have neither economic nor familial stability and comprise the basic group Miller feels should be defined as *lower class*. However, Miller points out that this group, too, includes several variations and degrees of stability and strain; and that "not every family is a 'hard-core case' or has a 'multi-agency problem.' "[17] For example, many in this group may be recently urbanized farmers whose personal instability arises mainly from readjustment difficulties. Similarly, Negroes who have migrated north from cell 1 families in the South may become only temporarily unstable as they learn to cope with the wholly new set of conditions attached to Northern life. On the other hand, cell 4 is also likely to include the mentally ill, criminals, broken families, the physically handicapped, and the otherwise hard-core cases.

Of the two forces, family stability has a substantially greater effect on a child than does economic hardship alone. To be sure, when a family has to worry about money matters and low income, it may have difficulty in meeting the various emotional demands of its developing children; yet, emotional solidarity within the family can offset significantly the adverse effects of poverty on a child's personality development. Further, we infer from Miller's analysis that, regardless of the family's economic status, children reared by stable, well-adjusted parents have a greater chance for a happy life than do children from unstable families, and that the *extent of economic insecurity a family unit suffers only compounds the problems encountered by the child from an unstable family.*

Despite what seems an implicit assumption to the contrary among educators, middle-class families are not automatically

[17] *Ibid.* p. 12.

stable; just as there are stable families among the poor, there are unstable families among those who suffer no economic hardship. Thus, in mustering its forces to deal especially with the disadvantaged poor, the educational system may, at the same time, overlook the existence of very real needs among children of the middle-class society.

URBAN VS. RURAL DISADVANTAGED

Today, over 60 percent of the nation's population lives in 212 metropolitan centers; it is estimated that, by 1980, 80 percent of Americans will live in urban areas. However, as the city's residential areas become more densely populated, the more prosperous city dwellers migrate to the suburbs. Consequently, urban areas are becoming more and more the habitat of the socioeconomically disadvantaged. In the larger cities, the deprived are mostly Negro and other nonwhite groups—i.e. Puerto Rican or Mexican—as reflected by estimated school enrollments. In Philadelphia, Chicago, and Baltimore, for example, elementary-school populations are about 50 percent Negro and Puerto Rican; in Manhattan, about 75 percent, and in Washington, D.C., 85 percent.[18] Although there are no adequate statistics available, there are also the poor Orientals and the poor whites—those Italians, Greeks, Irish, and Jewish who have not managed to break through the cycle of despair, and the Anglo-Saxon indigents of Appalachia and other rural parts of the United States who migrate to the cities looking for employment. Based on current trends, the prediction is that, by 1970, one out of every two children in many of our major cities will be poor or disadvantaged. In New York City alone, the city school system reports that the number of predominantly Negro and Puerto Rican schools had increased from 118 in 1960–1961 to 187 in 1964–1965, while the number of predominantly white schools has decreased.[19]

The urban situation today constitutes a sizable problem for educators who find that city school systems are unprepared to

[18]B. Asbell, *op cit.*, p. 84.
[19]*The New York Times*, March 30, 1965.

meet the various problems these circumstances present. As Charles Mitchell of the Detroit Great Cities School Improvement Program writes:

> In . . . large cities across the nation are concentrated families whose children are severely hampered in their schooling by a complex of community, home, and school conditions. Change in the population of the inner core of most large cities has created areas where the majority of children have extraordinary needs which the public schools are not prepared to meet. These, the children with limited backgrounds, comprise one-third of the 3,200,000 children now enrolled in America's fourteen largest school systems.[20]

If this situation continues at the present rate, the cycle of despair will suck down ever-increasing numbers of our urban population and of our national population itself.

The cycle is not limited to the urban poor. Though proportions of the American population become ever more concentrated in urban areas, there remain large numbers of people in rural regions, such as the recently publicized Appalachia and the farming regions of the United States, in which small private farms are rapidly being displaced by corporate farming. And there are the approximately 2,000,000 migrant workers who derive a negligible living from seasonal crop harvesting. Sutton reveals the plight of the rural migrant and his children:

> Wherever the production of seasonal crops requires hand labor, migratory workers move with the crops. . . . These migrants work in what is usually the only type of labor open to them. They have no permanent homes; they are poorly clothed and nourished. Inadequate wages trap them in a cycle of seasonal migration difficult to break. . . . The children of the workers suffer the greatest damage from a migratory existence. They are learning the way of life of their group and are coming to accept the goals and expec-

[20]C. Mitchell, quoted in "School Programs for the Disadvantaged," *Educational Research Service Circular*, American Association of School Administrators and Research Division, Washington, D.C., National Education Association, January, 1965, No. 1, p. 2.

> tations of their parents. They share, in common, mobility and its limitations, among them the limited opportunities open to them for getting an education and of using knowledge to gain a better way of life. . . .[21]

These children also "share in common" their parents' long working hours and hazardous working conditions. According to the government's Industrial Welfare Commission, about 500 migrant children are maimed each year from working in the fields with their parents. Child labor laws are difficult to enforce with this rootless population, and the families need every able member to supply their incomes. Thus, their children's education, such as it may be, is irregular and constantly interrupted, and it is not surprising that a study sponsored by the National Education Association found that, in some areas, as many as 75 percent of migrant children are "retarded."[22]

CULTURAL ORIENTATION

All groups of people have a culture of some sort. Although culture is not identical with environment, it is certainly a part of the environment to which the young are exposed. Culture must, however, be distinguished from the environment and defined as the aggregate of those attitudes, traditions, mores, and ethical codes peculiar to the particular society. For example, within a given urban slum neighborhood, several distinct cultures often coexist—Negro, Puerto Rican, Irish, and Italian—while in other parts of the same city an entire neighborhood might be composed almost entirely of one culture, such as the Chinese in New York's Chinatown.

Generally, cultural disadvantage in the United States has a geographical pattern: In the South, and in most of the urban areas of the North, cultural disadvantage is primarily a Negro

[21] Elizabeth Sutton, *Knowing and Teaching the Migrant Child,* Washington, D.C., Department of Rural Education, National Educational Association, 1960, p. 13.

[22] Shirley E. Greene, *The Education of Migrant Children,* Washington, D.C., Department of Rural Education, National Education Association, 1954, p. 8.

problem. Other groups—Mexican-Americans along the border states and in California, Puerto Ricans in New York, American Indians in the Southwest, the indigent whites of Appalachia and the rural South—also have been adversely affected by their cultural differences from middle-class America.

It would be impossible, of course, to identify every subculture in the United States and to define the various attributes which make it more or less incompatible with the middle-class mainstream. We can, however, describe some of the salient features and problems of the most notable subcultures—the Negro, the Spanish-speaking groups, and the American Indian. A brief profile of each of these groups should provide an indication of the width and diversity of the problems connected with cultural difference. In addition, we shall itemize a few of the less advantageous characteristics that are becoming more evident among constituents of middle-class society.

The Negro

Most disadvantaged minority groups are also segregated. Many schools reflect this pattern whether the group is Puerto Rican, Indian, migrant, Mexican, Italian, or Negro. However, the plight of the disadvantaged Negro deserves special attention.

Studies in population shifts point to a clear pattern of Negro movement to the large cities:

> From 1950 to the present, it is estimated that some 5 million Negroes moved to the heart cities. It is assumed that most of this movement was from the rural South to the largest cities outside that region. Meanwhile, a white exodus was taking place. Between 1950 and 1960, St. Louis lost 22 percent of its entire white population, San Diego 15.4, and Newark 23.7 percent.[23]

According to the 1960 census, the following percentages of Negroes lived in the 25 largest heart cities.[24]

[23]F. Crossland, "Education and Urbanization," Unpublished memorandum, March 24, 1966, The Ford Foundation, New York.

[24]*The World Almanac and Book of Facts*, New York, The World-Telegram and Sun, 1966.

1. Washington, D.C.	53.9%	13. Dallas	19.0%
2. Atlanta	38.3	14. Pittsburgh	16.7
3. New Orleans	36.2	15. New York	14.0
4. Memphis	37.0	16. Los Angeles	13.5
5. Baltimore	34.8	17. Buffalo	13.3
6. Detroit	28.9	18. San Francisco	10.0
7. Cleveland	28.6	19. Boston	9.1
8. St. Louis	28.6	20. Milwaukee	8.4
9. Philadelphia	26.4	21. San Antonio	7.1
10. Chicago	22.9	22. Denver	6.3
11. Houston	22.9	23. San Diego	6.0
12. Cincinnati	21.6	24. Seattle	4.8
		25. Minneapolis	2.4

These percentages gain importance when one realizes that Negroes now constitute about 11 percent of the total American population. It also must be noted that the median age for Negroes is lower than that of whites; hence, even larger percentages of Negroes are of school age in these cities. Sixty percent of all Negroes are poor, and the cycle of economic despair, combined with the often extreme prejudice which has forced them to remain in poverty, has driven them into a virtual social prison. *The New York Times* states it this way: "The cycle of discrimination that confronts the Negro . . . is hard to break. There is job discrimination, resulting in low Negro income. The low income plus housing discrimination condemn the Negro to living in the slums. There is apathy toward education, disqualifying many Negroes for many jobs that might otherwise be available."[25] Or, as *Time* Magazine says of the situation in New York: "The tragedy of Harlem is that yet another generation of such men is being bred because they cannot break out of the vicious cycle of the ghetto. Poor schooling leading to a low-paying job or no job at all, leading to housing in a run-down neighborhood, leading anew to poor schooling for children. . . ."[26]

[25]*The New York Times*, July 26, 1964, p. E4.
[26]"No Place Like Home," *Time* Magazine, July 31, 1964, p. 16.

As serious as are the consequences of racial discrimination upon employment and residential opportunities for those discriminated against, there is another, more insidious, and farther reaching effect of such prejudice—the negation of the victim's ego. Psychiatry and psychology have amassed quantities of evidence that the human organism intrinsically strives toward healthy personality integration and self-realization, and that self-hatred is one of the major factors impeding this process. Thus, confinement to low-paying and irregular jobs, to urban ghettoes with their decrepit and often hazardous dwelling units—each a debilitating factor in its own right—also leads to self-deprecation when contrasted to the standards of white middle-class life. When the Negro is further confronted by hatred, resentment, injustice, and apathy on the part of his white fellow human, his feelings of personal worthlessness become even more fixed, and he is even less likely to find the energy and purpose necessary for upward mobility.

Many educators and other professionals who work with the disadvantaged are fully sympathetic with the Negro's social reality and are keenly aware of the social destructiveness of poverty, slum life, unemployment, and of the institutional discrimination which forces these conditions upon the Negro; yet, in attempting to help the Negro to lift himself above these conditions, they complain that the Negro is unwilling to help himself. Few realize that the Negro too often fails to see that such self-aid is possible or even morally right in the scheme of things, so ingrained has he become with a basic feeling of worthlessness and so accustomed is he to the notion that he is "bad." Among many Negroes, particularly in the South, this attitude toward self and race manifests itself explicitly in the religious view that once upon a time the Negro people did something "terrible" to God, and God is now "punishing" them. In other cases, self-hatred leads to a projection of this hostility toward society as a whole.

Though such projection phenomena in human psychology are familiar to most educators and behavioral scientists—and even to many middle-class laymen—how many would be likely to connect

Negro violence and crime with Negro *self*-hatred? Indeed, one possible explanation (or at least partial explanation) for the increasing endorsement of "Black Power" among Negroes might well lie in the aggregate effect of Negro self-negation. In any case, no consideration of the culturally different should overlook both the causes and the effects of a negative self-image produced by social antipathy, particularly in the case of the Negro.

The Spanish-speaking minority

Spanish-speaking minority groups have been an American social problem for a good portion of the nation's history. The Mexican population in Texas, California, and the other Mexican-border states still comprises a major segment of the culturally different. Although many Mexicans have been assimilated into American society—particularly those who have migrated to Northern cities, have completed high school (and even college), and have succeeded in white-collar jobs—there are still vast numbers of poverty-imprisoned, uneducated, unskilled, and non-English-speaking Mexicans who are imprisoned in the cycle of despair. A good many of these are migrant harvesters who compete for their negligible living with the similarly impoverished "Anglos" (indigent white Americans), and the Negro migrant workers. This economic conflict with other migrant workers forces them to work for even lower wages than the non-Mexican, and their pay averages about 50 cents per hour, or less. This, in turn, infuriates the non-Mexican workers, and intercultural hatred among the migrants magnifies the historical discrimination that still exists against the Mexican in the border states.

This hatred and discrimination has particularly delimiting consequences for the Mexican-American child:

> As a rule there exist social and residential segregation where-ever there are large numbers of Mexican-Americans, although where their number is small there usually is little or no segregation. Throughout Texas, California, and the other states with large Mexican-American populations, the Mexican-American child suffers a special and serious handicap in becoming a successful American citizen as the result of

being segregated by Anglos and of segregating himself from Anglos.[27]

Mexican-American children, like children of other disadvantaged groups, are educationally handicapped. Children of migrant workers lack continuous education because their families must follow the crops. Even those children who are able to attend school regularly from the primary grades on are handicapped by language or because their parents have not been able to convey to them the importance of continuous schooling. In one study conducted in San Antonio, only 6 percent of such children completed high school, while 30 percent had a maximum of three years of any school.[28]

Thus, the factors which keep all of the disadvantaged in the cycle of despair are at work on the Mexican-American. But there are also cultural factors which have retarded full assimilation of the Mexicans:

> The assimilation of the Mexican immigrants has been further slowed because many of them are folk people. That is, they have a common body of tradition which is passed on from generation to generation which determines much of the pattern of their lives, and to which almost everyone conforms. This body of tradition is made for the next and expects to be followed. The child in a folk society receives his education by experiences from within the circle of the extended family. Although the individual has fewer choices than in a civilized culture, life has much continuity and social change is rare and slow.[29]

In many of our large northern cities, the Puerto Rican population comprises almost as large a segment of the culturally different as the Negro. Because many of these people—like the Mexican—are dark-skinned, anti-Negro prejudice has found expression against these people, as has the prejudice that is tradi-

[27] J. H. Burma, *Spanish-Speaking Groups in the United States*, Durham, N. C., Duke Univ. Press, 1954.
[28] Sister Mary John Murray, "A Socio-Cultural Study of 118 Mexican Families Living in a Low-Rent Public Housing Project in San Antonio, Texas," *Studies in Sociology*, **38**, 84.
[29] J. H. Burma, *op. cit.*, p. 123.

tionally directed against foreign-language-speaking peoples. Oscar Handlin describes the effects of this color stigma on the Puerto Rican:

> By island definitions, some 75 percent of the population of Puerto Rico were white, some 25 percent were colored. Whatever data we have indicates that a larger percentage of white than of colored Puerto Ricans came to the mainland. There they found themselves in a dilemma, for color which was of slight importance back home was crucial in New York. The effect has been to strengthen the character of the identification of the Puerto Rican in the case of those who were colored and to weaken it in the case of those who were white. The colored Puerto Rican wished above all to avoid the stigma of identification with the Negro and he could do so only by establishing himself as a Spanish-speaking Puerto Rican. On the other hand, whiteness became an important asset to the remainder of the Puerto Ricans in this country. As soon as some improvement of status enabled them to escape, there was an incentive to dissolve the ties with the group and to lose themselves in the general category of whites.[30]

In addition to the color and immigrant stigmata, the Puerto Rican may face a serious language barrier. These conditions obstruct or preclude employment for them and force them into low-paying jobs and into life in the city slums, where even their non-Puerto Rican neighbors reject them. Many of these other slum residents are unaware that the Puerto Rican is a United States citizen.

Yet the Puerto Rican is anxious to succeed economically in the American mainstream. Faced with the obstacles he meets in mainland cities, the adult Puerto Rican may become pessimistic about his own opportunities, but he does not project this pessimism upon the opportunities he wishes for his children. This outlook was reported in a study conducted in Philadelphia:

> A strong desire on the part of the migrants for any steady work was indicated. About a fifth of the sample said the

[30] O. Handlin, *The Newcomers*, Cambridge, Harvard Univ. Press, 1959, p. 59.

> kind of work they would like is "any steady job." This finding might be interpreted to indicate a pessimistic vocational outlook on the part of the migrant sample. However, if the migrant is pessimistic for himself, he is not pessimistic for his children. When asked "What kind of job would you like your children to have?" most respondents replied in terms of white collar or professional jobs.[31]

The effects of the mainstream culture on children from Mexican or Puerto Rican families have often disrupted the smooth functioning of the subculture. As we have earlier defined it, a culture includes the institutions, the structures, and the methods of organization of the people involved, all of which have evolved to meet the traditionally expected conditions for survival. In both the Mexican and Puerto Rican tradition, the family (usually a large one), is a closely knit unit in which loyalty is not only encouraged, but demanded. The father generally enjoys supreme authority over his wife and children, and working members of the family are expected to contribute substantially to the immediate family and to help support other relatives in need. In the mainstream American culture, however, these values are considerably diminished; the emphasis is on the autonomous individual. When Mexican or Puerto Rican children have been acculturated sufficiently to reflect this greater freedom, their behavior is viewed as unfilial by the older generation, and misunderstanding and estrangement between the generations arise. This has been a traditional pattern among immigrant groups to this country. For the children, this new freedom is sometimes interpreted as a tacit approval of flagrant behavior, and this interpretation is reinforced by the father's declining authority, thus undermining the few effective remaining home controls for child behavior. The school, on the other hand, accustomed as it is to viewing the conduct of children as the basic responsibility of parents, tends to attribute flagrant misconduct to cultural deprivation. In the case of Spanish-speaking groups, at least, such

[31] A. Siegel, H. Orlans, and L. Greer, *Puerto Ricans in Philadelphia: A Study of Their Demographic Characteristics, Problems, and Attitudes*, Institute for Research in Human Relations, 1954, p. 38.

behavior may well be the result of the collision of two distinctly different cultures and the consequent breakdown of the family structure within the minority culture.

The American Indian

Despite the romantic glamour attached to the American Indian by Hollywood movies, TV western, and adventure tales of the Old West, the modern American Indian poses one of our gravest cultural minority problems, and is "perhaps on the average the most impoverished and poorest prepared of all our minority groups."[32] Although they have been United States citizens since 1924, the various tribes are still treated by the federal government as "domestic dependent nations" and are left to themselves to regulate their conduct and affairs according to ancient tradition. With limited land and resources available to them on their reservations, many tribes have faced crises arising from increasing populations, poor agricultural conditions, and a deficit in marketable products and skills for extrareservation commerce. Thus, without enough food, clothing, and other material, they lack adequate means of gaining sufficient revenue to purchase these commodities from the outside world. Heline reveals the extreme crisis that developed during the 1940s as a result of this state of affairs:

> In 1948 the plight of Navajo and Hopi tribes in Arizona and New Mexico was so serious that, had it not been for trainloads of food and clothing supplied by private charity and an emergency relief appropriation later made by Congress, untold numbers would have died of starvation and exposure. Such want existed in our midst without our general knowledge because the Indians live out of public view and their sorry condition is not widely publicized.[33]

In addition to their often severe economic plight, many of the 200 tribes face equally severe cultural crises. As peoples whose entire social structure is built on tradition and custom, the tribes

[32]W. T. Hagen, *American Indians*, Chicago, Univ. of Chicago Press, 1961.
[33]T. Heline, *The American Indian: Our Relations and Responsibilities*, Los Angeles, New Age Press, 1952.

have found the surrounding modern society not only incomprehensible and hostile, but eroding as well: "With a majority of them, the old culture has broken down, social controls have become ineffective, and we find individual tribal officials struggling with the problems of local government with which they are ill-equipped to deal."[34]

The federal government, on the other hand, faced with the increasingly difficult and complex problems of administering to a burgeoning modern society, has found its Indian responsibilities trivial and bothersome. During the 1950s, more and more Indian affairs were shifted to state and local governments for administration. These local governments, in turn, have found themselves ill-equipped to deal with the situation. Poverty-bound Indians have created an added burden on welfare and relief agencies and have added heavily to the local governments' health and education responsibilities.

Attempts to train the agrarian Indian in industrial skills and to acculturate him into a highly technological society have been, in the main, unsuccessful. One reason is the tenacity with which the Indian himself clings to his proud heritage of tradition; another, closely related, is the general approach used in such efforts. Laura Thompson illustrates this approach in her classic study of the Hopi:

> Most Hopi children on entering school understand little or no English. Hopi has been their mother tongue from the cradle. Suddenly they are confronted with the stupendous task of learning about an alien culture in what to them is a foreign language, and of learning usually from a strange white teacher who herself often knows little of their own background. They can hardly be expected to appear to advantage. The progress of even the most gifted, compared to white children of the same age level, seems slow.[35]

Thus, a cultural clash results when subcultures such as the

[34]D. A. Baerreis, *The Indian in Modern America,* Wisconsin Historical Society, 1956, p. xiv.

[35]Laura Thompson, *Culture in Crisis,* New York, Harper & Row, 1950, pp. 114–115.

Mexican-American and the American Indian come into direct conflict with the mainstream culture reflected by schools. Such differences in cultural values are summarized in Table 1.1.

TABLE 1.1. Differences in cultural values

Value orientations	Anglo-American teacher[a]	Southwestern Indians	Spanish-Mexican Americans
NATURE	Mastery	Harmony	Subjugation
TIME	Future	Present	Present
ASPIRATION	Success	Follow old ways	Work a little—Rest a little
WORK	Hard	To satisfy present needs	
SAVING	Everyone should	Sharing instead	
SCHEDULES	Clock watchers	Unhurried	
CHANGE	Accepted as model behavior	Follow old ways	
EXPLANATION FOR BEHAVIOR	Scientific natural law	Non-scientific explanation	
COMPETITION	Aggression	Cooperation	Humility
INDIVIDUALITY	Self-realization	Group sanction	Obedience

[a]Represents a teacher with a mainstream orientation.
SOURCE: E. R. Leighton (Ed.), *Bicultural Linguistic Concepts in Education*, Tucson, Arizona, E. Roby Leighton & Associates, 1964, p. 9.

The middle-class disadvantaged

Thus far, we have considered the groups which are disadvantaged in relation to a more advantaged population. Yet the middle-class is disadvantaged, too, although we do not see it. Its deficiencies are concealed behind a façade of green lawns, quiet streets, well-furnished homes, clean hands and faces, new clothes, and polite speech. But for him as well, the institutions are all too often inadequate to his needs. Too often his experiences are protective and limited, his adult models dull and unstimulating. Through death or divorce, one or the other parent may be missing. Too often adequate parental attention is lacking.

While all of this creates a less obvious disadvantage, it is nonetheless serious, especially since the middle-class child's strategies for coping with his environment attract less attention and make fewer demands upon adults. These children are less likely to be defined as social problems, and their disadvantage is not as discernible because many appear to be succeeding, both in school and in work. Indeed, because most middle-class children appear to succeed in school, the schools seem to work *for* rather than against them. If this is the case, how can they, by any stretch of the imagination, be considered disadvantaged? The irony is that because of their favorable status and apparent success no one questions seriously their handicaps and the effect of the school on their development.

However, it is becoming more evident that the school process is not cultivating their talents adequately. For example, one Minnesota school teacher took out a full-page advertisement in the local newspaper to publicize his assessment of his affluent suburban students. He claimed that they were bored, indifferent and dull, and that in general they were a mass of superficial human beings interested only in having a good time at any cost. For many of these suburban students, this teacher predicted a go-nowhere future. Later, in a news interview he said:

> I believe that the students are frozen with sophistication, that they are unable to act and react virtually to anything. . . . In a suburban community like this one they have already achieved their goals of good food, good shelter, rapid transportation, but now they're going to have to find some other struggle, something that will give meaning to their lives, because now they seem to be more interested in just securing what they already have.[36]

In a CBS-TV news special "Sixteen in Webster Groves," the 96-percent-white, middle-class suburb of St. Louis was examined from the perspective of a 16-year-old. This news special made use of the results of a survey conducted by the National Opinion

[36]© Columbia Broadcasting System, Inc. 1965. All Rights Reserved. From CBS Evening News with Walter Cronkite broadcast April 8, 1965. Published with the permission of Columbia Broadcasting System, Inc.

Research Center at the University of Chicago which revealed, among other things, that:

84 percent of the 5- to 6-year olds say they are expected to go to college
96 percent of the 16-year olds indicate they are worried about getting good grades
77 percent feel it difficult to live with the pressures to do well in classes
54 percent admit they have cheated in order to pass a test.[37]

Parental pressure which gives rise to the anxiety indicated in these findings is only one aspect of middle-class life. A more serious condition, cultural ignorance, is illustrated by these 16-year-olds from Webster Groves:

BILL: This past summer I took a course downtown, and it was in another bad section of town, and I—I drove down there and I came in contact with people I've never seen before in my life, and they—I just couldn't believe it. They were from the slums, and they were mentally retarded, and they were all sorts of people, and they—it just helped me to understand people much better, and I mean, when you see people in Webster—people in Webster Groves are generally very—well, they're well off in a sense, and you just get—you get the kind of view that everybody's happy all the time, and we're all normal, and we all don't live in too dumpy houses—and—you get down and you see these people, and they've got all these pressing problems, and it just kind of makes me think of what a sheltered life I really have had. I—I've never really seen anything that bad before.

GIRL: Well, I think that's one of the reasons why teenagers do challenge what's been told them all their life because it seems to me, you know, up until you hit high school everything just seems to go pretty smoothly. Everything's all nice and rosy, and no one ever has any problems, and you aren't exposed to them, at least in the kind of environment we

[37]Reported in Sixteen in Webster Groves broadcast, February 25, 1966, and published with the permission of Columbia Broadcasting System, Inc.

grew up in. And once you begin to have experiences like Bill said, you begin to wonder whether people have been honest with you all your life in presenting this kind of picture and if you see people who aren't living such a happy life you challenge what has been told you. I mean—all these people—you don't—you never know what a depressing place it is until you go down there, and it's just—that's just an example, but things like that I've never been into contact with really.

GIRL: I—I hate to drive even down into the slums. I always feel guilty that I should even have decent clothes to wear. I really feel guilty because why is it that some people are so rich—they throw their money around—and then they end up—they end up having a bad home life, and some of these people have nothing. I—it almost seems like communism.

GIRL: But what can you do to help them? You just go through and turn your head and say you don't want to go down there, and you do nothing about it.[38]

One need only mention that the members of the privileged group have had access to leadership and power as an almost natural consequence of their status; yet their utilization of both leadership and power among their fellow men has been far from impressive. By virtue of their socioeconomic status, many inherit leadership, but have they been prepared adequately for this role? How many really ask fundamental questions about their world and its social institutions, and how these institutions might be improved? How many ask "Why are slums permitted to continue? What can be done to eliminate the poverty and ignorance that exists in my country?" And once having raised these questions, how many are willing to act to alter such social conditions?

The answer is that too few do; too many still cling to the destructive prejudice that reinforces the cycle of despair of the socioeconomically disadvantaged. Even among those who pay sympathetic lip service to the plight of the poor, there appears

[38]© Columbia Broadcasting System, Inc. 1966. All Rights Reserved. From Sixteen in Webster Groves broadcast, February 25, 1966. Published with the permission of Columbia Broadcasting System, Inc.

to be an almost passive acceptance of the existing human injustice. Few middle-class individuals seem even to understand the true meaning of the word *prejudice*—to judge without reference to the facts, or before all the facts are in—believing instead that it simply means to "dislike someone." On the basis of this erroneous definition, it is easy for many prosperous and successful people to justify their prejudice, claiming that it is their inalienable right to dislike whom they please. Yet there is psychological evidence which shows clearly the relationship of bigotry to an inability to cope with ambiguity and uncertainty.[39] Human beings are complex animals, and human relations are, at best, difficult. To be successful, human interaction must take into account and reconcile the myriad aspects of each of the individuals involved. For many—too many—it is easier to categorize their fellow humans according to stereotypes that are based upon obvious and irrelevant characteristics.

An educational system which graduates students, even from colleges and universities, with only an intellectual understanding about prejudice, democracy, justice, dignity, equality, and humanity is graduating half-educated persons. Simply knowing about democracy does not mean *performing* in a democratic manner. Many citizens who score well in intellectual understanding of democratic concepts at school later resist integrated schools and communities. The great irony of prejudice and socioeconomic disadvantage is that few of the middle class are actually aware of their own disadvantaged status and the small likelihood of perpetuating such advantage as they do have as long as social institutions remain segregated and outdated. Coles makes the following observation:

> One by one in crucial times in our history various immigrant groups have come to lend a diversity and richness to our culture. Nevertheless, this same culture has plenty of rot in it—cheap abundance, anxious conformity, smug carelessness.

[39]See, e.g., J. and Jeanne Block, "An Investigation of the Relationship Between Intolerence of Ambiguity and Ethnocentrism," *Journal of Personality*, 1951, **19**, 303–311; and R. Taft, "Intolerance of Ambiguity and Ethnocentrism," *Journal of Consulting Psychology*, 1956, **20**, 153–154.

> Money and work are what the poor people I know demand and need, but I am not so sure that some of the qualities that they already have are not in turn needed by the rest of us—the unmasking humor, the caustic distrust of fake morality, hypocritical authority, and dishonest piety. If most of the poor have been terribly crushed by our society, then in other ways so have many from our nervous acquisitive middle class.[40]

Thus, the middle-class child who comes to school prepared to succeed in a mediocre, outdated educational process may also be crushed; he too is disadvantaged, despite the fact that he passes his course work, does his homework, and is promoted upward through the system. There has been relatively little concern for the fundamental effect that this system has on the individual's personal understanding of life—his own and that of the others among whom he must live. Having prepared him for college and employment, we have given little thought to how well he will perform as an adult, how much he will be responsible toward other human beings and cognizant that a concern for the welfare of others is ultimately a concern for one's own welfare.

Although the focus of attention currently devoted to disadvantage among the lower socioeconomic groups overshadows the more privileged segments of society, the symptoms of middle-class disadvantage are becoming more and more evident. The very institutions we have established to perpetuate our democratic society—and to provide for the health, education, and welfare of its citizens—will surely fall short of their purposes unless the people who administer and operate them are themselves fully educated, thinking adults. Our attempts to improve the lot of the poor, the Negro, the Puerto Rican, the migrant, the American Indian, and the various other socioeconomically disadvantaged can amount to little more than an expensive waste of public and private funds unless these attempts stem from an encompassing and realistic approach to the assets as well as to the problems of

[40]R. Coles, "The Poor Don't Want To Be Middle Class," *The New York Times Magazine*, December 19, 1965, p. 58.

the disadvantaged. Yet, surely, we cannot expect such an approach as long as middle-class individuals—those who become our housing authority personnel, employers, realtors, social workers, and teachers—are themselves deprived of the full benefits of an educational process which prepares them for their personal and social roles.

Having expanded our concept of the disadvantaged to encompass the range of the social continuum, the next fundamental question is, "How did they get that way? By what process or processes does a person become disadvantaged?" For some insights into this question we turn to the "hidden curriculum" of the disadvantaged.

CHAPTER 2

THE HIDDEN CURRICULUM

Hays, Monkmeyer

THE HIDDEN CURRICULUM

Most of us think of the term *curriculum* as referring to the content to which the learner is exposed in a formal school situation. In the large sense, the school curriculum is a sequence of activities—an environment—through which the learner passes. It is hoped that, when the learner has passed through this sequence, he will have acquired certain facts, skills, and attitudes which are appropriate for his role as a mature adult in our society. In this way, the school curriculum is actually a deliberate attempt to transmit to the learner those cultural aspects which will reflect the dominant culture of the society and yield the most benefit to the society as a whole.

Miller, Monkmeyer

Fujihira, Monkmeyer

All American children, regardless of their social class, are required by law to spend significant portions of their early lives in the formal school setting. Yet, at the same time, these children go through another, less formal curriculum for an even greater portion of their lives. We shall call this second curriculum the "hidden curriculum," because most Americans cannot see it, although it strongly affects the children's reactions to the formal curriculum. Dewey alerted the schools to the hidden curriculum earlier in the century when he stated:

> The school has the function also of coordinating within the disposition of each individual the diverse influences of the various social environments in which he enters. One code prevails in the family; another, on the street; a third, in the workshop or store; a fourth, in the religious association. As a person passes from one of the environments to another, he is subjected to antagonistic pulls, and is in danger of being split into a being having different standards of judgment and emotion for different occasions. This danger imposes upon the school a steadying and integrating office.[1]

Today, the extraschool forces at work on shaping the child have greatly increased, as various social agencies and institutions have focused their attention on youth. Churches have stepped up their youth programs; recreation agencies (such as PAL, Boys' Clubs of America, and community or neighborhood centers) have proliferated and offer a multitude of leisure, cultural-education, and character-building programs; control and protection agencies (the police, courts, traffic bureaus, and safety agents) have expanded their youth efforts as juvenile crime and vandalism spread; psychotherapeutic and social-welfare services have become increasingly youth oriented; and vocational guidance and job-training agencies that operate more or less independently of the school are more and more in evidence—all of these represent a melee of extraschool vested interests geared to act upon and to influence the development of children and youth. Moreover, a host of diverse political organizations, ranging from the extreme right to

[1]John Dewey, *Democracy and Education,* New York, Macmillan, 1916, p. 22.

the extreme left, operate intensive youth movements devoted to recruiting the ideological bents of young minds, and commercial enterprise spends billions of dollars annually on youth-aimed campaigns—not merely to sell the products that are specifically designed for youth, but also to instill brand and product loyalty at an early age.

As Lippitt has also pointed out, each of these factions represents a deliberate and specific attempt to mold the interests, attitudes, and emotions of America's future citizens:

> In our studies of community functionings, we have identified a number of clusters of personnel that have a vested interest in influencing the behavior and values of children and youth. Each of these clusters has a program of socialization, more or less planned, and more or less formally presented as a program to influence the growth and development of information, attitudes, values, and behavior of the younger members of the community.[2]

As Lippitt further observes:

> The daily socialization mazeway of the child and youth is indeed a medley of intervention. Many of the inputs are competing for attention and time. Some are conflicting in their messages. There are great variations in the types of relationship offered and expected with the socialization agents.[3]

Of no small consequence on the budding personalities of the nation's young are the mass media themselves: newspapers, magazines, billboards, comic books, and especially the electronic media, such as radio and TV. Marshall McLuhan has pointed out that it is not merely the content communicated by these media which influence children, but also that, technologically, the very *nature* of each medium shapes the growing child's perceptual orientation: "The young student today grows up in an electronically configured world. It is a world not of wheels but of circuits,

[2]R. Lippitt, "Improving The Socialization Process," in John A. Clausen (Ed.), *Socialization and Society*, New York, Little, Brown, (in press).
[3]*Ibid.*

not of fragments but of integral patterns."[4] What overall impact this new electronic environment will have on the child has only recently been the subject of serious investigation. At this time it is sufficient to say that the electronic age is yet another aspect of the hidden curriculum that places all children at a disadvantage when they are forced to deal with an educational system which reflects the "old world of the wheel and nuts and bolts."

Yet, if the hidden curriculum includes these deliberate and relatively more obvious attempts to influence child development, it also includes the less obvious but perhaps more effective influences found in the steady sequence of affairs to which the child is exposed during the course of his daily life. The physical appearance of his neighborhood and his home and the routine modes of behavior exhibited by those who share these physical surroundings with him are likely to carry far more weight in shaping the child's orientation to himself and society than is any deliberate attempt by a group with vested interests.

Clearly, the education and socialization of any given child is far from limited to the four walls of a classroom but, rather, occurs in vast measure from a multifarious array of extraschool factors to which the child is exposed from the moment of his birth. To examine each of these factors and its consequence upon child development would, of course, be a formidable task, and certainly far beyond the scope of this chapter, which shall limit itself to three key agents of socialization: the neighborhood, the family, and the sibling and peer group. For, just as the formal curriculum has a school setting, so the hidden curriculum has a neighborhood setting; just as the formal curriculum is subdivided into classroom units, so the hidden curriculum is subdivided into family units; and, just as the school curriculum produces a student culture, so the hidden curriculum produces a sibling and peer culture. Further, just as the formal curriculum has a key teaching agent, the teacher, so has the hidden curriculum a key agent, the parent. Because of the obvious importance of the parent to the

[4]M. McLuhan, *Understanding Media: The Extension of Man*, New York, McGraw-Hill, 1966, p. vii.

shaping of a child's development, however, we shall reserve discussion of this key teaching agent for Chapter 3.

Both the formal curriculum and the vaster hidden curriculum serve to teach and to socialize the individual, and to equip him with the skills, knowledge, and attitudes which will underlie his adult functioning in society. Obviously, if the formal curriculum is to achieve its purpose, it must be consistent with, or at least accommodating of, the learning imparted by the hidden curriculum. The central questions, then, are: *How* does the child learn from this hidden curriculum, and *How* is he taught? And, once these questions are answered, *Who* teaches him? and *What*, indeed, does he learn?

Language and cultural transmission

That language is the chief medium through which a person learns his world may seem absurdly obvious. We praise our children through language or we scold them; we answer their questions or explain right and wrong to them through language; in the classroom, we expose them to the world of learning through both oral and written language. Indeed, so much do we take language for granted, that perhaps we have overlooked the real impact on learning that language makes.

Fundamentally, of course, it is through the mechanisms of sensory perception that the diverse aspects of the environment are made "known" to the individual. However, without language, this knowledge would remain largely implicit. A word label for an object enables the perceiver to abstract that object, so that a mental image of the object comes to mind when its word label is presented. Similarly, a label, or word symbol, for any *property* of that object enables the perceiver to abstract that property—and thus to distinguish it from the object as a whole. For example, the word *dog* may cue in a child's mind the gross image of a brown collie dog which he has seen, but the words *brown* and *collie* enable him to distinguish that *particular* experience of dog from another, quite different experience with, say, a black Labrador retriever. Thus, verbal symbols enable an individual to articulate in his mind the differences which exist among objects and their properties, among different objects within the same class, and among different classes of objects. Without the use of these symbols, the perceiver could only vaguely "sense" the differences among the diverse objects and relationships that confront him; he would have no way of cognizing (knowing) them explicitly, or of discriminating one object or its properties from another without their being in his immediate perceptional environment.

This verbal processing of sensory experience begins when the child "can respond to, but not make, verbal signals."[5] That is, before the child himself has learned to speak, he learns to associate certain speech sounds made by older individuals in his environment with the objects referred to. As sound labels for objects and persons—and their properties and characteristics—become identified with the objects, persons, and properties themselves, the child's sensations are made explicit for him, and the complex aspects of his environment become articulated in their similarities, differences, values, and various relationships. In this way, *language serves to shape the child's very perceptions:* "Speech marks out what is relevant—affectively, cognitively, and socially—and experience is transformed by that which is made relevant." In short, "spoken language powerfully conditions what is learned and how it is learned, and so influences future learning."[6]

But the speech sounds to which the preverbal child is exposed are normally made within a sociocultural context, and thus the child comes to know not only the objective meaning of the words, but also the cultural or social contexts in which the words are used. This, of course, places the persons or things for which the words stand within the same sociocultural contexts. Culture, therefore, defines and delimits what in his environment the child may come to know, and how he may know it.

Basil Bernstein, sociologist at the University of London, has

[5]B. Bernstein, "Social Class and Linguistic Development: A Theory of Social Learning," in A. H. Halsey, J. Floud, and C. A. Anderson (Eds.), *Education, Economy and Society*, New York, Free Press, 1961.
[6]*Ibid.*

pointed out that modes of speech and linguistic codes—apart from differences in dialect—will vary substantially from culture to culture, and among subcultures. The vocabulary in popular use in any one culture or subculture—and its arrangement into sentences—will lay stress on some objects at the expense of others and will place different values on different objects, as compared to the popular vocabulary of any other culture or subculture. Since the particular sociocultural group one is born into will determine the language code one comes to know and to use, this language code will, in turn, influence the way in which one processes his sensory experience. In other words, what is made available for learning will vary—as a function of the language style used—among different sociocultural groups.

Bernstein identifies two general modes of speech which exist within any given language: elaborated and restricted. An elaborated linguistic code tends to be highly articulated in both its vocabulary and its syntax, while a restricted code has limited syntactical variation and limited vocabulary usage as well. The child exposed at an early age to an elaborated style of speech learns to associate a relatively large number of verbal labels with their corresponding referents, and thus he learns to *perceive* a relatively wide array of objects within his environment. Further, since an elaborated code tends to draw upon adjectives and other descriptive modifiers, the child so reared also learns to perceive a relatively well-articulated environment; for example, the light green sweater as distinguished from the dark green sweater, the harsh voice as distinguished from the loud voice, and so forth. Finally, the relatively broad spectrum of syntactical alternatives for expressing objects and their relationships provides the child with a relatively wide and complex set of contexts in which the objective environment may be understood: "Your brother is doing his homework and mustn't be disturbed until he has finished!" communicates a great deal more than, say, "Don't bother your brother," though both statements may be made with the same goal in mind.

By contrast, a restricted linguistic code is characteristically rigid in its syntactical expressions and tends to avoid descriptive modifiers and, in many cases, specific verbs and nouns. "Don't do that," "Put this on," "Not that sweater, this one," are likely to suffice for "Put the vase down before you break it," "Put your coat on so that you won't be cold," "Please bring me the light green sweater, not the dark green sweater which is lying next to it."

Bernstein further suggests that users of these two modes of speech tend to develop a qualitatively different perceptual orientation to their environment—and to themselves in relation to that environment. Restricted code users develop a perceptual orientation to the *content* of perceived objects, while elaborated code users become oriented to the *structure* of objects. By *content*, Bernstein means "a function of the learned ability to respond to the boundaries of an object." *Structure* refers to "a function of the learned ability to respond to an object perceived and defined in terms of a matrix of relationships in which it stands with other ojbects."[7]

The relatively wider and more articulated perceptual orientation attained by the child reared in an elaborated linguistic code leads to a wider awareness of the environment itself, including many of those aspects which as yet exist outside the child's explicit frame of reference; consequently, such a child is likely to be more explicitly curious than his age counterpart from a restricted language home, who had become accustomed to living with unlabeled, and therefore ill-defined, aspects of his environment. Further, with a more articulated perceptual orientation, a more articulated and well-ordered cognitive structure develops in the child from an elaborated language home; the child is able both to perceive and to think *deductively*, identifying specific objects from general classes of objects—and *inductively*, identifying generalities by abstracting the common properties among groups of specific objects. In this way the child's ability to develop conceptual thinking is established; on this ability all abstract learning is predicated. By contrast, the child equipped with a restricted language code, and a consequently more limited perceptual orientation, is relatively more dependent upon his immediate percep-

[7]B. Bernstein, "Sociological Determinants of Perception," *British Journal of Sociology*, 9, 1958, p. 160.

tual experiences, as gross and generalized as these may be. He has a relatively limited ability to think deductively and inductively, a more limited capacity for abstraction, and consequently, a more limited capacity for abstract learning.

In terms of the intellectual development of children, Bernstein's sociolinguistic theory sheds some valuable light upon the perplexing problem of nature *vs.* nurture as it applies to observable intelligence, and helps to explain the relationships that exist between innate potential and attained achievements among children in school. Educators have traditionally considered children with limited verbal ability as having low capacity for scholastic achievement, and indeed, on the face of the matter, this has all too frequently seemed to be true. School instruction itself has been based on a certain measure of verbal ability, and those with less than this measure have been unable to sustain themselves at the level required by the formal curriculum. Intelligence and aptitude tests geared to determine intellectual potential are to a large extent also based on a certain measure of verbal ability. Results from these tests have largely reinforced the notion that children with limited verbal ability are innately less capable of intellectual learning. Extraverbal intelligence tests have been helpful in this regard; yet when one considers that a child's very mode of perception is shaped by the speech style to which he is exposed, it becomes probable that a large number of children are passed off as virtually uneducable merely because they have not yet acquired the ability to articulate and order their perceptions, or to abstract the relationships that exist among them.

The consequences of linguistic code upon cognitive development is but one aspect of Bernstein's sociolinguistic theory. Social roles also develop out of the contexts made available by a particular culture or subculture, and the linguistic code utilized in social interplay becomes the means by which these roles are learned. An elaborated linguistic code permits a more definitive awareness of one's own behavior in relationships to other objects and persons in the environment. "Don't play with that vase or you'll break it," for example, indicates to the child a host of behavioral possibilities and their possible consequences: Vases—as distinguished from a number of other objects—shouldn't be touched. Why? Because they might break; therefore, objects which will not break are potentially more "touchable" than are vases. And if, through careful handling, vases are not broken, even vases may be touched.

When related to a series of similar experiences, such as "See? You have broken your milk glass; next time be more careful," such expressions lead the child to understand a complex system of behavioral alternatives that are interconnected with various sociocultural contexts: glassware breaks, therefore be careful in handling all such objects; the risk is greater with vases than with milk glasses, for a greater premium is placed upon vases than on milk glasses.

Contrast the behavioral alternatives that become available to the child reared in a restricted mode of speech: "Don't touch that!" merely indicates to the child that the object he is handling at the moment is not to be touched. He has no understanding of why, and therefore cannot apply this learned behavior to any other object. Only through trial and error—touching and being told not to—does he learn which objects he may touch and which he may not. He has no way of classifying each specific event into a general rule which will guide his future behavior. Similarly, "Look what you've done!" in reprimand to his breaking his milk glass only tells the child that the behavior which caused this immediate experiential event is not desirable; he is given no means of developing a sociocultural hierarchy of different objects and his behavior in relationship to these objects. Thus, at best, a restricted language code limits the child's cognition of the behavioral alternatives open to him, and this in turn restricts the number of acceptable behavioral roles he can choose in any given social context.

Further, because of its more formally articulated structure, an elaborated linguistic code permits of a relatively definitive sense of time: "Present decisions affecting the [behavior] of the growing child are governed by their efficacy in attaining distant ends, affectually and cognitively regarded. Behavior is modified by, and oriented to, an explicit set of goals and values. . . . The future is conceived in direct relation to the educational and emotional life of the child."[8] For example, "Your brother is doing his homework and mustn't be disturbed until he has finished," communicates to the child that, while he should refrain from contact with his older brother *now*, he need not do so in the relatively near future—that is, when his brother has finished his homework. The child thus also develops an awareness that when another person is concentrating on an activity, that person is not available for social interplay. Of course, the orientation to all that "homework" implies in this context which ultimately derives from repeated situations of this sort is obvious. The comparable situation as expressed in a restricted speech mode is likely to be more like, "Don't bother your brother." The young recipient of such a directive is left without a specific reference to time and circumstances, and though he implicitly understands that this does not mean that he won't be able to relate to his brother in the future, he is not made explicitly aware of any future, to say nothing of the particular segment of the future insofar as it affects his own behavioral role within this and similar contexts.

This orientation to time and its changing circumstances as applied to different modes of behavior has important consequences upon the child's ability to regulate his own behavior. Without an explicit rational structure to guide him, the child can perceive little more than do or don't behave *this* way, *now*, in this *particular* situation. Moreover, he can acquire few general rules which can be applied in new but similar situations. Such abstractions as he is able to make are likely to be gross and overgeneralized, often leading to socially inappropriate behavior.

Still another aid to the achievement of self-control provided by an elaborated code lies in the verbal tools such a code provides for the child to mediate his own internal feelings:

> Within middle-class and associative levels, direct expressions of feeling, in particular feelings of hostility, are discouraged. The word mediates between the expression of feeling and its approved social recognition, that is, a value is placed

[8]B. Bernstein, "Social Class and Linguistic Development: A Theory of Social Learning," *op. cit.*

> upon the verbalization of feeling. This is so in all societies, but the important determining factor here is the organization of the words and the type of language used; not necessarily the size of the vocabulary, but the degree to which the social emphasis on an aspect of the language structure mediates the relation between thought and feeling. Language exists in relation to a desire to express and communicate; consequently, the mode of a language structure—the way in which words and sentences are related—induces a particular form of the structuring of feeling and so the very means of interaction and response to the environment.[9]

To illustrate, the frustrated or overtired child may express an accompanying hostility through his physical behavior, but an articulated reprimand helps him to identify, simultaneously, (1) his inner feelings, (2) the causes of them, (3) the particular behavioral airing of them, (4) the unacceptability of this particular behavior, (5) the reasons for this unacceptability, and (6) possibly even an alternative mode of release. Such a reprimand might go something like this: "Johnny, you should not hit your little brother; he is much younger than you. I know, you are angry but that is no reason to hit him. Come, you are just overtired. Let's have your nap, and when you wake up you will feel much better."

A comparable reprimand made by a parent using a restricted code might merely be "You bad boy, you know better!"—which, of course, the child probably does not. Or there might be no verbal reprimand, but merely a slap of reprisal by the parent. Thus, physical expression of hostility is not translated into verbal expression, and often is reinforced in the child as an appropriate mode of release for such feelings by the example of the parent's own behavior.

Clearly, then, language becomes the medium through which the child learns his physical and social surroundings and his own role in relation to these surroundings. The specific ways and contexts in which a child is acculturated, however, are complex and must be explored in more detail. We turn, therefore, to the over-

[9] *Ibid.*

all setting of the hidden curriculum, the subdivision of that setting, and the culture which evolves from it: the neighborhood, the family, and the peer group.

The neighborhood

From his birth, the child's environment has a strong effect upon his development. As an infant, of course, he sees little of this environment and is probably aware of even less of it. He is affected by it nonetheless, if only through its effects on his parents. The relative physical comfort in the family dwelling or the number of family members per room tend to be associated with general neighborhood conditions and have an influence upon the mother's state of mind. This state of mind, in turn, plays a part in her behavior toward her child. As the child grows, the neighborhood affects him more directly. The adults he sees (postmen, merchants, servants, maintenance men, or bill collectors), their relationships to his own parents, and their roles in the neighborhood, all serve to shape his developing view of the world, and to comprise a substantial part of his hidden curriculum.

The setting of the hidden curriculum may vary, especially for the socioeconomically disadvantaged child, whose neighborhood is likely to be a slum of uninhabitable dwellings, and human frustration and torpor. For the urban disadvantaged, the problem is compounded by overcrowding, violence, prostitution, and drug addiction. The disadvantaged rural child may live in a one- or two-room shack set among scarred hills and shared with pigs or chickens, as is the case for many in Appalachia. Migrant children may know no neighborhood as such, but only an endless series of cramped dirty rooms and strange faces. The Negro or Puerto Rican child may learn that his neighborhood has strict physical "boundaries" across which he dare not pass for fear of attack from other cultural groups. For the American Indian, the neighborhood is the reservation, and it is unlikely that he will encounter any other environment during his formative years.

The hidden curriculum of the middle-class child, on the

other hand, may be set among expansive rural lawns, tree-lined roads, and safe backyards filled with playground equipment; or it may be among stretches of clean concrete, high buildings, and city noises which are relatively subdued compared with those in the inner city. The urban middle-class child may spend fairly sizable portions of his day in the well-kept neighborhood park or playground.

THE CITY SLUMS

James B. Conant, in describing an *all-white* slum of a large city, quotes a report made by a school principal:

> When a residential area composed of large, old homes, formerly occupied by owners and single family groups changes economically and socially, conditions of general deterioration begin. Absentee owners rent the property by single rooms or small so-called apartments of two or three rooms to large families. . . . Such conditions attract transients (who either cannot or will not qualify for supervised low income housing), the unemployed, the unskilled and unschooled, and the distressed families whose breadwinners have either been committed to prisons or mental institutions or who have but recently been released from such. The only possession most of these families have is children. . . . In such an environment all forms of evil flourish —the peddling of dope, drunkenness, disease, accidents, truancies, physical, mental and moral handicaps, sex perversions involving children . . . at least 100 children are on probation to the Juvenile Court. There has not been a day since I've been at the school that there has not been one or more children in detention at the Juvenile Court. . . .[10]

Time Magazine, in 1964, vividly portrayed New York City's central Harlem, which is virtually *all Negro:*

> . . . [central Harlem] occupies only a 3.5 square mile wedge of upper Manhattan, but 232,000 people are packed into it, 94% of them black. Its worst streets are so crowded that if

[10]J. B. Conant, *Slums and Suburbs,* New York, McGraw-Hill, 1961, p. 16.

> the same density prevailed throughout New York City the entire population of the United States could be jammed into just three of its five boroughs. . . . There is no glamour here, there is little excitement even in the violence and sin. The black bourgeoisie live much as their middle-class white counterparts do. . . . But there are also the tenements where the mortar is so fatigued with age that hoodlums had merely to peel the bricks from crumbling chimneys last week for ammunition to heave at the cops. Half of Harlem's buildings are officially classified as deteriorating or dilapidated, but no classification, official or otherwise, can adequately describe their garbage-strewn hallways and rotting rickety staircases, their rat-infested rooms, and grease-caked stoves where the roaches fight one another for space, their crumbling plaster and Swiss cheese ceilings.
>
> On some streets men who cannot find jobs sit on stoops playing pinochle and coon can and George's skin, or drinking "dirty bird wine" at 60¢ a pint from the bottles hidden in brown paper. Buzzing around them are children who frolic unsupervised far into the night wearing latchkeys on strings around their necks because there is nobody around at home to care for them. Half of Harlem's children under 18 live with only one parent or none, and the juvenile delinquency rate is more than double that of New York's, and the venereal disease rate among Harlem's youth is six times higher than in the rest of the city.[11]

The two descriptions are strikingly similar. Both indicate physical deterioration of living quarters and stifling congestion; both imply a high rate of unemployment; and both spotlight the pervading filth, disease, and vice. Lack of adequate care for children and a high juvenile crime rate are also evident in each description, indicating that city slum conditions are essentially similar no matter what cultural or racial group dominates the neighborhood—white, Negro, Puerto Rican, or Mexican-American. When several cultural groups share a slum neighborhood, or live in adjacent neighborhoods, intercultural antagonism exists, and the sometimes extreme exchanges of hostility, too, are likely to be

[11]"No Place Like Home," *Time* Magazine, July 31, 1964, pp. 11–12.

fundamentally similar, despite any differences in the particularly disputed issues.

Role models

The child defines himself in terms of what he is exposed to and how he is exposed to it. The negative effects upon the child of slum conditions cannot be minimized. It is not untypical, for example, to find on a weekday mid-morning scores of unemployed adults lingering on street corners. Although the young child can hardly interpret this consciously to mean that he won't have to work when he is an adult, neither can he be expected to have the same attitude toward regular employment as the middle-class child, who daily sees his father leave for work and return every evening. Also, the employed adults the child does see may very well be engaged in garbage collection, dishwashing, streetsweeping, and other menial tasks; the vocational ambitions of such a child are thus likely to be severely limited at an early age.

Small wonder that many of these children find it difficult to be motivated by a teacher's appeal to "work hard in school because you will need education for a job some day." The Negro, Puerto Rican or Mexican-American may very well ask himself: "What job? a street cleaner? a porter? a migrant worker?"

Or, the child may be sufficiently exposed to "successful" adults who are numbers writers, racketeers, or "con" artists to cause him to aspire to similar occupations. After all, in his eyes, they are successful adults. Such exposure over a significant portion of the child's life, or during a particularly impressionable phase of his development, will prevent him from accepting the dominant society's evaluation of such occupations.

Ironically, during the school's attempts to broaden horizons through field trips, the child may not see what the school hopes he will. For example, when a group of predominantly Negro children were escorted through the physical plant of a major urban industry in an attempt to expose them to the changing world of work, they viewed the different roles which comprise the particular industry. They saw that most of the key positions were held by whites and that Negroes were the custodian, the sweeper, and the file clerk. The school authorities could not understand why the children were not more enthusiastic after such an "enrichment trip."

The adult models in the hidden curriculum of the slum also indoctrinate the child to the mainstream culture, and he identifies himself in relation to it accordingly. The Negro child, for example, tends to identify more with Negro adults, many of whom —if employed at all—are engaged in subservient tasks that keep them in soiled work clothes much of the time, while the white people he sees are more likely to be clean, well-dressed, and generally prosperous. His own father (if he knows him) may be a janitor or handyman for an office or apartment building in a middle-class neighborhood; his mother may be a domestic in a middle- or upper-class home. Or the child may know the white man only as a bill collector or process server who seems to threaten his family's security. The contrasts these situations present to the child harm both his self-image and his view of the dominant society.

The orientation of the slum child to the police is a particular case in point. In a slum, where incidents of crime and violence are frequent, the policeman is the outstanding authority figure. A young child, free much of the time to wander the streets, may see a policeman dispersing a group of teenagers or unemployed men loitering on a corner. The child cannot interpret, as does society, that the loiterers may be fostering some evil scheme; on the contrary, the child only sees a uniformed man (perhaps a white one) as a troublemaker among familiar and relatively trusted faces. The child's own mother may draw on the authority image of the police for disciplinary purposes: "If you don't keep quiet I'll call a cop," or, "You better not let a cop see you do that or he'll put you in jail." Hostilities of the slum child toward the policeman are therefore not surprising.

Such an authority figure can play another role in a child's life, particularly if the child's paternal parent is weak or missing: The child may see the power and force of the police as desirable characteristics in their own right and may emulate his own version of a policeman's bravery, strength, and authority. In this way, perhaps, exposure to the neighborhood policeman may account for some of the "toughness" displayed by children and youth in slum areas.

The views held toward the police among many who live in slum neighborhoods are expressed by Juan Gonzales, a young Puerto Rican in New York:

> The police are the most crooked, the most evil. I've never seen a policeman that was fair or that was even good. All the policemen I've ever known are hanging around in the liquor store or taking money from Jim on the corner, or in the store on the avenue. They're just out to make a buck no matter how they can do it. OK, maybe if you gave them more money they wouldn't be so crooked, but what do you need to qualify for a policeman? I mean, if you have an ounce of brain and you have sturdy shoulders and you're about six feet one, you can be a policeman. That's all.
>
> I mean you've got to fight them all the time. A policeman is supposed to be somebody that protects people. You're supposed to be able to count on them. You're supposed to look up to the policemen and know that if anything goes wrong, if any boys jumped me, I can just yell and the policeman will come running and save me. Around my block, you get jumped, the police will say, "Well, that's just too bad." He just sits there.
>
> Even the sergeants are crooked. It's the whole police force is rotten. There was a man, I don't know who he was, way out in Brooklyn somewhere. He broke down a whole police station, a whole police force, the detectives, the policemen, the rookies. Everybody that was on that police force was crooked. Everybody in the precinct was crooked. He had to tell them all to go home."[12]

Against this education which the slum child gets from his hidden curriculum concerning the law and its enforcement officers, consider how the Bank Street Readers, for example, present the policemen to the child when he enters the formal curriculum.

[12]Charlotte Leon Mayerson (Ed.), *Two Blocks Apart: Juan Gonzales and Peter Quinn*, New York, Holt, Rinehart and Winston, 1965, pp. 39–40.

Policemen walk.

Policemen ride in cars.

They fly over the city.

They go in boats.

Policemen go all over the city, by day and night.[13]

Crowding

The congestion of slum life, together with the crowded family living imposed by such a neighborhood, also affects the child's development in significant ways. Hunt suggests that crowding may not be a negative influence during the child's first year of life:

> Crowding . . . may be no handicap for a human infant during most of his first year of life. Although there is no certainty of this, it is conceivable that being a young infant among a large number of people living within a room may actually serve to provide such wide variations of visual and auditory inputs that it will facilitate development more than will the conditions typical of the culturally privileged during most of the first year. . . .[14]

Hunt goes on to say, however, that after the first year of life, crowding may cause deprivation:

> During the second year, on the other hand, living under crowded conditions could well be highly hampering. As the infant begins to throw things and as he begins to develop his own methods of locomotion, he is likely to find himself getting in the way of adults already ill tempered by their own discomforts. . . . The fact that his parents are preoccupied with the problems associated with their poverty and their crowded living conditions leaves them with little capacity to be concerned with what they conceive to be the senseless questions of a prattling infant. With things to play with

[13]Irma Simonton Black (Ed.), *Around the City*, New York, Macmillan, 1965, p. 118.

[14]J. M. Hunt, "The Psychological Basis for Using PreSchool Enrichment as an Antidote for Cultural Deprivation," *The Merrill Palmer Quarterly*, **10**:3 (1964), 237–238.

and room to play in highly limited, the circumstances of the crowded lower-class offer little opportunity for the kinds of environmental encounters required to keep a two-year-old youngster developing at all, and certainly not at an optimal rate, and not in the direction demanded for adaptation in the highly technological culture.[15]

Asbell suggests that the constant cacophony of noises and confusion of perceptual and olfactory stimuli that result from congestion may have the effect of conditioning the child to "tune out" his environment:

> Psychologists are beginning to discern that the slum child's inattention may be a high skill, the result of intensive training. When the child lives with 11 people in three rooms . . . sharing their toilets, knowing when the man is drunk next door and [that] the baby is awake downstairs—a child must *learn* to be inattentive to survive. His ears become skilled in not hearing, his eyes at not seeing. . . .[16]

There are, no doubt, many additional factors connected with slum living which also have strong effects on developing children, and which should be studied seriously by those concerned with tapping the human potential that exists in these areas. This chapter, however, is not concerned with an exhaustive analysis of slum conditions, but with the thesis that the educational setting provided by the slum dweller's hidden curriculum is indeed conducive to learning, and that the slum child does learn about a real world in a real way. To the child raised in this setting, the formal school curriculum must seem strange indeed.

THE RURAL SETTING

For some children, there is no neighborhood as such. Sutton describes the mobile life of the rural migrant child:

> . . . The migrant child lives for short periods of time during each year in several communities, sometimes in two, four,

[15]*Ibid.*, p. 238.
[16]B. Asbell, *The New Improved American*, New York, McGraw-Hill, 1965.

> six, and eight different states. Even though his family may have a well-established migratory route, there is no assurance that while on the trek he will reside in the same communities year after year. To some migrant children home is the location where they live the longest time during the winter—to others, home has no meaning whatsoever, and in response to questions regarding it they answer, "Nope, ain't got no home. Just any place we're at, that's my home." Or, "I don't know. You see we move a lot."[17]

This life provides the child with little that he can call his own; it gives him neither a home nor small personal items. It is not surprising that such children find it difficult to grasp the middle-class value of ownership and property. The adult models for them are predominantly fellow migrant workers and, since the children themselves generally work in the fields as soon as they are old enough, migrant work is all they come to know. Michael Harrington reports the case of one adult migrant worker reared in this fashion who claimed he has been "quitting for twelve years now. It just gets in your blood," he explained.[18]

The migrant child's setting also exposes him to interracial strife. Whether he is white, Negro, or Mexican-American, he sees the adults in his own group competing desperately against the others for a place in the fields, and the resentment experienced by the members of his group is passed on to the child.

On the other hand, the migrant's life on wheels provides the child with a rich variety of experiences, many of which potentially equal those provided in the formal curriculum. The difficulty is that, because of a lack of adult guidance, the child learns little from these experiences. Sutton, for example, describes the travels of a migrant child.

> The children see much of the United States while on the road, but they have little understanding of what they see. "I saw fields and fields of pretty grass when we went through

[17]Elizabeth Sutton, *Knowing and Teaching the Migrant Child*, Washington, D.C., Department of Rural Education, National Education Association, 1960, p. 14.
[18]M. Harrington, *The Other America*, Baltimore, Penguin Books, 1962.

> Kentucky. Is that where they raise those race horses?" "We crossed a lot of water on a big boat when we went to Virginia. Was that the Chesapeake Bay?" "We went through a long dark place; they said that the road went under a river. Where was that?"[19]

However, the rural migrant child does learn from this hidden curriculum. Some of his learning might be itemized in this way:

1. Extensive travel gives him some idea of geographic areas.
2. Crop picking from childhood gives him a criteria of adequate work performance. He knows who is or is not considered a good worker, who is or is not a good boss. He can describe in detail the different processes utilized in crop picking and which type of harvesting is the hardest work and why.
3. A life on wheels and enrollment in numerous schools may not give him a clear picture of *his* school, but he can describe how schools differ.
4. Borderline subsistence teaches him hunger, long hours of toil, and living from day to day. He becomes sensitive to the significance of weather change.

Whether this knowledge is utilized by the schools to foster new learning is not clear. What is clear is that, when the rural migrant child meets with the formal curriculum of the school, he is unprepared. He may not start school at the usual age, and, if he does, he may be far behind the intellectual development of even the slum child. Worse, his life seldom allows him to remain in any one school for very long; thus, when he reaches the minimum age required to quit school altogether, he has probably completed substantially less than the eighth year.

THE RESERVATION

In many respects, the average American Indian today is the most disadvantaged of all our minority groups, and, due to the

[19]Elizabeth Sutton, *op. cit.*, p. 15.

historical circumstances peculiar to the Indian, the neighborhood setting has played a particularly significant role in determining and maintaining his disadvantaged state. With few exceptions, Indian reservations are situated on barren or semiarid lands which are unsuitable for agriculture or cattle raising, and many are in regions affected by extreme climates. In the midst of a rapidly growing technological America—in which indoor plumbing with hot and cold running water, central heating, and even air conditioning are taken for granted by most—the typical reservation is largely made up of the most primitive of dwellings: Tents, mud huts, one-room board shacks, log and grass wickiups, and sun-baked clay adobes still shelter a substantial majority of Indians under all sorts of weather conditions. Disease—particularly tuberculosis—is widespread, and infant mortality is three times the national rate. The average life expectancy for the Indian is no more than 41 to 46 years, depending on the geographical region in which he lives—more than twenty years shorter than the life span of the typical white man. The unemployment rate is placed at about 40 percent, and the average family income—some of it deriving from public support—is $1500. Ben Bagdikian reports the following statistics for one group of Indians:

Life Expectancy: 17 years
Infant Death Rate: 258 out of every 1000
Yearly Income: Less than $500[20]

The following description of the American Indian of the Pacific Northwest amply illustrates the general surroundings of the hidden curriculum of the American Indian:

> The general economic, social, and physical conditions on these reservations are pathetic. The traditions of fishing and minor agricultural pursuits are not sufficient to maintain any adequate standard of living. The homes of the Indians are generally in very poor repair with inadequate facilities for sanitation, heating, and water. A state of general depression exists and has existed for a number of years. . . .

[20]B. H. Bagdikian, *In the Midst of Plenty,* New York, Signet, 1964, p. 30.

> Approximately 30% of the Indian families are on public welfare, and this is six times the rate for the local community.
>
> The health and welfare of the Indian American in the Pacific Northwest . . . is extraordinarily depressed. The overriding statistic which blots out all others is the average life span of the Indian. In 1960 the median life span of all Indians was not more than 41 years and in the Pacific Northwest it was not more than 46 years. In essence, this means that the Indian child looks forward to approximately 25 years less of life than his non-Indian counterpart.
>
> The other statistics follow a dreary trail after this first shocking realization. Indians are hospitalized twice as frequently; tuberculosis occurs at four times the rate of the whites; infant mortality is triple. One is not reassured by the accurate observation that in the area of health and welfare, conditions have improved in the past 10, 20, or 30 years. All in all, one can say that the circle of poverty, disease, and depression has hit home with a vengeance on these people.[21]

It is in this kind of physical setting of the hidden curriculum that most Indian children spend their preschool years and the bulk of their nonschool lives. Many grow to school age speaking only their tribal language, and even those children who acquire a familiarity with English before entering the formal curriculum have as their cultural frame of reference the social context, customs, traditions, and attitudes peculiar to their tribe. As one example, in Arizona, the scarcity of water forces some Indians to obtain it at sources very distant from their dwellings. This scarcity determines a priority in its use, with survival taking precedence. Consequently, there is not enough water to keep children clean at all times. When status in school depends on the child's cleanliness, a survival priority becomes a social and psychological need.

[21] V. F. Haubrick, "Indians in Two Public School Systems, Deprivation and Disadvantage," paper presented at Fourth Annual Oregon Program Workshop, "Teaching the Disadvantaged Child," Summer, 1965, Salem, Ore.

On many reservations, customs and traditions—and the formal rites and ceremonies through which they are expressed—are still carried out with great determination, despite the fact that the living conditions which once gave them their relevance ceased to be long ago.

Unlike the adult models of the slum child or the migrant, those provided by the reservation setting are not merely the more or less arbitrary socializing agents who quite unwittingly acculturate the children away from mainstream society; on the contrary, Indians tend to make a special effort to indoctrinate their offspring in tribal ways, and to cultivate tribal loyalty at an early age. In other words, Indian children are quite *deliberately* socialized in the traditional culture, and this process often ingrains in the child a different view of his future from that held by a middle-class white child. Thus, from the start of his formal education, the average Indian child has at best a severely limited perception of the larger American community, and he is likely to be wholly unprepared for its vastly different cultural orientation as it is explicitly and implicitly presented by the American school.

The problem of conflict that results is severe. On the one hand, the Indian child's whole socializing identity has been formed by the tribal culture; on the other, his attendance at school represents entry into an entirely different culture. The tug of war between his tribal orientation and the orientation of the school poses severe identity strains on the Indian child. If he moves toward the institutional orientation he may be viewed as trying to be a white man; if he accepts the tribal orientation he limits his mobility in the mainstream society. Adding to this conflict is the fact that the school, as an institution which reflects the mainstream orientation, is often insensitive to the values inherent in Indian culture. For example, when Indian children enter school they are told that they may no longer speak their native tongue. Many schools have passed a rule making English the only acceptable language. What educators have in essence been saying to the young children is, "We disapprove of your parents, your people, and everything you have been able to do with your language. We're going to teach you another language that from now on you must use."[22] Many educators now believe this has done much more harm than good.

THE SUBURB

In Chapter 1 we indicated that the mobility pattern of the United States is increasingly from rural areas to cities, and that, as the cities become more and more densely populated, those with the economic means to do so, in turn, move to the outlying residential areas of these cities, the suburbs. This latter population comprises the bulk of the mainstream of society, and thus, for most middle-class children, the setting of the hidden curriculum is suburban.

To travel from a city slum to a suburb would, in one sense, be going from the hidden curriculum of the disadvantaged poor to the hidden curriculum of the affluent disadvantaged. The transformation in setting is striking: from congestion to spaciousness, from concrete to grass, from noise to quiet. In the suburb, the difference between the setting of the informal curriculum and that of the formal curriculum is narrow, if it exists at all. The suburban neighborhood is virtually homogeneous, both in appearance and in cultural characteristics, and the neighborhood school blends in well with this background. The tree-lined streets, individual front lawns, and spacious backyards filled with swings, slides, and plastic wading pools are well matched by the tree-lined streets, wide green lawns, and large play areas that surround the local school. The residents are clean, well-dressed, and usually white, as are the local teachers. These are the surroundings and people that the child sees portrayed on television, in his picture books, and in the primary readers he will use when he begins school.

The fact that the suburban school and its residential community tend to provide nearly identical learning situations does not mean, however, that they are geared to the reality of adult living; nor is the suburban setting necessarily that which produces

[22]Caryl Steere *et al.*, *Indian Teacher-Aide Handbook*, Temple, Ariz., Arizona State Univ., Bureau of Publications, December, 1965, p. 78.

cultural, experiential, educational, or even economic advantage. That the suburban community may provide a severely restricted culture for the growing child is suggested by Peter Wyden:

> . . . More and more kids come to know only their neatly manicured, fumeless, comfortably monotonous bedroom communities where there are almost no old people, no poor, no childless, no Negroes, either no Jewish families or many, no sidewalks, no places to explore except by mother-chauffeured car, no houses or incomes too different from those of their parents.[23]

This homogeneous and limited setting is far from representational of settings elsewhere in the world today, or, for that matter, in this country. Indeed, the bland monotony of suburban living may limit the growing child's experiences, and lack of exposure to different cultures, values, and attitudes may have serious consequences on his role as an adult in society. For a child who has spent his formative years in such a setting, later school studies of different cultures and peoples are likely to be remote and meaningless and to make little permanent impression. Further, the emphasis placed on "conspicuous consumption" and affluence by suburban residents may give the child a highly unrealistic orientation to the value of money.

A major area of disadvantage for the middle class is its segregation from other cultural and ethnic groups. Since they do not know the poor, the middle-class parent and child may be insensitive to their plight. Many, indeed, of the middle class find it difficult to comprehend why help and assistance offered the economically less fortunate are not received enthusiastically. As the poor explain it:

> They keep on telling us, those welfare ladies, to take better care of our money and save it away, and buy what's the best in the stores, and do like them for dresses, and keep the children in school, and keep our husbands from leaving us. There isn't nothing they don't have a sermon on. They'll tell you it's bad to spend your money on a smoke or a drink;

[23]P. Wyden, *Suburbia's Coddled Kids*, New York, Avon Books, 1962, p. 14.

> and it's bad to have your kids sleep alongside you in the bed; and you're not supposed to want television because you should be serious with your dollar, and it's wrong for the kids, too; and it's bad for you to let them stay out after dark, and they should study their lessons hard and they'll get way ahead and up there.
>
> Well, I'll tell you, they sure don't know what it's about, and they can't, not if they come knocking on my door every week until the Lord takes all of us. They have their nice leather shoes, and their smart coats, and they speak the right order of words all right, so I know how many schools they been to. But us? Do they have any idea what us is about? And let them start at zero the way we do, and see how many big numbers they can become themselves. I mean, if you have got nothing when you're born, and you know you can't get a thing no matter how you tries—well, then you dies with nothing. And no one can deny that arithmetic.[24]

Although the suburban child sees his father and the others in the neighborhood leave for work each morning and return home each evening—thus automatically conditioning him to the "natural" fact of adult employment—he frequently, as Wyden points out, has little idea of *how* his father spends his working days. The mystery enshrouding the suburban father, who rushes off with early-morning commuting crowds— not to be seen again by his family until the evening (perhaps just before the children are put to bed, perhaps when they are already asleep)—can offset the effects that this male model would otherwise have on the child. In contrast, the part-time gardener or handyman, the cleaning woman, and the municipal garbage collector and maintenance man who serve the neighborhood are available relatively continuously for the child's observations. These people dress, not in the style of the suburban father, but in soiled overalls or work clothes. Their faces may be dark with soil and perspiration or they may be Negro. Indeed, the only Negroes a child from an all-white neighborhood sees may be menial workers, and these early as-

[24]Quoted in R. Coles, "The Poor Don't Want To Be Middle Class," *The New York Times Magazine*, December 19, 1965, p. 55.

sociations may provide the basis for gross generalizations made later in life. A child who lives in a white suburb may see a Negro collecting the trash and garbage. If this child sees another Negro he may tend to call him "garbageman." Already the stigma of color has been subtly communicated. The following situation is also revealing:

> A lone Negro child in a suburban nursery school was getting along famously, but the parents of the white children were chronically embarrassed because their youngsters kept insisting that the colored child's mother, who called for her boy just like the other mothers, must be the family maid.[25]

As with the slum children, the policeman is an image of authority to the suburban child, but the suburban child sees police force and power as always directed against the "bad guy" (who, incidentally, frequently conforms to the physical appearance of neighborhood maintenance people). The authority that the policeman represents to the middle-class child is of protection and helpfulness—the policeman is an all-around "good guy."

When the overall setting of the hidden curriculum of the middle-class child meets that of the formal school curriculum, the latter reinforces the former, and the child's understanding of reality—to say nothing of his values—is likely to be severely warped.

The family

The neighborhood, like the school, is only part of what the child learns. More important is the subdivision within the setting, where the child spends most of his time; for the hidden curriculum it is the family.

A family is more than a group of people more or less related to one another; it is, in a sense, a vibrant living organism, composed of constituent organisms who must constantly interact for the mutual health and equilibrium of one another and of the family as a whole. When these interactions break down or become

[25]P. Wyden, *op. cit.*, p. 11.

in some way destructive, the family unit and each of its members will suffer. Therefore, the family is of vital importance to the developing child.

Some friction is bound to occur in any family, of course. Without such interpersonal friction the family would become static—its members phlegmatic—and this would have a highly deleterious effect on an individual's survival ability in the real, conflict-ridden world. A relatively happy family, therefore, will have a fundamental stability based on mutual love, trust, and warmth which will ameliorate times of dissension and crisis. It is through just such stability that the child learns to trust the world even in times of crisis. Frequent or protracted antagonism, however, disrupts family stability and, with it, the child's sense of security.

The degree of stability a family enjoys is communicated in a variety of ways to the child from the time of his birth. At first, it is through physical contact and care provided by his mother; later, it is transmitted by other members of the household, the father, siblings, and resident relatives.

As the child is learning to trust or to mistrust his world through his family's stability, he is also learning *about* his world. Even before he can speak, he learns to respond to words, and thus to the objects they stand for, through the language used in the family. This language bears emotional as well as objective content, and through it the child's inner and outer worlds are shaped for him.

Of course, family variables which affect the development and education of children are numerous, and this discussion can sketch only some of the major factors involved in familial subdivisions of the hidden curriculum.

THE EXTENDED FAMILY

Society thinks of the typical family unit as composed of a mother, a father, and from two to five children. Rarely does the average individual imagine a "normal" family of more than seven or eight members. Yet, among the lower socio-economic groups, the family may be composed of many children and many parents and parent-substitutes: "The home typically includes aunts, uncles, grandparents, all of whom may, to some degree play a parental role. . . . In the Negro family the grandmother often plays the most decisive role."[26] A single Puerto Rican home may shelter a man and his wife, their five or six younger children, two or three older offspring, their spouses and their children, and perhaps a brother, sister, or parent of the first man or his wife. Among American Indians, the blood relatives are considered very close; aunts often are considered to be mothers, and uncles, fathers. Cousins are thought of as brothers and sisters, and even other clan members are considered to be relatives. In contradistinction to these cultural values, the typically mainstream American considers only the nuclear family to be most important.

The lower economic classes tend to have what we call extended families, partly because more members of a household mean more earning potential. Adult relatives living with the basic family can supplement household income and help care for the children when the parents are working. For some ethnic groups, the extended family is largely a continuation in the United States of a long cultural tradition. In many cases, the economic and housing pressures imposed on families from these groups provide strong encouragement for extended-family living.

The extended family is likely to have a considerably different effect on a child's development from that of the single nuclear family, whose structure intensifies interrelationships among its relatively few members. The extended family dilutes these interpersonal relationships and reduces the chances for close bonds between any two members. The child from the extended family is likely to have not one but several male and female adult models with whom he can identify. His older siblings or his aunts and grandmother may care for him and responsibility for his nurturing may be more or less equally divided among several persons. The child may not spend sufficient time with any of his male models to develop a close bond of identification. Even where there is a key male or female figure, the child may have to share this rela-

[26]F. Riessman, *The Culturally Deprived Child,* New York, Harper & Row, 1962, p. 36.

tionship with numerous siblings, and may grow up detached in his interpersonal relationships and lacking a clear-cut understanding of himself and his role in his social environment.

It is significant to note that, although the characteristic structure of the suburban family is nuclear (the parents and children only), there are aspects of modern suburban life which resemble the pattern of the extended family. In many suburban neighborhoods, care and supervision of children are frequently shared by other parents of the block, and neighbors frequently take turns in sitting activities while the mothers go out to shop or to club meetings. Wyden hints at the suburban substitute for the extended family:

> I don't know any mothers who usher their kids out of the house in the morning and tell them, "Go out and let the neighbors bring you up." But I have met quite a few ladies who hope that effortless exposure of their children to the wholesome suburban environment and the "nice" parents and kids in the neighborhood will relieve them of some of their own responsibilities.[27]

Nevertheless, when a lower-class child, whose understanding of the typical family includes aunts, uncles, brothers- and sisters-in-law, cousins, and even nephews and nieces, is confronted with the formal curriculum of the school, he may find it difficult to understand some of the material to which he is exposed. For example, most primary readers include stories about neat, clean, and happy families which have one mother, one father, and perhaps two or three brothers and sisters; and the central plot of many of these stories concerns travelling some distance to see Grandmother or Cousin Bill.

THE BROKEN OR INCOMPLETE FAMILY

Current statistics put the divorce rate for first marriages at approximately 25 percent of the total.[28] This rate, added to mar-

[27] P. Wyden, *op. cit.*, p. 12

[28] *Statistical Abstract of the United States*, 1965, Washington, D.C., U.S. Department of Commerce.

riages which are legally or illegally separated, or which are terminated by death of a partner, brings the proportion of broken homes to a considerable sum. Include the incomplete families in which there never was a legal father, and the total becomes still higher.

The broken family is not a phenomenon limited to the lower socioeconomic classes; on the contrary, divorce alone is common to the middle and upper classes. Thus, a broken family "represents a social problem that is independent of the economic conditions under which it operates."[29] The feelings of loss, failure, guilt, and shame that affect children and parents of broken families also cross all social barriers. Often the family's economic security is disrupted by the loss of the breadwinner; and the combined effects of economic insecurity and family instability can have unfortunate consequences, particularly for growing children.

Divorce, separation, and desertion as sources of family disruption are frequently preceded by arguments between the parents and general tension in the home. Children tend to assume the burden of blame for their parents' stormy relationships, especially when the parents compete with one another for the child's favor or use him against each other. In addition, the hostilities between the parents often find outlet against the children as scapegoats of marital failure. Such an environment affects the child's developing ego structure, often with harmful consequences to intellectual and personality functions. Similarly, when death takes one of the parents, the sense of loss is sometimes translated into resentment by the remaining parents and this resentment, in turn, is communicated to the child. The child, without adequate guidance, is likely to feel that he is in some way guilty for the parent's death, especially where the remaining parent's grief denies the child full satisfaction of his needs.

The family which was incomplete in the first place is found primarily in the lower segments of society, especially since the illegitimate babies born to middle-class women are usually adopted

[29] O. Pollak, "The Broken Family," in N. E. Cohen (Ed.), *Social Work and Social Problems*, New York, National Association of Social Workers, 1964.

into other middle- or upper-class homes. For many nonwhite babies, there are no such placements, and yet, these children too must encounter the formal curriculum of the school. There are also those fatherless babies who remain in the care of their mothers. Miller gives some idea of the scope of this problem:

> The . . . fatherless home is another major segment of the poor. There were one and a half million families like this in 1960, and virtually all concentrated in large metropolitan areas. About one million of these families were white and one half million were non-white.
>
> The large portion of non-whites within this group reflects the instability of family life among the Negroes. Every fifth Negro child is born out of wedlock and mothers of many of these children are left to fend for themselves in a hostile world. . . .[30]

Helen Perlman describes the plight of the unmarried Negro woman:

> When a Negro unmarried mother gives birth, she has three economic alternatives: she can depend, with her baby, on her family's (or the putative father's) support, she can go to work to support herself and her baby, or she can apply for ADC (Aid to Dependent Children). In the last two instances she must have someone else care for her baby. If it is not her mother or grandmother, this care must be paid for, and her earnings are rarely enough to buy adequate child care. If she applies for ADC, she and her child become a burden to the taxpayer. . . .
>
> The state of economic dependency on a regular relief grant is not the ummitigated pleasure that it is sometimes made out to be. The fact is that this money grant to child and mother is a minimal one that meets only marginal food, shelter, and clothing needs. It may be said that this grant is good or better than what this woman had before, and it cannot be argued but that it is a dependable, regular source of support. Nevertheless, it cannot be said that it allows either unwed mother or her growing child opportunity for expansion of their experience, or pushing back the constrict-

[30] P. Miller, *Rich Man, Poor Man*, New York, Signet, 1964, p. 88.

> ing walls that poverty without end imposes, or for looking forward with hope. . . .[31]

The child reared by only one parent faces many developmental difficulties. He is lacking not only a key model with whom he can identify, but also the chance to be a child *to* that parent. A child who has both a mother and a father is exposed to two different behavioral modes, feminine and masculine. Such a child tends to identify his own role most closely with the parent of his same sex and to imitate the general behavior of that parent, especially in relating to the parent of the opposite sex. Yet it is through interaction with each model as well as through imitation, that the child assimilates his understanding of the role behavior of the sexes. Thus, a boy who exhibits unmasculine behavior will be discouraged in that behavior by *both* his mother and his father, though each in a different way. The child who is without one parent lacks this opportunity for contrast in interaction. Further, the remaining parent who must fill a double role is likely to become confused in his own behavior; thus, the behavior typical of even the represented sex becomes unclear for the child.

This child's problems are compounded when he encounters the school curriculum. In most broken or incomplete homes—particularly among the lower socioeconomic groups—the missing parent is the father, and, since most primary grade teachers are women, the formal curriculum tends to reinforce behavior patterns the child has learned as a result of being reared solely by a mother. In many cases, the child's classmates do not lack parents, and this alone presents him with significant adjustment problems. When he is confronted with elementary readers, in which there are always a happy father and a happy mother, he is further hindered in his adjustment.

Family rituals and rearing patterns

The cultures of both the family and society are transmitted to the child largely through the daily habits and rituals of his

[31]Helen H. Perlman, "Unmarried Mothers," in Cohen, *op. cit.*

family. Washing before meals, bathing at bedtime, learning to say "please" and "thank you" reflect the myriad details common to the life of the "average" American. For some children, however, the family keeps alive certain cultural traits which are, quite literally, foreign to most Americans. Many Puerto Rican children are taught very early to show respect to their elders by bowing their heads. In the classroom, the Puerto Rican child may find that the opposite conveys respect; the teacher may insist, "Look at me when I'm talking to you," or "Look me squarely in the eye when I call on you." The whole orientation, the "machismo," for many Puerto Rican children constitutes a basic frame of reference toward masculinity. Certain types of physical contact between the adolescent boy and male adult are frowned upon. Thus, a teacher attempting to show friendship by putting his hands on a boy's shoulders might cause the child to jerk away; the teacher, in turn, may interpret this as defiance or unfriendliness and further widen the gulf between teacher and learner. Similarly, an illness in the migrant worker's family requires everyone to remain at home—despite the meager family income—until the person's health is regained, and teachers may interpret the resultant absenteeism of the migrant child as a lack of interest in school.

Indian family life differs considerably from the middle-class American life. For example, in Indian cultures, time is relative and clocks are not watched. The family starts the day with sunrise and ends it with sunset. In the culture of the school, the whole day is often regulated by bells, and the concept of time is made very explicit. Children are penalized for minor deviations from the prescribed time schedules; e.g., tardiness to class, handing in reports late, etc.

To a large extent, the culture imparted to the child is a function of his parents' educational background. The educational level is considerably lower for parents in the lower socioeconomic strata. Conant reports:

> Only 10 per cent of the parents [in a slum] had graduated from high school and only 33 per cent had completed elementary school. In contrast is the situation in which a third of the parents have completed elementary school to a high

income suburb where as many as 90 per cent of the parents have bachelor's degrees if not graduate degrees from the university. [32]

Formal education, as well as general culture, determines the types and extent of family rituals. Conversely, these rituals may have a strong bearing on the child's later understanding of the formal educational process. One family ritual which has important implications to later learning is the bedtime story. LaBrant suggests that pieces such as the "Mother Goose Rhymes," *Alice in Wonderland*, and Anderson's *Tales* develop familiarity with characters and events which appear repeatedly in both current and historical English prose.[33] Children who are familiar with these stories, and who have seen pictures and heard phonograph records of these favorites, have established strong foundations for later appreciation of literature. The school too frequently overlooks the fact that the hidden curriculum of the disadvantaged child may ignore this supposedly common heritage. Also, children from middle- and upper-class homes are exposed to books, magazines, and classical and popular music, which condition their artistic tastes.

In many homes, mealtime is a time for learning attitudes and skills. In theory, at least, middle-class families eat meals on a fairly regular schedule—an important factor in orienting the child to a time concept. Moreover, the parents may use the dinner table as a family forum for conversation and personal expression. Mealtime thus becomes an important social context for language development, and the child learns that he is expected to contribute to the conversation as his parents discuss such things as cleanliness, the nutritional aspects of food, money, current events, neighborhood events, respect for property, the care of pets, or success at school. The parents' expectations of the child and their personal values are also communicated to the child in this way. Significantly, these family seminars, which also include instruc-

[32]J. B. Conant, *op. cit.*, p. 19.

[33]L. LaBrant, "The Goals for Culturally Different Youth," in A. Jewett *et al.* (Eds.), *Improving English Skills of Culturally Different Youth*, Washington, D.C., U.S. Government Printing Office, 1964, p. 27.

tion in etiquette and deportment, become lessons in language and articulation.

Among some subcultural groups, however, mealtime is seldom utilized as a discussion and training vehicle if, indeed, meals are regularly scheduled at all. The unsupervised slum children may come and go as they please, raiding the icebox whenever they are hungry. Family members may eat hastily, alone, and with little communication with the others. In a study conducted in New York, for example, only one half of the lower-class children studied regularly ate one meal with both parents. The other children took their meals either alone or with their brothers and sisters.[34] In some families, meals may be eaten while watching television, thus precluding the need to speak. Such verbal communication as does occur may be laconic and to the immediate point: "There's soda and cake in the refrigerator. Get some and eat." Or, "I'm gonna get me some more cake." Or, "Hey, you're blocking my way—move your head." If a radio is available it will be tuned to a station for popular music, and if a news broadcast begins, a parent is likely to say, "Put some music on, will you?"—again diminishing verbal stimulation. Such lack of verbal communication and interaction seems to restrict the language learned by the child.

Among some socioeconomic groups, the deficit in adult-child communication is manifested in other ways. The naturally curious child may ask questions that merely annoy the already overburdened adult, who dismisses him with as brief an answer as possible. The previously mentioned restricted language code and the lack of adult response to the child's curiosity combine to hinder his later functioning in the classroom setting. Hunt sums up these two factors:

> Beginning in the third year, . . . imitation of novel patterns should presumably be well-established, and should supply a mechanism for learning vocal language. The variety of linguistic patterns available for imitation in the models pro-

[34]Suzanne Keller, "The Social World of the Urban Slum Child, Some Early Findings," *American Journal of Orthopsychiatry*, October, 1963, p. 826.

> vided by lower-class adults is both highly limited and wrong for the standards of later schooling. Furthermore, when the infant has developed a number of pseudo-words and has achieved the "learning set" that "things have names" and begins asking "what's that?", he is all too unlikely to get answers. Or, the answers are all too likely to be so punishing that they inhibit such questioning.[35]

In contrast to the "ideal" family patterns attributed to the middle class, the child of the lower socioeconomic level is indeed disadvantaged, and, theoretically, a child with such rich family relationships is indeed advantaged. But what values and insights are *actually* being projected to many of the middle- and upper-class children through their family rituals?

Peter Wyden presents convincing and shocking evidence that families living in restricted suburban atmospheres are depriving their children of many desirable experiences. A few examples:

> A sixth grader tried to pay for his 35¢ lunch with a $50 bill.[36]
>
> A seventh grader boasted in school how his father had made him a vice president in three corporations to satisfy certain technicalities for income tax authorities.[37]
>
> A four-year-old boy was taken by his mother to St. Louis where he said of a Negro boy, "Look how dirty that boy's face is!"[38]
>
> Two boys, aged ten and fourteen, were taken by their father past some downtown slums. One of the boys demanded incredulously, "You mean people *live* in these places?"[39]
>
> In one public [suburban] park a pond was stocked with fish for the convenience of the resident fathers. "It's a quick fishing trip so they can get rid of their obligations to the kids," said a disgusted policeman.[40]

[35]J. M. Hunt, *op. cit.*, p. 238.
[36]P. Wyden, *op. cit.*, p. 11.
[37]*Ibid.*
[38]*Ibid.*, p. 24
[39]*Ibid.*
[40]*Ibid.*, p. 36.

> One bright kindergarten girl . . . could not identify a dishpan pictured in her reading test. She had never seen one. . . . Many children in dishwasher-equipped subdivisions haven't. [41]

Wyden also indicates that—popular myth to the contrary—many suburban children lack continuous contact with adult family members. Commuting fathers spend much of the working week away from home, and their free time is likely to be spent in a flurry of local civic activities, visiting and entertaining, or on the golf course. When they are home they may be too tired to be interested in their children, and suburban children grow accustomed to fathers hidden behind newspapers or transfixed by television. Frequently, phonograph records substitute for, rather than supplement, bedtime stories. By day, young children may be left alone or with other neighborhood children in a "maximum security" backyard. Or the television set may become a mechanical baby sitter while the suburban housewife tends to her own affairs. Such a mother, like her lower-class counterpart, may find it inconvenient to sit down and discuss with her children their curious questions.

Even family-centered mealtimes may too frequently be missing in suburban homes, as the busy mother ships her children off to the neighbor whose turn it is to give them lunch. Or perhaps she provides them with food and deposits them in front of the television set. When these children reach school age, their parents may schedule for them a full program of activities to utilize all free time. Thus, even suburban children are often deprived of personal warmth and close parental relationships, supposedly dominant in the middle-class family, and such children all too frequently have little understanding of the real world and its relationships. They develop unrealistic attitudes and values toward society and their place in it; they become ill-equipped to cope with a highly complex and rapidly changing world burgeoning with diversified populations.

[41] P. Wyden, *op. cit.*, pp. 63–64.

The sibling and peer culture

The third strategic socializing agent in the hidden curriculum is the group composed of the child's siblings and peers, a group which can exert considerable influence on the behavior of its members. It is largely through other children, especially those of his own age, that the child's budding self-concept is developed, reinforced, refined, and even reshaped. The number of brothers and/or sisters in the household, their ages, and the child's relationship to each comprise an important aspect of his early social experience. Peers, or friends, teach the child to interact with his agemates, to lead or to be led, and to cope with his social capabilities and inadequacies. Cultural values, too, are transmitted through these social groups.

Siblings and peers, however, can also cause the child to experience jealousy, competition, and a sense of rejection. Indeed, although the child may experience rejection from his parents or other adults, the methods used by his agemates are curiously more punitive, for to fail socially in this context is to be humiliated, ridiculed, taunted, ostracized, and stripped of all dignity.

Siblings are frequently the child's first social contacts on a more or less equal basis. An older brother or sister, because he or she is closer to the child's own age, can translate many of the parents' expectations and demands to meet the younger child's limited frame of reference. A younger sibling, in turn, provides the child an opportunity to pass on adult teachings in such a way that he himself can absorb more of the meaning. Where parental influence is weak, missing, or overpunitive, protective and mutually supportive bonds can develop between or among the children in the family. In many instances, it is an older brother or sister who becomes the main model for the child's sex identification. In large families, where the older children may assume major responsibilities for the care of the younger, the older children develop the senses of responsibility and independence early in their lives and acquire many of the skills required of adults.

Programs in early childhood intervention—such as Operation Head Start—raise the question of what effect children participating in these enrichment programs have on their siblings. The Early Training Project at George Peabody College asked, "How much do younger children learn from their older brothers and sisters?" The project hypothesized that children in the experiment would teach other children undergoing the early training program—including their own younger siblings—their newly acquired attitudes toward achievement and developing skills that would improve "attitudes for learning." Although the research is in progress preliminary evidence suggests that younger children do learn more effectively from their older brothers and sisters.[42]

Contacts with children outside the family also have especially strong implications for learning. Within the family, the child is relatively dependent and accustomed to his status as a child. Among his agemates, however, he must stand or fall on his own merits or deficiencies. Here the personality, skills, values, and emotional stability he has developed are put to test against those predominating in the peer group. To be accepted as one of the group, the child must meet the standards his group sets. If rejected, he must reevaluate himself, his standards, and his abilities.

To become established in a peer group, then, the child must, to a large extent, conform to the attitudes, values, and overall behavior patterns of that group. Where these standards match those in which he has been trained, group membership will only reinforce them. However, where standards conflict with those of the child, he must resolve the conflict largely on the basis of what he expects to gain from changing his old ways or from retaining them. Studies of children from highly sympathetic and secure homes indicate that they tend to be independent enough to withstand peer-group pressures rather than to change their values, while less secure children have a strong need for group acceptance and may quickly adopt the different values of their peers.[43] A

[42]E. H. Noyes, "Comparison of Early Training Project Groups and their Siblings on First Test, Stanford-Binet Scores," George Peabody College, Informal Report, Younger Sibling Study, Spring, 1965.

[43]P. H. Mussen, J. J. Conger, and J. Kagan, *Child Development and Personality*, New York, Harper & Row, 1963.

child who, during his preschool years, has not strongly identified with a model of his sex may also be quick to adopt peer values where they differ from what he has known:

> A second antecedent of susceptibility to peers has its origin in the failure to form a strong same-sex identification with a parent during the years 3 to 6. If the child has not made such an identification, he will be looking for substitute models with whom to identify, and he will be motivated to adopt the attitudes of peer-group leaders. Children who will be most likely to resist the peer group's values, if they contradict the parents', are those who view parents as nurturant, are anxious about violating parental standards, and have identified with these adult models.[44]

The formal educational structure hopes that peer association will transmit the values of self-realization, individual achievement, healthy competition, cooperation, neatness, "gentlemanly" or "ladylike" behavior, friendly extroversion, nonviolent leadership, conformity, creativeness, and academic proficiency. Parenthetically, there are many inconsistencies among the values and characteristics we expect of American children: Social pressures to compete sometimes lead to lack of team spirit; pressure to conform frequently suffocates individualism; and team spirit can cancel individual achievement. Nevertheless, the child who meets the school criteria in most standards will be considered appropriately socialized, despite the difficulties he may struggle with privately. Conversely, the child who does not match these values and characteristics in ways that the school and society can appreciate is often considered "culturally disadvantaged."

Yet tests and evaluations of social popularity in peer groups reveal the influence of differing cultural values of peer groups. One study, which measured traits considered popular among lower-class and middle-class children respectively, found that the lower-class children most admired belligerence, physical strength, "toughness," and bravado, and considered interest in school (and other middle-class values) "sissyish" and intolerable to the peer group. Among

[44]*Ibid.*

middle-class children, friendly, outgoing, neat, attractive, and academically inclined boys and girls rated highest.[45]

The authors learned of one class of American Indian children in which after one child had indicated he did not know the answer to the teacher's question, all the other children in turn indicated that they didn't know the answer either. The perplexed teacher did not know that one of the values of that particular tribe was that no member of the tribe should embarrass another. Because the first child had failed to answer the question, his friends would not embarrass him by indicating their superiority. The entire tribal ethic was basically one of humility and a sense of egalitarianism. Cooperation among Indians is stressed far more than competition. Consequently, the Indian child who does not respond as the teacher wishes becomes, in the view of the teacher, strong-willed or stubborn.

It is significant that children from the middle classes who fall significantly below peer standards may be viewed as "problem individuals" by their schools and cultures, and sympathetic attempts may be made to provide them with individual help. Children in the lower socioeconomic groups, however, may be considered "social problems" whose members are "culturally deprived." Members of this group who, because of "sissyish" attempts to meet school standards, fall significantly below their peer-group standards may be considered individually redeemable by the formal curriculum.

Among peer groups in general, extraverbal systems of communication are developed to convey meaning implicit to their members. Even children raised in elaborated language codes will tend to use more restricted codes with their agemates. This reflects, in part, the separation of the cultures of child and adult. Since adults have a "higher" status, from which children are excluded, children develop their own in-group norms to exclude adults. This is clearly illustrated in popular "rock-and-roll" songs, such as "Yackety Yak," which mocks parental authority, and "In-Crowd," which proclaims:

[45]B. Pope, "Socioeconomic Contrasts in Children's Peer Culture Prestige Values," *Genetic Psychology Monographs*, 1953, **48**, 157–220.

We have our own way of walkin'
We have our own way of talkin'[46]

Indeed, the way a member of the in-crowd walks, his facial expression, his gestures, his clothes, all convey meaning. The child can demonstrate "playin' it cool" merely by the way he walks and poses, and this nonverbal language, within the context of his particular situation, may tell his friends everything he wants them to know without his having to utter a single word. Spoken language is likely to be simple, short, and to the point in a vernacular which is quite esoteric to most adults. Peer-group members use these nonverbal and verbal languages among themselves both in and out of school.

A child raised in an elaborate code can switch communication styles according to the circumstances, particularly in dealing with his parents and teachers, and assume the behavior expected of him. The child accustomed to only a restricted code, however, may find it impossible to make such a change, for he lacks the necessary language. Changing roles through language has important consequences for school participation:

> . . . Because the working class child can only use—only know—a public [restricted] language, it is often used in [inappropriate] situations. The expressive behavior and immediacy of response that accompany the use of this language may again be wrongly interpreted by the teacher. This may well lead to a situation where pupil and teacher each disvalue each other's world and communication becomes a means of asserting differences.[47]

An elementary school teacher in conducting a spelling lesson began a sentence "Your mother . . ." Several students responded to this cue and began to whisper, "Your muthuh _____." The teacher, amazed at the response thus triggered, had to stop two boys from physically attacking one another. When order was restored, he was at a loss to understand how the word mother could have created such a response. He learned that, in one peer

[46]Printed with permission of Keys Popular Song Distributors, Inc., New York.
[47]B. Bernstein, "Social Class and Linguistic Development," *op cit.*, p. 303.

situation, "mother" has the personally insulting connotation of the mother as a prostitute.

Behavior leading to breakdown in communication between teacher and child is often unintentional, for, to all intents and purposes, two different languages are being spoken. The breakdown is compounded by the written materials used in school—books, charts, slides—which are all based on elaborate language.

The following sequence from the film *Phyllis and Terry* is illustrative of the difficulties children reared in a restricted code faced in understanding themselves and the cultural standards of the school:

TERRY: Umm. You see, I can't explain mine, but it's just that music is beautiful, you know. Music is art, music is texture. My teacher told me that in school and I remembered it. (Laughs) But, anyway, I like . . . I like music, you know. You know.

PHYLLIS: Mm-hmm. . . .

TERRY: Let's see, how can I put it? Talk to her for a while, while I try to think of what I have to say. I'll think hard. O, it sort of makes you let loose like a feeling, you know? You know, like you know, like, say, you know, say like if you should go up in a parachute, right? Or go up on the roof and you jump off. (Phyllis giggles). Listen. Well, as you're coming down, there's nothing there to hold you, there's nothing there to be pulling. You just going free—just going through, right? That's the way the music is, sort of.[48]

Words and phrases such as "you know," "like," "say," "sort of," are characteristic in the codes of many youngsters. Too often, such speech patterns are judged inferior and such esthetic statements as, "There's nothing there to hold you" or "There's nothing there to be pulling. You just going free," are ignored. Yet among the peer group, such phrases are meaningful and communicative, especially when they are accompanied by nonverbal forms of expression.

Many artistic virtues contained in restricted language codes are overlooked entirely by the formal school. The restricted lan-

[48]*Phyllis and Terry*, 16mm., B & W, Marner Films, N.Y.C., 1965.

guage "contains its own aesthetic—a simplicity and directness of expression, emotionally virile, pithy and powerful with a metaphoric range of considerable force and appropriateness."[49] A preservice teacher in Syracuse University's Urban Teacher Preparation Program noted, "The language of the kid is creative and rich in expression. Some of the expressions heard have a ring of poetry, much more so when spoken by the kids as they clown around and talk." This teacher listed some of the expressions:

Scream on—yell at a child, tease or insult him
Look hard at me—a mean facial expression, an insulting look
Toed down—being drunk
Lame—not hip, old fashioned, square
Threads—clothes, suits, dresses
The man—white person, policeman
Switchem—a girl who walks with a swing
Bread, Some Green—money
Make it on the scene—show up, appear
Your breath smells—a high-ranking insult[50]

Another student teacher, assigned to Harvard's Operation Second Chance in a Boston junior high school, wrote of her pupils' "not 'grammatically' correct" compositions:

> . . . But several [compositions] have the telling quality of some of the folk songs and spirituals we studied. Some would seem to reflect the compassion and awareness of reality that Reynolds' story stirred within them. All were written with verve and without apprehension.
>
> I think it is David Holbrook, the British poet and educator, who says that the creative efforts of such children may be compared with the artist's impulse that forges a work of literature. . . . I know . . . that the writing of these compositions represents an expression of themselves not unlike very real artistic creations.[51]

[49]B. Bernstein, "Social Class and Linguistic Development," *op. cit.*, pp. 288–314.

[50]Courtesy of Jack Barry of the Urban Teacher Preparation Program, Syracuse University.

[51]Gail Donovan, "The 'Lively Art' of Language," *Harvard Graduate School of Education Association Bulletin*, **10**:2 (Summer, 1965), 11.

Significantly, this teacher found that even the more enlightened teaching methods in which she had been trained had not prepared her adequately to meet the reality of these children, and "reflect our general unreadiness to adjust education programs in ways radical enough to meet the real needs and nature of such children."[52]

The implications for the classroom are discussed in Chapter 10. Our purpose here is to suggest that the school's traditional approach is not attuned to various cultural differences existing between the school and many of the children it serves, nor does it realize the role of the peer group in reinforcing these children's cultural values. By appealing to the child to conform to the alien and/or "adult" standards of the school, many or all of which may be beyond his grasp, the formal curriculum only strengthens his need for acceptance by his agemates and for adopting their frame of reference.

Yet limited attempts by schools to utilize the structure and control of peer groups in the hidden curriculum have indicated not only the strength of these groups, but also the potential value of such a strategy. In some cases, these have come about through the few isolated attempts made at school desegregation. In one predominantly Negro junior high school, for example, the principal reported that neighborhood gangs remained intact in the school environment and brought heavy pressure against any of their members who attempted to hit the books—study hard. It was largely this factor, claimed the principal, that explained the low achievement levels of the students. Later, shifts of students to other schools to correct racial imbalance broke up many of these peer groups in their new schools. Students who were assimilated into new peer groups which placed a higher value on academic achievement tended to make academic gains.

In another school, a group of near dropouts who cared not at all for school became active participants because school authorities identified peer leaders and tapped their organization and leadership skills. This agent of the hidden curriculum became a

[52]*Ibid.*, p. 8.

legitimate school club, complete with jackets for its members and its own song. Esteem given the leaders and their gang invoked the members' involvement in, and identification with, school functions. In still another situation, a teacher in training who had been unable to control her class of disadvantaged fifth-graders, achieved perfect control after she identified a peer leader and assigned to him much of the responsibility for class control.

Unfortunately, few such attempts have been made to equalize student populations in schools and to make use of peer groups and their leaders. The formal educational system, for the most part, ignores the social realities the disadvantaged child must face to be accepted as an equal by his associates. This was demonstrated when the highly competitive American sport of basketball was introduced to Hopi Indian children. Although the children took to the game rapidly and with great fervor, they would not keep score, nor could any amount of inducement make them keep track of which team was winning. This greatly perplexed the teachers until they realized that the Hopi do not share the competitive inclinations of most Americans, and peer pressure is brought upon the individual not to excel beyond the degree that can be achieved by the group as a whole. Refusal to compete is a cultural trait based on centuries of social evolution in a difficult desert environment where the solving of survival problems forced the tribe to develop a highly cooperative and interdependent social structure, in which individual efforts are devoted fully to the interests of the group.

There are obvious positive traits, largely overlooked by the educational system, that are developed and nurtured by the peer group. For many children forced to play in city streets, the peer group provides opportunities for constructing imaginative, original games in keeping with the limitations and possibilities of the environment. Lack of recreational areas and crowded conditions provide an environment for stickball, a kind of midget baseball in which the entire game is in proportion to the space available and adapted to the conditions of automotive and pedestrian traffic. Broom handles serve as baseball bats and, instead of a regulation baseball, half of an inflated rubber ball is used, which is less likely to roll under a passing car or to hurt a passerby. The rules and procedures of stickball may resemble baseball, but the game requires separate skills and thus takes on an entirely new dimension.

In depressed rural areas, children may improvise games and toys from old sticks, automobile tires, boxes, small streams, mud puddles, or trees. These games often require a degree of planning and ingenuity of which middle-class children would be incapable, yet their value tends to be underestimated or misunderstood because people lack familiarity with the lower-class frame of reference.

On the other hand, identification with the middle- and upper-class frame of reference frequently blinds school officials to the negative effects of peer influence on children from these homes. Newspapers regularly report a large incidence of juvenile crime, vandalism, and immorality which is startingly high considering that these "advantaged" areas should produce only children reflecting the values espoused by the school. Peer-group "dare" activities have sponsored too many tragic, reckless-driving accidents, and alcohol parties have resulted in many a drunken-driving accident. Escape from "Dullsville" has been the reason for marijuana and even narcotics parties, and has occasioned a good deal of pointless theft. Theft has also been prompted by attempts to "keep up with the rest of the kids," and "Everybody's doing it, why pick on me?" has been the response of many a child caught cheating in school. School officials are likely to be unaware of such behavior and the underlying value system which causes it until it becomes flagrantly obvious, because these children are equipped to play the external roles and to speak the language that the school expects of them.

Furthermore, the school typically fails to realize that any child who has not had social contact with siblings or peers can be considered—to some extent, at least—culturally deprived. A child raised without brothers, sisters, or early playmates may have a large adjustment problem when he enters the formal curriculum; this may affect his school performance whether or not the teacher notices the child's way of viewing such problems. On the other hand, in conforming to peer-group standards which are not acceptable to the mainstream society, a child may actually have made what, for him, is a suitable adjustment to the alien and hostile demands of that society. Disadvantages traceable to peer relations or lack of them are complex and, like those stemming from the other socializing agents in the hidden curriculum, cannot be assessed solely in terms of socioeconomic levels.

In examining just a few of the influences in the hidden curriculum which affect a child's development, we have provided the barest indication of the vastness and complexity of learning a child undergoes before he enters school and for a substantial portion of his life when he is of school age. Even so, we have not yet discussed the most important socializing agent of all, the parent. It is this final socializing agent who shapes to a large extent the experiences the child receives from the neighborhood setting of the hidden curriculum, the subdivision of the family, and the sibling and peer culture, for the extent to which the parent helps the child to understand and to interpret these experiences has a significant learning consequence in its own right. Indeed, the parent's own conscious and unconscious reactions to these environmental influences have far-reaching learning outcomes for the child. In addition, the parent's own behavior, attitudes, and notions provide a whole set of learning experiences in their own right. Thus, it is to this fourth, and most strategic element in the hidden curriculum that we now turn.

CHAPTER 3

THE LANGUAGE OF THE PARENT AS TEACHER

In examining the development of the child within the broad outline of his neighborhood, his family, and his agemates, we have only hinted at the effects on him of his major teachers; yet it is clear that the pivotal agent, the one most influential in the child's development, is the parent.

Under ideal conditions, there are two master teachers in the hidden curriculum, a father and a mother. Each assumes responsibility for different aspects of the child's learning. Generally, the mother satisfies the child's needs and administers to his comforts; she provides security and understanding, thus communicating to her child that his world is basically friendly and that he can feel relatively confident to explore its infinite and often frightening possibilities. Long before the child can comprehend the meaning of her words, his mother soothes and reassures with her voice, thus setting the patterns for his later speech as well as his cognitive and emotional grasp of his immediate environment. The father provides opportunities for his child to socialize through games, conversation, and other, often more physical, activities in which male interests and feelings are projected. These experiences open important learning channels for the child beyond those provided by his mother; through his father, the child has another resource for satisfying his needs for identification and learning, and for acquiring a sense of security.

However, these ideal conditions do not exist in all homes, nor have many parents had any formal training to prepare them for their role. A child from a large family may have several mother figures to care for him, or several "fathers" to teach him. In such cases, the influence of any one parental figure is likely to be diminished. A child from a broken home may have no mother or, more likely, no father figure. Even in families where both parents are present, one or both parents may provide weak or inadequate guidance for the maturing child, thus affecting the child's social development and understanding of his world.

The way parents teach and what they teach is undoubtedly influenced by their own formal education. In Chapter 2 we noted that large educational differences are likely to exist between slum and suburban parents, and the results of the different educational

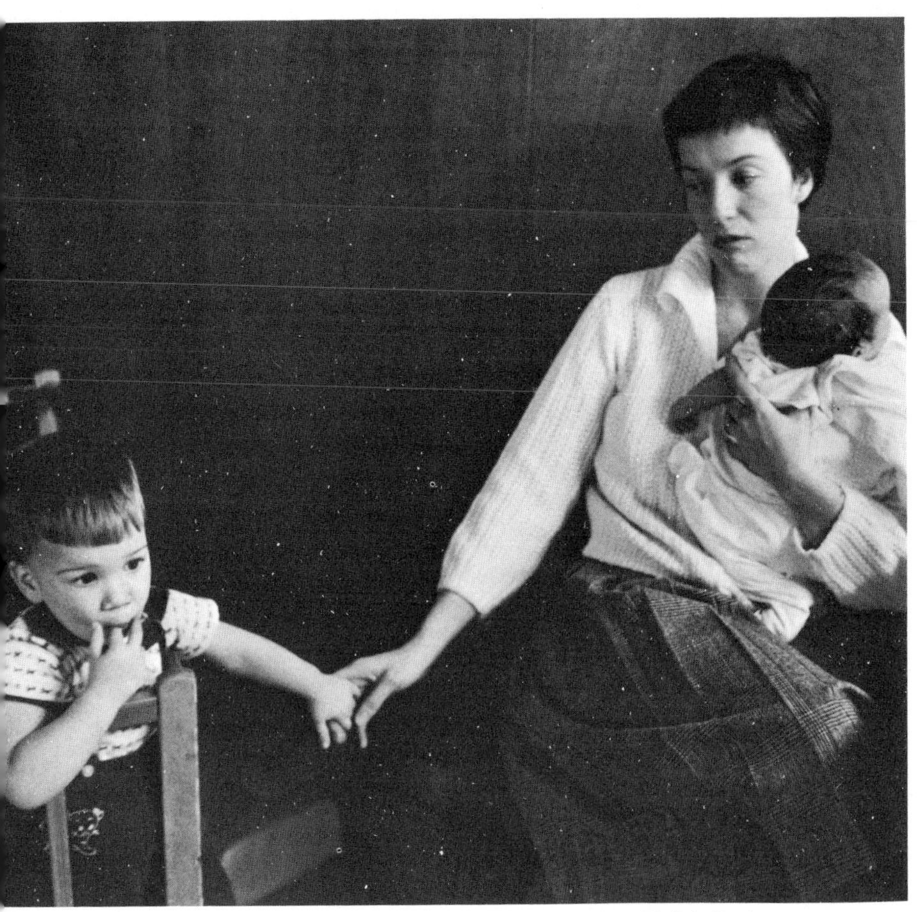

Zimbel, Monkmeyer

THE LANGUAGE OF THE PARENT AS TEACHER

attainments of parents are reflected in their influence on their children right from birth. For example, middle-class mothers and fathers run for Benjamin Spock's *Baby and Child Care* for the explanation of certain symptoms of their children's behavior.[1] It is less likely that Spock is a reference book in the lower-class home.

Parental sensitivity to the well-being of the middle-class child begins in the prenatal period when the parents follow the prescriptions of the attending obstetrician scrupulously in terms of

[1]B. Spock, *Baby and Child Care,* New York, Duell, Sloan and Pearce, 1946.

medicine, diet, and physical activity. Because of their economic and educational situation, the lower-class parent is less likely to develop this kind of activity as reflected in infant mortality rates. For example, in New York City, with its massive slums, the infant mortality rate per 1000 is estimated at 45.3 compared with 26.3 for most middle-sectors,[2] and, in 1948, infant deaths were 258 out of 1000 among a certain group of American Indians.[3]

Maternal teaching style

When both parents are present in the home, it is the mother who is with the child for most of the time and whose influence upon the child is the stronger, especially during the crucial period of the child's infancy. Thus, while paternal attention is desirable—even necessary—to healthy child development, our discussion of the parent as teacher of the hidden curriculum will focus primarily on the mother's teaching role.

Until recently, most of our understanding of the ways of maternal influence on infant development was derived from psychoanalytic inquiry and theory, and dealt primarily with the mother's emotional make-up and behavior toward the child. This line of inquiry has undoubtedly been valuable to both research and practice. Recently, however, educators have considered mothers as teachers of their children in much the same capacity as school teachers. The strategies, methods, and materials—as well as content—usually associated with the school teacher have been compared with those used by the mother in her daily interaction with the child.

Although these aspects of motherhood are only now being researched, Hess and Shipman propose that the essence of the mother's teaching style is in her characteristic mode of communicating with the child, and that the child's intellectual growth will

[2]F. Powledge, "Negro Riots Reflect Deep-Seated Grievances," *The New York Times*, August 2, 1964, p. E5.
[3]B. H. Bagdikian, *In the Midst of Plenty*, New York, Signet, 1964, p. 108.

be determined largely by the nature of the communication system established between mother and child.[4] It is mainly through this framework of communication, specifically through *language*, that we examine the parent as teacher. We will emphasize a view of language that is broader, however, than merely the specific set of verbal symbols she uses and teaches her child. What words a mother uses, the ideas she expresses with them, what feelings she projects when using them, what they objectively represent, and how she communicates them are all part of this very complex issue.

The objects and relationships to which a mother refers in the course of her daily routine with her child—and, significantly, those to which she does not refer—have important implications in establishing the boundaries of the child's field of learning. The content of her communication, both objective and emotional, offers a system of rewards and punishments in which the child acquires attitudes in connection with the objects and relationships he comes to know, and by which his own behavior toward these objects is either thwarted or encouraged. Indeed, this communication system may teach the child that it is more advantageous to know some things than others. In a broad sense, then, the words, content, and purposes of the mother's communication constitute her teaching style which to a large degree determines the nature and extent of the child's field of exploration.

THE WORDS

As noted in Chapter 2, a speech system controlled by a restricted language code is usually made up of many short commands, simple statements, and questions. It is a language in which the selection, combination, and organization of words and phrases are more predictable than in the elaborated language, and it is typically based on relatively concrete objects and relationships rather than on abstractions and conceptualization. Consequently,

[4]R. D. Hess and Virginia C. Shipman, "Cognitive Elements in Maternal Behavior," *The Minnesota Symposium on Child Psychology*, Minneapolis, The Univ. of Minnesota Press (in press).

a restricted code relies heavily on gestures, facial configurations, and other implications for expression of subtle differences in meaning. Its form, in general, does not facilitate the communication of ideas and relationships which require precise distinction. In short, it is a language of implicit, rather than explicit, meaning.

Contrast the words of the restricted-code mother speaking of the past to her child—"Things were different then, not so messed up"—with those used by the school teacher, an elaborate code user—"During the colonial period the pilgrims had a tendency to engage in outdoor activities." The child raised in an elaborated language may respond to the latter, while the child with a restricted language code may be unable to recognize the cues of "during, colonial, period, engage, tendency, and activities."

Moreover, the use of *which, because, when, before, although, who, while, but,* and *for* provide the elaborate code user with an important entry into more comprehensive thought patterns. Consider an elaborated-code mother playing with her daughter: "Which of your toys is your favorite, Trudy? Is it Kathy [doll] or could it be Teddy? [teddy bear]. Oh, I know, it's your dish set which you received from Santa this Christmas. But I suppose they are all your favorite toys, aren't they?" Through such language a child becomes sensitized to words which link ideas or expressions and consequently, he is equipped with important thought-coordinating devices. Such a child uses compound and complex sentences easily in his own speech and writing and is later rewarded in school, where both speech and writing becomes avenues to success in all subject-matter areas.

By contrast, the restricted-code mother does not possess the same facility for linking words. She may say, "This is a nice toy [doll] and that one [teddy bear] is pretty, too, and those dishes are nice, too." Here, *and* becomes the basic linking word, and often results in overuse of *and, like,* and *you know* in the school situation. For example, a child with limited verbal ability reported to the class on a movie she had seen: "And the monster came and beat up the girl and then the monster scared all the people and he fell in the ocean and couldn't swim and he died. . . ." Another child, explaining how he flew a kite said, "Like I took the rope and like the kite and you know, sailed up and I run and it like went way up."

The important process of labeling the many pieces of the child's environment is also conditioned by the language code utilized. Martin Deutsch, in accord with Bernstein, suggests that, in a restricted language code:

> Language is used in a convergent or a restrictive fashion rather than a divergent, elaborative fashion. An exclamation or an imperative or a partial sentence frequently replaces a complete sentence or an explanation: if a child asks for something the response is too frequently, "yes," "no," "go away," "later," or simply a nod. The feedback is not such that it gives the child the articulated verbal perimeters that allow him to start and fully develop normative labeling and identification of the environment.[5]

The elaborate-code mother will have more labels than will a restricted-code mother, and those labels will differ both qualitatively as well as quantitively. For example, the restricted-code mother might say, "Don't play with Mike, he's bad," or "That's a nice picture," or "She sure is lucky." The words *bad*, *nice*, and *lucky* are one-dimensional descriptions. There is no attempt to add the descriptive words which explain how or why a person or thing is "bad," "nice," or lucky." Usually there is no need to elaborate verbally because the simple words are meaningful within their immediate contexts. In school, however, the contexts demand verbal elaborations which were not made available previously. Hence, a child learns the responses, but when asked, for example, what "nice" or "bad" means, he might be puzzled and reply that "bad is bad" or perhaps "evil," and "nice is nice," or at best "good."

Now consider the approach of an elaborate-code user: "Johnny, would you be a good boy and get the juice from the refrigerator, please?" (The ingredients of a "good boy" are clearly implied here: Good boys help their mothers); "Don't touch that

[5]M. Deutsch, "The Role of Social Class in Language Development and Cognition," *American Journal of Orthopsychiatry*, **35**:1 (January, 1965), pp. 79–80.

bowl, dear, you may break it"; "I wish you wouldn't play with Mike; he doesn't say nice words" (Mike isn't nice because he doesn't use "nice" words); and "Sweetheart, would you please bring me my light green sweater?" In each of these examples, the specific object, deed, or quality is made clear. In the last case, the child is asked to perceive not only the boundaries of an object—the sweater—but also the properties of that object—the color green—and the subleties involved—the shade (lightness) of the green.

Other examples of the different emphasis in labeling occur daily. An elaborate-code user may actually explain to her child, "Eat the meat like a good boy. Meat is good for you. It will make you grow tall and strong. This meat came from a cow just like the one in your picture book. Now chew the meat well, Johnny, so that it will be easy to swallow and you will be able to digest it. . . ." This elaboration in the labeling process over time adds a number of properties to the object *meat*. In this case, the mother's teaching progressed from *meat* generally, to *kind* of meat (reinforcing this with a picture of a cow from a familiar book), to the personal *value* of meat (e.g., the health values of meat), to what happens to meat that is eaten.

The restricted-code mother simply may not have these verbal avenues open to her and is consequently limited to communicating the one label—*meat*—in a single-dimensional manner. If there is verbal communication at all, it may be as follows: "Eat your meat, Johnny. Eat or you'll be skinny. Do as I say."

Thus, the child raised in an elaborated communication system is more likely to develop a perceptual orientation geared to the complexities in his environment, causing his cognitive processes to develop along more analytic lines. Because of the structure and range of his code, this child will be able to formulate higher levels of generalization from these wider bases of particulars. Further, because an elaborated language code is explicit, the child is receptive to verbal cues. He learns to respond to words according to their meaning and also assimilates them as his own method of conveying meaning.

The child limited to a restricted language system, however,

has less acute perception of objects, limited discriminatory powers, and little practice in perceiving the complex relationships that exist among objects. Such a child can generalize only on a considerably less articulate level and the generalizations he does draw may be missing many important particulars. On the other hand, this child may become more sensitized to nonverbal cues, because his language code relies heavily on emotional supplements. The child learns the nature and meaning of nonverbal expressions and adopts them for his own communication, in which tone, facial expression, and gestures convey his real meaning.

In summary, the choice and extent of the words and phrases used by the mother shapes the child's cognitive and objective perception of the world. The mother who uses a restricted code limits her child's cognitive and perceptual awareness, although the child's emotional or affective perceptions *may* be more highly developed as a result of his developed ability to cue in on the unsaid and implied. The mother who uses an elaborated code with her child, on the other hand, tends to develop expanded perceptive and cognitive abilities in her child.

Bernstein and others have pointed out that restricted language codes tend to dominate the lower socioeconomic strata, while the middle and upper classes tend to draw on more elaborated codes. But restricted codes can be and are found among the middle classes, especially in mother-child relationships, even though the mother may use elaborated language with her peers.

Both the child's quantity and quality of labels predetermine the kind of verbal mediation in which he can engage. The school is marked by problem tasks which pose severe hardships on restricted-language learners, and the relation between language and verbal mediation offers additional clues to the discrepancies found in different school tests among advantaged children.

THE COGNITIVE CONTENT

By *cognitive content* we mean what the words objectively represent. It refers to language or thought that conveys what is there or happening *empirically*. It does not refer to the implicit feelings or emotional conotations of the parent's verbal interaction with the child.

All parents—as conscious or unconscious teachers, regardless of language code or socioeconomic background—have many subject areas open to them that can be used as cognitive content in communicating with their children. Family rituals such as mealtime and bedtime stories may offer opportunities for exploring simple common areas with the child. Also, cleanliness; current events in the neighborhood, community, and nation; the importance of school; and current TV programs are useful in orienting the child to the wide variety of subject matter in his life. Trips, vacations, and shopping excursions provide opportunities to introduce new areas for analysis. Another important factor in the selection and communication of subject areas is the mother's frame of reference or her knowledge of and familiarity with certain subjects. For example, an elaborate-code mother who is a musician may make music a more salient subject of her communication. Similarly, a father interested in sports might draw heavily on baseball, bowling, or football.

Questions posed by the curious child also determine much of the subject matter of mother-child communication, but again the content is a function of the mother's own knowledge of and *attitudes* toward the subject raised. For example, if a lower-class child asks, "Why does it rain?" the mother may respond with "What do you mean why does it rain? It rains because it rains!" On the other hand, the middle-class mother may avoid "unpleasant" content areas such as sex or death. If her child asks "Where did the baby kittens come from?" she may manipulate the words into a different context. This approach may divert the child's immediate attention quite successfully, but the question that was left unanswered will occur to him again. With repetition of such manipulations of the child's questions the child may become confused, or be discouraged from seeking answers from his mother.

Other content about members of the family and objects on the periphery of the child's environment may be adapted by the mother, but reference to them depends on their availability in the environment. In many homes, for example—particularly in the lower socioeconomic strata—there is no father. For this reason, unlike middle-class mothers who may use "Daddy" in the content of communication (e.g., "We'll show Daddy your drawing." "Tell Daddy what you said to me." "Daddy will take you to the movies."), lower-class mothers are less likely to employ a "Daddy" concept. In some homes, Daddy is away at his job and perhaps not in the immediate frame of reference of the mother. This is true even in some suburban homes where the father spends long hours—perhaps days—in the city, or away on business trips. Similarly, many homes are void of books, and the mother's own lack of orientation to books may preclude any reference to them during her relationship with her child. A child from such a home has little occasion to become familiar with the object *book*, or with the purpose of a book and its care, until he encounters the formal school curriculum.

Much of the content selected in any mother-child communication is about the child *himself*—his growth, his training, his needs—and the objects that stand in relation to his behavior, what he may or may not touch, what he does or does not need. The toddler who has discovered that there are all sorts of fascinating gewgaws in his world may seize upon a glass object causing the mother to respond with "Leave *that* alone," or even, "No, no. *Mustn't* touch." Or she may say, "No, no, *Johnny*, that's glass and if it *breaks* it will *cut* and *hurt* you." The italics indicate the kinds and degrees of objective content that can be communicated to the child as a result of his *behavior* in relation to the object involved. The first two sample responses are restricted. They are simple and typical enough to be as accessible to mothers with characteristically restricted language codes as to mothers with normally elaborated codes. The child exposed largely to this kind of response—which uses pronouns, rather than the particular labels of objects and their attributes—will come to recognize these objects and their attributes, but will do so largely without the benefit of early verbal associations and conceptualizations.

Thus, the selection and communication of this objective content is, to some extent, determined by the range allowed by the verbal code, and a restricted code will be unable to accommodate the diversity of content permitted by an elaborated code. The mother's language code and teaching style help to focus this content, and permit degrees of analysis and discrimination which make the child feel comfortably familiar with the content.

Much of the growing and rambunctious child's behavior in relation to objects prompts a maternal appeal for him to be "good" rather than "bad" or "naughty." This is certainly true in many lower-class homes where, "in the context of an overcrowded living space, 'being good' means being physically inactive, verbally non-participative, and non-observant."[6] This may also be true in some middle-class homes where the mother puts a great deal of emphasis on keeping her house neat and her expensive possessions on display. In both cases, these practices and the particular communication of them run counter to the child's need for early stimulation.

Along with the *specific* objective content communicated by the mother in her activities with the child, many important concepts are developed, one of which is the concept of time. For example, if the mother says, "Daddy will take you to the park this weekend," the child may explore the meaning of *weekend*; each day the child might ask, "Is today the weekend?" Whereupon the mother might reply, "No, dear, tomorrow is the weekend and Daddy will take you to the park then." Or, the mother might employ the strategy of delayed gratification or punishment: She may reward the child by saying, "You've been very good, Johnny, so Mommy will take you for a ride tomorrow," or "Because you have been so naughty you will not be able to go to Richard's house tomorrow." Repeated episodes of this sort literally force the child automatically to develop a present-future orientation.

Through language, the child begins to formulate a cognitive notion of time. Time references are much more likely to be made

[6]F. L. Strodtbeck, "The Hidden Curriculum of the Middle Class Home," in C. W. Hunnicutt (Ed.), *Urban Education and Cultural Deprivation*, Syracuse, N.Y., Syracuse School of Education, 1964.

in middle-class homes than in lower-class homes, however, for the lower-class mother tends to rely much more on responses dealing with the immediate. Consequently, the child is likely to become more oriented to the present and will be less willing to base his behavior on future rewards or punishments. Further, because the child taught in a restricted verbal communication system becomes sensitized to nonverbal cues, he is all the more likely to become oriented to the present, to which nonverbal cues inevitably pertain. He develops a present-time focus from his implicit language and a curtailed sense of the future from his restricted explicit language.

A present-time orientation is reinforced by the immediate nature of the punishment strategy employed by the restricted-code parent, which strategy is apt to be nonverbal or physical. A child with such an orientation may find it difficult to respond to a teacher who uses verbal means for punishment or who delays punishment by saying, "I'll keep you after school." Indeed, the child may not realize the relationship between his misdemeanor of earlier in the day and the act of punishment which takes place after school.

THE AFFECTIVE CONTENT

By *affective content* we refer to the feelings that are projected along with the words, for the meaning of a word cannot be divorced from the emotional quality with which it is said.

For the child raised in a restricted language code, the emotional content of communication is of particular significance, since nonverbal cues are a primary method of obtaining meaning. For example, if the child spills a drink on the floor, his mother may verbalize no more than "Clumsy! Satisfied?" or, "Clean it up!" The real meaning of her message is conveyed not so much by the words she utters as by the silent language of her facial expression, a slap, or the harsh tone of her voice. Or, if the child asks a question his mother can't answer, the inadequacy of her verbal response may cause him to seek an answer in her general behavior. At times the mother may communicate facially to the child that he is "showing off" or "acting big" by asking questions which the mother can't answer.

Because of his sensitivity to extraverbal cues, developed as a result of restricted verbal communication, the child becomes attuned to the expressive content of all emotions—the effect of pregnancy on the mother's feelings; the subtle undertones of his mother's relationships with him and with his father or other adults; the emotional response his mother may have to a neighbor or a bill collector.. He learns revenge, hate, pain, disgust, jealousy, sorrow, worry, and fear as well as love, pleasure, contentment, and joy, both through his own experiences with those feelings, and by observing these emotions as his mother experiences them. This learning remains largely implicit, however, as the child has not likely developed a verbal mediation ability.

Emotions are also communicated by the mother who uses an elaborated code, but because her communication system allows a greater range of verbalization, she tends to make the emotion understood through words rather than through facial or physical expressions. The kinds of emotional content that predominate such a mother-child relationship, therefore, teach the child to notice *the verbalizations* of feelings—perhaps at the expense of the feelings themselves.

Social control

Every mother employs a different approach to controlling her child's behavior. One may punish, one may reward; one may threaten, another promise; still another may avoid or neglect the problem altogether. Underlying each of these strategies is an expression of authority which may either strengthen or weaken the bonds between mother and child, and which may limit or increase the chances for verbal interaction between mother and child. Depending on the type of social control used by the mother, the behavioral choices available to the child in response to her authority may be uncompromising acceptance, withdrawal, rebellion, or trust.

Here again, the role of the mother's language code is an influential factor in the child's behavioral development. A mother who uses highly articulated verbalizations controls her child through verbal manipulation of his feelings, by citing reasons which link the child to the significance of his own acts, and by explaining his behavior to him. Such a mother provides avenues for verbal mediation between the child's motives and his behavior, between his behavior and its effects on his environment, and between these effects and his mother's behavior toward him. When a mother who utilizes a restricted language code disciplines her child, there is apt to be less talking through of acts, less verbal investigation of motives. Whereas one mother is likely to explain the rule and place it in context verbally—"No, Johnny, don't hit your little brother; you'll hurt him"—another is likely to announce the rule and to leave it at that—"I've told you, you don't do that! You know I've told you to leave your brother alone!"

PERSONAL VS. POSITIONAL CONTROL

There are at least two major reference points from which forms of control can be derived, *personal* and *positional*.[7] "How do you think Sam would feel if you did that?" or "You're making me very nervous so stop it," are illustrations of the *personal* derivations, while "Don't do that to Sam, it's not nice," and "We don't allow that here, so stop it," illustrate the *positional*. In the former case, rules are *achieved*; in the latter, they are *assigned*.

Because control which is personal utilizes more interpersonal dimensions and nuances, whole orders of learning are made available to the child which are not possible if the control is positional. Whatever the physical consequences of his behavior on

[7]Much of this discussion is based on the work of Basil Bernstein, particularly as set forth in G. J. Klopf and W. A. Hohman (Eds.), *Perspectives on Learning: Papers from the Bank St. Fiftieth Anniversary Invitational Symposium*, New York, Mental Health Materials, Inc., 1967, pp. 15–46.

his environment, the child reared in a personal control system learns that he cannot act without affecting with pain or pleasure the people in his social environment. For example, the child who has broken mother's favorite vase has not merely broken a valued object, he has hurt his mother, too. Similarly, if he interrupts his brother while the latter is doing his homework, he has not merely interrupted him, he has caused his brother some personal inconvenience at the same time. Thus, the personal approach to behavioral control elicits the child's identification with the feelings of others, at least to the extent that his behavior has been the immediate cause of those feelings. The child's behavioral guide becomes: If I do not want to be guilty of hurting mother (as well as of the misdeed), I will not do this deed.

With positional control, the child comes to accept power and authority, rather than the feelings of others, as guides to his behavior: These are the rules, and that's that. He is not to touch glass vases or to interrupt his brother while he is studying simply because mother *says* so. If he violates these rules he may incur his mother's wrath, to be sure, but this wrath tends to discourage empathetical identification with her. Thus, the motivation for obeying a rule given in a positional control system becomes essentially self-seeking: If I do not want to get punished, I will not do this deed.

In general, with positional control, the child is less likely to learn about objects, events, and persons—and his behavior in relation to them—than with personal control, although, in a restricted-language home, positional control is particularly likely to have this effect. In an elaborated-language home which uses positional control, the child's attention is focused on the physical effects his behavior has on the obects (including human objects) in his environment rather than on the emotional effects they have on other people. With the personal approach to control, this focus is reversed: The child's attention is generally oriented more to the emotional consequences which his behavior has on others than to the physical consequences of his acts. In an elaborated-language home, this personal control can develop in the child an explicit sense of empathy with others, while in a home which draws upon a restricted code, this empathy is likely to remain implicit and beneath the threshold of the child's conscious understanding.

It may be much easier to rebel against a positional control system, because authority is clearly defined and a sharp distinction between the child and the authority figure is maintained. Personal control tends to over-involve the child in the consequences of his acts, as the empathetical bond that is developed obscures the distinction between the child himself and the authority figure. To rebel against the authority figure in this case is tantamount to rebelling against oneself. The challenge to positional control is a challenge to the right of the authority figure to issue a rule, while a challenge to personal control is a challenge to the right of the authority figure to have feelings similar to one's own. Thus, parental rebellion among children raised with a personal control system is likely to be much longer in coming, if it occurs at all. Since healthy child development depends on periodic stages of rebellion in order that the growing child learn a sense of his own autonomy and identity, personal control can have damaging consequences to the child's personality.

On the other hand, positional control can have damaging effects on the child's ability to control his own behavior properly. Since the primary reason for obeying a rule handed down by authority is to avoid punishment rather than to avoid the act itself, the child may feel perfectly free to commit the wrongdoing in the absence of the authority figure. Or, if rebellion is successful, the need to refrain from obeying further rules assigned by the authority figure disappears. In other words, a misdeed becomes no misdeed at all as long as one can get away with it.

Because personal control develops in the child a sense of guilt—his own inner feelings of guilt being the primary reason for avoiding an act—the child so raised will refrain from doing the misdeed even in the absence of the authority figure. The empathetical bonds developed between the authority figure and the child lead, in effect, to an incorporation of the authority figure within the child's own personality configuration.

A further consequence of positional control on an individual is paradoxically to engender in that individual a strong dependence on positional authority. Without an inner structure of behavioral rules to guide him, the individual finds himself unable to control his behavior, or to see the various values of his different acts under different circumstances. Thus, while such an individual may attempt to render impotent any given authority figure, he may unconsciously be seeking a reliable authority which cannot be rendered impotent through his rebellion. Such a child is likely to choose a peer group in which his identity is confined and defined for him by the status arrangements in the group, and where rules are provided by each level in the hierarchy of authority to pertain in specific contexts. By contrast, the individual accustomed to subtler and less clearly defined lines of authority, as provided in a personal control system, may find it difficult to assume a role dictated and regulated by sharp lines of authority. Though such an individual may never have fully extricated his own identity from that of the parent he has incorporated into his own personality, the behavioral mode exhibited by an authoritarian regulator is likely to be so out of keeping with that of the personality he has incorporated as to become incompatible with and intolerable to the individual.

The implications for classroom control are obvious: For example, some types of classroom control may lack meaning for children taught to respond to the authoritarian nature of positional control, because the teacher draws on a personal approach. Conversely, children raised in homes which emphasize personal control may be bewildered or angered by control where positional mandates are used by the teacher. The relative strengths of peer groups within the classroom may also be diagnosed and dealt with more realistically in terms of the type of social control which underlies them. The peer group which is cohesive because clear lines of leadership and authority prevail may provide a stronger influence on the behavior of its members compared to that of the teacher who used a personal approach to classroom discipline; while the egalitarian peer group may exert a stronger influence on its members than the teacher with authoritarian tendencies.

REWARD AND PUNISHMENT TECHNIQUES

Closely interwoven into the mother's method of social control is her use of reinforcement techniques. All mothers employ—consciously or unconsciously, randomly or systematically—some sort of reinforcement technique. Some mothers place the emphasis on rewarding their children for good or desirable behavior; some fail to reward for good behavior, but stress punishment of undesirable behavior, some use both reward and punishment with equal emphasis. Although rewards are actually the reinforcers of behavior, a child reared in an essentially punitive home may learn to find reward in the absence of punishment; he may tend to avoid those acts which will bring punitive measures, and to do those deeds which will not bring punishment. As we shall see, however, sometimes children actually find reward in punitive attention from adults.

The more the child's needs are satisfied, the more reinforcing are the acts that lead to the satisfaction of those needs. Essentially, reinforcement techniques can be classified into two kinds, *positive* and *negative*. Positive reinforcement reinforces *desirable* behavior, while negative reinforcement actually serves to reinforce the *undesirable* behavior. If, for example, a child learns that his mother will pay attention to him only when he misbehaves, he will continue to misbehave even though the attention may be in the form of punishment. Adult attention itself can serve as a negative reinforcer; as Harris, Wolf, and Baer point out:

> . . . While it seems reasonable that for most young children adult attention may be a positive reinforcer, it is also conceivable that for some children adult attention may be a negative reinforcer. That is, the rate of behavior may decrease when it is immediately followed by the attention of an adult, and rise again as soon as the adult withdraws. Actually, for a few children observed at the preschool, it has been thought that adult attention was a negative reinforcer.[8]

[8]Florence R. Harris, M. M. Wolf, and D. M. Baer, "Effects of Adult Social Reenforcement on Child Behavior," *Young Children*, **20**:1 (October, 1964), 15.

Although it is often overlooked by parents and teachers themselves, they are often less likely to notice or to relate to children who are quietly occupied and causing no disturbance. As soon as the children's behavior becomes disturbing in some way, however, the adult is forced to notice it and to deal with it. Thus, even the wise mother or teacher who manages, without scolding or punishing, to engage the children in another, less disturbing activity may actually be providing the incentive for the children to repeat the disturbing behavior which has brought the adult's attention.

In many homes, children are given virtually no attention unless they are actually misbehaving, in which case anger and punishment are bound to follow. Without the contrasting frame of reference of rewarding attention, such children may learn that there is no point in trying to incur mother's favor. From this the child can acquire a primarily negative self-image and an unconscious desire to punish himself. Thus, a cyclical, self-fulfilling prophecy can develop in which both the desire to punish himself and the desire to receive the only kind of adult attention he knows lead the child to ever more severe types of misbehavior. This cycle can be carried into school, where the teacher may feel that the child simply cannot perform as well as others, and in living up to her negative expectations, the child reinforces the teacher's lack of faith in his native abilities.

As in all modes of mother-child interactions, the mother's language code brings to bear important influences which are integral with her use of reinforcements. Regardless of the particular reinforcing techniques she is most inclined to use, the elaborated-code mother is more likely to use verbal rather than physical reinforcements. If she stresses rewarding techniques, she is likely to do so with such words and phrases as "Fine," "Excellent," or "That's a good boy." While she may accompany these with a wink, a pat on the back, a kiss, or other nonverbal supplements, her child learns to seek approval through words.

Such a mother may also provide specific tangible rewards or favors—such as candy or allowing him to do something he looked forward to—but, in verbalizing her reasons, the child acquires a highly articulated conceptualization of his behavior. For example, she may say, "What a good boy! You have cleaned up your room very nicely! Just for that I'll take you to the zoo today." Or perhaps: "You have been so good about eating all your dinner, you may have as much chocolate pudding as you want."

The essentially punitive mother with an elaborated language code also helps the child to acquire a more articulated conception of his behavior: "You naughty boy! Just look at your room! Well, you can just stay in here until it's all cleaned up." Obviously, if the child wants to leave his room, he will do as his mother wishes, even though that may bring no particular reward from her. If the mother is consistent in her demands that he keep his room neat, he will acquire tidy behavior, even though he may, through lack of rewards from his mother, acquire a sense of hopelessness about pleasing her. It should be noted that essentially punitive mothers who rely on punitive words unsupported by deeds may leave the child in an ambiguous position as to how he should behave, even though he may fully understand her words. For example, many middle-class mothers are likely to say, "Oh, Johnny! Just look at your room; it's a mess! Haven't I told you not to be so messy? You are a naughty boy." Whereupon the mother herself may proceed to clean it up, or she may leave it as it is. The child knows, both from her words and from her tone of voice that she is displeased, and that he has done wrong. Yet little or no incentive is provided him actually to change his behavior, or even to remedy the displeasing situation. Such a child is fully able to comprehend, but not to respond.

Another undesirable effect of social control expressed through an elaborated-language code can occur when too much content is "packaged" into one message. For example, the mother might say, "Johnny, you are forever leaving your toys in here. Take them upstairs immediately, and don't leave your room is a mess, either. You never keep your room clean, and oh, just look at those hands! They're filthy, and your clothes, they're a mess. And who gave you that gum? You know you're not supposed to chew before dinner. Go get washed up right now!" The child becomes verbally overloaded and may find it difficult to decipher just exactly what it is that his mother is attacking. In addition, he may leave the scene feeling that he is generally bad, rather than that he did any specific thing wrong.

In restricted-language homes where the mother provides positive rewards, these may be in the form of a wink, a kiss, or a nod of approval. The mother might supplement these with a word or two, such as "Good boy," or "That's nice," but the full comprehension of his behavior which led to the rewards is not developed in the child. As he seeks to repeat the behavior, he must rely on trial and error; if he errs and brings disapproval on himself, he is perplexed. Worse, the mother, having shown him that she approved once, may feel that now he should know what to do, and accept the right behavior without further reward. This, too, may leave the child hopelessly confused.

Unfortunately, since restricted codes tend to be used more in lower-class homes where poverty, overcrowding, and other tension-producing conditions prevail, punitive measures are more likely to be the primary means of social control in these homes. The combination is unfortunate: The only means for gaining maternal attention is to misbehave, and the attention it brings—a slap, harsh words uttered loudly and perhaps at a shrill pitch, ominous threats—do little to help the child become explicitly aware of each form of his behavior. Lower-class mothers are particularly likely to utter rash threats which have little likelihood of being carried out, yet which leave the child uncertain and anxious. "Cut that out or I'll break your arm!" "Do that again and you'll have your head handed to you," and similar verbalizations are frequently the fare. To be sure, such a child learns, but what he learns has little direct relationship to the behavior which evoked these words, and virtually no relationship to the content of the words themselves.

In general, regardless of whether the primary mode of social control is punitive or rewarding, the reinforcement positive or negative, elaborated language codes offer the child more behavioral alternatives. In addition to providing him with articulated conceptions of his various forms of physical behavior, elaborate language codes help the child to learn various forms of verbal behavior with which he can express himself. The child learns to translate much of his physical aggression into verbal aggression, and to seek attention through verbal rather than physical means.

Developing learning styles

Of considerable significance in the mother's communication strategy—consciously or unconsciously employed—is the influence she has on the child's learning how to learn. Bloom, Davis, and Hess point out that this involves:

> . . . a far more basic type of learning than coaching the child on school learning. It includes motivating the child to find pleasure in learning. It involves developing the child's ability to attend to others and to engage in purposive action. It includes training the child to delay the gratification of his desires and wishes and to work for rewards and goals which are more distant. It includes developing the child's view of adults as sources of information, and ideas, and also as sources of approval and reward.[9]

The mother's willingness and ability to provide guidance for the child, and the means by which she provides this guidance and makes knowledge available to him, are crucial in this regard. Does the mother as teacher process information by *telling* the child? Or does she ask *questions* so that he may reason through to the answers himself? In the first case, the *deductive* approach is involved; the second centers around an *inductive* approach. Recent research into cognitive functioning suggests that a combination of deductive and inductive methods comprises the most effective teaching strategy.

If the mother's strategy is predominantly one of *telling* the child, of "putting in" information, she is apt to stifle his imagination and curiosity before they can develop. Also, the "telling"

[9]B. S. Bloom, A. Davis, and R. Hess, *Compensatory Education for Cultural Deprivation*, New York, Holt, Rinehart and Winston, 1965, p. 15.

mother is prone to overload the child with more information than he can assimilate and retain at a given time. At the very minimum, a persistently deductive approach may discourage the child from seeking out the mother—and other adults—as information resources. On the other hand, if the mother's teaching style focuses too strongly on *asking* the child, of "drawing out," her demands may overtax his limited knowledge and prompt him to acquire a defeatist attitude toward learning. In this case, the child's imagination and curiosity are overburdened to the point of frustration. Clearly, if either the "telling" or the "asking" mother includes primarily punitive emotional content in her teaching style, her effect on the child's learning attitude will be destructive.

Even something as seemingly simple as how mothers view the role of toys in the child's development adds to the inductive-deductive orientation. An interesting phase of a study being conducted by the Sociological Research Unit of the University of London involves the different perceptions of toys by middle- and working-class parents.[10] Although the study was still in progress at the time of writing, the data collected suggested certain important differences. The middle-class mother is likely to view toys as active educational or discovery items which "permit the child to find out about things" (to discover *inductively*), and "to help them when they go to school." The lower-class mother is less likely to see toys as tools of exploration and considers them most useful in keeping the child busy and involved passively so that she is "free to do other things."

Preliminary research in communication styles of mothers suggests that effective communication conducive to learning must involve the student in both talk and participation. An experiment on the teaching styles of 60 urban mothers conducted by Jackson, Hess, and Shipman at the Urban Child Center, University of Chicago, suggests the importance of feedback to child learning.

[10] B. Bernstein and D. Young, *Social Class Differences in Conceptions of the Uses of Toys*, London, *Sociology*, Sociological Research Unit of the London University Institute of Education, March, 1967.

> It seems justifiable to conclude at this preliminary phase in our work that teaching styles, which encourage the child to talk about the material help him learn. Why? Because they provide much more accurate feedback information for the mother to use in deciding on the next step in her instruction of her child.[11]

The "drawing-out" maternal teaching strategy, when carried out carefully, causes the child to develop an inductive style of learning from which he is more likely to inquire information independently.

The drawing-out strategy has other benefits in addition to helping the child develop an inductive learning style. It may give the child practice in developing a more elaborate communication system which offers him a broader linguistic repertoire for "thinking out loud," for verbal mediation. So Jensen points out: "Verbal mediation consists of talking to oneself in relevant ways when confronted with something to be learned, a problem to be solved, or a concept to be attained.[12]

The process of verbal mediation enables the child to use language in pursuing higher levels of generalization and to transfer learning to different settings and situations. The importance of verbal mediation to cognitive development is only now being investigated, but it has been hypothesized that the more restricted the language code of the child, the more restricted will be his habit of verbal mediation. Jensen concludes:

> Though spontaneous mediation will be deficient when innate capacity is poor, it will also be deficient when innate capacity is good but the social environment is impoverished in the kind of verbal interactions which inculcate mediational habits.[13]

[11]J. D. Jackson, R. D. Hess, and Virginia Shipman, "Communication Styles in Teachers," paper presented at the annual meeting of the American Educational Research Association, Chicago, February 12, 1965.

[12]A. R. Jensen, "Verbal Mediation and Educational Potential," Invited address presented at the annual meeting of the American Psychological Association (Div. 16), Chicago, September 4, 1965.

[13]*Ibid.*

The mother who uses language to think through a particular problem-solving sequence with a child may be developing this cognitive skill of verbal mediation. Consider the mother and child playing with a puzzle; the mother might verbalize as follows: "Let's see, Johnny, where shall we put this round piece? . . . Do you think it will fit here? . . . No, because it's too big? This spot looks round, too. Let's try it. . . . It works! Let's see if there are any other round pieces. . . . Good! There is another. Where would you place that one? . . . That's right! That fits the other round groove. You are a smart boy, Johnny. Now what will we do? . . . Let's look for a color that we can match. This piece is red. . . . See? It matches the red already in the puzzle."

The child, in this case, was given a model of problem solving through the application of verbal strategies and reinforcements. He was exposed to the actual problem-solving process simultaneously with the verbalization of this problem-solving process. This, as Jackson, Hess, and Shipman suggest, may help the child to think the problem through or it "may be a rehearsal for thinking."[14]

In summary, we have attempted to illustrate the role of language use in parent-child interactions, and to suggest some of the resulting possibilities in the development of the child, including his own language development. While some maternal teaching strategies tend to be somewhat more associated with some socioeconomic levels than others, it must be made quite clear that the relative adequacy or inadequacy of maternal teaching in terms of the instructional strategy used in the schools cannot usefully be defined solely according to traditional socioeconomic criteria. Mothers under economic hardship are not, *ipso facto*, mothers who have restricted language codes or essentially punitive communication styles. Similarly, mothers who are college graduates are not necessarily those who maintain a close communicative relationship with their children and a happy combination of inductive-deductive teaching strategies. Every child is an individual with his own intrinsically unique emotional and intellectual characteristics, which are shaped by a unique

[14]Jackson, Hess, and Shipman, *op. cit.*

combination of factors, under the guidance of a mother or mother figure, who, during her own growth, was shaped by a unique combination of factors.

Of major significance in this chapter is the important way in which language actually controls both the quantity and quality of roles that an individual can appropriately perform. Conversely, roles can determine what language is appropriate. The superiority of one language code or another depends on the context in which each of them is used. Usually, social contexts characterized by states of "intimacy," or closer relationships, utilize restricted language regardless of educational level or socioeconomic background. For individuals who are familiar with each other, it is less necessary to state intent explicitly as much of the implicit communication is understood. In such contexts, a restricted code is not only acceptable but is the normative speech pattern. Thus, an elaborated-code user may become considerably less verbal in some social settings, and more articulate in others, as he is usually able to adapt his language in accordance with the setting and to play the different roles expected in the family, the school, and the neighborhood.

The person who knows only a restricted code, however, is not equipped with this flexibility. The school creates a variety of social contexts necessitating alternative roles and, in general, an elaborated language communication system which the restricted-code child may find difficult to understand because he lacks previous experience. His inability to assume these roles and to use elaborated language places the restricted-code child at an institutional disadvantage. Seldom, if ever, is his inability viewed by the school and other mainstream-oriented institutions as anything but a negative trait; rather, it is yet another condition which reinforces the school's notion of "uneducable" children. Yet, to expect such children to assume the "proper" roles and language—and to evaluate them as failures or successes on the basis of their performance—is to expect them to alter their own ideas of reality and social existence.

Certainly the restricted code child is "himself"—he is literally forced to be the only self he knows by his early learning.

Such authenticity could be the basis of a positive view among school people, although the school generally overlooks this. Further, in his sensitivity to what he considers "phoney," such a child might actually be pointing to genuine flaws in the educational process. Thus far, the school has failed to acknowledge this as a possibility, also.

By contrast, the child socialized with an elaborated communication system, being equipped to assume the roles demanded of him, may actually reserve expression of his real self for outside of the classroom and among his peers. Though the school overlooks such a possibility, this child may actually be exposing only a superficial veneer imposed over this real self, a veneer which shows little of his real feelings and motivations, his real abilities, his real and meaningful learning. He dutifully memorizes the facts, provides the correct responses, and exhibits the right behavior that the school expects—perhaps only to shed it all once he is outside of the classroom.

What happens when the child exposed to these influences of his hidden curriculum—as shaped by his main teacher, his parent—confronts the formal curriculum? School dropout and cultural "disadvantage" are salient symptoms among the lower socioeconomic strata, but what of the middle-class pupils? For some insights into how pupils themselves view the school, we turn next to "The Phoney School."

CHAPTER 4

THE PHONEY SCHOOL

All of us view the world through our own cultural spectacles, to which we become so accustomed that we fail to notice a kind of "fog" which gradually accumulates and obscures certain details in our way of life. We come to take our own perspective so much for granted that it is difficult to distinguish between what really *is* and what is only a distorted image. When someone wearing different cultural spectacles confronts us point-blank with his vision of reality—or questions us about something which has blinded us with its presence—we are forced to take another look, and perhaps even to wipe our own spectacles. For example, when citizens from other nations visit the United States, they often raise questions about inconsistencies which we have overlooked in our culture. Similarly, many Americans travelling abroad are able to take a "fresh look" at American institutions and values as a result of their experiences. Such people share what we might call a "cross-cultural perspective" from which we can obtain an objective picture of our own lives.

In the same way, children—who have yet to be blinded by the accoutrements of culture—are apt to make stunningly accurate observations of what adults say and do. Indeed, we often remark on the disarming honesty and unique clarity of perception of young children. We react with shock, surprise, and amusement as children point out elements of our daily lives, suddenly giving them a new twist or putting them in a new light. Like foreign visitors, children look at our culture before they have become entirely immersed in it. The fogging-up of their spectacles is still in the early stages.

The most pervasive criticism that many of our children, and particularly those we term "disadvantaged," have leveled at adult society has concerned what they call the "phoniness" of our conventional educational system. What these children mean by phoniness was clearly revealed to the authors when a group of ninth-grade boys refused to read in English class. The teacher inquired why, and when the boys insisted that the books assigned to them were "phoney," the teacher probed further:

TEACHER: What do you mean, *phoney?*
CLASS: Corny.

Bob Adelman

THE PHONEY SCHOOL

TEACHER: What does *corny* mean?

[*No response*]

TEACHER: Can you give me an example of what isn't corny? In a TV program perhaps?

CLASS: "Naked City."

TEACHER: Why isn't "Naked City" corny or phoney?

CLASS: Well, one Sunday you see a kid with his mother walking to church and the next day he gets into trouble.

TEACHER: Why isn't that phoney?

CLASS: Because he isn't all bad or all good. He isn't one-way.

TEACHER: Are you saying then that a one-way character is phoney?

CLASS: Yeah!

[*Teacher writes "phoney" on the blackboard and under it "one-way" character.*]

CLASS: If you'd give the kids in this school the choice, they'd all read comic books.

TEACHER: Why?

CLASS: They're a lot more fun.

TEACHER: But I thought you said one-way characters were "phoney." I never heard of Batman doing anything nasty.

CLASS: The big difference is we know the comic books are going to be phoney, and that's why they're fun. But you tell us the stuff you give us in school isn't phoney and it always is.

TEACHER: I see. . . . What else do you see on TV that you don't think is phoney?

CLASS: "Divorce Court."

TEACHER: Why isn't that phoney?

CLASS: We don't know; it's just that they talk like real people. That's the thing about school books, they're not about life like we know it.

TEACHER: Would you agree, then, that another thing that makes books phoney is the fact that the characters and events, or things that happen, aren't really believable to you.

CLASS: Yeah!

[*"Unbelievable talk" and "events" are written on the blackboard.*]

TEACHER: Suppose there was a science-fiction story about a man travelling to Mars. Would that be phoney?

[Some disagreement here by the class.]

CLASS: It wouldn't have to be if the guy really acted like someone would act if he were really going.

TEACHER: So, you're saying that the situation wouldn't have to be real if the persons in it were acting in a believable way? [Agreement][1]

At this point, some literary criteria—albeit simplified—were established by the pupils: "Phoniness" meant one-dimensional characters, unbelievable situations, and dialogue: in other words, that which has little or no connection with the children's reality. For example, read this excerpt from a widely used workbook; imagine two 10-year-old boys—any two 10-year-old boys—in the following situation:

> "I hope we don't have to wait much longer for the arrival of the school bus," said Sammy. "This icy wind is choking me!"
>
> "I'm convinced that the bus is stalled in a snowdrift somewhere up the valley," said his schoolmate, Phil. "It's fairly level along here, and the snow hasn't drifted. But on that curving mountain road it's a different story. Let's go home and get out of this bitter cold."
>
> "What you say may prove to be right, but I think we ought to wait a little bit longer," argued Sammy. "Don't you remember how the bus driver fought his way through the snowdrifts last year?"[2]

Ironically, the title on this page of selections is "Where Could This Happen?"! Where indeed could you find two 10-year-olds who speak like this? Even in ordinary circumstances it would sound unreal, let alone in the predicament they were in.

[1]The incident was experienced by the authors in the course of their work with the Madison Area Project in the public schools of Syracuse, New York, during 1962–1965.

[2]From *Think-and-Do Book to Accompany More Times and Places*, by W. S. Gray *et al.*, p. 19. Copyright © 1962 by Scott, Foresman and Company.

The prevalence of school dropouts is symptomatic of the system's phoniness.

> The dropouts, by and large, don't like middle-class culture; and they know quite well what we can do with it. Dropping out is one way of telling us, and it is about time we turned our attention to the things about the school that are bugging them. . . . Core values of both their culture and that which the school represents are at issue; any one that we start by considering will lead to others.[3]

It is true that the first situation cited involved a group of disadvantaged boys, and it could be argued that only such children as these become dropouts. Yet such implicit complaints are not limited to the lower socioeconomic strata: "Contrary to some popular beliefs, dropouts are not exclusively from working-class and lower-class, low-income families. In Syracuse, New York, for example, 30 percent of the parents of dropouts were in white-collar occupations."[4] Further, "the current college dropout rate is between 50 and 60 percent."[5]

Equally revealing testimony to the phoniness of the educational system as far as children are concerned are the shocking but "practical" strategies pupils have discovered for *non*learning. Holt describes some of the techniques employed by economically *privileged* children in private schools:

> [The child] knows that . . . the teacher's attention is divided among twenty students (and that the teacher is more likely to call upon) students who seem confused or not paying attention. (The child) therefore feels safe waving her hand in the air, as if she were bursting to tell the answer, whether she really knows it or not . . . When someone else answers correctly, she nods her head in emphatic agreement.[6]

[3]E. Z. Friedenburg, "An Ideology of School Withdrawal," in D. Schrieber (Ed.), *The School Dropout*, Washington, D.C., National Education Association, 1964, p. 33.
[4]S. M. Miller et al., *The School Dropout Problem (Part I)*, Syracuse, New York State Division for Youth, 1963, p. 44.
[5]S. S. Carlson and K. W. Wegner, "College Dropouts," *Phi Delta Kappan*, **56**:7 (March, 1965), 325.
[6]J. Holt, *How Children Fail*, New York, Pitman, 1964, p. 12.

Holt goes on to say:

> A teacher who asks a question is tuned to the right answer, ready (and) eager to hear it . . . He will assume that anything that sounds close to the right answer is meant to be the right answer. So, for a student who is not sure of the answer, a mumble may be his best bet. If he's not sure whether something is spelled with an *a* or an *o*, he writes a letter that could be either of them.[7]

In a similar vein, *Time* Magazine reported a technique for passing courses with flying colors with minimum studying. That technique was developed by liberal-arts students at Princeton and, at the time it was reported, was creeping across U.S. campuses." Called "ceptmanship," the technique requires only that the student document pithy statements and weave them together in an elaborate manner on essay exams in order to get top grades. Such verbiage is designed to impress the busy professor, who more than likely will not check each paper carefully for knowledge and understanding. Said *Time*, "Superlative ceptmanship amounts to a canny duel between teacher and student. . . . [Consequently] we may be getting a generation of illiberal liberal arts majors who think of ideas as symbols to be manipulated rather than as important issues to be serious about."[8]

These nonlearning strategies, the high dropout rates at all social levels, the widespread incidence of academic cheating by students of all ages and socioeconomic backgrounds—to say nothing of the persistence of discipline problems in elementary and high schools and the increasing campus revolts and demonstrations—are all ways in which our children are trying to tell us that our educational system is phoney.

Why is it that these pupils call our revered American school *phoney?* Unfortunately, today many parents and educators still explain this with such statements as: "Only delinquents feel that way," or "Such children come from bad parents," "They're too young to know what the world is all about. They'll find out

[7]*Ibid.*, p. 7.
[8]The Use and Abuse of the Cept," *Time* Magazine, March 26, 1965, pp. 46, 49.

when they grow up." "TV is at the root of it; children watch TV too much," "Children today are just lazy," "Children have too much freedom today," or even "It stems from a complex social problem; there are too many factors involved to provide a simple answer." In other words, despite our increasing concern with all children, we still seek answers in irrelevancies. We have not yet wiped the fog from our cultural spectacles.

The predicament, of course, is that the child's own "hidden curriculum" is far more oriented to reality than the school's method and materials are prepared to face. For lower-class children particularly, life is no "crystal stairway"; it isn't sugar-coated; it hasn't been screened of unpleasantness for them. Even middle-class children are exposed to larger slices of reality than we allow ourselves to believe. And, for any child, life is what is *here* and *now:* what he can see, hear, touch, and feel through his direct experience. Incidents related to his direct experiences will have meaning for him; those which are remote and not related to his experience will soon tire him, if they don't stymie him altogether.

Yet the school insists on presenting *all* children with a picture of a world that, in its perfection, exists for *no* child. In the primary and middle grades, the basic skills of reading, grammar, spelling, and arithmetic are taught within the context of stories about Mommies and Daddies who are always white, always attractive, always together, always loving, always happy, always successful, always good, and always wise—and about their children who are *almost* always good, but whose "naughtiness" (when it occurs), seems to stem more from childish whimsy than from the genuine drives and emotions that children actually experience. Also, and especially in the early grades, these stories may be presented in language that is quite unlike actual speech.

In school, as the child acquires basic educational skills, he is asked to use them to memorize subject matter that has little or no bearing on his immediate life: In what year did Vasco Da Gama reach India?, Who was the thirteenth President of the United States?, and What are the most important products of Chile? are the sort of questions upon which the child is asked to focus his attention.

Meanwhile, the child is becoming increasingly aware of the confusing complexities that exist in his real world; yet the school, which keeps insisting that it is teaching him to understand this world "when he grows up," does little to explain those complexities to him. Why are girls more shy than boys? If the water can disappear like that, can we? Why do I live in the slums? Why do people fight so much? Why aren't there any Negroes living on our block? Why do I get so angry when someone takes something that belongs to me? Why do we have to hide certain parts of our body? These and many other questions that may perplex the child usually go unanswered in school.

Further, most of the school's resources for student motivation depend on delayed gratification and punishment. If, for example, Johnny persists in disrupting the class, his teacher may appeal to him with, "If you don't pay attention now, you will be sorry when you grow up and need this information," or with, "Johnny, please pay attention now so you can get a good mark on your test next week." If such long-term verbal threats or promises fail, the teacher can always make Johnny stay after school or apply some other punishment long after the misdeed has been forgotten by Johnny himself.

In presenting a world almost totally divorced from reality, the school adheres to what we shall call the *Antiseptic Curriculum*. In some cases, the school does expose the child to portions of his own reality, but it is too often without adequate interpretation; we shall attribute such cases to the *Semiantiseptic Curriculum*. To the vast stores of irrelevant or meaningless facts and figures with which we program our children we shall apply the term the *Nonessential Curriculum*; and finally, the long-range promises we give children as vital reasons for learning nonessentials shall be considered the *Remote Curriculum*.

The antiseptic curriculum

Recall the description of the economically deprived, minority-group urban child as presented in "The Hidden Curriculum"—the large family, the uninhabitable dwellings, the battle for daily survival—and imagine that child coming to school, where his first assignment from his neatly dressed teacher is: "Open your English workbooks to page four, children. Now, I want you to read the paragraph very carefully to yourselves and when you have finished, answer the questions on the bottom of the page."

And so, the child opens the book and reads the following:

> Does everyone in your family have a different idea of where to go for a vacation?
>
> A vacation on the sea coast will make everyone happy.
>
> There are thrills and fun for all the family in this wonderland of golden sun and silver sand.
>
> Dad will find deep-sea fishing, sailing, and other he-man sports. Mother can visit the exciting shops and take the guided sightseeing trips. Or she can take sun baths on the beach.[9]

Or consider the life of a migrant worker's child. Everything that the family owns can fit into an old rusty pick-up truck which carries the child, his mother and father, and his several brothers and sisters from state to state, from field to field. He has been entered in a dozen or more schools so far in his short life, only to be whisked out again when the crop has been harvested and the family is ready to move on. His activities and life must, of necessity, revolve around hard, physical labor.

In order to teach this child to read the teacher assigns the following selection from a popular reader:

> Molly's whole family was busy. Her father was busy with a rake in the yard. Grandfather was watering flowers and vines around the house.

[9]From *Think-and-Do Book to Accompany More Times and Places* by W. S. Gray *et al.*, p. 1. Copyright © 1962 by Scott, Foresman and Company.

> Grandmother was in a bedroom upstairs making a coat for Molly. Mother was in the kitchen fixing supper for everybody.
>
> Only Molly had nothing at all to do.[10]

This is accompanied by an illustration of a lovely white house with purple shutters, bordered by beautiful flowers and vines, and surrounded by a good-sized lawn on which Grandfather (dignified and white-haired), Father (vaguely featured, brown-haired), and Molly (looking exactly like Shirley Temple did when she sang "The Good Ship Lollipop" in the movie) are dressed as if they were department-store mannikins advertising what the "well-dressed" suburban gardener might wear.

In short, basic readers which are widely used throughout the country depict life as though it were lived only by happy, neat, wealthy, white people whose intact and loving families live only in clean, grassy suburbs. These families rarely have over four members, and the most serious crises they have to face are the loss of the family pet or who in the household will have use of the car. In this storybook world, there are no crippled children, no blind, no deaf, practically no disease, and hardly even a broken arm or a skinned elbow. Further, the ethnic groups comprising so much of our population are often omitted, or else they are included in such units as "Understanding Children from Other Lands." Even though many text publishers are now using more multi-racial characters, the plots tend to remain antiseptic and the characters one-dimensional.

How can we expect children who are subjected to such distortions of reality during their formative years to become mature and enlightened adults, well-equipped to lead the nation in a world of increasingly complex political, economic, and sociological problems? As Ezra Jack Keats, author and illustrator of children's books, says: "If any group of people is to be pictured as always fashionably thin, with children who never misbehave,

[10] W. S. Gray et al., *The New More Friends and Neighbors*, Chicago, Scott, Foresman, 1965, p. 178.

and all of them improbably perfect, we are denying a people's right to deal with reality and [to] assume the very responsibilities for which they struggle."[11]

The phoniness of the antiseptic curriculum is communicated to children not only in the reading materials assigned, but in a variety of ways throughout the daily school routine. It is communicated by the way the teachers dress, speak, and act; by *what* they teach, and by *how* they teach it. Imagine, for example, a teacher telling a disadvantaged child:

"The reason we are studying the Middle Atlantic states is so that *when you grow up* [always "when you grow up"], you'll know where to go on vacation."

OR

"Our first unit this year will be 'Your Friend, The Policeman.' "

OR

"Yes, I know you failed only science and math this year, but when you're left back, you have to take *everything* over again."

OR

In a science class when a pupil blurts out, "I watched my ma have a baby last night at our house": "You watch your mouth. We don't talk about *those* things in school!"

Thus as Jean Grambs states, "The school demands of children that they deny what their own sense experiences tell them and accept instead the school's version of reality. [The children] may be making such an effort to meet this demand that in the process they have little energy left with which to learn the content that is offered them."[12]

The great distance between the school's assumptions and the pupil's reality was amusingly illustrated in the following situation.

[11]E. J. Keats, "The Right To Be Real," *Saturday Review*, November 9, 1963, p. 56.

[12]Jean D. Grambs, *Schools, Scholars and Society*, Englewood Cliffs, N.J., Prentice-Hall, 1965, p. 80.

The teacher was working on initial consonant blends, and held up flash cards of words containing "Tr": *tree, trip, true, trim*. The class responded accurately to each card until *trim* came up, whereupon the class dissolved into laughter and general disorder. "I don't understand it," the teacher reported later. "I've never had any trouble with that class." The answer was that the word *trim* had a special meaning for the class of which the teacher was not aware: For the children, *trim* referred to sexual intercourse.

Such occurrences are, unfortunately, not rare, and many a teacher has been similarly embarrassed. It would be impossible, of course, for anyone to be familiar with all the meanings pupils have for common words in our vocabulary; yet a more sensitive awareness to pupil reality and peer norms would enable many teachers to handle such situations more comfortably for themselves and more educationally for the children.

It can be argued—and frequently is—that not all children are "disadvantaged," and that, in any case, the school must hold up the highest ideals to its young charges. Yet, as we have said, even the most "privileged" children are exposed to a larger slice of reality than the school recognizes. On television alone children are confronted with realistic representations of childbirth, illicit love, mental and physical illness, violent emotions, and crimes. In a seventh-grade unit on juvenile delinquency, the authors assigned a television documentary as homework. The day after the program, an irate parent came to school complaining, "Why did you assign such a program for homework? Isn't there already enough horror and violence around without my child having to observe more?" Indeed, there is a great deal of horror and violence in the real world, to say nothing of the fictional world, but children are exposed to it whether or not we choose to face that fact, and it is the school's responsibility to help interpret the child's experiences. If we are to impart to our children "noble ideals" we must do so in terms of the antitheses of these ideals, because these antitheses are the basis from which ideals must be evolved, clarified, and implemented.

Thus, the antiseptic curriculum, in which reality is ignored, in the long run damages any child. The effects on a child from the lower extreme of the socioeconomic continuum are particularly harmful. In bypassing the living reality of the slum child, a Negro, or a Puerto Rican as though his world did not exist, the school deprives the child of a means for dealing with his reality, and an implicit confusion will haunt his mind as he struggles to grasp some meaning from his hours at school. At best, the child is bored and restless in class; at worst, he assimilates a destructive interpretation of the contrast between the world depicted by the school and that of his parents and the other teachers in his hidden curriculum. He may be severely resentful of the conditions imposed on him by the white, middle-class world, and thus hostile to its values, traditions, institutions, and to its way of life generally. In any case, the child cannot be expected to absorb the school's teaching to become the "solid American citizen" of the middle-class scheme of things. Further, the child's developing ego is bound to be damaged to a large degree by the gulf between his own reality and the school's. As long as the school deprecates the child's own sense experience, it removes the incentives necessary for the child even to try to learn what the school offers, for, in rejecting the child's view of reality, it rejects the child.

In short, the school cannot close its eyes to those aspects of life that it does not like; rather, it must learn to deal with them more effectively than it has in the past.

The semiantiseptic curriculum

It would be unfair to imply that all educators rigidly espouse the antiseptic curriculum; indeed, many teachers—particularly those working in depressed areas—are aware of the need to deal with pupil reality. Unfortunately, however, attempts to present school matter in more realistic contexts have too frequently resulted in exposure without interpretation, which can be even more confusing to the child than no exposure. The same is true of partial exposure, which attempts to introduce adult reality to the child in "safe" doses. But, as a *New York Times* review of teen-age literature said, there are no safe doses of experience:

> Teen-age literature attempts to provide experience of the adult world in safe doses. But there are no safe doses of experience. Achilles' mother dipped him into a river to make him immortal, but it was the heel she held him by through which he sustained his mortal wound. Teen-age literature, holding on to more than the heel, leaves more of the teen-ager vulnerable to such mortal wounds.[13]

There are many areas in which teachers may attempt to deal with pupil reality, yet fail in utilizing the feedback constructively. For example, we know of teachers who, in trying to avoid a completely antiseptic curriculum, may have reinforced the distorted social attitudes their pupils had already learned. In raising such topics as: "What are slums and what effect have they on people who live in them?" "What is school integration and why do some people want Negroes to move to all-white schools?" or "What is social or ethnic discrimination and how does it come about?" these teachers may have given middle-class children a negative attitude toward people from slums, or strengthened previously acquired antipathy. Worse, exposure to such topics may really have added the exclamation point to lower-class children's already well-entrenched negative selves.

In a well-intentioned attempt to get her pupils to express their own feelings, one teacher confronted her Negro class with such questions. The pupils wouldn't quite admit that they lived in slums, but they talked about what it might do to those who did. They also expressed anxieties about attending an all-white school. Why should *they* do all the moving? Many felt they would rather stay where they were. The teacher met with resentment, defensiveness, and hostility: "How come we're doing these things?," "Do other kids talk about these things in school," "Why do you pick on us to bring up these things?," and "Why aren't we studying our regular subjects?" The teacher could not produce

[13]Carolyn Heilbreen, "Life in Safe Doses," *The New York Times Book Review* (Children's Book Section), May 9, 1965, p. 3.

an answer that was satisfying to the pupils, who were hurt and resentful.

A similar situation arose in another class of lower-class youngsters. The teacher was aiming at pupil familiarity with an understanding of the various kinds of neighborhoods within a community, and decided to arouse interest by taking the children on a tour of the city. During the trip, he pointed out contrasts in living conditions, and the children were asked to consider the following questions: "How do you like this street?" "What do you like about it?," "Would you like to live on a street like this?," and "Who do you think the people are who live in this neighborhood?" The basic structure for the class discussion never actually formed, for in this case, too, the children became restless and unruly when the subject came up in the classroom. It could be inferred, of course, that during the trip they contrasted their own neighborhoods with the better ones they saw. Was the real message of the trip, "Now, kids, you can see how really bad off you are!"?

Thus, when such well-intentioned attempts to help the disadvantaged child understand his bewildering reality are made without supportive interpretation, the child actually becomes cognitive of what he already senses emotionally: that he is himself socially inferior and unworthy. The lower-class Negro is in a particularly difficult plight. He realizes consciously that he is at the bottom of the heap, financially and socially. He knows that, as a Negro, he is set apart from the rest of society and excluded from its privileges (though somehow he is expected to comply with its moral and social values!). The propaganda of white society has had its effect; indeed, there is no way for him to escape it. The message—which is communicated to him almost from his birth—is all too clearly that he and his kind are poor, dirty, lazy, stupid, irresponsible, and generally worthless, and this message is only brought home all the more powerfully by the teacher who tries to incorporate the child's social situation into the semiantiseptic curriculum.

This is not to say that the school should abandon all attempts to make contact with the child's experiences, however, but only to draw attention to the fact that the semiantiseptic curriculum is oriented from the white middle-class perspective which views slums as "bad," and minority groups as "different" or "deprived." It is as though we shake our collective heads and say, "tsk, tsk" to any child who does not automatically match our standards of living, of taste, of habits. It should not surprise us that children exposed to this attitude shrink from and even rebel against us. Only when the school (including the teacher-training institutions) fully identifies itself with the children's own perspective will the formal curriculum be equipped to handle social reality to the advantage of pupils and society both.

The nonessential curriculum

Considering that so many of the largest problems facing the world and the United States today are predominantly a matter of inadequate human relations and lack of cooperation among different peoples, one wonders why we spend so much time trying to get our young children to memorize such facts as the order of American Presidents, the precise dates on which this or that event occurred, the area in square miles of this or that state (or nation, or continent), and the locations of natural resources in the world. We do not deny the importance of knowledge in these areas, but we become concerned when schools emphasize these areas to the exclusion of others.

How many of us can remember these facts now? Can you, right now, name even two products of Chile? Can you "right off the top of your head," so to speak, list all the Presidents from Washington through Johnson in perfect order? Can you remember the year in which Texas was admitted to the Union? And, if you can answer these questions correctly, is it because you remember these facts from your grade or even high-school education? Probably not. Even though such facts and figures were drummed into us repeatedly in grade school, again in high school, and perhaps still again in college, most of us cannot recall particular details at a moment's notice. In any case, it is unimportant, since they can easily be found in reference books.

Moreover, most of these facts have no personal usefulness to us. True, the child who is forced to memorize the products of Brazil or India may grow up to become a manufacturer of packaged nuts—in which case, the knowledge that he can obtain his raw product economically from these countries may be useful—but it is doubtful that his grade-school exercises laid the foundations for his adult career. On the contrary, he probably acquired his knowledge of nut crops in Brazil and India from working experience, for within this context such information has *personal meaning*. But for those of us who have no similar context, such matters are of no consequence.

If these trivial facts and figures are, in the main, of little or no relevance to adults, how can we expect them to have meaning to children, whose primary concerns are their own behavioral values in relation to their expanding social environment and their cognitive understanding of the increasing complexities that unfold before them? Chile, Andrew Jackson, and 1492 are not a personal part of their individual experiences, and become only remote aspects of their peripheral experience, solely because of the dictates of the formal curriculum.

It should be remembered that, to a young child, even issues which are currently in the news are relatively meaningless unless the child has a vested interest in them. For example, if Negro children are interested in integration topics, it is not because they are "civic minded." To be sure, the roots of civic mindedness can be planted by drawing upon current affairs in this area, but their intrinsic concern is that they are themselves Negro, that their closest adult models are strongly involved in the issues for personal reasons, and that the emotional attitudes of these models are communicated to the children. Thus, in many cases, well-meaning attempts to draw upon current affairs or to associate them with historical, geographical, and other formal subjects of the curriculum may be just as nonessential and phoney to the children as the purely historical facts and figures. In a class composed primarily of children from white-collar families, for example, the subject of automation may seem remote and irrelevant to the pupils (unless social concern has become their personal concern), while in a class composed predominantly of children from blue-collar families, automation might be a timely and interesting subject—provided that it is presented in a *personally meaningful* and *constructive* way.

If there is a preponderance of useless subject matter in the formal curriculum, it is at the expense of content which could be very useful, both to the growing, seeking child, and to society itself. Havighurst and Peck remark on the absence of content dealing with human behavior:

> The idea of giving any formal place to the phenomena and laws of human behavior in the curricula of elementary schools as yet seems to strike many people as bizarre. If only because of the tradition-bred familiarity it seems more "sensible" to spend years studying the geography of foreign lands, the construction of sentences, and the mysteries of the multiplication tables, rather than spend some time each day teaching children how to understand about the behavior of themselves and others.[14]

In light of current rates of crime, juvenile delinquency, alcoholism, drug addiction, mental illness—to name just a few important problems—is it not more bizarre that we don't enlarge the behavioral content of our curricula? Indeed, has our best economic, scientific, and technological advancement reduced the prevalence of hate, greed, lack, fear, or the various degrees of warfare that stem from such problems? On the contrary, our prowess in science and technology (which, interestingly, is due to the contributions of relatively few individuals as compared to the population we have processed through our educational system) has only increased the numbers of people who hate, lack, and fear, and the destructiveness of the tools used by them.

Because of children's own most compelling needs, the ab-

[14]R. F. Peck and R. J. Havighurst, *The Psychology of Character Development*, New York, Wiley, 1960, p. 195.

sence of subject matter in the behavioral sciences seems even more ludicrous. A child's strongest concerns (whether or not he realizes it) are with understanding and handling his own emotions and behavior with respect to himself, his parents, his siblings, his agemates, and society in general. To do this, he needs an adequate reference system in terms of the emotional and behavioral patterns of other individuals in his environment. Yet, in presenting the child with nothing but the happiness, loving kindness, and goodness associated with the "American Dream"—in the hope of conditioning him in these values—and by forcing him to memorize strange names and meaningless dates because they are part of "our great American heritage," the school does nothing to help the child to understand the painful sensations of his own unhappiness, resentment, and fears, or to prevent him from observing hostilities in others who share this American heritage with him.

Interestingly, despite the vast psychological evidence that the child's younger years are his most "formative"—that is, the child is then most vulnerable to the shaping of his personality and attitudes—the schools persist in concentrating the teaching of meaningful knowledge in the later years. For example, in junior or senior high-school the child suddenly is confronted with discussions of family relations, marital responsibilities, sex topics, job-finding, and similar personal problems of "life-adjustment." Such attempts as are made by the school are usually inadequate since they are nearly always presented in the emasculated, sterile, and idealized version of middle-class life. Yet, to introduce these topics when the basis of the child's adjustment and understanding has already been laid—or mislaid—is absurd. Formal psychology (generally presented on a "this-can-help-you-to-understand-yourself" basis) is seldom introduced before the college level, by which time the child, if he gets to college, is already firmly entrenched in defense and self-deluding mechanisms which obstruct his ability to "turn round" on himself. Consequently, the potential personal and social values of such subject matter are likely to be lost, and the facts and principles acquired remain on a peripheral and purely academic level instead of being integrated into the individual's behavior.

The middle-class children who succeed in school do so because they have the role alternatives and verbal skills. With little apparent difficulty (as far as the middle-class-oriented educator can see), they comply with the school's insistence that they memorize apparently meaningless content, at least to the point where they can pass the tests and get promoted. But have they been really prepared for adult life? The divorce rate, the incidence of ulcers and other psychosomatic illnesses, the vast sums spent each year on psychotherapy, indicate that they have not. The rigidity with which political parties are adhered to without respect to issues is another symptom, as is the startingly low percentage of the population that votes even in presidential elections.

If we have managed to remain blind to the symptoms of inadequacy and phoniness in the nonessential curriculum for the middle and upper classes, we must no longer fog our cultural spectacles where it concerns the disadvantaged. The low educational level, the high dropout rate, the increasing incidence of crime and violence, and widespread poverty have forced us to examine this group, and to listen when its members call our educational system "phoney." Many of them lack the verbal and other skills that comprise so much of "readiness" for today's formal curriculum. Faced with a far more pressing reality than the order of American Presidents, it is hardly a wonder that these children get more meaning from the television programs "Naked City" and "Divorce Court" and from comic books than from their formal education.

The remote curriculum

Thus far, we have tried to show how far out of reach is a mastery of the formal curriculum for many, if not most, pupils. Even "privileged" children with the skills that constitute the school's view of readiness must be badgered into attentiveness and participation, as teachers in suburban schools know all too well. The artificial idealism of the "American Dream" comprising the all-pervasive theme of the curriculum, the tidy attempts to deal with such aspects of reality as the school recognizes, and the overwhelming emphasis placed on trivia—of which the vast bulk will remain forever useless—conspire to bore and to alienate the child. For the child who has not even developed the basic school readiness, these aspects constitute an anathema.

To motivate these restless children, the school can think of little better to offer than equally meaningless promises:

Because when you grow up you will have to know this.
When the time comes for you to look for a job, you will need these skills.
Studying colonial times will help us understand our lives today.
When you are old enough to vote, you will be glad you studied about this.
We are studying nutrition so that when you have a family you can keep them healthy.
If you study hard now, you will get a good mark on your test.
Pay attention in class, now, at the beginning of the term, and you will be promoted.
Stay in school and you will be able to find a good job.

It is unlikely that these far-off "reasons" inspire even advantaged children to become interested in school, and they definitely discourage pupils from disadvantaged homes. How is the slum child—whose father, if he knows him, may be a sometime dishwasher and whose mother may be a cleaning woman for wives of white-collar or professional men—to believe that learning history and hygiene will enable him to find a "good" job? How is the migrant-worker's child to become interested in getting a good mark on a test? How is the child of non-English-speaking, immigrant parents to acquire an interest in voting? How is the child who must fight or steal his way to recognition in the home to consider the colonial period relevant to his life today?

Middle-class children go along with the game because they have been conditioned to merge with the adult world and its educational system. They respect adult authority, but often only superficially. Real learning isn't their concern; getting along with the system is. Keep "big people" happy, and there will be time enough to have your own fun; get the "right" answers on the tests, and teachers won't notice what else you do; bring home a good report card, and Dad will buy you that car you want.

But lower-class children have not been so trained. "Dad" may not even care whether the child brings home a good report card, and even then he's not likely to provide material rewards. Dad may have a high-school diploma, but being Negro, does *he* have a good job? Also, lower-class children tend to have different perceptions of time, long-term goals, and means-ends relationships from those of middle-class children:

> School is an institution where every item in the present is finely linked to a distant future, and in consequence there is no serious clash of expectations between the school and the middle-class child. The child's developed time span of anticipation allows the present activity to be related to a future. . . . [However, among the working classes] The specific character of long-term goals tends to be replaced by more general notions of the future. . . . Thus, present, or near-present, activities have greater value than the relation of the present activity to the attainment of a distant goal. . . . This environment limits the perception of the developing child of and in time. Present gratifications or . . . deprivations become absolute gratifications or . . . deprivations, for there exists no developed time continuum upon which present activity can be ranged. Relative to the middle classes, the postponement of present pleasure for future gratification is found difficult.[15]

Thus, the disadvantaged child may not even comprehend these "phoney" reasons for learning sterile irrelevancies, much less be motivated by them.

In this chapter, we have attempted to show what happens

[15] B. Bernstein, "Social Class and Linguistic Development: A Theory of Social Learning," in A. H. Halsey, J. Floud, and C. A. Anderson (Eds.), *Education, Economy and Society*, New York, Free Press, 1961, pp. 296–297.

when the product of the hidden curriculum meets the formal curriculum of the school. For the disadvantaged poor, there are at least three major points of conflict:

1. Their learning style is different from the teaching style of the school.
2. What they already know is not utilized by the school.
3. The school manages to avoid helping them with those things with which they are really concerned.

The message of these three areas to the disadvantaged poor is: "You can't learn very well, you don't know anything, and *we'll* tell *you* what you should be concerned about." It is small wonder that these children find the conventional education system—and the middle-class society it represents—"phoney."

However, in helping us to see why they think our school system is "phoney," the disadvantaged poor have helped us to understand better why it might be considered phoney by all children. We accept the typical complaints of middle-class children toward school as perfectly normal for their age—did we not also recite gleefully "No more teachers, no more books . . ." when a school session came to a close? As long as their marks are acceptable, their behavior not too flagrant, their appearance fairly neat, we think our middle-class children are doing well scholastically; i.e., that our system is perfectly fine as it is. But on closer scrutiny it becomes tellingly clear that these "privileged" children, too, hold the school to be "phoney," and for some valid reasons. Let us examine the educational system next in terms of how its products compare to its stated educational goals.

CHAPTER 5

FROM PURPOSE TO PRODUCT

Our society through its policy makers appears to be increasingly aware that fundamental discrepancies exist among the purpose, process, and the product of one of its key institutions—the school. Although these discrepancies have been with us for some time, their existence has become a matter of national concern because of the growing international implications posed by the depletion of our human resources. Schools are now viewed as the main institutional vehicles for cultivating the human resources of the country.

Two revolutionary events have illuminated the difference between the schools' purpose and the products they are turning out. The launching of Sputnik in 1957 and the Civil-Rights movement focused attention upon the relationship between the schools and the students they have produced. It is now clear that the schools have to a large extent failed both the economically privileged and the poor student, and that the philosophical ideal of educating all the children of the society has become a political and social necessity.

Symptoms of the schools' failures, which have been manifest for some time, are now being subjected to careful study. School dropouts are viewed with alarm even though their numbers are decreasing. During the 1960s, the Department of Labor estimates that 7.5 million will drop out of our schools. Two thirds of them will go no further than tenth grade.[1] Rejection rates for military service and the problem of low scholastic achievement of the poor and minority groups are of great concern. When these symptoms are analyzed they show that: (1) We are not educating all the children, and (2) a large reservoir of human resources remains untapped. Clearly, the product of the schools still is not reflecting its purpose. For the first time the nation is becoming aware that human development makes good political and economic sense as well as human sense.

When the Russian Sputnik beat the U.S.'s efforts to launch the first space satellite, strong criticism was aimed at curricular inadequacies in the educational system: Why were the nation's

[1]D. Schreiber (Ed.), *The School Dropout*, Washington, D.C., National Education Association, 1964, p. 2.

Stevens, Ford Foundation

FROM PURPOSE TO PRODUCT

schools producing so few fully qualified scientists and technologists? Under great pressure from society, educators quickly focused their attention on ways of cramming college material—particularly mathematics and the sciences—into elementary-school programs. At the same time, publicity given to Appalachia and other economically depressed regions, mounting tensions erupting in urban slums, and increasing outbreaks of violence and civil disobedience by Negro pressure groups converged on the Federal government. Educators in turn have been asked to devote special attention to educating the millions of the poor, "culturally deprived," and otherwise disadvantaged segments of the Great Society.

The fundamental issue behind the nation's new, spectacular focus on education is the cultivation of human resources, without which the nation cannot maintain its leadership role in the world. The successful launching of Sputnik immediately revealed that the Russians—who had progressed from an essentially feudalistic country into a modern technological society in fewer than fifty years—had managed to tap and to harness their human resources to a far greater extent than had the United States. The emergence of this unexpected and powerful competitor for world superiority made American society realize that our scientific, commercial, industrial, and technological advancements depend upon the efficiency with which we develop our human resources. A depletion in this resource would affect the very core of the nation. College, once a luxury for the few, has now become essential for the majority if we are to maintain a lead in technological innovation. Further, as an increasingly automated industry diminishes the availability of low and semi-skilled jobs, school dropouts, who comprise much of the labor force in these jobs, threaten to become an even greater drain on the taxpayer through their dependence on welfare support, and on the economy through their low purchasing power. Thus, fully educating everyone in our diverse population is no longer a democratic ideal to be expounded by a few philosophers, but a vital and immediate necessity. The business of education is to "yield benefits to the households of the society," explains economist Benson.

First, there are generalized or social benefits:

1. Economic productivity is increased.
2. National defense is strengthened.
3. Our democratic society operates more effectively under the control of a literate and informed electorate than it would if the voters were mostly uneducated.
4. For an educated person it is more stimulating to be able to share intellectual interests with others through communication.
5. The cancer of abject poverty is cured—that is, the occupational mobility that public education provides is a guarantee that household poverty is not passed along from one generation to the next.

Second, there are specific or private benefits that accrue to households having children in public schools. The children receive the basic preparation to undertake a line of work, and they are encouraged to use their minds and bodies in ways that will help them to live a good life.[2]

Another role of education, that of being an instrument for social reconstruction, is becoming clearer, and the question which Professor George Counts (a philosopher and educator at Teachers College, Columbia University) raised in the 1930s—Dare the Schools Build a New Social Order?—has been answered affirmatively in the 1960s.[3] Education is being viewed increasingly in society as the instrument for social renewal and for developing the Great Society. Brameld, one of the key reconstructionist philosophers, asserts: "Reconstructionism is thus a philosophy of magnetic foresight—a philosophy of ends attainable through the development of powerful means possessed latently by the people. To learn how to exercise that power for these ends is the first priority of education."[4]

In addressing the White House Conference on Education

[2]C. S. Benson, *The Economics of Public Education,* Boston, Houghton Mifflin, 1961, p. 23.
[3]G. S. Counts, *Dare the Schools Build a New Social Order?,* New York, John Day, 1932.
[4]T. Brameld, *Education for the Emerging Age,* New York, Harper & Row, 1965, p. 25.

in 1965, President Johnson said, "Education will not cure all the problems of society, but without it, no cure for any problem is possible. It is central to the purposes of this administration and at the core of our hopes for a Great Society."[5] At the same conference, the President presented his view of the kind of educational product that is needed for the Great Society:

> Most of all we need an education which will create the educated mind. This is a mind—not simply a repository of information and skills, but a source of creative skepticism—characterized by a willingness to challenge old assumptions and to be challenged, a spaciousness of outlook, and convictions deeply held; but it is a mind which new facts can modify. For we are a society which has staked its survival on the rejection of dogma, on the refusal to bend experience to belief, and in the determination to shape action to reality as reality reveals itself to us. This is the hardest course of all to take. Without education it is an impossible course.[6]

Education finds itself in a state of major transition today. If it is to meet the demands placed on it by an increasingly technological society, it must modernize along each of the intricate lines which compose the complex of the overall educational system. To be sure we have instituted such innovations as educational television, teaching machines, and programed materials, but these have yet to penetrate beneath the surface of the educational system. In any case, the fundamental principles and content involved remain virtually unchanged. It is not enough merely to adapt automated machinery to classroom use, to condense four years of college work into two, or to tailor college material to fit elementary school minds; on the contrary, we must reconsider the very substance of the subject matter itself.

Massive changes in educational institutions, from nursery

[5]L. B. Johnson, quoted in "The White House Conference on Education," *American Education*, U.S. Department of Health, Education and Welfare, 1:17 (July-August, 1965), 28.
[6]*Ibid.*

school to the university, must be made suitable and efficient for meeting the present and future needs of society. Teacher-training institutions, especially, must streamline their teaching methods as well as the methods they teach.

Clearly many complex renovations are required of the new age of education. If the current spotlight on educational reform is to result in strengthening the existing educational process, more careful findings must be formulated to move education to a new stage of operation. We must take a long, hard look at even our most cherished assumptions. Perhaps the first glance should be cast in the direction of the purposes for which our educational system exists.

Purposes

The outstanding educational aim in this country has always been equal educational opportunities for all. In 1944, and again in 1948, the Educational Policies Commission, one of the key voices of the teaching profession, reiterated authoritatively that American education was for "all the children of *all* the people."[7] So dearly have we cherished this ideal, so long have we expounded it, that perhaps we have substituted the ideal for reality. The fact is that this country has never provided equal educational opportunities for everyone in its diverse population. On the contrary, education commensurate with the times, and the adequate preparation of people to cope with the times to come, has, throughout this country's history, been available primarily to the children of the wealthy and the favored few receiving their support.

Although at least some form of public elementary instruction was a reality as early as 1635 in the town of Boston, it was not until the nineteenth century that even the primitive "three R's" public schools existed to any significant extent outside New England and a few communities in the West. Even when they

[7]Educational Policies Commission, *Education for All Children*, Washington, D.C., National Education Association, 1948.

did spread, their effect on society was limited. They excluded, for example, Negroes, American Indians, many of the newly immigrated peoples, and the children of the many farmers who valued their offspring's productive labor over their schooling. The first public secondary school, moreover, did not appear until 1821, when Boston established a precedent that was soon followed elsewhere in the land. However, 3.8 percent of the 14 to 17 age group were enrolled in high schools.[8] The dropout rate was high then as it is now, particularly among the lower classes. Higher education, especially, has been the privilege of a few; until World War II—when Federal funds provided tuition and subsistence for those veterans who wished to pursue their studies—it was reserved chiefly for the upper and upper-middle classes.

Perhaps one clue to the reason why the schools have never educated all lies in the qualitative purposes for which public education has stood. These have differed greatly from age to age; during the seventeenth century, for example, the Deluder Satan Act of 1647 in Masschusetts established that the main purpose of the school would be to teach reading and writing so that the Bible could be read and understood, thereby thwarting the devil. In 1862, when America was still largely agrarian and the industrial revolution was just beginning to gain momentum, the Morrill Act donated large grants of land to each state, to "teach such branches of learning as are related to agriculture and the mechanic arts . . . to promote the liberal and practical education of the industrial classes in several pursuits and professions in life."[9] For today's technological and primarily urban society, the Elementary and Secondary Education Act of 1965 states that: "In this decade Federal interest has been greatly magnified because of the educational implications inherent in technological developments and the relation of education to national preparedness."[10]

Probably everyone would agree that the schools *should* pro-

[8]W. Rudy, *Schools in an Age of Mass Culture*, Englewood Cliffs, N.J., Prentice Hall, 1965, p. 147.

[9]C. B. Swisher, *American Constitutional Development* (2nd ed.), Boston, Houghton Mifflin, 1954, pp. 381–382.

[10]"*Elementary and Secondary Education Act of 1965*," Report No. 143, House of Representatives, 89th Congress.

vide equal educational opportunities for all in our population, and that the prime qualitative objective of education should be to equip its products to meet not only the challenge of today, but also—and particularly—those we might reasonably expect in the future. Toward these ends, the overall purpose of the public schools might be summarized this way: *To help all children to assume mature adult roles; to equip them with those academic vocational, and avocational skills, understandings, and attitudes which will enable them to develop fully their individual potentialities; to achieve the greatest possible degree of social and economic mobility, and to contribute effectively to the improvement of our democratic society.*

So defined, this statement of purpose is overgeneralized. It raises some questions: Have educators been interpreting this purpose to mean to help all children to assume mature *middle-class* adult roles? Are they trying to equip them with those academic skills that are required for college, those vocational skills that are necessary for white-collar jobs, and those avocational skills helpful in *playing golf, fishing,* and *carrying on cocktail party conversations?* Are they not encouraging children to acquire "white skins," material insatiability, and a preference for neat, look-alike, lawn-fringed, and automatic-appliance-furnished houses so that they *can* achieve the greatest possible degree of social mobility? And, toward the improvement of our democratic society, do we implicitly encourage only those contributions which will further entrench *middle-class* culture and values both in this country and in the rest of the world?

Ironically, as the middle-class culture is reinforced, the continuation of this mainstream orientation becomes a threat to its own participants. In light of current national and international problems the American middle-class stand is in precarious balance and is being faced with a growing confrontation with a non-middle-class world.

In view of this, it is ironic that there is a strong argument that the role of the school should be linked only to academic content—subject-matter mastery—and that all other tasks are not part of the school's function. However rational this point may appear, education's new role in modern society must be to develop *all* of the human resources of the society and to serve as the key institution for reconstructing the society. The evidence for this definition appears clear as education is called upon to solve such problems as social mobility, manpower and employment, poverty, social injustice, and segregation. The argument that the schools should retain a "three R's" orientation appears irrelevant to the demands of modern society.

The United States cannot entertain a middle-class centered educational purpose and maintain its position in a culturally and politically diverse world. Nor can it espouse such purposes and hope to achieve harmony among the diverse peoples in its own population. On the contrary, it is not difficult to realize that, to be effective, the aims of education today must fully recognize and *accommodate* the heterogeneity of the American people as well as the diverse needs of an increasingly complex age. Properly tapped and directed, the unique resources of each individual should amply meet the divergent demands of the present age to the mutual satisfaction of both individual and society, and lay a solid foundation for the developments to come in future eras.

To accomplish this, however, the school must aim to supply *each* child with as many alternatives for decision-making as it is possible for him to assimilate; to expose him *impartially* to as many ways of interpreting a situation as we can; to develop and to extend his *meaningful* perception of the structure and content of his expanding environment; and to widen his repertoire of role performance and action involvement. In other words, whether a student is wealthy or poor; white or Negro; Puerto Rican, Mexican-American, or American Indian; of migrant or industrial parentage; from a rural, urban, or suburban home; verbally restricted or elaborated; fast or slow in learning, the educational process of the modern age should be capable of making *contact* with the child. It should be able to move him forward in his development toward becoming all he has within him to become.

Further, if this process is carried out, the disadvantaged child can choose to become as middle-class as he desires, but he would at least have the skills to make the choice and to assume the necessary roles. The American Indian could remain as loyal to his tribal values and customs as he wished without having, at the same time, to prefer isolation from the society at large. The Negro, too, would be free to devote his life primarily to the Negro community, or to the white, or to society generally, according to his leaning, but he would simultaneously be free to come and go in the overall society as his enterprises led him. Similarly, the middle- or upper-class child could choose his central life role—perhaps even several—from among a variety of possible alternatives. It is this element of *choice* which is so crucial.

In eliminating the middle-class orientation of its educational aims, therefore, the school would not merely substitute lower-class or subcultural values, but would focus upon those elements of *all* classes and cultures which are classless and vital to the very core of humanity. As Paul Goodman, psychologist, put it, "Our philosophic aim must be to get each one out of his isolated class and into the one humanity."[11]

The products

Assuming that our purpose has been to educate *all* children, how have our products turned out? The Elementary and Secondary Education Act of 1965 gives this assessment:

> . . . A national problem . . . is reflected in draft rejection rates because of educational deficiencies. It is evidenced by the employment and manpower retraining problems aggravated by the fact that there are over 8 million adults who have completed less than 5 years of school. It is seen in the 20 percent unemployment rate of our 18 to 24 year olds. It is voiced by our institutions of higher learning and our vocational and technical educators who have the task of building on elementary and secondary education foundations which are of varying quality and adequacy.[12]

[11]P. Goodman, "The Universal Tray," in D. Schreiber (Ed.), *op cit.*, pp. 44–45.

[12]*Elementary and Secondary Education Act of 1965, op. cit.*

Of course, these statistics are largely weighted by the disadvantaged segments of the population who are the casualties of both the American society and the schools which represent this society. That these schools are widening rather than diminishing the gap between their purposes and their final products among deprived groups is clearly revealed in a progress report to the U.S. Commissioner of Education:

> By all known criteria, the majority of urban and rural slum schools are failures. In neighborhood after neighborhood across the country, more than half of each age group fails to complete high school and 5 percent or fewer go on to some form of higher education. In many schools the average measured IQ is under 85, and it drops steadily as the children grow older. Adolescents depart from these schools ill-prepared to lead a satisfying, useful life or to participate successfully in the community.[13]

These children are the first to take their places among the ranks of the unskilled and unemployed. They are the chief drain on public welfare funds, and they become dependent on public relief at an early age. They cause the highest portion of crime and mental-illness statistics, and thus become a drain on tax-supported, law-enforcing agencies and penal and mental institutions.

Kenneth Clark made a study of school performance in Harlem:

> In reading comprehension, the ability to understand what one is reading, 30 percent of the Harlem third grade pupils are reading below grade level, compared to 21.6 percent who are reading above. For sixth grade pupils, the story is even more dismal; there 80.9 percent of the pupils score below grade level in reading, while 11.7 percent score above, indicating a rather rapid relative deterioration in reading comprehension within three school years.
>
> Between grades three and six, word knowledge falters also; in third grade, 38.9 percent score below grade level,

[13]Panel on Educational Research & Development, *Innovation and Experimentation on Education*, Washington, D.C., U.S. Government Printing Office, 1964, p. 30.

> 18.7 percent score above; in sixth grade, 77.5 percent are below, 10.6 percent above. Arithmetic shows a similar pattern of underachievement, though figures are only available for the sixth grade (57.6 percent are below grade level in "computation," 66.6 below in "problems and concepts"). By eighth grade, three-quarters of the Harlem junior high school students score below grade level in reading comprehension and word knowledge; in arithmetic, their performance is even more discouraging—83.8 percent are now below.
>
> The academic performance of Harlem pupils in reading and arithmetic is still more depressing when compared to the performance of other children in New York City and in the nation as a whole. In the third grade, New York City pupils, on the average, are about equal to those elsewhere. By the eighth grade they have slipped almost a half grade behind. During those same grades, the pupils in Harlem slip further and further behind the achievement levels of both the city and the nation. In the third grade, Harlem pupils are one year behind the achievement levels of New York City pupils. By the sixth grade they have fallen nearly two years behind; and by the eighth grade they are about two and one-half years behind New York City levels and three years behind students in the nation as a whole.[14]

At the 1965 White House Conference on Education, this indictment of the American educational system came during deliberations upon education in the world of work: "Education is the only industry in America which continues in business despite the fact that it is producing a million products unfit for consumption."[15] Sidney Marland, Superintendent of Schools in Pittsburgh, Pennsylvania, points out the discrepancy between the goals of equal opportunity and the development of all human resources and the actual outcomes:

> One of every three students in fifth grade drops out of school before high school graduation. While the proportion of dropouts has been declining for the past 50 years, it is

[14]K. B. Clark, *Dark Ghetto*, New York, Harper & Row, 1965, pp. 120–121.
[15]Joan Bowers, quoted in *American Education*, *op. cit.*, p. 15.

still large enough to indicate that, for far too many young people, the schools have failed dismally to provide a relevant education.

More than 20 percent of our high school students in the 80–90 percentile of academic attainment do not enter college in the year following their graduation—many of them never get beyond high school.

Fewer than 2 young citizens in 10 now graduate from college.

While 69 percent of our young white adults have graduated from high school, only 42 percent of our young non-white adults have done so.

While 14 percent of our young white adults have completed college, only 4 percent of our young non-white adults have done so.[16]

Frank Cordasco, the sociologist and Professor of Education at Montclair State College, discusses the Puerto Rican and Negro products of the New York City schools:

> A 1961 study of a Manhattan neighborhood showed that fewer than 10 percent of Puerto Ricans in the 3d [*sic*] grade were reading at their grade level or above. The degree of retardation was extreme. Three in ten were retarded 1½ years or more and were, in the middle of their third school year, therefore, reading at a level only appropriate for entry into the second grade. By the eighth grade the degree of retardation was even more severe with almost two-thirds of the Puerto Rican youngsters retarded more than 3 years.
>
> Of the nearly 21,000 academic diplomas granted in 1963, only 331 went to Puerto Ricans and 762 to Negroes, representing only 1.6 percent and 3.7 percent respectively, of the total academic diplomas. In contrast Puerto Ricans received 7.4 percent of the vocational school diplomas, and Negroes, 15.2 percent. For the Puerto Rican community these figures have critical significance since Puerto Rican children constituted in 1963 about 20 percent of the public elementary school register; 18 percent of the junior high

[16]S. P. Marland, Jr., "Ferment in the Schools," *Children*, U.S. Department of Health, Education and Welfare, p. 62.

school register; and in keeping with long discerned trends, Puerto Rican youngsters made up 23 percent of the student body in vocational schools and 29 percent of that in special (difficult) schools.[17]

ADULT MATURITY

More difficult to assess are the broad social behaviors of the school's product. Of those who are graduated by the conventional educational process and assume important adult roles in the society, many have not exhibited sensitivity to emerging social problems—such as equal rights for minority groups—or demonstrated commitment to the democratic value of equality of opportunity. Certainly the passivity of the vast middle-class product, when confronted with a social injusice, has to be recognized.

A central question for educators to raise is, "Does the school have a responsibility for developing products who have a sensitivity to social injustice?" If the answer is no, then the schools can look to other institutions for the answer. However, if the schools look elsewhere they will only be postponing the inevitable. The role of the school as an instrument for social change has been assigned by the demands of societal reality.

In failing to reach the deprived segments of society, the schools are not helping *all* children, obviously, nor are they helping disadvantaged children to "assume mature adult roles." The statistics on dropout and unemployment are cogent testimony that the schools are not developing "academic, vocational, and avocational skills" in these children.[18] If anything, they are disabling them in the development of their individual potentials. Further, it is quite clear that neither the society nor the schools

[17]F. Cordasco, "The Puerto Rican Child in the American School," *Congressional Record*, Reprint 3:195 (October 19, 1965).

[18]Daniel Schreiber, former Director of "Project Dropout" of the National Education Association, indicated in a conversation that he believes that most of the dropouts who returned to school through Operation Second Chance dropped out again. To invite a child to return to the same program which may have been responsible for his dropping out initially does not offer him enough incentive to remain in school. The cycle of returning to school and dropping out again is depicted in the film entitled *Jimmie* produced by the National Education Association.

even *permit* much social and economic mobility for such individuals, much less enable them "to achieve the greatest possible degree" of such mobility. But worse, if we may judge from the incidence of crime, violence, drug addiction, and rioting among the discontents, the schools seem to be enabling these children to contribute destructively to our democratic society.

The disparity between the educational system's purpose and its products is by no means limited to the lower classes and subcultures in our nation. Indeed, considering that the middle-class oriented schools are supposedly best geared to middle-class children, the number of high-school dropouts in this segment of the population is shockingly high, as indicated in earlier chapters. In addition, enrollment in college, one of the chief status symbols espoused by the educational system, falls far short of what one might expect from a democratic nation which puts so much emphasis on education:

> Anyone concerned with the admission of potential college dropouts must keep cold facts in mind. In 1962 only about 22 percent of the males and 17 percent of the females over 25 in the United States had attended college. Of these only about 12 percent of the males and 7 percent of the females had completed one or more degrees. This and other studies indicate that approximately 50 [to] 60 percent of those students who enter four-year college degree programs fail to complete them.[19]

If we consider the entire educational system from nursery school through college and the proportion of individuals who drop out of this system at any point along the way, we can hardly go on believing that we are providing all of our children with even remotely equal educational opportunities. But of those we do process through any portion of the system, how many emerge ready "to assume mature adult roles"? How many are equipped with the various *skills* they will need to develop fully their individual potentialities? How many can achieve expansive social

[19]S. S. Carlson and K. W. Wegner, "College Dropouts," *Phi Delta Kappan*, **66**:7 (March, 1965), 325.

and economic mobility? How many can contribute—or even are interested in contributing—to the improvement of our democratic society? Furthermore:

> . . . What about the other 80 percent who will not graduate from college? Unfortunately, the "pursuit of excellence" has left most of them behind. At the junior high school, high school, and junior college levels, most students, whatever their abilities, aptitudes, and interests, study those subjects that form the high road to the baccalaureate degree. More than a few of them have difficulty appreciating the logic of this course. Despite propaganda about the importance of staying in school, they drift out of educational institutions in droves: the system loses 35 percent of its enrollees during high school, then 45 percent of its high attrition is unavoidable, of course, but, still, large numbers of these dropouts are simply early leavers who are capable of considerably more education than they received.[20]

James Coleman, a sociologist at Johns Hopkins, gives further evidence of the failure of the schools in his study of adolescent culture in high schools. His sample represented a cross section of socioeconomic students. Boys and girls were asked "If you could be any of these things you wanted, which would you want to be?", and "If you could be remembered here at school, how would you want to be remembered?" The answers reveal that students view education as vocational preparation and that the areas that students identified as relevant are not shared by the conventional educational process (Table 5.1). In fact, the assumption could be made that middle-class students fail to identify with the conventional subject-matter curriculum because it is "phoney" to them also. Jobs and popularity are more real to them than goals which are defined solely in academic subject matter terms. In 1957, the *Look* Magazine Educational Survey by Audience Research Inc., attempted to answer the question, "Just how good is the product of our educational system?"[21] Assuming that the

[20] G. Venn, *Man, Education and Work*, Washington, D.C., American Council on Education, 1964, p. 2.

[21] *Look Magazine Educational Survey*, Princeton, N.J., Audience Research, Inc., 1957.

goals of education are good citizenship, intellectual curiosity, attainment of basic skills, knowledge of facts about the world—the survey of representative samples presented a profile of a less than adequate educational product.

TABLE 5.1

	Boys		Girls	
	Fall	Spring	Fall	Spring
Most want to be:	(N= 3892)	(N= 3746)	(N= 4057)	(N= 3992)
BOYS				
Jet pilot	31.6%	31.3%	—%	—%
Nationally famous athlete	37.3	36.9	—	—
Missionary	5.7	5.9	—	—
Atomic scientist	25.6	25.9	—	—
GIRLS				
Actress or artist	—	—	18.4	19.8
Nurse	—	—	29.2	26.0
Model	—	—	32.0	33.5
Schoolteacher	—	—	20.6	20.6
Want to be remembered as:	(N= 3696)	(N= 3690)	(N= 3955)	(N= 3876)
Brilliant student	31.3	31.5	28.8	27.9
Athletic star (boys)	43.6	45.1	—	—
Activities leader (girls)	—	—	36.1	37.8
Most popular	25.0	23.4	35.2	34.2

SOURCE: J. S. Coleman, "Social Climates in High School, *Cooperative Research Monograph No. 4*, Office of Education, U.S. Department of Health, Education and Welfare, pp. 11–12.

Finally, the product of our present educational process at best can just *adapt* to or *cope* with the environment. That is, the student does the best he can to live with what is. Lacking in his orientation is the crucial dimension of *acting upon*, or *reconstructing* the environment which he finds. It is simply not enough to adapt to an environment which may in turn be exercising negative influences on the person who is doing the adapting.

SKILLS

The skills best suited to develop individuals' potentialities will vary according to the era and the society in which the individuals are to spend most of their lives. It would be absurd, for example, to train our children extensively in the shaping of arrowheads and stone implements, the shoeing of horses, and other skills that at various earlier times were important. Yet, many of the skills we have foisted upon our children are just about as obsolete or inappropriate. For example, by the time training in agriculture and the mechanic arts was established in the land-grant colleges, a good many of the people at whom this program was aimed had moved to urban industrial centers to become factory workers. When courses in manual and industrial arts became widespread the particular skills taught were already outmoded or otherwise inadequate, and employers were often forced to institute their own apprenticeship courses to insure themselves efficient and appropriate manpower for a goods- and service-oriented society.

Meanwhile, the skills that *are* needed, and which perhaps will always be appropriate, are either omitted from the curriculum or fail to be transmitted effectively to the pupils. For example, reading and writing skills, which might reasonably be expected to remain useful for a long time to come, are considered to be severely limited among even those "advantaged" students who continue through the higher learning phases of the educational system. William C. Warren reported that "We have found that few of our entering [law] students, however carefully selected, possess these skills to the extent needed for law study."[22]

Further, though we live in a scientific age, it is astounding how few really basic scientific skills are imparted to our young in the classroom. At the very moment in 1945 when the first chain nuclear reaction was being tested in Chicago Stadium, chemistry students across the land were memorizing the table of "immutable" elements and atomic weights. Even today, in some

[22]Quoted in J. Barzun, *The House of Intellect*, New York, Harper & Row, 1959.

science classes in elementary and high schools, children are learning to define *matter* as "that which has *weight* and occupies space." Recently in one large New York City high school, mimeographed sheets containing the chemical equation for photosynthesis were passed to students in all the biology classes of both the academic and the general (noncollege preparatory) curricula. The students were told to memorize the equation. But the right side of the equation was missing something like 10 atoms! No one in the entire student-faculty body involved had questioned it. The job of memorizing chemical formulae is one which *might* be reserved for a computer, but surely science courses should develop in human beings the ability to understand the basic principles of conservation of matter.

Testimony pointing to the disparity between what skills we *say* we want to develop through education and what we actually *do* develop could comprise an entire book in its own right. But these examples force us to realize that we can no longer view only the socioeconomically disadvantaged as educationally deprived; rather, virtually the bulk of our population is made up of faulty educational products.

SOCIAL MOBILITY

We are accustomed to viewing social mobility as proceeding in one direction—upward. Such mobility as occurs in the opposite direction is viewed with rue, disgust—and a sigh of relief that it "didn't happen to us." But we do not view as social mobility the abilities to make and to retain genuine and affectionate friendships among, and to relate personally with, individuals in different cultural, social, or economic circumstances from our own.

There are, and always have been, those individuals who are as comfortable in one social setting as in another, but these persons have been far too few. How many non-Indians have really achieved close personal relations with members of an Indian tribe? How many white people can count among those in their social circle Negroes of the same tastes and interests? How many Negroes can achieve a truly warm relationship with their white "brothers"?

How many economically secure people can enter the home of someone in less fortunate circumstances and feel at ease, or vice versa? To be truly socially mobile, one would have to have at least some flexibility in these directions, but this aspect of social mobility seems to have escaped us altogether.

The ability to choose our friends from among the rich variety of human beings available in our heterogeneous society is virtually nil. We are limited to only those few individuals in our own homogeneous social class who happen also to reflect the same interests and share the same concerns as we do. In this regard, education has failed in realizing its purpose to enable its products "to achieve the greatest possible degree of social mobility."

Certainly it has been our cherished belief that America is the "land of golden opportunity." As "proof," we generally spout a dozen or more names of famous, self-made men who rose from extremely humble origins to positions of great wealth and power. But sociological studies made during this century clearly indicate that such men are now the rare exception indeed, and that upward social mobility, where it takes place, has become limited.

One of the most widely used criteria for assessing social mobility is occupational status, as it "is closely related to amount and source of income, to education, . . . and occupational information is more precise and more available than other relevant data."[23] However, as Mayer points out, occupational mobility does not reflect movement in the prestige or power hierarchy, about which little is known. Further, occupational mobility is strongly affected by a variety of technological and other factors connected with the overall economy of the nation, as distinguished from the efficiency of the educational institution. In fact, it has long been understood that an industrial society will foster more mobility than a preindustrial society largely because of the occupational needs dictated by industrial development. Significantly, when the industrial United States was compared to contemporary preindustrial societies, social mobility due to nonindustrial factors was found to be sorely lacking.

[23]K. B. Mayer, *Class and Society*, New York, Random House, 1955, p. 69.

Thus, our cultural faith in our "golden opportunities" to climb socially seems unwarranted, as does the widespread belief that it is through education that upward mobility is acquired. Moreover, even to the extent that there has been occupational demand in this country (from which those at the lower extreme of the socioeconomic continuum have largely been excluded), resultant mobility has been limited. As Mayer points out,

> . . . Most of the mobile sons who have left the father's level have not gone very far up or down the occupational hierarchy; . . . [and] most of the movement is one step up or down the ladder. Thus, mobile sons of semiskilled workers are most apt to become either skilled workers, if they move up, or unskilled laborers if they move down; relatively few of them will rise into the ranks of major business executives or become professionals. . . . Over two thirds of the sons work at occupations on the same level or one immediately adjacent to that of their fathers.[24]

Mayer also indicates that while manual workers may now be able to move upward within the general category of blue-collar workers, they are not very likely to become white-collar workers; those who do enter white-collar jobs from blue-collar origins usually become clerical employees, salesmen, and small-business proprietors. Yet even this limiting upward movement may be on the decline:

> It has become harder to make spectacular rises in the business world. Many fields, the main province of giant corporations, are denied to small new businesses. Similar situations are also found in farming, where subsidies are given on the basis of *previously* planted acreage; in the professions, where younger men are sometimes barred from lucrative practice by various means and even in labor, where immigration restrictions and the closed shop sometimes make it hard for newcomers.[25]

For Negroes, Mexican-Americans, and Puerto Ricans, opportunity for mobility is particularly restricted. These groups are the

[24]*Ibid.*, p. 71.

[25]J. B. Biesanz and M. Biesanz, *Modern Society* (2nd ed.), Englewood Cliffs, N.J., Prentice-Hall, 1959, p. 187.

first to be excluded from job openings, and hold a disproportionately large number of the dirty and badly paid jobs available to nonskilled workers. Thus "it may be claimed that there are two working classes in the United States today: a white one . . . and a Negro–Mexican–Puerto-Rican working class which is socially insulated and forms a kind of lower caste working base which facilitates the upward careers of white, especially those who are native born.[26]

Our society, therefore, does not foster the social and economic mobility to the extent that we have believed true, nor does the school play an extensive role in fostering whatever mobility does occur. It is worth noting, too, that since the availability of the education necessary to achieve a higher socioeconomic status is largely a product of the prior attainment of an already relatively high status, education has been less the perpetrator of upward social mobility than upward social mobility has been the perpetrator of upward educational mobility.

SOCIAL CONTRIBUTION

The economic, political, intellectual, cultural, and social maintenance of any society depends on the constructive participation of its members; for its growth and progress, the society needs more than mere participation, it needs the willing effort of its people to make special contributions. Often these contributions require dedicated and selfless efforts on behalf of a cause that will benefit others in the society, the society itself, or perhaps even mankind generally. A nation composed largely of people who are out for their own personal gains—especially when sometimes it is to the detriment of others—cannot expect to progress at a rapid and smooth rate, nor can it expect even to function harmoniously.

That our population has, to a large degree, been incapable of the socially dedicated efforts necessary to help the United States progress rapidly and smoothly became clear to us when our scien-

[26]K. B. Mayer, *op. cit.*, pp. 74–75.

tific and technological leadership in the world seemed threatened. It was not only that relatively few individuals had been properly trained for these areas, but also that the scientific and research fields had themselves failed to attract sufficient numbers of workers. One of the main reasons for the "unattractiveness" of these fields was the low level of the salaries they offered. Similarly, public administrative agencies—particularly those at the national level—have complained that they have been unable to attract talented and well-trained staffs, and that highly qualified potential personnel have been lured to business and industry by higher pay and better personal benefits. Educators, too, decry the lack of dedicated teachers at all levels. These and other vitally important institutions have lost to private enterprise because the latter can afford to offer the desired personal rewards to those with the human resources which will further benefit the corporate economy. Such trends are indicative of a population which seeks personal gain over social contribution. While such self-seeking aims have accrued favorably to the overall national economy, the by-products of an expanded economy have only increased the necessity of efficient public-service agencies, and thus the need for dedicated people who put social contribution above their own personal gain.

To be sure, the losing agencies have, to a limited extent, instituted salary-level and other material reforms, but it is not likely that the funds necessary to compete with private business will be fully available, or that the lure of individual personal gain can much longer be relied upon as a panacea for motivating social contribution. It is certainly doubtful that material rewards alone will elicit the full power of socially oriented efforts. In any case, that material rewards must be emphasized in order to entice talented and well-educated people to contribute to their society is shockingly revealing of the social apathy that prevails in a democratic nation which has always expounded lofty, altruistic ideals. This social apathy and its commercialistic foundations are described by Richard Poston:

> . . . With the coming of the Industrial Revolution . . . human values were lost. . . . Neighborhood life in any meaningful sense [and] initiative, civic integrity, and social

> responsibility began to grow sterile. . . . Bigness, commercialism, professionalism . . . became the gods of worship. . . .
>
> Slowly but steadily the new technology with its mass methods gnawed deeper and deeper into the foundations of community life . . . until men and women by the millions lost their motivation for community responsibility. An attitude of what's the use anyway spread like a plague across America. . . . The majority became by-standers in public affairs, and in all parts of a great nation men and women had assumed an attitude of leaning on someone else.
>
> Millions are pieces of men living a kind of existence from payday to payday in great mass of anonymous and socially isolated human fragments. That spirit of . . . identity and true participation in community life . . . has diminished until millions live side by side without speaking to each other, without caring what happens to the family across the street. . . .[27]

The malignant growth of social apathy in our supposedly democratic society is reflected in a variety of ways. It is exposed in the many incidents of violence which have taken place while "respectable" citizens looked on. It is revealed in the numerous organized charity drives that must promise contributors the tax deductibility of donations in order to raise funds; often these organizations must provide expensive feasts and entertainment for the "charitable" contributors as well. It is illustrated in the relatively low proportion of adults who volunteer their time as youth workers, hospital aides, and other important nonpaid personnel. Richard Corbin comments on the remoteness of the charitable contributions we do make:

> As individuals the vast majority of us prefer agencies to personal charity. We prefer making a donation to the Society of the Blind, Inc., to dropping a quarter in a blind man's cup. We would rather contribute to "Disabled War Veterans" than push wheelchairs two hours a week in a nearby veterans hospital . . . as we grow more compulsive

[27]R. W. Poston, *Democracy Is You: A Guide to Citizen Action*, New York, Harper & Row, 1953.

> in our sharing and more determined to wipe out human suffering, we are in effect putting greater distances between the sufferer and ourselves, until, at last, he becomes an abstraction.[28]

Such social apathy threatens not only to destroy our already challenged spirit of democracy, but also to annihilate the structural foundations of our national existence. To maintain our national identity among countries that are modernizing at an extraordinary pace we must be able to count on the fully harnessed energies of a socially dedicated population; to maintain our position of leadership in such a world, this necessity becomes critical.

But if social apathy is a grave danger, consider how much more dangerous are the socially *destructive* efforts of our citizens. Syndicated crime has so profited from widespread individual weaknesses that many of its high-level personnel have taken to sidelining in respectable enterprises as they continue to administer its narcotic-disseminating activities. In turn, the "weak" individuals who comprise the various markets for syndicated crime steal, molest, beat, and even kill to get the money required for their destructive needs. The financial and human resources that are being wasted in these two sectors alone—the crime administrators and their markets—is drain enough on the human resource potential of the country, but the legal, law-enforcing, and other social agencies required to deal with just these problems comprise an even greater drain on the truly socially constructive energies that might otherwise be put to advantage.

When the diverse problems which face our country today—the outcomes of which ultimately shall determine the fate of the United States—are examined in relation to the purpose of our educational system, it becomes all too clear that our education has been severely deficient in achieving its purpose, quantitatively and qualitatively. Yet education is the only institution upon which we, as a nation, can rely to provide us with a population which has a significant proportion of truly democratic, socially oriented,

[28]R. Corbin, "Literacy, Literature, the Disadvantaged," Report of the Incoming President to the Executive Committee, National Council of Teachers of English, Cleveland Convention, 1964.

dedicated adults who will contribute to our country's welfare. The powerful socializing agent of the hidden curriculum is itself made up of individuals who have, to a major or minor extent, been processed through the formal curriculum, and thus the school can no longer afford to blame faulty products on parents and other human influences in the background. Nor can the school afford to grumble about "community pressures," for until the community is itself composed of desirable products, the extent of responsible leadership available in the community will at best be questionable:

> A free democratic society at the higher levels—state, regional, national—is but a myth unless the initiative, the controls, the ideals and the direction come clear and uninterrupted from the people in their home communities. This is where it must be practiced, this is where it must have meaning in the personal everyday lives of men and women if it is to be practiced and have meaning anywhere. . . . If our communities are strong, America will be strong. If they are weak, America will be weak.[29]

If, when it comes to hard, practical facts, our revered educational system has failed to deliver products that measure up with those it promised, is it perhaps because its promises have themselves been unrealistic? There are those who would answer in the affirmative, claiming that we should revise our educational purposes. Yet it is not the *aim* of any enterprise which causes a faulty product, but rather the process used to shape the product. The end result will resemble the original intent qualitatively and quantitively only if the process itself is in keeping with that intent. Obviously, the process must also be geared to the reality of the raw material used to make the product.

So it is with the educational enterprise. The "raw material" of human potential, with all of its wide and rich variation, lends itself well to shaping; indeed, almost too well, for, as we saw in earlier chapters, the child has already been molded to a large extent by the time he enters school. Even so, this sensitive material is still pliant, and the process through which it passes in the formal

[29]R. W. Poston, *op. cit.*, pp. 8–9.

curriculum can either etch deeper the patterns already traced, or effect significant changes. But if the final outcome is to compare closely to the original aim, the process of education must in all of its aspects correspond both to the purpose set forth and to the nature of the material from which the product is to be made.

What we have done so far is to illustrate how certain groups are disadvantaged within a given educational system without assessing the quality of that system. Our next task is to show how the standard system actually makes everyone disadvantaged.

CHAPTER 6

THE PROCESS

The American educational process today is no simple matter. From the child's viewpoint, its most important single constituent is the teacher, but the school's influences upon the child are by no means limited to her. As noted in Chapter 2, school peer groups, both in and out of the classroom, can strongly affect the child's educational development, as can the subject matter taught, the methods by which it is taught, and the materials used to present it.

But if classroom activities have traditionally occupied center stage in the learning process, the backdrop of the school's organization and administrative policies have played an equally, if not more, significant role. Many school policies and procedures confront the child directly; for example, the graded system, by which a child is arbitrarily grouped according to his age with other pupils of varying interests and capabilities, is a function of the school's policy. Or a child in primary school who has not done well in some subjects may be advised by the principal that he has been "left back" because it is school procedure. Or a high-school student may have to wait several days to join his classes because the administration has not finished processing his schedule cards. However, policy has its greatest effect on the child indirectly, through its influence on and control of the teacher, the subject matter, the rules and methods used in the classroom, and the paper work that accompanies all administration.

Behind the individual school, furthermore, lies an even more powerful force: the massive, adult-centered, national educational "system." The proportions and complexity of this establishment are staggering (Fig. 6.1). It is this system which determines what the individual child is to be taught and how, with whom he is to be grouped, and how fast he will progress—indeed, it all but determines what the child's future will or will not be.

The nonsystem

Structurally, this giant establishment is anything but organized; according to strict definition, it cannot truly be called a

Fujihira, Monkmeyer

THE PROCESS

The Institutions

Elementary	93,000
Secondary	31,000
Universities, Colleges, and Junior Colleges	2,168
	126,168

The Teachers

Public School Teachers	
Elementary	1,026,000
High School	783,000
Non-Public School Teachers	
Elementary	159,000
High School	77,000
College and University Teachers	
Public Institutions	257,000
Non-Public Institutions	209,000
Total Teachers	2,511,000

Administrators and Supervisors

Superintendents of School	13,784
Principals and Supervisors	98,616
College and University Presidents	2,168
Other College Administrative and Library Staff	51,700
Total	166,268

Board Members

Local School Board Members	129,000
State Board Members	492,000
College and University Board Members	35,000
Total	656,000

The Learners

upils in Elementary Schools (Kindergarten through grade 8)	
Public Schools	31,200,000
Non-Public (Private and Parochial)	5,400,000
Total Elementary	36,600,000
econdary School Students	
Public High Schools	12,000,000
Non-Public	1,300,000
Total Secondary	13,300,000
ollege and University full- and part-time students enrolled for credit toward degrees	
Public Institutions	4,000,000
Private	2,000,000
Total Higher	6,000,000
Grand Total Students Enrolled	55,900,000

The Cost (in billions)

Current Expenditures and Interest	
Elementary and Secondary Schools	
Public	$24.4
Non-Public	3.2
Higher	
Public	7.6
Non-Public	5.6
Capital Outlay	
Elementary and Secondary Schools	
Public	3.9
Non-Public	0.5
Higher	
Public	2.4
Non-Public	1.2
Total	$48.8

More than 58,500,000 Americans are engaged full-time in the nation's educational enterprise as students, teachers, or administrators. Nearly another 557,000 make education a time-consuming avocation as trustees of local school systems, state boards of education, or institutions of higher learning. The breakdown is given here. Figures are based on latest available estimates from the U.S. Office of Education and the National Education Association.

Fig. 6.1. *The magnitude of the American educational establishment (1966–1967). (Reprinted with permission from the* Saturday Review, *October 15, 1966, p. 75.)*

system. We speak of a "national" educational establishment, or system, because the United States comprise a national entity, and as such, are dependent on the resources—human and other—existing in all states and communities within the nation. Most of our country's internal problems are national concerns, and we face the rest of the world as a nation. The effective handling of all our diverse national and international affairs depends on the effectiveness of our national agencies—and on those who administer them. If our public or private officials are ignorant or ill-advised, their effectiveness will be limited. Further, since the management of public affairs is largely determined by popularly elected officials, ignorance should not prevail *anywhere* in the nation. Education is thus perhaps the most vital of our national concerns. Yet there is no *national* system of education.

The closest thing to a national coordinating agency is the conglomeration of organizations such as the United States Office of Education, the National Education Association, the United States Office of Economic Opportunity, and the sundry "committees," "groups," "studies," and "projects" which comprise the curriculum-reform movement. Further, to the extent that individuals trained in teacher-education institutions in one state find jobs with schools in different states, teacher-training institutions are also in a kind of national coordinating position. Private associations and foundations—such as the National Science Foundation, which provides financing for the curriculum-reform movement, and the Fund for the Advancement of Education, which contributes to experimentation with and implementation of new methods—also affect the national educational establishment (Fig. 6.2).

Each of these diverse public and private agencies is an autonomous unit. While each has liaisons with many of the others, and most are dependent on the others for funds, materials, and information, such interdependence and interaction are haphazard on the broad scale. There is no systematic coordination of their various functions nor of their collective body of knowledge; rather, the aggregate of these sundry enterprises comprises the "brain" of the educational establishment. As a result, many of the innova-

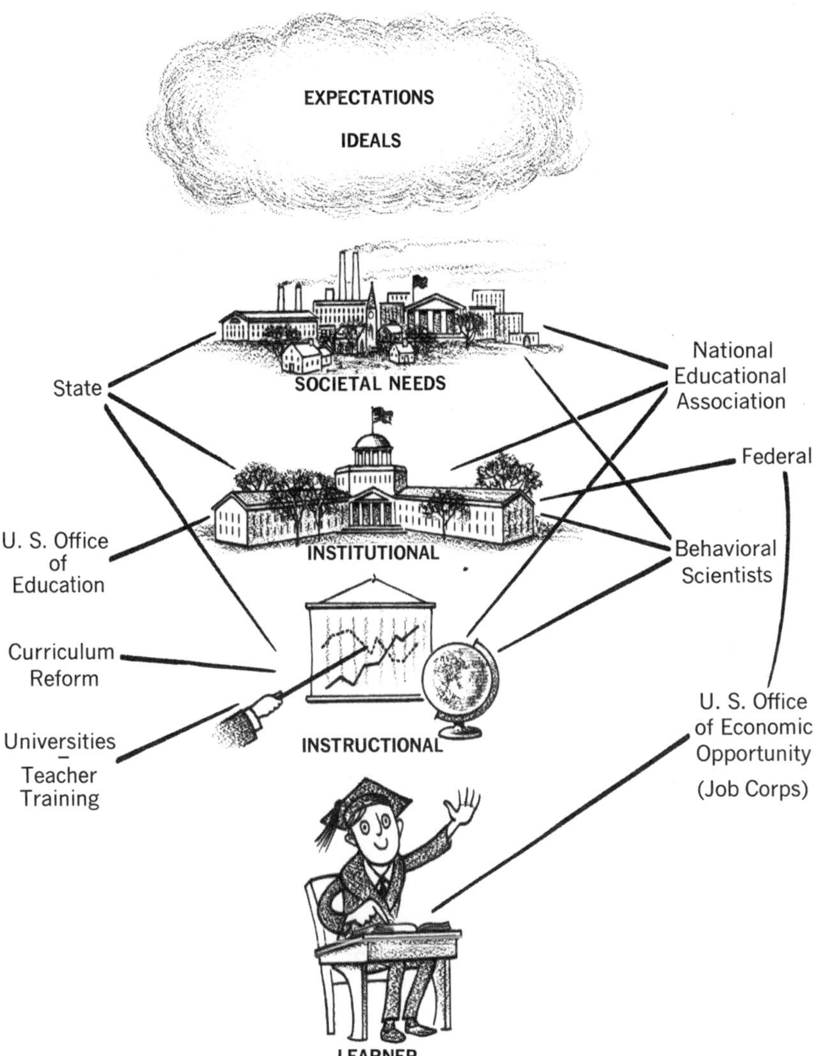

Fig. 6.2. The decisionmaking levels of the educational establishment.

tions and developments believed to be typical of today's education remain at the upper level and do not filter down through the rest of the system.

Responsibility for control of the educational process is about equally divided among the 50 states, Puerto Rico, and the District of Columbia, each of which purports to oversee its own educational standards. Such decentralization adds at least 50 different educational systems to the national structure. Many state officials who are in policymaking positions—that is, who set teacher certification requirements, influence textbook adoptions, and affect curriculum decisions—either have had no classroom experience or have long been far removed from actual pupil contact.

Specific control of educational procedures and policies rests with local educational officials. Usually a panel of from three to ten members comprises the school board which, in turn, hires a school superintendent. Although the superintendent is usually a professional educator trained in school administration, school-board members are apt to be "average" citizens. In some communities, school-board members are elected; in others—particularly New York and Chicago—they are politically appointed. Studies by Neal Gross have shown that the political orientation of the school board can negatively affect educational practices as can lack of educational sophistication among board members.[1]

Since each local community represents an educational system in its own right, there is a wide divergence among local processes, and since each district is administered by its own superintendent, gaps can exist even among districts of a single county or municipality. Each school within a district is guided by its principal, and, as demonstrated by recent Negro protests, schools within a single district can provide vastly different qualities of instruction. There is often little specific coordination between elementary and secondary school programs, and the administrators of these two levels may work at cross purposes. Consequently, the so-called "national" educational establishment is wholly disunified, and processes students more or less at random.

Assessment of the results of this nonsystem was a topic of considerable concern at the 1965 White House Conference on Education. John I. Goodlad, speaking on the dimensions of national assessment, indicated a need for:

[1]N. Gross, *Who Runs Our Schools?* New York, Wiley, 1958.

> . . . Some kind of test that would tell us what is needed . . . how a school system in Arkansas, for example, measures up to one in Oregon; how ninth graders across the Nation compare in their grasp of American history with the ninth graders of two years ago, and how eight-year-olds differ from 13-year-olds in what they have learned, feel and believe."[2]

Goodlad, approaching the educational structure from the decision-making level rather than from the point of view of institutional hierarchy, revealed the confusion and cross-purpose efforts resulting from the fragmentation of the current educational establishment.

The U.S. Office of Education, through its control of Federal funds, indirectly contributes to this confusion and cross-purpose functioning. Although this agency has no direct control of curriculum content, conditions attached to financial grants determine in large measure the emphasis a given state puts on different areas:

> In California more than half of the personnel in the state department of education is in the highly specialized areas for which federal assistance is given. New York State reports that its state department of education has one specialist in vocational agriculture (federally supported) for each 4,000 students in this field of study, while it has one specialist in English (state supported) for each 1,000,000 English students. Similar facts could be brought out in almost every state.[3]

It is at the instructional level, however, that these assorted pressures are strongest. The "new" math, physics, and biology are thrust upon teachers and curriculum planners, and proponents of each demand a prominent place in the school program. The arts and humanities compete with the sciences for prominence in the curriculum. The behavioral scientists—especially educational psy-

[2]J. I. Goodlad, quoted in "The White House Conference on Education," *American Education*, 1:7 (July–August, 1965), p. 17.

[3]H. P. Allen, "Here is the Basic Answer to Federal Control," *Nation's Schools*, March, 1951.

chologists—offer a host of theories and experimental findings on learning processes, teaching methods, and curriculum programs. Still other agencies also recommend audiovisual materials, nongraded and flexible scheduling, computerized instruction, educational TV, staff-utilization patterns, and public relations.

The result, of course, is that the good is mixed with the bad, valuable scientific findings become lost in the shuffle, and small-scale, but widely publicized workable methods are the first to come under attack when this chaotic establishment is criticized. Such lack of coordination actually obstructs change in the individual school systems. The isolated, sporadic, and often short-lived attempts at innovation—often considered representative of the status of education today—reach very few schools; instructional television, team teaching, and ungraded primary instruction are used in only a fraction of the nation's schools, and sometimes only minimally in even these schools.

Significantly, the so-called "progressive" movement which received widespread and often controversial publicity from the 1920s through the 1940s has never been implemented except in a few experimental schools, most of them privately financed. That these programs have not, in 30 years, had a significant impact on the actual educational process is indicative of the lack of change below the establishment's theoretical realm. Even schools reported to be "progressive" in an eight-year study (1932–1940) were found by 1950 to have lost their progressiveness.[4]

Uncoordinated efforts at curriculum reform serve only to fragment the educational process and further complicate approaches to the various subject-matter areas:

> This . . . compartmentalization has carried over into education, where schools are still so honeycombed with separate subject matters that students seldom have anything but the haziest notions of how, if at all, the courses they pursue are connected with one another.[5]

[4]Frederica Redefer, as reported in Crisis in the Transformation of the Schools—The Eight Year Study—Eight Years Later, unpublished doctoral thesis.

[5]T. Brameld, *Education for the Emerging Age*, New York, Harper & Row, 1965, p. 134.

Indeed, as Theodore Sizer, Dean of the Harvard Graduate School of Education, has pointed out:

> The major weakness of the reform movement today, is its tacit acceptance of the way the schools are presently organized. Virtually all of the curriculum reformers assume that their subjects will be taught for a certain number of hours per week in classes of a certain size, that there will be little interrelationship between subjects, that each class will be taught by a single teacher, and that this teacher should be made as much like other teachers of the same subject as possible.[6]

The effectiveness of "national" reforms is further confounded by their uneven adoption and by the inadequacy of the teachers who use them:

> It is dangerous . . . to assume that curriculum change has swept through all of our 85,000 public elementary and 24,000 public secondary schools during this past decade of reform. Tens of thousands of schools have scarcely been touched . . . especially in areas of very sparse or very dense population. Tens of thousands have had little opportunity to realize what advances in knowledge and changes in subject fields mean for them. Tens of thousands hold emergency certificates or teach subjects other than those in which they were prepared. In elementary schools, teachers with backgrounds in science and mathematics constitute a species that is about as rare as the American buffalo.[7]

Each institution, department, and division in various pockets of the disorganization is designed to meet a specific educational need but none are coordinated with the main process or with one another. Many innovations are purely additive, aimed at squeezing the disadvantaged child into the middle-class mold. One relatively recent example of such purely additive programs is the compen-

[6] T. R. Sizer, "Reform Movement or Panacea," *Saturday Review*, June 19, 1965, p. 52.
[7] J. I. Goodlad, *School Curriculum Reform in the United States*, New York, Fund for the Advancement of Education, 1964, p. 10.

satory-education movement. Most of these programs have dealt with the rehabilitation of faulty educational products so that they might be better prepared to meet the demands of the conventional process. Viewed from a long-range perspective, such programs point to the development of an entirely separate educational system for certain members of our society. In other words, it is not enough that we have one hodge-podge establishment, now we would devise another. At the very least, the implementation of a compensatory movement introduces a host of additional factors into an already unmanageable framework. Thus, the solution to the problems of a fragmented process becomes more fragmentation, with stop-gaps added as new pressures emerge.

The increased role of the federal government in education will, of course, necessitate a public accounting of the educational product. At the 1965 White House Conference on Education, United States Commissioner Francis Keppel revealed that:

> The Federal Government, through the Congress, may still be a minority stockholder in education, but its investment is nonetheless substantial. In an educational structure that now costs America $35 billion a year, the Federal share is more than 15 percent, the Nation's taxpayers and their representatives in Congress will want to know—and have every right to know—whether that investment is paying off. . . . Clearly the American people want an accounting. The language of the law in the new act is explicit and pointed on this score.[8]

But what will these changes be? More additive programs that cost more and fragment the nonsystem still further? And how is change to be brought about in such a system? Certainly, the implications are enormous and difficult, and, at this time, change is being stimulated mainly through forces outside of the educational system itself—for example, from the Civil Rights movements and various programs sponsored by the Federal government.

[8] F. Keppel, quoted in "The White House Conference on Education," *American Education*, 1:7 (July–August, 1965), 14.

Assumptions of conventional education

Many of the components of the conventional educational process are, in essence, assumptions based on nineteenth-century ideas of man and his environment. The rigidly graded system and measurement of intelligence (IQ) which characterize the process are based on mechanistic, fixed notions which fit the "Newtonian" model of man. This absolute model has since been replaced by the more flexible twentieth-century "Einsteinian" model of man and universe. Gordon schematizes this changing model:[9]

NEWTONIAN MODEL MAN	EINSTEINIAN MODEL MAN
A mechanistic, fixed closed system characterized by:	An open-energy, self-organizing system characterized by:
1. fixed intelligence	1. modifiable intelligence
2. development as orderly unfolding	2. development as modifiable in both rate and sequence
3. potential as fixed, although indeterminable	3. potential as creatable through transaction with environment
4. a telephone-switchboard brain	4. a computer brain
5. steam-engine driven motor	5. a nuclear power plant energy system
6. homeostatic regulator (drive reduction)	6. inertial guidance and self-feedback motivation system
7. inactive until engine is stoked	7. continuously active

[9] I. J. Gordon, "The Task of the Teacher," *Studying the Child in School*, New York, Wiley, in press, pp. 2–3.

ASSUMPTIONS ABOUT LEARNING

One of the major assumptions of the old process concerns learning. Carl Rogers describes the fundamental assumptions upon which the educational process seems to be based:

> 1. Some learning appears to be primarily cognitive, primarily the fixing of certain associations. A child can learn his letters and numbers in this fashion; at a later date he may learn to rattle off the multiplication tables; at a still later date he may learn the rules for solving a binomial equation, or the irregular verbs in French. Only very imperceptibly do any of these learnings change him.
>
> 2. The student cannot be trusted to pursue his own learning. The attitude of most teachers and faculty members tends to be one of mistrustful guidance. They look suspiciously on the student's aims and desires and devote their energies to guiding him along the pathways he should follow.
>
> 3. Presentation equals learning. This is evident in every curriculum. It is especially clear if one observes a faculty committee . . . that what is presented or "covered" is what is learned. This assumption is that the aim of education is to accumulate brick upon brick of factual knowledge [and the] building blocks must be assimilated before the student can proceed to learn on his own.
>
> 4. "The truth is known." In almost every textbook, knowledge is presented as a closed book. These are the facts, about chemistry, or history, or literature or whatever. The student has almost no opportunity to realize that in every field it is the *search* for knowledge which is important and that the "knowledge" already gained is only the best working hypothesis we can formulate at the moment.
>
> 5. That constructive and creative citizens develop from passive learners. There seems to be a great unanimity in the verbalized aim of producing good citizens, able to act constructively with an independence and originality adequate to the complex problems of today. It is equally evident that the main virtue encouraged in our classrooms at

all levels is that of passively learning what is presented by the instructor, which in turn has been selected by some educational group as being material important for the student to learn.

6. Evaluation is education and education is evaluation. Taking examinations and preparing for the next set of exams is a way of life for students. There is little or no thought of intrinsic goals; the extrinsic have become all important.[10]

ASSUMPTIONS ABOUT BUREAUCRATIC EFFICIENCY

Each school system in the United States is to some degree bureaucratic, and the extent of bureaucracy throughout the national system can be legitimate cause for concern. Although the term *bureaucracy* is now synonymous with rigidity, red tape, and authoritarianism, its origin was in efficient organization to produce a specialized product. Consequently, any organization with a hierarchy of authority, a system of rules, a specialization, and an amount of impersonality can be viewed as bureaucratic.

The key to success or failure of an organization is efficient production—and inefficient production gives reason to examine closely the components of the organization. Policies intended to be efficient often have the opposite result in bureaucracies, and certainly this is true in educational bureaucracies. Haubrick cites, for example, the case of one teacher who required a state license, the granting of which is contingent on completion of student-teaching experience. The teacher, with six successful years of classroom experience, had never gone through the formal process of student teaching. As a result, the bureaucracy of another state denied him a license: "nothing against the individual, you understand, just that the rule has not been met."[11]

Bureaucracy is still tied to the nineteenth-century mechanistic concept of a big machine with many parts, all fitting neatly to-

[10]C. Rogers, "The Facilitation of Significant Learnings" in L. Siegel (Ed.), *Instruction: Some Contemporary Viewpoints*, San Francisco, Chandler, 1967.
[11]V. Haubrick, "Cross-Cultural Approaches to Behavior and Learning," speech given before the Fourth Annual Oregon Program on Teaching the Disadvantaged Child, July 28, 1965.

gether to form an organization where the individual's task is solely to keep the machine running smoothly. Unfortunately, individuals become so concerned with keeping the machine running that they cannot assess its efficiency or lack of it.

The problem, then, is in introducing reforms to make the organization more efficient. The present procedure is to add new divisions or departments as new needs emerge. When, for example, the problem of the disadvantaged became both visible and abrasive to the organization, colleges and universities responded by adding courses in culture and poverty, state departments developed compensatory education to handle the special educational needs of the socially deprived or educationally handicapped as a result of social, economic, cultural environment in which they live, and the public-school systems developed remedial programs. All this has only made the educational establishment more ponderous, and the results are dysfunctional.

Business and industry have been aware for some time that the old model of bureaucratic operation cannot guarantee efficiency for an indefinite period of time, and that it can, in fact, be economic suicide. As a result, they incorporated units for research and development. Research and development divisions function as change agents for the corporate system, and, through systematic testing and innovation, new practices replace the old on a regular and continuous basis. Outside of a few regional centers for educational research and development, there is no corresponding method in the present public-school educational system. Although it is too early to evaluate the Federally initiated regional research and development centers, there is to date little evidence that the findings and recommendations of these units have been incorporated into the areas' public-school systems.

The second critical problem is the hierarchial arrangement which causes decisions to proceed from the top down—from a state department of education through the school board, superintendent, and principal, to the teacher. The assumption is that those farthest from the actual situation are best equipped to make relevant decisions, and that the teacher is merely a technician not really qualified to make key decisions about the curriculum. At the same time, the system proclaims the importance of the teacher, causing considerable ambiguity about teachers' real professional status.

In centralized, urban bureaucracies, change is very difficult. Inbreeding perpetuates and strengthens the operation and few, if any, administrators are selected from outside the system. Often, teachers are rewarded for long years of good classroom teaching by "promotion" to administrative posts, thus effectively removing from the classroom many of the best teachers. Attempts to decentralize these large city school systems have been primarily administrative, with little regard to the needs and sentiments of the local community and its parents, and consequently have not been conducive to quality education.

ASSUMPTIONS ABOUT PARENT INVOLVEMENT

For the most part, parent and community involvement in school-related matters are limited to Parent-Teacher Associations and their meetings which have become an integral part of the conventional educational process. The school assumes that one way for the schools to get closer to the parents is to invite them to the school on a regular basis, and to meet on a variety of topics. This approach seems to work in middle-class communities where there seems to be a congruence between the orientation of the parents and that of the school. What actually transpires in these P. T. A. meetings, however, is not altogether clear, nor is it clear just what educational value they do have for the parents and teachers. One can judge only by the performance of the parents, and it is difficult to evaluate the effectiveness of the P. T. A. as an educational tool when these same parents decide to move out of the neighborhood at a time when school desegregation occurs. The fact remains that many middle-class parents define a good school not by the quality of the program offered in the school, but by the socioeconomic composition of the children who attend.

On the other hand many of the lower-income parents do not

respond to P. T. A. programs. Again, schools are expecting the parents to adjust to their processes rather than attempting to reverse the procedure. Further, the school assumes that it is the responsibility of the parent to assume an orientation befitting the middle-class type of P. T. A.s. Many low-income groups see this as nothing more than sheer talk. Consequently, school officials often rationalize the poor attendance at parent-school meetings as lack of interest of parents in the school.

There is another way in which the schools fail the community. For the most part, schools remain an 8:30-to-4:00 operation and as centers for children only. Schools which serve as centers for all community activities and community residents remain largely an unrealized notion, as does the notion of civic participation in school policy. The need for stronger community involvement in the educational process is most apparent in large cities where the casualties of the system are most startling.

Recently, however, certain dramatic incidents have demonstrated the trend toward parental and community concern for more active involvement in school affairs. Parents and other community groups in ghetto areas appear to be saying, "You professionals have failed to educate our children—they are two to four years behind in reading. We can no longer sit back and watch our children fail under your system. We want to make sure our kids get quality education. In order for this to happen we must have more authority in shaping school policy. We want to make public schools more public anyway."

However, any attempt to expand parent and community participation in the school system will meet with resistance, as Marilyn Gittell, Professor of Political Science at Queens College points out in her study of school policy in New York City:

> Any effort to change the school system and expand civic participation must face the concentration of power in the professional bureaucracy and the resistance by the bureaucracy to any plan that would erode its power. Thus, any plan for change must have as its first objective the diminution of bureaucratic power. Meaningful plans for the reorganization of large city school systems must embody a

formula for the decentralization of bureaucratic authority and the expansion of outside nonprofessional influences.[12]

Administration

Clearly, to get at the root of the problem with education today is no simple task. Just as the nonsystem is multifaceted, so are the problems inherent in each segment of the nonsystem. However, in order to clarify our view of the present process it will be necessary to review the educational establishment from several main perspectives, each oriented from a different level of decision making. To begin with, let us examine the administrative aspects of education, from the school board to the individual school principal.

THE SCHOOL BOARD

Generally, a panel of trustees comprises the school board, which oversees the administration of the public schools. The trustees are lay citizens selected either by popular vote or by political appointment; they are not professional educators. These trustees meet periodically to hire and fire school personnel, to consider construction of new schools, to decide on school and administrative policies, to determine sources of revenue, and to prepare and to adopt the annual budget.

Unfortunately, the budgetary procedures employed in most public-school systems do not usually operate in the best interests of educational-program development, but rather, according to fiscal limitations. The budget starts with what the system can afford to spend, as determined by available revenues. The allocation of these revenues is often based on how the money was spent during previous years rather than with actual program needs. Consequently, although the school board may consider that they have purchased the "best education for the money," the result

[12]Marilyn Gittell, *Participants and Participation*, New York, Center for Urban Education, 1967, p. 57.

is often inferior education for the children. Very few school systems, for example, have adapted Planning Programing Budgeting System (PPBS) in which the budget is measured in terms of how well each program achieves its stated objectives.

Recent national concern over this inferior education has, of course, brought more public pressure on school boards, but the net effect of this pressure has too frequently been to elicit defensive reactions among school trustees. This situation is unfortunate, for instead of inviting suggestions from professional educators—particularly those at the teacher-training level—too many trustees have become the more closed to outside professional direction. Unequipped to sort out and to evaluate the many and various theories, methods, and innovations which are presented to them from all sides with regard to fundamental reform, defacto segregation, the dropout problem, cultural deprivation, and the many other educational themes prevalent today, these lay citizens are all the more likely to cling to the policies they have always known and acted upon. In response to public pressures, they may impose merely additive or superficial changes upon these fundamentally outworn and inadequate policies.

The irony is that these public pressures to reform often actually serve to strengthen the rigid and inefficient bureaucracy. Called upon to make changes, the school board has been forced to act with more autonomy; thus increasing the amount of decisionmaking that occurs at the upper levels. Armed with more power but with little (if any) more ability to make the necessary professional decisions, the school board has acted primarily to reinforce the traditional machinery behind the faulty educational process.

THE SCHOOL SUPERINTENDENT

The school superintendent is a professionally trained and experienced individual who is hired by the school board to implement school-board policies and to administer the schools' operations. It is the school superintendent, therefore, who wields the most *professional* power in the school system.

However, the problems and pressures brought to bear on the school superintendent can be overwhelming. The school may select or reject him for his views on school integration, teachers' unions, or other factors which might affect the public-school system; he may be selected to maintain the status quo or to bring about a vast change. He is expected to maintain a good public image for the school system and for the trustees who head it, and thus he must continually face both public pressures and those imposed upon him by the board. Often his job depends on making sufficient reforms in educational policy and methods to keep the public satisfied that they have a good educational system, and yet without offending this or that particular pressure group. In addition to these difficulties, the superintendent must somehow manage to act as public-relations man—attending dinners or special programs, making speeches, writing news releases, and the like—and, at the same time, oversee the management of the schools.

Emburdened under these weighty demands on his time and personal resources, it is not difficult to realize why many good school superintendents have been unable to implement important educational innovations, and have often become buried in the bureaucratic machinery. As public attention to education has mounted, however, the superintendent, as the professional in charge, has often borne the brunt of the criticism aimed at the school system. The turnover in superintendents since the educational-reform movement began has been noticeably high, especially in the larger school systems, and appears to be increasing.

While in theory, current focus on the problems of integration, cultural deprivation, and school dropouts make these excellent levers by which the superintendent might effect truly fundamental reforms in the conventional educational process, it is considerably difficult to mobilize the existing bureaucratic machinery for these purposes. The school superintendent is thus largely limited to superficial reforms such as the introduction of educational television and other instructional equipment or the supervision of the design of new school buildings, while the fundamentally faulty conventional process sustains.

THE CENTRAL OFFICE

The substance and body of the entrenched bureaucracy is comprised of the central office, which stands as the controlling unit for the school system. Various supervisors, curriculum coordinators, psychologists, purchasing agents, and other administrative personnel have their offices here, and it is to them that the individual-school personnel must turn for guidance, assistance, supplies, and other "services."

Indeed—in theory, at least—the central office exists to provide such guidance, assistance, and supplies for teachers and other personnel engaged in the specific tasks of educating children. In practice, however, assistance and guidance are typically given in the form of mandates dictated by those in the central office rather than offered as suggestions in the spirit of cooperative teamwork toward the end of quality education. Supplies, when they are available, are often meted out sparingly and almost resentfully by those in the central office, except when certain equipment and supplies are forced upon local school personnel. From the teacher's point of view, the central office is a distant giant from which emanates a variety of inappropriate or difficult demands. The attitudes which result from such circumstances are regrettable, and cause a serious breach between those who are ostensibly working for the same cause. Certainly the respective viewpoints held by teachers and central-office staff are not conducive to facilitating exchanges of information and ideas.

Contributing to these attitudes is the proximity to power and authority those in the central office enjoy. An employee of the educational establishment is rated according to his distance from the "office," and this distance is measured in terms of social status as well as in physical or geographical terms. A generally condescending attitude among central-office officials toward local-school personnel only adds to the resentment felt among the latter. Meanwhile, pressures brought upon the central-office staff members from the school board and their school superintendent increase the need for a feeling of authority among those in the central office, and the breach between the central office and the local schools is entrenched.

THE PRINCIPAL

As the chief administrator of the local school, the principal is responsible for everyone and everything in his school building. The principal is thus likely to see himself as part of the "management team," as a representative of the central office with the governing powers of the system in so far as they apply to his school. Yet, in executing his administrative duties, the principal must interact with teachers, parents, students, clerical workers, and maintenance employees. Ideally, therefore, the principal's role could be strategic in mediating the viewpoints of local-school personnel and central-office staff, and in effecting basic reforms in educational practice.

In fact, however, the principal's role is likely to have a different effect, for the principal is likely to find himself caught in the middle. Student problems, teacher problems, and parent problems bombard him from one side, while policy directives from the central office hit him from the other. In addition, the principal is confronted with an overwhelming number of sundry tasks such as conducting staff meetings, ordering supplies for the school building, approving requisitions from teachers, attending conferences at the central office, and so forth. He, like the school superintendent, is often required to attend dinners, special award programs, and other public-relations duties, and certainly he is required to maintain a good public image for his school and for the system as a whole. Added to all of this is a plethora of paper work and bureaucratic red tape to execute in connection with his administrative duties. All of these various pressures leave little time for the principal to effect basic reforms even in his own school, much less in the operations of the system.

Another reason the principal is not likely to become the strategic change agent that his position potentially enables him to be is that most principals, particularly in the larger systems, are promoted from within, and are thus more likely to be protectors of the status quo rather than reformers. Such a principal's orientation is likely to be from the point of view of the local school rather than from a more comprehensive viewpoint, and thus, such changes as he does effect are likely to be made purely at the local-school level.

Basic educational reforms in the overall public-school process have little chance of occurring without basic reforms in this administrative machinery. From school board to principal, these reforms are impeded at each rung of the administrative ladder and public pressures upon the schools to produce better educational products will have little influence upon this machinery unless administrative reforms are forthcoming.

The teacher

Within this paradoxically unstructured yet rigid educational establishment, the teacher is at a particular disadvantage. Of strategic importance to the heart of the educational process itself, the teacher himself is a more or less faulty product of the very process he must perpetuate. Long before he begins his professional training, he is conditioned to his role by his own early education. The middle-class culture in which he has been reared has taught him to accept the system that taught him, and for 15 or more years—the most impressionable of his life—he has been exposed to and taught by those who provided the models for his own teaching behavior. There is more truth than truism in the adage "you teach as you have been taught."

Thus, underwriting the formal professional curriculum to which the teacher is exposed in teachers' college, is this "hidden" curriculum, which fosters preconceived notions about the absolute values of age-grading, for example, or the reward or punishment advantages of good or bad grades. Throughout this hidden curriculum, the teacher may also have assimilated the notions that children who fail are stupid, stubborn, or naughty; that children who use slang or poor grammar are slow, uncouth, ill-bred, or delinquency-bound; or even that Negroes, Puerto Ricans, Mexican-

Americans, and American Indians are dirty, inferior, worthless, and lazy. Moreover, many teachers unconsciously employ a "self-fulfilling prophecy" with minority group students, i.e., they have limited expectations of performance from them. This leads to a cycle of low expectation–low performance which further handicaps the learner.

TEACHER TRAINING

The operational and instructional practices in most teachers' colleges are, in the main, merely a continuation of those the student teacher has come to know during his own elementary and high-school education: lectures, assignments, and mark incentives. His professional course content—which emphasizes the grade- and high-school curriculum, instructional devices and methods, and achievement and aptitude tests—only serves to reinforce explicitly the procedures to which the student teacher was exposed during his earlier years. This is especially true as teacher preparation is generally oriented to the middle-class child that the student teacher himself probably was not too long ago. The recent emphasis on dropout remediation and cultural deprivation generally tends to accentuate the orientation.

Significantly, this professional focus limits the student's concept of his teaching role:

> The idea of the education of teachers has been narrowly conceived to fit a narrow concept, and the teacher is less an intellectual or cultural leader than an agent of social service. He prepares himself, not to serve as an example of man thinking . . . but as a man transmitting a curriculum. It follows that his education as a teacher need consist of nothing more than a knowledge of the material in the curriculum. . . .[13]

The student teacher is, of course, given subjects other than those concerned with pupil curriculum, how to impart it, and how to measure its effect upon the child. Educational psychology and child development, for example, go beyond what is taught *to* the

[13]F. Keppel; *op. cit.*, p. 15.

child, and deal with the child himself: his intellectual, emotional, and physical nature and growth; his motivation, his behavior, and so forth. But in most schools of education, little is done to help the student teacher to understand his *own* nature, his *own* motives, and his *own* behavior. Studies have shown that the personality characteristics of the teacher—and the emotional tone of his teaching behavior—are of vast significance to his effectiveness in the classroom, perhaps more so than his intellectual competence and professional skills. Yet educational psychology courses emphasize the problems of pupil psychology at the expense of teacher psychology. Rarely does the educational-psychology professor communicate to his students that the very undesirable traits to watch for and to handle among the pupils they will face may well be a strong part of their own personalities. At best, general and theoretical statements are made to the effect that "psychology helps us to understand ourselves." Certainly those individuals who are accustomed to hiding their emotional inadequacies even from themselves can hardly be expected to understand the personal relevance of such a presentation.

Despite explicit verbal emphasis on "individual differences" among children, these psychology and other courses in the professional curriculum tend to assume implicitly that most children will submit willingly to any teacher's efforts if, as a student, the prospective teacher just absorbs this professional curriculum. This assumption is all the more likely to become an integral part of the teacher's implicit frame of reference because professors of education tend to impart their subject matter with a heavy use of "pedaguese"— a jargon which incorporates a large proportion of abstract words of no clear, specific meaning. Such terms as "whole child," the "needs and interest of pupils," "learning outcomes" are used wholesale without much further description of just *what* is meant by "whole" child, or what *specific* needs and interests might be implied in different, concrete situations. Certainly one child's "individual differences" are going to make him a different "whole child" from another pupil, with a whole set of different "needs and interests" which will certainly affect his "learning outcomes." Yet these items are likely to be taught in purely abstract and theoretical terms to the student teacher, and he gains little in the way of a concrete conception of exactly how children might differ in their personalities. Thus, the teacher learns to accept all "individual differences" as perfectly normal as long as they are appropriate and amenable to the narrowly conceived conventional education process he has known all his life. Consequently, though he learns this educational language well in order to pass his courses, the student teacher emerges from his professional training with little relevant understanding of real teaching situations for which this training has ostensibly prepared him.

THE JOB SETTING

When the graduated teacher leaves the training institution and confronts his first real, on-the-job school, he is unprepared for the forces which assail him in daily reality. Idealized theories about modern instructional equipment give way to problems of how to get a torn and antiquated projection screen replaced, how to get hold of one of the school's two or three overworked tape recorders for just one hour a week, or even how to acquire a few packages of colored paper for a class project—short of buying it with one's own pocket money, that is. Here, in this real setting, the results of long hours spent studying the advantages of team teaching are replaced by the myriad difficulties connected with just getting along with one's fellow teachers. High-sounding abstractions concerning "positive pupil reinforcement" translate into the baffling problem of how to keep the class quiet enough merely to be heard (by oneself!), and elaborate course work in curriculum planning disintegrates into a desperate struggle to cover just the superficial aspects in prepackaged syllabuses before the end of the term. The ways and means of "creative and imaginative teaching" a well-indoctrinated and ambitious beginning teacher may have thought out before starting the term are tossed aside in the attempt to deal with the *one* curriculum, the *one* set of methods, and the *one* set of tests and measurements with which the teacher is presented by the school. "Individual differences" and the "whole child" become useless phrases as the teacher faces the bewildering sea of 40 or more strange faces.

It is not surprising, therefore, that so many accredited teachers are overwhelmed by the circumstances in slum schools, in segregated schools, or in schools on Indian reservations. Indeed, as Allison Davis asserts:

> We know what actually happens to new teachers. Going from . . . theory [and] sheltered practice teaching into the schools of the masses, the new teacher experiences a cultural shock, a trauma of fear, disillusionment, and frustration. . . . College preparation [is] useless in a classroom where her pupils appear to come from . . . a world of different values and goals [and] she does actually suffer a period of deep anxiety, resulting from both moral and emotional shock.[14]

Nor is it surprising that there is a shortage of teachers willing to work in such schools. Despite the fact that teacher-preparation institutions have been called upon to place more of their students in these schools for their practice training, the professional talk on campus is still irrelevant to the slum reality. Professional course work on campus becomes an end in itself, as revealed by the testimonies of teachers-in-training:

> As to my own experiences and reactions to Harlem teaching, let me say that I was initially totally unprepared and totally at a loss.
>
> My experiences at Harvard were centered mainly around curriculum improvements (or "How to get College Level Concepts down into the Elementary Schools") and around middle-class suburban children. Harvard's assumptions, methods, and approaches simply did not prepare me at all and are totally irrelevant to the lower-class urban Negro children I am now teaching.[15]

[14]A. Davis, "Teaching Language and Reading to Disadvantaged Negro Children," *Elementary English,* November, 1965, p. 791.

[15]Betty Levy, "Classroom in the Slums," *Harvard Graduate School of Education Association Bulletin,* **10**:2 (Summer, 1965), 18.

> For my student teaching experience . . . I was assigned to a class known as Operation Second Chance. . . . The program calls for homogeneous grouping of boys according to reading ability for . . . intensive remedial work. . . . The format is certainly a departure from traditional procedure; yet one wonders whether the total project does not still reflect our general unreadiness to adjust education programs in ways radical enough to meet the real needs and nature of such children.[16]

Even in middle-class schools, all of the key instructional decisions—for which the student teacher has been so laboriously prepared by the school of education—are made by authorities who are separated by a considerable social and physical distance from the working classroom. Policies on texts, curriculum change, instructional aids, and teaching methodologies flow down to the teacher from the higher echelons of the organization. If, in so many words, at least, the teacher's college has provided for the diversity of individual differences, the local school system has not. Nor has the system accounted for any creative inventiveness the teacher may try to employ in his classroom, or the particular ways in which he, as an individual *teacher*, will relate to his pupils.

The beginning teacher's ambition to become an innovator quickly goes down the drain in the living reality of his occupation. Unrealistic syllabuses to follow, tests and questionnaires to administer to the pupils, subject-matter tests to prepare and mark; forms and notices to distribute at frequent intervals, announcements to make, fire drills to explain and to practice, attendance records to maintain—all make heavy demands on the teacher's time. Requisition forms and "channels" to follow further occupy the by now mildly frantic teacher.

Frequently assailed by criticisms of syllabus requirements, the school administration generally protests that these are merely guides, not bibles, and that every teacher has the right—nay, the obligation—to adjust the guide to meet the needs of the class.

[16]Gail Donovan, "The 'Lively Art' of Language," *ibid.*, 7.

Yet when pupils fall below the "norm" on examinations, both the teacher and school are censured by the central administration. Indeed, the only real flexibility allowed the teacher is within the classroom. But just let the teacher fall short in record keeping or unintentionally prompt a complaint from an irate parent, and his "obligation" to teach as he sees fit is soon forgotten by school authorities.

As classified by the conventional educational system, all teachers are alike. In any public-school system, all beginning teachers start at the same pay, and receive salary raises, promotions, and other benefits on the basis of tenure only, on the assumption that all teachers are performing similarly. No attempt is made to reward the teacher on the basis of his individual merit and actual performance in the classroom. To be sure, in many school systems holders of advanced teaching degrees are paid on totally different salary scales, but this blindly assumes that M.A.s or Ph.D.s are automatically better teachers than those with their baccalaureates only, despite the fact that many teachers with advanced degrees are considerably less effective than some who have only a bachelor's degree.

Furthermore, the system does little to reward the innovative teacher, but rather, forces such a teacher into the mold of sameness which permeates the educational process. A system that is accustomed to sameness becomes concerned by deviations; conformity is equated with good education. The conforming teacher is expected to perform all classroom tasks equally well—making up assignments, collecting milk money, composing subject-matter tests, taking roll, and maintaining discipline. That some teachers might have special areas of strength and weakness is overlooked by the conventional process.

Thus, teachers become "boxed in" by the organization, and even the most imaginative of them are forced to conform to the status quo. Many certified teachers give up teaching early in their careers, and those who remain are all too likely to become so ingrained with the bureaucracy that they reinforce its rigid resistance to change.

TEACHER ORGANIZATIONS

The low salary levels of teachers; the impediments to good teaching, especially in certain urban schools; the impracticalities and working disadvantages that result from the social and physical distance between administrative staff and teachers; and many other working hardships have all served to make the amelioration of these conditions the focus of attention among teachers. Toward the end of solving some of these difficulties, teacher organizations have come into being, the two largest being the National Education Association and the American Federation of Teachers.

While the rapid growth in and constructive efforts made by such organizations has been impressive, it is as yet unclear as to just what extent these collective efforts will influence the general improvement of the educational process. The present orientation of school boards, school superintendents, and administrative staffs still reflect a typically managemental position *vis à vis* the teacher as an individual, despite reforms in salary standards, retirement plans, and other benefits that have accrued to the teaching profession generally. In any case, it is relatively less a question of personal benefits for the professional teachers at this point, than it is of improvements in actual working conditions which remain at issue. For the teacher to do even an adequate job of classroom teaching, many changes in administrative orientation and procedures must be effected; for the teachers to go beyond merely adequate teaching to inventive and creative teaching, administrators and teachers will have to form a cooperative team. Significant in this regard is the fact that several state legislatures—Massachusetts, Michigan, Wisconsin, Connecticut, and Washington among them—have already passed statutes directing local school boards to enter into shared-policy relationships with teacher organizations. The effect that such collective negotiations may ultimately have on school programing, however, remains to be seen; to date, teacher organizations have not had an appreciable impact on educational policy at the local level.

The curriculum

Underlying the entire educational process—the backbone of the establishment—is the curriculum. The curriculum comprises the content of the educational process; that is, the subject matter that is to be imparted to the pupils.

In keeping with centuries of tradition, this curriculum is essentially academic, with few changes in the basically classical notions of what makes the "educated" man. In elementary schools, English, science, mathematics, and social studies compose the fundamental "three R's;" in the higher grades, these are elaborated into more specialized subjects: Science becomes physics, biology, or chemistry; the social studies become American, world, or ancient history; mathematics becomes algebra, trigonometry, or geometry. At the college level, the curriculum is still further elaborated, as completion of an array of specific academic courses leads to the baccalaureate degree.

This fundamental curriculum can in no way be considered a social curriculum which imparts sound conceptions of human emotions, social values, or personal ethics. To the extent that social problems arise in history or English units, they are treated as intellectual facts, to be memorized for tests. Little or no effort is made to get pupils to understand the feelings and motivations of the historical or literary characters involved. Little or no attempt is made to get pupils to understand their own feelings and motivations and those of the others in their immediate daily environment until, perhaps, high school when remote and abstract treatments of hygiene, family relations, and similar subject matter are appended to the academic curriculum. Courses in psychology and sociology are not offered until the college level, when the students' notions about human behavior—including their own—have already been implicitly shaped or misshaped.

The educational process proceeds on the assumption that this basically academic subject matter must be mastered before the student can be considered to have been educated. The learner who is unable to meet these academic requirements—that is, to master the content at a prescribed rate—is considered to be a failure and is not permitted to proceed up the graded hierarchy. Of course, so many pupils, particularly among the lower socio-economic strata—have not fulfilled these academic requirements, that the educational process appended a host of nonacademic or "vocational" courses at the high-school level. But the grade-school curriculum, which purports to prepare pupils for secondary school, remains academic in orientation.

Most of the innovations which are getting so much attention today only reinforce this academic orientation of education. The burgeoning field of audiovisual learning materials, for example, is aimed at providing pupils with concrete experience which is related to the same academic subject matter to which education has always been restricted, and other learning aids—educational TV, programed learning, and similar technological advances—have become the media for basically the same traditional academic content. This is also true of the curriculum-reform movement, for, as Goodlad points out, of all the recent educational reforms, "the current curriculum reform movement is and has been the most influential. . . . The movement is discipline-centered, the ends and means of schooling being derived from the academic subject."[17]

The idea of academic mastery is founded on the classical assumption that the purpose of education is to produce a person who is learned in the bulk of knowledge that man has accumulated over time. Since, according to this assumption, the aim of early education is to prepare the pupil for his much more difficult higher education at the college level, the institutions of higher learning have largely dictated the curriculum requirements for the lower grades. If the high-school student wishes to enter a good college, he must have a better-than-average scholastic record in each of three years of English, three of history, two or three of math, and so on. What is more, he must acquire this record at a high school with a good academic rating. In order to be ac-

[17]J. I. Goodlad, "Directions of Curriculum Change," *NEA Journal*, December, 1966, 33–37.

cepted by such a high school, therefore, he must have a better-than-average scholastic record in his grade-school academic subjects. If his grade-school record is average or below, his chances at one of the "better" high schools are likely to be minimized, and he will probably be encouraged to attend a technical or vocational high school in his community. This situation has only been reinforced as colleges become more and more crowded. With increased competition for entry into college, the curriculum dictates of higher education will continue, and will achieve an even greater stranglehold on the traditional, academic curriculum.

The consequences of these curriculum dictates on true learning are great. The criterion for success in an academic program is the acquisition of facts and the repeating of those facts on tests and quizzes. This leads to rote learning of verbal and other symbolic material with a deemphasis of conceptual skills—the results of good rote learning passing as the same thing as good conceptual skills. Indeed, institutions of higher learning have complained to the public-school system that their enrollees are deficient in the conceptual and other cognitive skills necessary to their courses. Yet, as their entrance requirements become ever more demanding, the public-school system, in turn, boosts its own standards in the academic curriculum. Further, the fear of jeopardizing chances of being accepted by the colleges has made both students and their parents intolerant of any changes in the public-school curriculum which might deny them this goal.

Is there an alternative? What would happen if students were admitted to college from a different curriculum? Significantly, the now famous "Eight Year Study" showed that students with "progressive" programs did as well as if not better in college than did students prepared by the conventional educational process. During the years 1932–1940, the college performance of students who had graduated from thirty progressive schools was compared with the performance of students prepared by more conventional schools. The participating colleges agreed to waive their usual admission requirements for the study. Chamberlain and others report on the results.

> The experiment might have been judged in many different ways; after all, the ultimate proof of an education is in the lives people lead when they have left the classroom. But the Commission was determined to test the results in terms of how well graduates of the thirty schools performed in college. Under . . . Ralph W. Tyler, of the University of Chicago, a team of measurement experts set out to compare these graduates with other college students with similar background and ability. The team's technique was to set up 1,475 pairs of college students, each consisting of a graduate of one of the thirty schools and a graduate of some other secondary school matched as closely as possible with respect to sex, age, race, scholastic aptitude, scores, home and community background, and avocational interests.
>
> . . . The evaluation team found that graduates of the thirty schools (1) earned a slightly higher total grade average; (2) received slightly more academic honors in each of the four years; (3) seemed to possess degree of intellectual curiosity and drive; (4) seemed to be more precise, systematic, and objective in their thinking; (5) seemed to have developed clearer ideas concerning . . . education; (6) more often demonstrated a high degree of resourcefulness in meeting new situations; (7) had about the same problems of adjustment as the comparison group that approached the solution with greater effectiveness; (8) participated more and more frequently in student groups; (9) earned a higher percentage of non-academic honors; (10) had a somewhat better orientation toward choice of vocation; and (11) demonstrated a more active concern with national and world affairs.[18]

This Eight Year Study has become a classic in the literature of education, but unfortunately its results did not have serious consequences on the admissions policies of colleges and universities, or in admission policies or the program aspects in public schools.

In 1940, Dean Hogart E. Hawks of Columbia College, made

[18]D. Chamberlain *et al.*, "Did They Succeed in College?" in L. A. Cremin, *The Transformation of the School*, New York, Knopf, 1961, pp. 255–256.

the following observation to the Association of American Colleges:

> The results of this study seem to indicate that the pattern of preparatory school program which concentrates on a preparation for a fixed set of entrance requirements is not the only satisfactory means of fitting a boy or girl for making the most out of college experience. It looks as if the stimulus and the initiative which the less conventional approach to secondary school education affords sends on to college better human materials than we have obtained in the past.[19]

It appears that if higher education is preparing for the universality of higher education beyond high school, [there is a need] for developing a system of community colleges. This, in essence, might become the buffer between high schools, colleges and universities. The educational process of colleges and universities is simply not geared to diverse groups. Colleges and universities are not equipped to deal with the so-called "disadvantaged" learners, nor do they feel that this is their role. The community college, on the other hand, could conceivably be viewed as an extension upward of the high school and an extension downward of the college.

Among the many twentieth-century curriculum reforms is the institution of an increasing number of such community and junior colleges. It is hoped that these two-year colleges will develop unrealized college potential among those who did not pass the traditional academic curriculum, and yet screen out those who really do not have college potential. However, the community college faces numerous problems: Well-trained staff members are scarce, and the basic philosophy which underwrites the conventional curriculum threatens also the community college. If the students were unable to master the academic curriculum in the lower grades, how are they to suddenly master it in two years at the community college?

It may be argued that the public-school system has altered its curriculum in the lower grades through such means as the "unit method," the "project method," the "core curriculum," and the "curriculum-reform movement." As already indicated, however,

[19] L. A. Cremin, *op. cit.*, p. 256.

these have become new means to achieve old ends. The unit method, for example, has been adopted as a teaching technique to make more efficient the coverage of traditional subject-matter areas. The core curriculum, which received a great deal of publicity during the late 1930s and early 1940s, is today viewed as a combination of English and social studies into one large block of time. The "curriculum-reform movement" is, in essence, a revising of traditional subject-matter areas to include more major concepts and up-to-date knowledge. While, to be sure, this was a much needed change, it, too, may be viewed as merely another attempt at making more efficient what already exists, rather than as a truly basic change in curriculum orientation.

What the traditional curriculum—complete with its modern appendages and reforms—still lacks is a focus on the real and immediate problems of our times. As Phenix has asserted:

> We must above all teach them [our children] to meet the problems of our time with courage and competence. And what are the problems of our time? Are they not the role of intelligence, the mass media, standards of taste, sex, race, politics, and religion? . . . [They] are problems only because values are at stake, because people *care* about the outcomes, because these are questions on which decisions of moment must be made. They are real problems because most people are not neutral toward them but, on the contrary, hold firm convictions about them. Thus, the use of genuine issues as the criterion of what shall be taught affirms that education is a moral enterprise, where the term "moral" refers to purposeful conduct based on consideration of values.[20]

In emphasizing the intellectual facts, the present curriculum proceeds at great expense to the emotional understanding which is so necessary to the proper *interpretation* of facts. Indeed, inadequate emotional comprehension is as poor a learning outcome as is the learning of misinformation at the intellectual level, or as nonlearning itself. Kenneth Clark states as follows.

[20]P. H. Phenix, *Education and the Common Good,* New York, Harper & Row, 1961, p. 4.

> To obtain the truth of Harlem one must *interpret* the facts. Certain social truths can be more painful and disturbing than facts, and this truth may account in some measure for social science's seemingly endless preoccupation with statistics. Statistics may be manipulated and played with, analyzed and treated in a way calculated to lead to minimum pain or personal involvement. They are "manageable." Figures on the extent of malnutrition in Southern states or rural areas are impersonal and are not especially disturbing. Direct encounter with a starving child, on the other hand, is a truth which is personal; it remains personally disturbing until the child is fed. To face social truths seems to require empathy, social sensitivity, and a peculiar type of courage.[21]

Goodlad begins to point to the new direction:

> Some educators claim that this cycle of *discipline-centered curriculum* is over. For the next several years, educators' concern will focus more and more on the total *curriculum* rather than on bits and pieces of it. . . . What will be the third cycle of curriculum change in the second half of the twentieth century? I believe it will be what one might call the *humanistic curriculum* and that it may become significantly evident by 1990 or 2000. . . . Perhaps I can best sharpen what I mean by a brief discussion of what humanistic education is not. . . . First, we do not value education for the right reasons. The central force in our striving for more formal education is our expectation that it helps in the acquisition of worldly goods and in gaining access to certain circles of power and influence. The school mirrors this expectation. Nowhere is this observation more clearly substantiated than in our marking practices. The system of rewards and punishments, which is extraneous—and probably deleterious—to learning, is based on society's materialistic conception of education.[22]

Only when our pupils are taught from an early age to recognize, to think out, and to understand basic human values and

[21] K. B. Clark, *Dark Ghetto*, New York, Harper & Row, 1965, pp. xxiii-xxiv.
[22] John I. Goodlad, "Directions of Curriculum Change," *NEA Journal*, December, 1966, pp. 33-37.

problems common to all in our age will our curriculum begin to nurture the kind of teachers who can foster this diversity for the benefit of both individual and society. It is therefore crucial that the present academic curriculum be made relevant to meaningful ends—those of individual and societal growth.

THE AGE-GRADED SYSTEM

Providing structure and form for the traditional curriculum is the age-grading system which assumes that all children of the same age are alike, and have the same developmental achievements, the same frames of reference, the same rates of development and learning in all areas, the same abilities and potentialities, the same interests. All in a given grade are expected to learn best when they are studying the same thing at the same time for the same length of time.

There are always those children who do unusually well according to the stringent criteria of the age-graded curriculum (these are the "gifted" pupils), and there are always those children who do unusually poorly (these are the "failures," the "pòor students," the "disadvantaged"). As Goodlad points out:

> A child can be in the fifth grade for arithmetic computation, the sixth for arithmetic reasoning, the seventh for spelling, the eighth for word meaning, the ninth for paragraph meaning, and the tenth for language—and yet be officially registered in the sixth grade, in the same class as Jean whose scores range from high second to low fifth; Pat from fourth to tenth. Children are downright ornery. They refuse to grow up all of a piece.[23]

The "gifted" pupils are sometimes rewarded by the school for their individual differences by being skipped a grade ahead of their agemates, a procedure which assumes that because the child is capable of learning the material the school has found most suitable to a higher age, he is therefore older than his own age

[23] J. I. Goodlad, "Meeting Children Where They Are," *Saturday Review*, March 20, 1965, p. 57.

in all ways. The "failures" are punished for their individual differences by nonpromotion or even demotion, a procedure which assumes that because a child is incapable of learning the material the school has found most suitable to his chronological age group, he is therefore younger than his chronological agemates in all ways.

The difficulties inherent in these school procedures are many. The "gifted" child has often been found to have several personal and social difficulties when put in a class of older children—perhaps his physical development is considerably behind that of most of his new classmates, perhaps his emotional and social development is lagging. Or, the skipped child may have done exceptionally well in all his subjects but one, in which he was doing only satisfactorily. In his new class, the child may find himself so far behind in this one subject that his struggles detract from his performance in the others. Often the "rewarding" implications of his promotion throw his self-image out of kilter with his realistic abilities, and his consequent lack of equilibrium may take its toll in his academic performance. On the other hand, the nonpromoted child may have done adequately in some subjects and poorly in others; exposed to this material for the second time, the pupil may find himself generally bored and unchallenged, and begin to drop further behind in all his subjects. The "punitive" effects of nonpromotion, furthermore, tend to have seriously damaging effects on the child's self-image, which effects generally permeate into the whole of the child's behavior and school performance.

Recently, and because of the difficulties found in skipping or nonpromoting children, the school has tried other approaches. One of these deals with individual differences by regrouping children of the same age-grade within the classroom, so that the teacher relates to several subdivisions rather than to the group of 30 or more children as a whole. For example, a first-, second-, or third-grade teacher might have three or four different reading groups, classified as "fast," "medium," "slow," and "poor." In addition to imposing extra demands on the teacher, however, this method also implies reward and punishment values, and fails to get at the root of the problem.

Clearly, the age-graded system assumes that "individual differences" are actually "individual deviations"—from some norm. When normative psychology came under attack and individual differences became part of the literature in child growth and development, attempts at basic reforms in the graded system were made by a few schools. However, most of the schools remained unaffected, and the movement has met with considerable opposition. Unfortunately, efforts to evaluate the relative effectiveness of these basic reforms have yielded no clear-cut evidence to date in support of nongraded systems, team teaching programs, and the like, and the conventional educational process continues to claim that it can achieve as much through age-grading as through any other method with considerably less inconvenience to the school.

Although the educational establishment is said to serve the students, the students are too often the forgotten clients in the educational process. They are the least actively involved in the adult-oriented school system, a school system that requires the learners adjust to the process rather than adjusting the process to the learners. No provision is made for the pupil as a unique individual, with real interests, real problems, real thoughts and feelings, but rather only for that undividualized mass of pupils whose interests, problems, thoughts, and feelings square with what the school expects.

When the various factors involved in the educational establishment are examined separately and together, it is evident that the present, outmoded process, even with its many-faceted attempts at reform, cannot hope to achieve the quality products that our present society in its present age needs for its health and growth. Very few of the innovations indicated by modern theory and research evidence are actually implemented to any appreciable degree, and many of those which are remain isolated pockets in the unwieldy overall establishment and are unable to effect any basic educational reforms. Those reforms which are essentially additive or supplementary in nature may have somewhat more impact on the public-school system—thus making the educational establishment even more cumbersome—but those which are targeted at the underlying status quo are particularly likely to remain at the much discussed but nonimplemented level.

What then, is the solution? Shall the bureaucratic resistance to change forever impede quality education for all? Must we cease to nurture our ideals and adjust to the status quo? What sort of changes can create a basic reform? In the following chapters we shall attempt to answer—or at least point in the direction of possible answers to—these and other specific problems. Before we outline some of the specific remedies which are possible, however, it is necessary to explore what forces can be mobilized to get these specific remedies implemented; for, as already pointed out, few changes are likely to have their desirable effects unless the core of the educational establishment itself can be moved. In the next chapter, we shall examine some possible strategies for moving the seemingly immovable establishment.

CHAPTER 7

STRATEGIES AND POLICIES FOR CHANGE

Our times demand that institutional changes be effected with the rapidity of revolution and rendered with the subtlety of evolution. At the same time, our institutional structures have grown grotesquely large and inflexible. When these rigid structures—and the people who run them—are pressured with demands for reform, they react with even greater rigidity; our organizations are simply too overgrown and too unwieldy to meet these demands. This is precisely what has happened in and among our various educational institutions.

Fortunately, periods of crisis offer unusual opportunities for accomplishing change. When former U.S. Commissioner of Education Francis Keppel exclaimed, "Thank God for the civil rights movement!" he was lauding the opportunities it afforded for teachers and educators to improve education.[1] Further, the Civil-Rights crisis brought into the foreground many related concerns which have forced the school's attention on the existing educational process and its inadequacies for growing numbers of our population. These crises have provided many opportunities to disturb the existing educational equilibrium, but perhaps none so much as that concerning the disadvantaged learners. This problem has become so pressing and so perplexing that it has necessitated departing from long-accepted school procedures. As possible solutions, a vast array of "revolutionary" projects and programs have been recommended, and educators who have become involved in these projects and programs have been forced to reexamine *everything* they know about teaching and learning in the attempt to find ways of educating these so-called "uneducable" disadvantaged. Significantly, many of their findings are relevant and transferable to learners in settings other than those concerned with the disadvantaged poor.

In a sense, then, social crises are themselves an effective strategy for mobilizing rigid institutional structures for change. But social crises alone are not sufficient to effect the kinds and degrees of change needed if our society and its organizations are to keep up with the times. We have already indicated in previous

[1]F. Keppel, speech to the American Association of School Administrators, Atlantic City, Spring, 1964.

Botwick, Monkmeyer

STRATEGIES AND POLICIES FOR CHANGE

chapters that many of the educational programs implemented to serve the disadvantaged are not fully adequate to their purposes, and some may, in the long run, actually make the overall educational establishment *less* efficient than it has been. The main problem has been that, while these social crises have forced education to accommodate and to effect reforms, those changes which have been made have remained at the fringes of the educational establishment, and have not influenced the core of the bureaucracy. In addition to—and in many cases, as a result of—existing social crises, there are many conditions which can be utilized to mobilize established convention, and many of these lie within the rigid core itself. In this chapter, we shall examine some of these crucial conditions, and suggest how they might be utilized to serve as strategies for reforming the bureaucratic machinery itself.

It is important to emphasize that this is not a how-to-do-it chapter. A detailed, step-by-step account of how to implement change is not given here, nor is any attempt made to define specifically just what changes should be made in any aspect of the establishment. Rather, several broad areas which lie both within and without the formal educational structure are pinpointed for their possible usefulness in serving as "keys" to open the doors which have been locked against any true and basic change. No real or basic change—for better or for worse—can be implemented as long as these doors remain shut. Thus, the term *strategy*, as used in this chapter, should be interpreted broadly and as referring only to those areas which, when properly harnessed, can serve as vehicles for effecting the very process of change, whatever specific direction the changes themselves may take.

Selecting the arena for change

While it is not our aim at this point to specify what particular changes should be made in any aspect of the educational bureacracy, it is desirable to know what general area of the educational enterprise as a whole is to be most affected by whatever changes are made. Specifically, since the educational enterprise is comprised of three basic parts—its purpose, its process, and its product—it is necessary first to select which of these arenas should be the prime target of change. The purpose-process-product discrepancies in education were noted in Chapter 5, and, as already mentioned, the visible consequences of these discrepancies among the poor and disadvantaged have already led to the implementation of a variety of public- and private-sponsored educational programs. Let us examine these movements and see which of these three arenas have been the prime targets of reform.

CHANGING THE PURPOSE

An interesting illustration of a proposal to change the *purpose* of education occurred as an immediate response to the first Russian Sputnik during the late 1950s. Although the stated purpose of American schools was then, as now, to develop human potential, America's technological lag was attributed to the schools' failure to emphasize academic subject matter. Many critics pointed a finger at the "life adjustment" purposes of the schools, blaming this "nonacademic" area of the curriculum for the paucity of scientists and other top-level personnel. These critics wished to restate the purpose of education to include academic mastery only; courses in family and human relations, home economics, sex education, vocational training, and the like were considered by these critics as "frills."

Ironically, it has always been the practice of most schools to emphasize academic mastery. With few exceptions, the nation's children have always started their educational careers with classical drilling in the "three R's," and continued through the primary and intermediate grades with intensive instruction in arithmetic, science, and the social studies. Only in the secondary grades are pupils likely to be exposed to the "life adjustment" courses, and these courses are especially aimed at those children who were at a sufficiently low level of academic achievement as to make college beyond their reach. The critics who proposed that the schools "return" to a strong emphasis on academic subject matter were under the mistaken impression that the educational process was "too progressive," believing that the widely publicized but little implemented progressive-education movement was actually an integral part of the nation's public schools.

To be sure, the educational system was not producing sufficient numbers of scientifically and technologically proficient products, but a lack of academic orientation could hardly be blamed for the schools' failure to cultivate the human resources of the country; rather this rigidly academic orientation itself was forcing growing numbers of children to fall behind or to drop out altogether, and a good many of those who succeeded, even through college, were severely lacking in conceptual skills. Therefore, by advocating that the purpose of the schools be "changed" to put even greater stress on academic mastery, these school critics merely helped to further entrench the rigid and outdated system.

Another example of an attempt to change the purpose of American education lies in the response with which conventional educators have traditionally met the problem of "uneducable" pupils. Although the purpose of our schools has always been to provide equal educational opportunities for all in our culturally diverse land, the repeated failure of children from certain types of cultural backgrounds to take advantage of the opportunities provided by the school has led many to feel that certain cultural and socioeconomic groups are uneducable. It is this belief which has led to the institution of manual and industrial-arts training programs and the low-level "general-education" courses that are geared to youth from low socioeconomic backgrounds.

The idea that perhaps the academically unqualified can be steered into vocational courses does not offset this change in purpose. Unfortunately, these vocational courses *also* produce large numbers of educational failures, leading to the notion it is simply a waste of time to keep some children in school. This, too, reflects the hidden purpose of education as being only for those who can qualify. In this way, there emerge two levels of the "elect"—those who qualify for college and the professional life, and those who qualify for vocational training and the skilled or clerical labor force. The remainder are abandoned to whatever personal resources they may have to eke out a living and to live their lives. Yet it is entirely possible that, given a new process, we can develop in *every* child capabilities which heretofore have gone unrecognized.

In both of these examples, the change deals with the purpose; the process and the faulty products remain the same. Yet to change the purpose only shifts the responsibility, it does not cure the problem. While education for the elite may be the prerogative of private and parochial schools, it cannot be justified in the public schools which are maintained for the purpose of preparing *all* the people to become successful, productive, and socially committed citizens of a democratic society.

CHANGING THE PRODUCT

Since the crisis of the disadvantaged learner in our society is essentially one of a faulty product, at first glance, the most likely change would deal with the product itself. This form of change accepts the purpose of education as equal opportunities for all, but proposes rehabilitation of the disadvantaged student so that he will fit the existing process. Remedial instruction in reading, math, and other basic subjects is expected to bring the failing student up to his grade level; special supplementary courses, field trips, and other experiences related to his weak subject areas are expected to make him more receptive to his academic courses; and special guidance and therapy from vocational counselors, social workers, and psychologists are expected to convince the student of the personal importance to him of his schooling, and to render him emotionally more amenable to the conventional educational process.

This form of educational intervention is called "compensatory education." In essence, compensatory education programs attempt to get the child "ready" for the regular school program. The rationale is simple and direct: The disadvantaged child's deficiencies are diagnosed and programs of concentrated remediation are planned to correct the deficits. For example, Head Start, the Office of Economic Opportunity's preschool program, attempts to prepare the disadvantaged child for school by starting him at an earlier age. Similarly, Upward Bound, another OEO Project, is planned to help prepare the disadvantaged high-school student for college without requiring the colleges to change their conventional admissions standards. The assumption in each case is that, once compensatory efforts are accomplished, the student is rehabilitated and can join the normal or regular learners in the standard educational process.

This movement dates back to the mid-fifties with the

Demonstration Guidance Project at PS 43 in New York City which, in turn, led to the Higher Horizons Project and to the Great Cities—Grey Areas project of the early sixties involving the Ford Foundation and ten major American cities. Currently, Title I of the Elementary and Secondary Education Act of 1965 has spread compensatory education to every state in the Union. Evidence of the compensatory movement can be seen in the creation of special departments and divisions at local and state levels. For example, the General Assembly of Ohio enacted special legislation creating an Office of Compensatory Education to handle the "special education needs of socially deprived who are educationally handicapped as a result of the social, economic and cultural environment in which they live."[2]

Advocates of one school of thought believe that there would be less need for compensatory education programs geared to pupils in the middle and upper grades if children were reached during the preschool period. This current preschool movement (not to be confused with the nursery-school movement of the 1930s and 1940s) has been stimulated by Project Head Start. Child-development research, important to this movement, contends that there are optimal periods of development and learning in the human organism. Benjamin Bloom, Professor of Education at the University of Chicago, reported, for example, that intelligence is 50 percent developed by age 4 and 80 percent developed by age 8.[3] The idea behind the recent preschool movement, therefore, is that if children are exposed to a special educational program during the critical period of early childhood—from birth to age 4—they will be equipped for the formal school process they meet later.

This preschool movement and the other forms of compensatory education are additive to the conventional process, and most of them remain outside of the established educational system. In other words, they do not attempt to alter the funda-

[2]*Proceedings of Ohio State Legislature*, 106 General Assembly regular session, February 22, 1965.

[3]B. S. Bloom, *Stability and Change in Human Characteristics*, New York, Wiley, 1964, p. 68.

mental process, but merely add new layers to the old. Further, compensatory education implies that there is nothing wrong with the traditional program, but that there is something wrong with the learner. Clearly, rehabilitating the product to fit the standard process is less threatening to those who are involved with the existing process than are attempts to change the process, as it does not focus upon them and the program with which they are identified. The children are not responding because of certain inadequacies in *their own* backgrounds.

When disadvantaged learners are given a more concentrated dosage of what they have not been able to swallow the first time, many proceed to drop out again, while the program which had originally frustrated them remains virtually unchanged. Although progress reports from compensatory programs do not always lend themselves to evaluation, people who are responsible for such programs often reveal that progress is less than satisfactory. In discussing a compensatory program in Pittsburgh, an article in the *Wall Street Journal* states: "Compensatory education, unfortunately, has yet to yield measurable results."[4] A recent survey of compensatory programs by a team from Yeshiva University reveals, moreover, that such programs have at best a limited impact on the disadvantaged.[5] Similarly, reports from the U.S. Commission on Civil Rights have concluded that "programs of compensatory education—special efforts to upgrade the education of children in ghetto schools—have been of limited effectiveness."[6]

Yet books such as *Compensatory Education for Cultural Deprivation* tend to reinforce these remedial programs which seek to change the product. Its authors maintain:

> What is needed to solve our current as well as future crises in education is a system of compensatory education which

[4]R. L. Bartley, "Pittsburgh Attacks City School Problems," *Wall Street Journal*, June 17, 1966, p. 16.
[5]E. W. Gordon and D. Wilkerson, *Compensatory Education for the Disadvantaged, Programs and Practices: Pre School Through College*, New York, College Entrance Examination Board, 1966.
[6]Quoted by F. M. Hechinger in "Integrated vs Compensated," *N.Y. Times*, Feb. 26, 1967, p. E9, from U.S. Commission on Civil Rights report, "Racial Isolation in the Public Schools."

> can prevent or overcome earlier deficiencies in the development of each individual. . . . Compensatory education as we understand it is not the reduction of all education to a least common denominator. It is a type of education which should help socially disadvantaged students without reducing the quality of education for those who are progressing satisfactorily under existing conditions. . . .[7]

The major failure of this and similar books—and the entire compensatory movement—was pointed out by Harry Passow, Professor of Education at Teachers College, Columbia University: "The disappointment of the book is that none of its proposed major revisions would drastically modify conventional school patterns."[8]

Attempts to change the product *before* he reaches the conventional process have been somewhat more successful, but as the children proceed through the early grades of the conventional process, the good results of these programs tend to disappear.[9] Certainly early-childhood education is extremely important, and an extension of public education to include these early years is a valuable innovation, but it cannot be considered a substitute for changing the conventional process.

The fallacy in trying to change the *purpose* or the product of education, rather than the process, can be seen in an analogy of a similar problem in automobile production. Let us suppose that we are in the business of manufacturing cars, and that our advertisements read, "Buy the car that will be free of mechanical difficulties for five years." Sales increase rapidly, but it is soon reported that our new cars are being brought back for repairs after only three months, and that the number of new cars in need of such repair is increasing drastically.

[7]B. Bloom, A. Davis, and R. Hess, *Compensatory Education for Cultural Deprivation*, New York, Holt, Rinehart and Winston, 1965, p. 6.
[8]A. H. Passow, "Diagnosis and Prescription," review of Bloom *et al.*, *op. cit.*, in *Saturday Review*, May 15, 1965, p. 82.
[9]M. Wolff, *Six Months Later: A Comparison of Children who had Head Start, Summer 1965 with their Classmates in Kindergarten: A Case Study of the Kindergartens in the Public Elementary Schools in New York City*, sponsored by the Graduate School of Education, Yeshiva University and supported by funds from the United States Office of Economic Opportunity.

As manufacturers, we consider the solutions to the problem. One is that the advertisements be changed to read, "Buy a car that is free of mechanical difficulties for three months." In this case, we would be changing the purpose. We reject this alternative, however, because we must keep up with the needs of the consumer; we would not sell cars that lasted three months only. Our company has already been associated with a five-year mechanically perfect car, and thus, we vote in favor of continuing the advertisements that reflect this claim.

Further discussion brings consensus for creating a special division to rehabilitate all faulty cars. In short, we decide to change the product. In a very short time, this division is flooded with cars to repair and it becomes evident that we must *expand* the program of automotive rehabilitation. New services are established, and additional mechanics are hired to carry out the program. Three months after the repairs, however, our car owners experience more mechanical difficulties. Again the cars are rehabilitated and after three more months, the same cars will again be in need of automotive repairs.

After a while, several disappointed car owners ask, "Why don't you do what you promise? These cars don't last for five years. Your special rehabilitation division is okay, but it's bothersome to bring the car back every three months. Change the way you're building cars and perhaps the automotive rehabilitation division will be unnecessary."

Just as the automotive rehabilitation division would not solve the problem for the car manufacturer, compensatory education cannot solve the problems of educating the disadvantaged. Further, to rely on compensatory education to solve the problem is to create two separate systems—one for the advantaged and one for the disadvantaged—although, as shown previously in this book, both groups are disadvantaged vis-à-vis an outmoded educational process. Only by changing the institutional process itself can we improve education for any group.

The danger is that compensatory education may become an *end in itself*. The current impetus in Federal legislation has made compensatory education so widespread that it may actually become part of the same unwieldy educational process which must be reformed.

Yet despite its failure to solve these problems at their roots, compensatory education has served usefully; it has brought needed attention to the problem of the disadvantaged, and it has shown us that the present generation is not prepared to sacrifice people while we search for more adequate solutions. It has also made contact with the problem and the people. Undoubtedly, too, it has helped many children who might otherwise have been totally forsaken. Consequently, compensatory education must not be considered a mistake, but rather as a first step in a series aimed at structural overhaul of the entire educational process.

CHANGING THE PROCESS

The third alternative in selecting the arena for change is to change the *process* of education. Many reformers have said that process change is drastically needed, because the present institutional model was forged at a time when the purpose of the schools was different and it had never been planned to deal with so wide a diversity of pupils and subject matter. Many of these same reformers are devoting their efforts to achieving such process innovations as programed learning, educational TV, team teaching, curriculum reform, and similar modern innovations.

The difficulty is that, while certainly these innovations are valuable and may be expected to do a better job than the old practices they replace, their potential is not fully realized because they, too, are attempts to make the *existing* system more effective, rather than to alter the outdated system itself. Moreover, they are introduced piecemeal and unsystematically, making the dysfunctional educational system more fragmented, and the already uneven process even more uneven.

True process change involves changing the institution of education at its core—the entire system of education, from teacher techniques, curriculum content, and teacher training to administrative organization and personnel; from the physical plant to the very attitudes and philosophy which underlie the entire educational system. In short, an up-to-date process can only come about by constructing *a new model,* a model based on the belief that institutions must adjust to *people,* rather than the other way round. In essence, this requires a change in the behavioral roles among educational personnel within the system. Educational personnel must be willing and able to recognize that there are *no human failures,* only program and institutional failures.

What is needed, then, if we are to achieve true process change, is an across-the-board reform which will affect the total educational system, rather than the piecemeal implementation of these sundry devices, programs, and techniques. In any true system, all subparts of the system are related functionally to each other, and are integrated for the good of the whole. The synthetic interrelationships of these subparts comprise a total system with both purpose and direction. Therefore, to feed innovations into any part of the educational system (usually the classroom), cannot be an efficient change unless all of the other parts of the system are similarly affected. Indeed, the unwieldy and rigidly entrenched educational establishment may engulf these helpful but relatively superficial devices.

The faulty assumption which underlies the recent enthusiasm over programed instruction, educational TV, and the like was humorously but cogently revealed in the theoretical case study which appeared in the *Harvard Educational Review.*[10] The article describes how the latest in instructional reforms—team teaching, ETV, and programed instruction—were used skillfully to improve instruction. The subject matter that was so effectively taught, however, was composed of the content of the telephone directory! Obviously, these instructional devices are useless if they are merely to increase the schools' traditional emphasis on rote rather than conceptual learning, or to teach meaningless curriculum content.

[10]M. Harmin and S. Simon, "The Year the Schools Began Teaching the Telephone Directory," *Harvard Educational Review,* **35**:3 (Summer, 1965), 326–331.

Thus, the development of a new educational process which will realistically accommodate the diverse needs of a diverse student population, and simultaneously develop the human resources needed by a diverse technological society, cannot hope to be achieved by the mere substitution of one set of orthodoxies for another, or one cumbersome and inflexible structure for another. The new educational process needed for the maintenance and growth of modern America must be flexible, adaptable, and self-revitalizing. It will have no final answers, but will ever engage in a continuous search for better and better ways of educating people; and such a process will be the first to find fault with *itself* as its accustomed procedures emerge as inadequate.

The creation of an educational system of this sort is no easy matter; ironically, the people on whom we must rely to produce this new process are themselves the faulty products of the conventional system. These human resources are in many cases what lead to bureaucratic rigidity. Thus, the largest problem facing education today, and the one with which this chapter is chiefly concerned, is that of how to move the rigid educational bureaucracy; in other words, how to get the faulty products to reverse the cycle.

As indicated earlier in the chapter, there are many conditions extant today which can be of enormous use in getting a toe-hold in the doors to the bureaucratic core, providing they are used properly. The following recommendations comprise only a few of these, but they are fairly representative of the kinds of entry strategies available to those involved in educational reform. It should be pointed out here that no one strategy is a final key, but rather each should be used, as appropriate, with each of the others. A case study of how these "vehicles" were actually used in one public-school system is presented in Chapter 8.

Tapping the power sources

Before any specific change can be implemented, it must have a strong endorsement and financial backing from a noted and accepted authority or organization. These "power sources," in effect, provide the "energy" by which the specific change can be mobilized. There are many power sources behind education today, both within and without the formal educational system, and the imaginative use of these sources can make the difference between merely gaining attention for the specific change and actually achieving the change. Financial backing as well as concerted interest and cooperation can come from the Federal and state governments, private foundations, business and industry, and even from the community. Most of these may be considered sources *extrinsic* to the formal educational system. But colleges and universities also have potential as valuable power sources, and these and other sources intrinsic to the educational system should not be overlooked.

THE FEDERAL GOVERNMENT AS A POWER SOURCE

At present, the Federal government is the only power source of sufficient magnitude to enable significant and widespread changes to be effected in educational practices across the land. It has both the dollars and the legislative authority to support educational research and reform, and to ensure that the nation's schools are actually producing healthy, well-informed, and critically thinking citizens. Until recently, however, Federal support of education has been minimal. The Morrill Act of 1862 endowed states with large land grants for agricultural and technical colleges, and the Smith-Hughes Act of 1917 and the George Barden Act of 1946 stimulated the institution of vocational education in secondary schools. But outside of these measures, the government has generally maintained a hands-off policy with regard to state-controlled education.

With the National Defense Education Act of 1959, Federal involvement in education has since been substantially increased. This bill cut across every level of education, from preschool through college, and it was followed in succession by the Vocational Education Act of 1963, the Civil Rights Act of 1964, the Economic Opportunity Act of 1965—and various amendments to each of these—adding up to an investment in 1966 of over $5 billion, or 15 percent of the total cost of education in the United States.

The question of Federal control vs. states rights is always a potentially explosive one, and this increased involvement in education on the part of the Federal government has caused some controversy. For this reason, the recent educational legislation is carefully worded to avoid implications of Federal control, and to assure the state and local authorities extensive leeway in deciding the specific programs they will implement with Federal funds. The legislation does require that the funds be used for certain types of educational programs, however. If the specifications outlined in the act are not followed in the use of the money provided, the government can curtail the flow of these funds to the area or project involved. Thus, the government does have the power to influence the educational process.

Nevertheless, the Federal government, as an agent extrinsic to the educational process, cannot accomplish what professional educators are in a position to do. It is one thing to make money available for a general purpose; it is quite another to use this money to implement specific programs which will have an effective and enduring influence on the basic educational process. Thus, the key question is in just what direction the Federal influence on education will take.

A case in point can be drawn from Public Law 89-10, passed by the 89th Congress on April 11, 1965. The purpose of this act is to "strengthen and improve educational quality and educational opportunities in the Nation's elementary and secondary schools."[11] Title I of this act provides over $1 billion for the education of children from low-income families, and Title III authorizes appropriations of over $100 million (fiscal ending June 30, 1967) to stimulate and to assist in the provision of vitally needed educational services not available in sufficient quantity and quality, and to stimulate and assist in the "development

[11] *Elementary and Secondary Education Act of 1965*, Report no. 143, Washington, D.C., U.S. Government Printing Office, 1965, p. 1.

and establishment of exemplary elementary and secondary school educational programs to serve as models for regular school programs."[12] Clearly, there are certain restrictions as to how these monies may be used—for example, they cannot be used to build new schools which will merely replace older buildings, or which will house middle-class suburban children for the purpose of exposing them to exactly the same educational pattern that exists in standard mainstream schools. On the other hand, the stipulations are not so stringent as to indicate the precise nature of the educational services which will "serve as models for regular school programs" or which are not available in sufficient quantity and quality. There is nothing under either of these titles to prevent local authorities from interpreting them as an encouragement of compensatory—and thus merely additive—programs; indeed, to date this has been the main use to which the available funds have been put. If the act has been so interpreted, it is because schoolmen themselves have endorsed compensatory education as the solution to disadvantaged education, rather than an overhauling of the basic conventional process as it affects *all* children. Some plans are now being formulated for the construction of regional centers which will serve as models for education generally, but it is too early to determine the direction they will take.

The large sums available to almost every school system in the country under this and similar acts (as long as the system must contend to some extent with a disadvantaged population) can serve as strong forces behind the implementation of across-the-board school reform. Or they can be expended to institute programs which do not ultimately accomplish their purposes and which may make the current process even more cumbersome and ineffective than it has been. The choice lies with professional educators. If schoolmen expand their vision beyond compensatory education, innovations in instructional devices and technology, and similar trends in vogue today, to encompass *institutional*

[12]*Ibid.*, p. 16.

reform, true and sweeping process change can become a practical and effective reality.

For example, under Title I of the Elementary and Secondary Education Act of 1965, funds are distributed to virtually every school system which can offer some sort of "demonstration" project or model school. Properly used, these funds could lead to a demonstration project in which research, development, and staff training—relevant to curriculum, teaching methodology, instructional technology, and administrative functions—are simultaneously carried out, not merely among the typically segregated, lower socioeconomic student population, but also among all children, including a proportion of white middle-class pupils. From these demonstration schools, effective procedures in administration, teacher training, pupil diagnosis, and classroom techniques could pass gradually to the other schools in the system.

Similarly, funds appropriated in connection with Project Head Start could be used for more than a compensatory preschool program to prepare low-income children for traditional schooling; they could be used to implement similar preschool programs for integrated groups composed of children from an array of cultural, ethnic, and socioeconomic backgrounds. Further, the more effective techniques used in these preschool programs—team teaching which uses volunteer teachers and older children, experience stories aimed at developing positive self-concepts, and other process innovations—could serve as models for changing the outmoded procedures used in the older grades. Significant in this regard is the new "follow through" project, presently sponsored by the U.S. Office of Economic Opportunity, which recently has been initiated to carry out procedures found effective in Head Start from kindergarten through the third grade. While initially these broader applications of Head Start would be executed on an experimental basis, gradually they could become integrated into the school system as a whole, not only to coordinate the educational opportunities provided for children of a certain age level, but also to coordinate the education provided at *each successive rung* of the education ladder.

Further, many antipoverty, community-action programs sponsored by the Office of Economic Opportunity are developing a wide range of after-school and evening programs for both children and adults. Educators could avail themselves of these funds to finance community programs in the schools. A variety of educational, cultural, and recreational programs could be offered toward the aim of bringing the school and the community it serves more closely together, affording closer communication and understanding between teachers and parents, the business community and school administrators, and so forth. Such a plan would provide much more effective public relations than the press-releases, special and sporadic dinners and other occasions, and the other means usually relied on by school boards and their school administrators to maintain their public image. What is more, while these typical publicity measures generally require that key school personnel spend much of their valuable time in activities that have little to do with the educational process directly, such school-community programs would involve them integrally with the educational process they purport to oversee.

Federal legislation on behalf of education and related enterprises is so vast, and the various titles so diverse, that it rests with professional educators to keep informed of the specific purposes for which Federal monies may be obtained, and to consider the most effective ways these funds may be utilized under each title. To the extent that schoolmen fail in these responsibilities, needed tax dollars will be wasted and valuable opportunities missed.

THE STATE AS A POWER SOURCE

While the Federal government has only recently become strongly involved in education, it has been the state government which has traditionally borne the chief responsibility for educational matters. The state government has always appropriated a relatively large percentage of its revenues for education. While local school systems must also contribute to their own financial support, most states provide more than 40 percent of local educational financing. (Some states—such as Delaware, North Carolina, Louisiana, and Hawaii—provide more than 70 percent, while in South Dakota and Nebraska, state aid comprises less than 10 percent of school support.) In addition, state governments have generally assumed the responsibility for setting curriculum standards, certifying teachers, and deciding other matters concerned with education. Indeed, an entire department of the state governmental machinery is organized to administer educational policy.

In addition, state education departments usually operate a system of state supported colleges and universities—including teachers colleges—in which affiliated child-development laboratories, learning laboratories, nursery schools and kindergartens, and educational research and development centers are maintained by professionally trained personnel. This relationship between university staff and the governmental administrators also holds potential for positive leadership in educational policy making in the public schools.

Unfortunately, however, this leadership has generally been exercised to strengthen the traditional status quo, rather than to encourage the streamlining of the conventional process into an up-to-date institution which can keep up with, and even set the pace for, a modern and rapidly developing society.

The Civil-Rights issue, the disadvantaged learner, and similar social crises that have arisen in our "Great Society"—and the Federal legislation and funds they have stimulated—have offered unusual opportunities to alter this situation. Anxious to obtain some of these funds, state education departments have instituted their own specific educational programs, making portions of their own educational budgets available for these purposes. Colleges and universities, too, have appropriated Federal funds for research and development projects, special teacher-training courses, and the instituting of small-scale model schools. The difficulty is that most of these state and university plans have been concerned with the primarily additive innovations, such as compensatory and preschool education for low-income pupils, the development of programed learning materials and ETV courses, and similar measures which attempt to make the outdated conventional process more effective, but which do not affect the faulty core of this process. Moreover, there has been relatively little synthesis of these efforts, with the result that there is much duplication of effort and cross-purpose functioning between the state educational departments and their affiliated colleges and universities.

Again, efficient utilization of state funds and resources rests with the professional educators. State support could be especially effective in mobilizing college and university efforts on behalf of the disadvantaged to encompass public education generally. The state's unusual power and prestige in influencing its universities could be used to initiate a closely knit partnership with the local school systems. Such a partnership with teachers' colleges would, for example, provide the schools with badly needed assistant teachers and personnel for teaching teams and, at the same time, provide the teacher-training institution with a ready-made training ground for its student teachers. Similarly, graduate programs in school supervision and administration could be conducted in part in the actual public-school system. Such a policy, if implemented, could offset educational costs considerably, for more administrative and teaching staff could be added for the money expended in salaries and benefits. Indeed, school systems frequently complain that they cannot add more personnel because the money is simply not available.

One example of how the state's power and authority can be tapped occurred in Boston, where a group of parents and professional educators pooled their efforts to overcome obstacles imposed by the local school system. They proposed state legislation and funds to create a school which was outside of the local school system's jurisdiction and directly under the state's authority. The school is community oriented and includes a host of educational practices that would not be possible in any local public school.

In short, educators can profit greatly from tapping the state's power and authority to change the fundamental educational process. But it is the responsibility of the educator to do so, and to enlighten state legislators and administrators as to how it behooves them to allocate funds toward this end.

PRIVATE FOUNDATIONS AS POWER SOURCES

Privately endowed foundations and charitable institutions have always been active supporters of education and educational enterprises. Libraries, learning institutes, museums, and similar undertakings by such foundations have sprung up all over the nation for the purpose of making learning available to citizens. In addition, private foundations have sponsored or initiated many educational and cultural projects which have pioneered new methods and approaches to societal upgrading. For example, beginning in 1960, the Ford Foundation gave a series of grants totalling to more than $3.2 million to establish several educational experiments in ten large cities.[13] Known as the Great Cities School Improvement Program, this effort focused on the educational needs of culturally disadvantaged children. Although the program details differed in each city, common to each were experimentation with a broad range of teaching materials, innovation in administrative approaches that would be geared to reaching the disadvantaged learner, implementation of ways to encourage and to use community resources, and experimentation with ways to increase the effectiveness of teaching skills and teacher attitudes. Later, this effort mushroomed into a large scale attack on all aspects of deprivation: employment, housing, community planning, recreation, and health, as well as education. The Great Cities Project has amounted to more than $12 million in Ford Foundation grants.

In addition to accomplishing their specific aims, the Ford Foundation and some 15,000 other private foundations, in their various projects, have served as an overwhelming influence on initiating public support from both governmental and private sources, and have encouraged these sources to engage in similar

[13]Buffalo, Chicago, Cleveland, Detroit, Milwaukee, Philadelphia, Pittsburgh, St. Louis, Washington, D.C., San Francisco.

undertakings. As Henry T. Heald has summarized it, foundations "yield returns to society far exceeding the dollar amount of their grants. They help with the risks and the costs of getting things started."[14] The very fact that a foundation supports an idea gives the idea status and may make the change more readily acceptable to the public.

Significantly, the pioneering attack on urban problems by Ford and other foundations has set the stage for the Federal Government's recent active involvement toward similar objectives. Much of Title I of the Elementary and Secondary Education Act of 1965 and the model for compensatory education grew out of Ford's Great Cities Project. The Gray Areas Project—also initiated by the Ford Foundation—has served, in part, as the model for later Office of Economic Opportunity community-action programs. Due largely to the work of private foundations, the government has also become actively involved in teacher-training programs which are geared to the teaching of disadvantaged pupils.

Now that the Federal government has taken over a large part of such foundation-sponsored programs, there is some question about the future role to be played by the private foundations in the United States. Very likely, foundations will continue to engage in the kinds of projects thus far discussed, forming a kind of partnership with the Federal government. But more likely, they will begin to finance projects that are even more innovative, experimental—and potentially controversial—which the government cannot fund because of public disfavor. Certainly it should continue to be the task of private foundations to exert the initiative they have shown in the past, and to support potentially worthwhile educational and cultural programs that do not as yet have public support.

In any case, the professional educator can utilize foundation funds which are available for existing projects, and, by carefully planning his proposals, he may also be able to entice foundation officials to participate in new areas. The educational reformer should apprise himself of the current interests of the many

[14]H. T. Heald "American Foundations and the Common Welfare," address given at Columbia University, March 5, 1967, p. 7.

private foundations, and, in capitalizing on these interests, he may be able to open up related but new areas of potential interest to these foundations.

BUSINESS AND INDUSTRY AS POWER SOURCES

Increasingly, business and industry have come to realize that the schools are essential to their own growth and development. The economic health of business and industrial concerns—indeed, of the nation as a whole—is dependent on the purchasing power of the national citizenry, and, to the extent that there are unemployed or low-income families, the economy will be impaired. Further, these business and industrial concerns must compete with one another and with those of the rest of the world in pioneering new goods and services, methods of marketing and distribution, and so forth; to compete successfully, they must have top personnel in research and product development, management, and manufacturing.

Such manpower has been scarce and hard to find, and more and more corporations have taken to instituting and to expanding their own training programs. In addition, many companies and corporations include in their budgets, tuition costs for those of their employees who enroll in higher-education courses which are likely to have relevance to their work.

Recently, however, this interest in trained manpower has taken on even greater proportions, with large industrial concerns financing, planning, and participating in the public education of their communities. For example, in Huntsville, Alabama—headquarters for many NASA programs and aerospace industries—a group of space-industry contractors formed the Association of Huntsville Area Contractors (AHAC). In order to develop fully educated, trained, and skilled manpower for their own interests, these contractors pool their efforts to close the gap between the public-education program and the actual knowledge and skills required of those who would be employed in aerospace and related technological projects. AHAC officials are spurring experiments and innovations in teacher training, curriculum revision, community involvement programs, and many other areas related to education. To illustrate, AHAC specialists supply instructional staff to teach specialized courses which pertain to the aerospace industry, and they set the curricula for these courses. In addition, they review standard school courses to see how they might integrate similar content into these courses and, at the same time, upgrade the general educational value of these courses. AHAC also uses its many community resources to serve as a catalyst in the alleviation of community problems which interfere with quality education, and thus, provides a vital overall community service as well as educational assistance.

In addition to their interests in developing the skills and abilities for their own manpower needs, business and industry are beginning to view education as a profitable enterprise in its own right. For example, the Federal government has actually offered contracts to industrial concerns to participate in the many Job Corps programs around the country. The companies are contracted to help train disadvantaged youths for employment. Further, more and more industries that are involved in technologically advanced communications are beginning to see education as a new market for their products and services. American Telephone and Telegraph has a number of services available to schools, such as the speaker-phone system by which a class may discuss a subject with an authority who is unable to visit the class in person. Firms such as Time, Inc., IBM Corp., RCA, and many of the major television networks are also beginning to woo the schools' commercial patronage. The products and services offered to education range from audiovisual equipment and hardware (electronic learning-laboratory systems, projectors, etc.) to new curriculum formats and instructional sequences which use integrated combinations of a variety of different media. Perhaps the resignation of Francis Keppel from the U.S. Department of Health, Education and Welfare to accept a post with General Learning Corp. symbolizes the seriousness of commercial enterprise's venture into the education market.

The opportunities afforded the professional educator by this upsurge in interest among businesses and industries are numerous.

For example, the educational reformer may be able to elicit the interest of major industries and industrial concerns both to finance educational programs and to supply trained personnel as instructors and curriculum planners for the schools in their home communities. By taking an active part in public education, industries can not only raise the quality of their potential labor force, they can also raise the economic and cultural standards of their communities, and probably the community purchasing power as well. Participating corporations can also enhance their corporate image within their community and to the public at large. When one considers the large sums of money industrial concerns spend for corporate-image advertising, the public-relations potential of active involvement in education may incur the interest of corporation officials.

The educational reformer may also take advantage of the burgeoning interest in education as a commercial enterprise. Anxious to find new consumers for their educational goods and services, such firms as Graflex, Inc., Basic Systems Corp., Systems Development Corp., and those mentioned above may be encouraged to participate in the implementation of true process change. The interest these companies have was reflected in a statement by R. T. MacFarlane of Graflex, Inc.: "We are now entering a phase in which we must address ourselves to improving new hardware and software systems in a way that is consistent with curriculum and educational needs. The problem we face in this regard is one not so much of equipment innovation, but of penetrating the educational process to learn the real needs."[15]

Companies which put out new instructional materials and curriculum systems, for example, might be invited to examine and to discuss specific curriculum needs in a disadvantaged school, and to experiment with new content formats, for a very low fee. Workable formats might then be sold to similar schools around the country, thereby profiting simultaneously the school, the company, and the larger educational system. In one situation, a company provided an educational consultant at an unusually

[15]R. T. MacFarlane, "Industry and Education," *Educational Technology*, January 20, 1967, p. 25.

small cost to the school in return for the opportunity to set up a demonstration model of an expensive piece of educational equipment. The model was used to demonstrate the equipment to other schools as potential buyers, and thus provided a mutual benefit to both school and company.

These, then, are an indication of how the resourceful educational reformer might capitalize on the power sources available in business and industry. The educational reformer must acquaint himself with specific goods or services supplied by the various companies and with the operating aims of business and industrial corporations, and then literally shop around for those agencies which might be most interested in participating in the given educational problem or facet thereof. When these business and industrial power sources are combined with the resources available through the Federal and state governments and private foundations, a powerful and concerted attack on the conventional school process can effectively be endorsed.

Identifying the vehicle for change

While the long-range objective of the change may be the entire school system, the educational reformer must have a more immediate and narrowly circumscribed medium in which he can develop his process innovations. Such a medium, or vehicle, can range from a single demonstration school to an experimental project conducted at a certain school level in several schools simultaneously. In some cases, the reformer may gain access to a standard school or to the public-school system itself through some particular need which the organizational bureaucracy recognizes.

THE DEMONSTRATION SCHOOL AS A VEHICLE FOR CHANGE

Schools which purport to depart radically from conventional practice become known as "demonstration" schools. Encouraged by the recent focus on education, and especially that in connection with the disadvantaged, more and more school systems have developed some sort of demonstration project. In theory, these model schools pioneer in new methods of teaching, which can range from novel ways of arranging the physical dimensions of instructional space, to new means of grouping pupils and/or teachers, to the technological equipment used to impart instructional content. Team teaching, nongraded pupil groupings, smaller classes and even individual instruction, programed learning equipment and machines, audiovisual materials, and similar innovations are incorporated in some combination in these schools. The idea is that authorities from other schools and school systems can visit these demonstration schools and transplant all or any part of these innovations into their own localities as they seem appropriate.

One illustration of such a demonstration project is the Nova Schools project in Fort Lauderdale, Florida. In this educational complex, education from early childhood through graduate school takes place on one campus. The architecture accommodates such features as decentralized resource centers, where an abundance and variety of learning materials are made readily accessible to teachers; advanced information-retrieval systems; a TV control center and studio; several audiovisual centers, where an array of projection and audio equipment can be used in combination, elaborate learning laboratories with telephone switching equipment, and similar technological facilities.

The newly built or remodeled buildings are, of course, departures from more conventional school architecture, and demonstration schools generally can boast more instructional equipment, such as television sets, movie screens, language laboratories, programed learning centers, and the like. Yet it is sometimes difficult to discern whether these obvious innovations represent a real process improvement or merely a new and more efficient way of enhancing the conventional process. Nongraded approaches, for example, generally manifest themselves as little more than subgroupings of pupils in a given age bracket according to level of ability in the standard curriculum. Fact learning is just as prevalent and is just as fraught with personally meaningless content. Books, films, and other learning materials are as antiseptically middle-class as ever.

Nevertheless, the demonstration school can be used as an excellent starting point for effecting basic process change throughout the school system. Money is generally available for testing innovations in these schools, and the school board and others in the organizational machinery are likely to be more receptive to changes and experiments in these schools than in others. In cities where no demonstration school exists, it may be possible to acquire the financing and the organizational backing to develop one. As will be indicated subsequently, the imaginative educational reformer can utilize the demonstration school to push one change project, and when that has been started on its way, to embark on another, closely related project which will reinforce the first. In this way, the change agent can initiate one "experiment" after another, until the demonstration school is indeed a successful and systematized working model after which other schools can be patterned.

THE EXPERIMENTAL PROJECT AS A CHANGE VEHICLE

There are many experimental programs currently receiving favorable attention which can be used as vehicles for introducing new changes. Project Head Start began as just this sort of program, and while this project still lies outside of the conventional process, it has been so successful that it has rapidly been expanded. Further, as mentioned earlier, the success of Head Start has motivated a similar, follow-through program which carries the instructional approach used in Head Start through the third grade.

In much the same manner, the educational reformer can build on one or more successful and accepted experimental projects. For example, in attempting to implement curriculum reforms—such as the "new" math, science, etc.—in the schools, the change agent would soon find himself confronted with teacher deficiencies, and he could proceed to obtain released time during the school day for teachers to convene for in-service training. Acquiring this release of time soon involves the change agent in school scheduling, however, and a host of other problems along with it. Thus, almost any currently accepted, albeit fringe, educational problem can be used as a staging point for effecting additional changes, each of which leads closer to the core of the conventional process. In each case, the reformer would expand his experimental programs to encompass a wider and wider range of the school system and its process.

ORGANIZATIONAL NEED AS A VEHICLE FOR CHANGE

A need on the part of a particular school or the school system as a whole can serve as highly effective vehicle for implementing pervasive changes in the core process. Any weak spot that is openly recognized by the bureaucracy provides a kind of Achilles' heel to gain access to those weak spots which are not formally recognized by the organization, provided that the change agent plans his strategy wisely. For example, a school system may have an immediate need to correct racial imbalance among its schools, and a plan which aims to solve this problem may be received with welcome. Such a plan, of course, can ultimately include a host of *process* changes, as well. Or, a particular school may have a high dropout rate, and the educational authorities may be looking for a solution in this area. A plan explicitly geared to reducing school dropout might be the means by which implicit plans to revise the core process—and the educational bureaucracy that perpetuates it—might be implemented. High rates of teacher turnover or a severe shortage of teachers are similar areas which can be tapped by the reformer to effect sweeping changes in the core process.

It is, of course, unlikely that large bureaucratic school systems would hire outside change agents on their own initiative, and thus, for an educational reformer to gain entry, the organization must be actively aware of its immediate problem and in search for a solution to it. If the problem is critical enough—and if the public is bringing a great deal of pressure upon the bureaucracy to solve it—the organization is likely to be quite receptive to outside help; further, in such a situation, the organization is likely to be relatively more flexible and tolerant of innovation (within limits) than it would otherwise be. Where organizational need is less pressing, financial backing from an outside power source can make the bureaucracy more receptive than it would be if it had to spend its own tightly budgeted funds. In cases where the organization is not likely to admit openly its weak spot, a nearby college or university can be called upon to bring the public's attention to the problem. For example, a sociology department might sponsor and conduct a survey in the school's community, the findings of which are generally published in the local news media. In the case study presented in Chapter 8, this actually occurred and led to the creation of a program jointly sponsored by the public-school system and the university.

The particular problem or project the reformer is engaged to handle, then, becomes the vehicle or operating base from which more encompassing changes may eventually stem. Once he has been engaged to solve the immediate problem, however, the reformer who wishes to effect a sweeping process change must become an integral part of the organization, and yet without developing the vested interests which sustain the rigid bureaucracy. Once he has gained the respect and confidence of both the teachers and the administrators, the change agent will be able to do much to implement, piece by piece, his overall strategy.

Developing reinforcement and expansion strategies

In tapping the appropriate power sources and identifying the vehicle for initiating his process changes, the educational reformer has taken the first two steps toward achieving his ultimate objective. If these two steps were all that were required to effect true and basic changes in the conventional process, however, these changes would have been already made. Federal, state, and private monies are already being expended in connection with demonstration schools, experimental projects, and school needs; but the evidence thus far suggests that basic changes in the conventional process have not been forthcoming. Rather, the results seem to indicate that a wide array of disconnected and piecemeal innovations are being executed at cross purposes with one another, and with much duplication and triplication of effort.

To eliminate this waste of money and effort—and simultaneously to effect true and pervasive changes which will streamline education for all children—both funds and innovations must be coordinated so that the best of any plan will contribute to the effectiveness of and strength behind any other. Team teaching, for example, can offer little hope for the improvement of education in any segment of the population if it merely results in a smaller ratio of pupils to teaching staff. Teaching teams can only profit education generally if the subject matter they teach is actually *learned* by the pupils, and pupils can be expected to learn subject matter only if it is meaningful to them and presented to them in a meaningful manner. In turn, the subject matter can be meaningful to the pupils only if it relates to pupil reality, and teachers, being closest to that reality, must therefore have a voice in instructional planning. But in order for teachers to be effective in this area, they must genuinely understand pupil reality as it actually is, and not how they deem it to be, based on middle-class and traditional ways of viewing children. Further, the organizational hierarchy must be willing to accommodate teachers' views in instructional planning if teachers are to participate in such planning, and so forth.

This highly intricate interrelationship among educational variables underlies all educational reforms, and the ultimate effectiveness of any single innovation will depend on how well these natural interrelationships are recognized and accommodated. If true process change is to occur, therefore, the educational reformer must be prepared to expand his base of operations to accommodate an ever-widening sphere. The professional educator with imagination and vision will not overlook any variable in the highly complex issue of education, and will keep alert for any that might emerge during the process of change. In the meantime, he will skillfully coordinate those innovations which are extant today and, where appropriate, use one to set the basis for embarking on and reinforcing another.

PARLAYING STRATEGY

By using what we have termed a "parlaying" strategy, the educational innovator can capitalize on and consolidate funds from several power sources more or less simultaneously. Beginning with a specific problem, he submits to an appropriate power source a proposal in which he outlines his remedial plan and its costs. Once he has been given the financial grant and authoritative support for executing his plan, he can then use this support as additional strength in submitting a different but related proposal to another power source. The endorsement the reformer has received from the first power source thus serves to bolster his image among those in the second power source, increasing his chances for gaining the additional financial grant. Having been backed by two power sources so far, the change agent then proceeds to a third with a proposal outlining the solution to still another but related problem, and so on, each time building on his funded "credit rating" for obtaining additional funds and support.

Of course, in order to obtain even the first grant, the educational reformer must have a problem which has been fully identified and recognized, and which falls within the interests of the power source. The first financing and endorsement can become a parlaying strategy for gaining access to the vehicle—e.g., a demonstration school or experimental project; then the vehicle plus the credit rating gained through the first grant of funds will serve as the parlaying strength for gaining further financial backing and endorsement. Thus, once the initial strategies have been successfully accomplished, both the vehicle and the financial backing become reinforcing instruments for similar parlaying strategies, and for expanding the radius of reform.

Let us suppose, for example, that a fully trained and experienced educator has been engaged by a local school system to solve a school-dropout problem, and that he has been given a limited and inadequate budget for the purpose. His first step might be to acquire additional funds for the immediate purpose, and thus he submits a proposal to an outside power source that makes funds available for the same purpose. His first proposal may feature more accepted approaches to the dropout problem, such as those involved in compensatory education. If he is given the grant, he then begins to initiate the strategies outlined in his proposal. Meanwhile, the dropout problem is partially contingent on a high rate of teacher turnover which leads to poor teaching as a factor in the low level of educational achievement throughout the school. This may lead the change agent to submit —perhaps in cooperation with a nearby teacher-training institution—a related proposal to another power source suggesting that a more intensive in-service training program might be initiated. This second proposal tends to be viewed the more favorably by the power source for two reasons: First, the agent has already proven his fund-raising ability, and second, he is linking two important problems, dropouts and teacher training.

Thus, through such parlaying strategies, the change agent capitalizes on the several interconnected needs involved in the single, immediate problem of school dropout by raising the financial backing needed from a variety of sources. Once he has his "experimental" program fully and successfully operating, he can then begin to parlay for more and larger grants to implement the program on a wide sphere.

PACKAGING STRATEGY

Closely related to the parlaying strategy is the "packaging" strategy, by which the educational reformer relates one problem area to another. While such packaging was indicated above—indeed, parlaying depends on the effective packaging of problem areas, at least implicitly—explicit packages are an effective means of gaining cooperation both from the educational organization and from power sources. Drawing on the theme, "look how much more you can get for your money," the change agent can make his proposal extremely attractive to the school system, and at the same time, gear his efforts to several areas of change simultaneously.

To illustrate, a change agent who has been engaged to institute or to streamline team teaching in a demonstration school can package into one plan:

1. A less severe shortage of fully trained and experienced teachers through the use of in-service practice teachers, volunteer teaching assistants, and pupil teaching aides
2. A more cost-efficient use of available payroll funds because these sub- and nonprofessional teachers and teaching assistants can free highly qualified teachers of much trivial detail
3. Higher-quality team teaching because, with the larger staff enabled by using these non- and subprofessional personnel, more time is available for team planning and information exchange
4. A more efficient and high-quality supervisory program, because the low cost of the sub- and nonprofessional staff frees some money for highly trained teaching supervisors to counsel the teams and their professional teaching leaders

At the same time, of course, the change agent will be initiating:

1. The beginnings of a community-school partnership through the use of volunteer and paid teaching assistants who are drawn from the community
2. A partial remedial-education program through the use of pupil teaching aides who learn as they teach
3. A potential lessening of pupil alienation, as pupils are more likely to relate successfully to the student aides, who are closer to their own ages
4. And—if pupil teaching aides are drawn from schools which serve "better" neighborhoods—the potential for a program of cultural integration in the schools

The packaging strategy, then, capitalizes on a set or series of organizational needs, rather than a single need. A packaging strategy may not incorporate *at one time* these several needs; it can be developed progressively, as each phase of an overall project contributes to a greater confidence on the part of the organizational staff. This developmental approach to packaging strategy is particularly desirable in rigid systems which are not immediately open to innovation, and which tend to resist changes which seem to the staff to be too radically deviant from the status quo. In such a case, the package may evolve naturally as each phase of the project uncovers new need areas which cannot be ignored if the interests of the organization itself are to be served.

Utilizing the available human resources

As stressed earlier, any basic change in the educational process can come only through an alteration in the behavioral roles played by those integral to the bureaucratic machinery. Such an alteration will not be forthcoming with sheer money or authoritative mandates. Rather, they must evolve slowly, subtly, and naturally, yet without undue delay. To accomplish this requires that the human resources—both within and without the formal educational system—be fully and properly utilized. The most immediately available human resources are the public-school teachers themselves, but, in addition, there are those perhaps not presently connected with the public-school system but who can be brought in from without to take active part in the formal educational process; for example, students and professors of education, volunteer teachers drawn from the community, teacher's aides drawn from the older pupil population, professional social workers, psychologists, and so forth. With strategic help from such people, the educational reformer can make significant inroads into the conventional status quo.

TEACHERS AS CENTRAL HUMAN RESOURCES

One of the most serious hindrances to improved education is the failure of the organization to tap the knowledge and decision-making potential of its teachers. The teacher is closest to the learner of all those involved in educational policy; he must interact with the pupils in daily reality and thus, he is most likely to be familiar with their needs, their problems, and their assets. The teacher has learned, perhaps through trial and error, what will and what won't work in the classroom, and what obstacles in the home or in the school lie in the path of pupil learning. Yet only in rare cases does the conventional organization permit the teacher to engage in any significant part of instructional planning. Decisions concerning what subject matter is to be taught, how much is going to be taught, in what grades it will be taught, and with what equipment and instructional devices it will be taught all flow downward to the teacher from those who are the farthest from pupil reality.

The recent emphasis on team teaching provides a valuable opportunity to change this one-way flow of educational policy. Although teaching teams have not yet become an integral part of the nation's school procedures, the wide attention this new instructional mode has received provides an avenue through which the educational reformer can effect some degree of teacher decisionmaking. Teams of teachers—whatever lines along which they are grouped, and whatever the specific purpose of their team—would meet regularly as a scheduled part of their teaching day to exchange information based on their experience, and to plan new classroom approaches. Through such conferences, obstacles imposed by school bureaucratic procedures would be aired and passed upward, perhaps through higher levels of similar teams, where head teachers and teacher supervisors convene with regularity, teams of principals do likewise, and so forth up the hierarchial ladder. Changes in the curriculum and its syllabuses, grading practices, instructional equipment and supplies, and organizational paperwork routines might be brought about with considerably greater ease through such team planning, and with greater confidence on the part of each individual teacher.

Armed with money and backing from a power source, the educational innovator could establish and utilize such teams in a demonstration school or experimental project, and from this point, effective methods and policies could be expanded gradually to the school system as a whole.

UTILIZING COLLEGES AND UNIVERSITY HUMAN RESOURCES

Although the college or university is as much concerned with teaching and learning as is the public school—and it prepares the teachers, counselors, and administrators for the public educational system—two different cultures have emerged, with considerable distance between them. The latest theories and practices in education, as well as in other academic fields, are likely to be found at the college level, but too often these innovations remain at this level and do not filter down through the rest of the educational establishment. For example, colleges and universities often maintain their own "laboratory" schools and child-development centers; yet the methods, materials, and curricula used in these laboratories—as well as the findings concerning their effectiveness—are restricted to the university and to a few esoteric journals. Meanwhile, the problems caused and/or experienced in real public schools go unattended by those who are most equipped to understand them. Such ties as do exist between the university and the public schools are often tenuous; for example, student-teaching programs, in which the teachers college places undergraduate teachers in public schools for practical experience, often fail to help the student teacher to relate to or to cope realistically with classroom and school administration problems.

Such connections do offer excellent potential for benefitting education generally, however, and the educational reformer can do much to tap this potential. Teacher-education institutions and other colleges need to understand better the actual state of affairs as they exist in the public schools, and conversely, experienced school staff need to be more thoroughly involved in the procedures and philosophy implemented at the college level. This gap can be significantly lessened through effective utilization of both student and professor at the college level.

While the public schools are interested in getting more and better teachers into their schools, their most immediate need is for the in-service training of their existing professional staff. The college of education, on the other hand, has a persistent need for locating the most suitable schools for their pre-service teaching trainees. The educational reformer can take advantage of both these needs simultaneously by establishing the role of "clinical professor," or instructional specialist. Such a person would be recruited from a nearby teacher-training institution and would serve as the leader for the teaching teams mentioned previously. As the experienced teachers in these teams became, under the guidance of the clinical professor, more sophisticated in working through their instructional problems according to the latest in teaching methodology, pre-service trainees from the teachers college could be introduced into this clinical setting as new teaching-team members. Thus, by using the public school as a clinical setting, a two-way training program could be established for the mutual benefit of the public school and the teacher-training institutions. Such a plan would work equally well for college students preparing for careers in such fields as school administration, counseling, clinical school psychology, school social work, and related fields.

The specific process changes which might be implemented through such coordinated planning are many, and would depend on the educational reformer's creative imagination and professional experience. But to involve college and university personnel integrally in the process would be of considerable value in accomplishing these changes.

CREATING NEW INSTRUCTIONAL ROLES

One of the most common complaints of teachers—particularly in schools serving disadvantaged areas—has to do with the size of their classes; teachers feel that they simply cannot cope with large groups of pupils. Through the community-action programs of the Office of Economic Opportunity, involvement of the disadvantaged in working out their own problems has opened up new possibilities for solving this problem of classroom size through the creation of paraprofessional roles. For example, nonprofessional assistant teachers drawn from the community can expand the basis of personnel resources available to schools. The potential involved in such a movement provides a number of valuable opportunities both for changing the core of the conventional process and for improving the educational level and involvement of the participants. By redefining the tasks of the professional teacher and allocating much of the multitude of clerical, routine teaching, and managemental duties to teaching aides and assistants, the professional teacher is freed to use his training and experience creatively both in the classroom itself and outside the classroom in planning more effective instructional strategies. Such a procedure would not only revitalize the educational process, but it would also contribute to teachers' self-esteem and job satisfaction, thereby reducing the rate of turnover in teaching personnel. Such a procedure would be especially useful in urban areas, where teacher dissatisfaction and turnover appear greater.

Moreover, by recruiting parents and others in the community as teaching assistants and volunteer teachers, the school-community breach could be sizeably reduced. In working closely together, parents and teachers would profit from one another's frames of reference, and many of the problems now blamed on the "home" would become mitigated as the teacher became more familiar with the cultural and familial realities of the parent and, similtaneously, the parent became more familiar with child development, the learning process, and other relevant concepts in which the professional teacher has been trained. In many cases—and particularly in disadvantaged areas where the breach between the middle-class oriented teacher and the culturally different pupils is large—the parent as teaching assistant might serve effectively to reduce pupil alienation.

A similarly effective strategy would be to engage older pupils as teaching aides. It is frequently easier for children to relate to those who are closer to their own age level and peer values, and thus, "junior" teachers would not only unburden the professional teacher of many of his routine tasks—such as reviewing, testing, marking short-answer quizzes, and operating film-projectors and other audiovisual equipment—but would tend to draw the younger pupils closer to the instructional process. Classroom discipline problems, if relegated to these junior teachers might also be substantially mitigated. Another and highly desirable side effect of such a strategy would be the educational benefits accrued to the youthful teaching aides. In tutoring younger pupils in their subjects and seeing to other teaching details, the junior teachers would be reinforcing their own learning of the subject matter at the same time; they would also be learning how to teach and to lead others; and finally, they might be encouraged through their teaching activities to pursue a professional teaching career.

UTILIZING COMMUNITY HUMAN RESOURCES

The power that a community can exert over a school has been demonstrated in the many protests against schools policies which have occurred in recent years. A case in point is the controversy waged over New York City's Intermediate School 201, in which members of the community, particularly parents, expressed their deep conviction that a school must somehow belong to its own community. The breach between the community and its schools can be a serious handicap to quality education, and it is most urgent that educators find ways to reconnect the school with the community it serves.

The essential strategy, and one the educational reformer can utilize, is to *involve* the members of the community in the school process. By so doing, the school will not only reduce the obstacles it faces as a result of negative community pressures, but it can also utilize the valuable human resources which are available in the community towards its own ends. Parents, businessmen, various community leaders, and ordinary citizens comprise a fundamental source of authority and support for the school which can no longer be ignored if education is to achieve its aims. We have already mentioned the use of parents and others in the community as volunteer instructional staff, but there are many other ways in which the school can utilize these human resources.

To begin with, greater latitude for community participation in certain areas of school programing and policymaking would serve to weld the school and its community into a harmonious and mutually sustaining partnership. Such a plan would familiarize parents and other community members with school procedures and the problems school personnel must face; it would simultaneously familiarize school personnel with the main cultural values extant in the community, and the real educational needs of the community. Community participation in school planning—particularly in large school systems—may be initiated through the creation of local school boards for each district, and perhaps for each school within a district. These boards would be smaller than the overall board of education, and they would report to the citywide board, but they should have substantial autonomy in the areas of personnel recruitment and program development. They should be free, for example, to make the school as much of a community center as the community itself desires, and to decide on the kinds of educational, cultural, civic, and recreational activities such a community center would provide. These local school boards would be responsive to the community interests, and would have the right to hold their professional school staff accountable for meeting their specific educational objectives. Similarly, the higher, citywide board would hold the local board accountable for meeting the goals of public education generally. Further, through a two-way communication channel established between the higher board and the local board, the true goals of public education can be maintained as a result of greater understanding, and sectarian misuses of power can be mitigated through the systems of checks and balances maintained between the two board levels. In other words, this kind of decentralization of schools can serve as the means for creating a self-renewing school system, and for balancing an overcentralized bureaucratic system.

This school-community partnership can be strengthened through various activities which might be held at the school as *community center*. Frequent meetings of parents and other community members with teachers and school administrators would yield a mutual educational program in which laymen were informed of good instructional methods, out-of-school obstacles to pupil learning, and school financial needs; and similarly, school personnel would learn the cultural and social realities of the community. For example, if it became evident that a large number of pupils were hampered in their studies because overcrowded living space prevented adequate concentration on homework assignments, a parent-teacher committee might be formed to solicit funds for, and otherwise implement, a plan by which these pupils can be afforded adequate study space. Or, if parents objected to the white middle-class nature of some learning materials, a committee might be formed to seek out or to develop more suitable materials. Through school-community activities, local businessmen might be persuaded to make available to the school their resources and facilities in the interests of education.

There are several advantages of community involvement to the school and to the educational process generally, and the wise educator will overlook no possibility of drawing on these resources. By tapping the human resources in the community to meet specific needs as they arise in his immediate project, the educational reformer can gradually strengthen his attack on the conventional process, and as effective programs emerge, he can integrate them into his program of expanding change.

Operating strategies

Equipped with initial backing from a power source; a vehicle for implementing his "experimental" changes; means of expanding and reinforcing his financial resources and areas of change; and the human resources with which he can strengthen and enlarge his efforts; the change agent is now ready to begin his actual operations. *How* he uses these four main factors during the actual process of change, however, will be the key to the success or failure of his endeavors. His approach must be slow and yet not too slow. He must work within the status quo and the administrative machinery—and thus he must become a part of this machinery—yet he must maintain a strong degree of autonomy if he is not to be swallowed by this machinery. He must win the confidence and support of those he is attempting to change, and even of those who resist his changes; yet he must also be able to wield power and authority, even over those who are in highest command. He must achieve his own needs as indicated by his objectives, and yet without violating the needs of those who would impede his achievements. He must penetrate deeply into any one problem area, and simultaneously survey the broad area of the overall problem; yet he must be careful to conserve his own energy and personal resources. Indeed, it is the actual dynamics of change which present the greatest challenge to the change agent's imagination and skill.

CHANGE-AGENT TEAMING

For a single individual to attempt to accomplish, single-handed, the breadth and depth of the process changes herein indicated would be folly at the outset. The number of facets involved in any single problem area can be enormous, and the number of people involved and with whom the change agent must relate closely in connection with several problem areas is prohibitive to effective reform by one person. For this reason, the educational reformer must have at least one partner, equally skilled, with whom he can cooperate and collaborate. While the addition of a third or more change agents may be desirable in some cases, we shall deal here with the pair of change agents as representative of the advantages of teaming. One disadvantage of having too many change agents involved should be pointed out, however. Too many change agents can impede rather than implement change. There will be enough difficulties encountered with the formal school personnel and, in order to overcome these difficulties, the members of the change-agent team must be absolutely bound together in their objectives and in their philosophy as to how to achieve these objectives. Any lack of cooperation or presence of dissention among the change agents themselves will only lead to malcoordination of efforts, which, in turn, can lead to failure of the project.

In a paired change-agent situation, effective results can be obtained when one agent operates at the instructional level and the other at the administrative. Working together, the former relates primarily to teachers and their assistants and supervisors, while the latter deals with the school board, the superintendent, the central office, and the principal. The administrative change agent may also deal with authorities in the community and officials in the power sources which finance the project. It is the administrative change agent, therefore, who is in the position of authority, at least explicitly. It is desirable that the agents work on parallel levels with respect to one another, however, in order that the chances of reaching their common goal will not be impaired as a result of hierarchical conflicts.

The administrative change agent's visible connections with the higher powers is a significant factor in effecting change. The principal himself is more likely to listen to policies which come from the administrative change agent, for he knows that the change agent has the backing of the higher-ups. When these policies concern changes and recommendations from the teachers (inspired by the instructional change agent), the principal, not accustomed to teacher involvement in policymaking, finds himself squeezed between two forces, and he must comply. This is a signal to teachers that the plans they develop with the instructional change agent will not be lost in the usual bureaucratic red tape, and that they can count on the administrative change agent's cooperation.

The instructional change agent's role is to gear the instructional staff to change. While encouragement to participate in school planning is a favorable inducement to teachers to accommodate innovation, there are, of course, those particularly resistant teachers. Some have enjoyed a particular status of authority, tenure, and respect, and may attempt to impede change through a refusal to cooperate. In this case, directives handed down through the conventional channels—channels which these same change-resistant teachers are accustomed to obeying—serve as the power for the instructional agent.

In this way, the two change agents aid and abet one another in their respective purposes toward a common goal, the one passing downward the policies most conducive to effecting the desired changes at the instructional level, the other passing upwards the information and desired policies on which the administration decisions must be made.

CAPITALIZING ON ORGANIZATIONAL NEED

Although, presumably, the school authorities have engaged the change agents—particularly the administrative change agent—to serve a particular need, they are not likely to be receptive to the sweeping nature of the change agents' ultimate objectives. For this reason, the reformer must carefully map out his underlying strategy so that the specific problem he has been engaged to solve is dealt with to the ongoing satisfaction of the school authorities, and, at the same time, not so swiftly and effectively as to eliminate his further worth to the organization.

As mentioned earlier, if the organization has clearly recognized a need for the presence of an outside change agent, it is more likely to put aside some of its conventional procedures and to adapt where necessary in order to enable the change agent to fulfil his purpose—at least insofar as the recognized problem area is concerned. This openness can serve as the door by which the agent can get the organization to recognize additional and closely related needs. Too often those inside the educational bureacracy are oblivious to the existence of real problems because they are too close to the trees to see the forest, as it were.

When, for example, the school system is confronted with community dissatisfaction and unrest over school programing, it is up to the change agent to capitalize on this fact to gain acceptance for further reforms in the educational process. It should be stressed, however, that uppermost among the change agent's motives should be the ultimate effect of the reform upon the *learner*. To capitalize upon an organizational need and to effect changes which will meet that need is not enough, and could result merely in a game of seeking power, prestige, and status for the change agent himself.

Artful persuasion on the part of the change agent can serve to open the eyes of the school officials to other needs, and these needs, in turn, can provide the rationale for prolonging the original project. Little by little the organization's needs are expanded as a related part of the original need, and the organization becomes more and more receptive to innovation in order to meet these needs. Thus, the imaginative reformer not only gains the time he needs to implement his more sweeping changes, he also obtains the organization's permission and endorsement to deal in these wider areas and, at the same time, he has its permission and endorsement to change the very core of the process through more and wider deviations from the organization's conventional mode of operating.

TIMING STRATEGY

As implied above, the change agent is generally expected at the outset to accomplish his initial project within a given time limit. Highly aware of this deadline and its inadequacy to the real demands of the problem, the change agent may have a tendency to rush things. He may be tempted, for example, to point out additional organizational needs too early in the game, or too many at one time. To do so can elicit the administration's resistance and lack of cooperation. Nor must the change agent implement approved changes with too much rapidity. It is in the nature of human beings to resist the unknown and to cling to the known, even though the latter may be highly inadequate and self-defeating to those involved. The natural process of evolution is gradual and slow, and even relatively minor changes wrought by the educational reformer at a moderate rate can throw the organization into a state of confusion. Irreparable damage to the entire organization can be done if major changes are made too rapidly.

On the other hand, the change agent must not allow undue delays to set in, for these can be equally damaging to the process of change. Reform which is too slow in coming is likely to fail to get a good grip on the bureaucracy, and the bureaucratic machinery is likely to grind such changes as have been implemented into features which reinforce rather than weaken the conventional process.

To solve this dilemna, the change agent must be highly sensitive to his environment, taking his cues to increase or to decrease action from the response of those with whom he must deal. He must look for the most effective ways of initiating change and proceed to concentrate on these ways so that change does not proceed too slowly; yet he must recognize symptoms of stress and alter his approach when necessary, giving school personnel sufficient time to accommodate and to adjust to the changes which have been implemented.

GAINING THE CONFIDENCE OF SCHOOL PERSONNEL

Closely related to the change agent's timing strategy is the degree of confidence he engenders among those with whom he must work. Unless he plans his strategy wisely, the change agent will have two strikes against him right from the beginning; his position as an "outsider" will muster the forces of the natural ingroup against him, and his objectives to "take over" will add fuel to this resistance. For this reason, it is probably wise for the change agent to obscure his real role as reformer at the beginning, although gradual exposure of this role will inevitably occur during later stages of his involvement.

During the initial stages of the operation, the change agent should spend most of his efforts sympathetically and supportively listening to what the teachers, principals, and other school personnel *perceive* to be their needs. This strategy accomplishes two purposes at once: The change agent can diagnose the specific problems involved and, by lending a sympathetic ear, gain the confidence of the school personnel. During this phase, the change agent can relieve any impressions of his being a threat to the staff members, and gradually become more and more trusted and accepted as a member of the ingroup.

Once he has achieved this basic confidence among school personnel, the change agent should be careful not to interpret it as the signal to jump into radical forms of innovation. His first reforms should be of the most accepted and familiar variety, such as those which have received widespread publicity, and they should be chosen for their ability to relieve the needs which the school staff perceive to be greatest. For example, large classes are a common complaint of teachers, and the school administration is likely to be sympathetic to a reduction in class size, also, provided it can be accomplished with relative ease. Since the accepted way of accomplishing this reduction is to regroup pupils within a given class, the change agent should capitalize on this or a similar method as an initial step toward a more pervasive and effective means of solving this and related problems. Similarly, teachers and administrators alike are familiar with the problem of lack of teaching materials, and the change agent can solve this problem readily within the framework of meeting his larger and more encompassing process changes. The wise agent realizes that, although such solutions are superficial and yield only limited benefits to learning, these concerns are vital to teachers, administrators, and parents; and, if he can satisfy these needs, he can later ask them to consider more radical and fundamental departures from the status quo.

Thus, by meeting teachers and school officials on their own terms, the change agent can gradually win their confidence and support to expand to greater and greater degrees of deviation from the accepted norm, and to ever widen his area of refom.

EXPLICIT VS. IMPLICIT ROLES

As we have said, it is well for the change agent to conceal his true role from school personnel until he has their full confidence and support. By no means should this be construed as a cue for the change agent to *alter* his true role, but rather, that he should disguise his position in such a way that his explicit role is immediately acceptable to school personnel. This leads the change agent to assume a kind of double identity, in which he can accomplish two or more objectives simultaneously. For example, an instructional change agent might be introduced officially as a Helping Teacher. In this case, the change agent's *explicit* role might be to help teachers to acquire additional or more suitable teaching materials and equipment.

His *implicit* role, and one which he would execute in connection with his explicit duties, might be first to assess the teachers' instructional modes and their competencies, and to identify the strengths and weaknesses of the instructional process in the school as a whole. In this way, the change agent's first implicit role is that of *diagnostician,* and he would carry out his diagnostic activities by sitting in on classes, ostensibly for the purpose of evaluating what kinds of materials would be most suitable for each subject, for the particular pupils involved, and so forth.

Next—and still in the pose of one who wishes to help teachers to obtain more suitable teaching materials—the change agent may become a *teacher coordinator*. After all, it is clearly necessary that, as Helping Teacher, the change agent can be truly helpful only if he holds teacher conferences so that he can learn what sorts of materials and equipment are most needed by the teachers. Through such conferences, the change agent leads discussions and exchanges of information which cover a large area, and which help teachers to work together better, to learn how their colleagues operate in the classroom, and to acquire other information.

During these same conferences, the change agent can adroitly uncover other problem areas which have nothing to do with teaching materials. He may, for example, capitalize on teachers' complaints about class size and, in his official role of Helping Teacher, there is nothing to prevent him from providing this service in the form of reduced classes. Thus, helpful soul that he is, the change agent sets the basis for team planning. This leads him gradually to assume the *explicit* role of Team Planning Coordinator.

In the meantime, his discussions of possible teaching materials lead to problems in the curriculum, and thus, another implicit role of the change agent is to lead, very subtly at first, a program of curriculum redefinition and development. However, since reductions in class size, the institution of team planning, and curriculum planning must involve administrative decisions, still another implicit role of the instructional change agent is to develop a communications channel between teachers and the administration, and ultimately to evolve a program whereby teachers take an active part in school planning.

Throughout this same process, the change agent also serves

implicitly as a retrainer and supervisor of teachers, for in artful ways he can get teachers to realize their strengths and weaknesses, and equally artfully and subtly, makes them aware of the latest in educational theory and practice. Significantly, through his own behavior and his strategy of meeting teachers on their own terms and dealing with their reality, the change agent becomes an implicit model on which teachers may pattern their teaching behavior with respect to their pupils.

It should be noted that the effective change agent can also get others to play both implicit and explicit roles without their awareness. An immediate case in point is that of the volunteer teaching assistant recruited from the community. Under the artful leadership of the change agent, this community member, perhaps a parent, becomes the "teacher" of the professional teacher to the extent that he or she makes the latter aware of the cultural and social realities which exist in the community. The volunteer also implicitly plays the role of "pupil," to the extent that he or she becomes familiarized in child development processes, the development of learning skills, good instructional techniques, and educational problems and their solutions.

The change agent can get the school psychologist, health specialist, vocational counselor, and others in the formal system to play implicit roles, too. By involving these people in teacher meetings, the exchanges of the respective frames of references of the teachers, counselors, and others can take place with various educational benefits to all concerned, including the pupils.

BUILDING THE CHANGE AGENT'S AUTHORITY

Although it is vital in the interests of effective and enduring process change for the reformer to gain the confidence and support of school personnel, it is equally vital that he maintain his authority and power to implement change. In other words, while the change agent may disguise himself as helper and "servant" to those in the establishment, he must also appear as a reliable professional authority who knows what he is doing.

Upon initial entry, he will be known as an "expert" who was

hired by the administrative powers. As such, his authority as a professionally trained and experienced educator is reinforced by his administrative backing. While these facts enhance the change agent's power with the staff, they can, as previously indicated, work against him if he uses this power unwisely. Thus, as "helper," the change agent's authority can serve him most usefully. As he proceeds to capitalize, step by step, on the organization's needs—catering simultaneously to those which exist on the instructional and administrative levels—his effectiveness at both levels will increase his image as an authority among school personnel. For example, his effectiveness in getting the administration to recognize and to satisfy the needs of the instructional staff will enhance his authority among teachers; similarly, his effectiveness in solving problems at the instructional level will increase his image as a reliable executive among the administrators. Further, the change agent's ability to tap additional outside power sources (through parlaying procedures)—the Federal and state governments, private foundations, and businesses and industries—will add significantly to his authority and power.

The values of this authority to the change agent's endeavors can be great. The more he is seen as a reliable authority, the more likely school personnel will cooperate; the more power he is able to yield, the more drastic the changes he will be able to effect. Further, in times of duress or in special cases of resistance, the change agent may overty or subtly remind the dissenters just who the "specialist" really is. Again, however, it must be stressed that the change agent should be very careful in exploiting this power, lest it engender more, rather than less, resistance.

MAINTAINING AUTONOMY

The final point in the change agent's operating strategy is that he must be sure to maintain his autonomous position in the bureaucracy. This can be difficult, as one of his immediate strategies is to become an integral *part* of the bureaucracy. As he becomes an accepted member of the ingroup, the social pressures both within and without the immediate ingroup which serve as a cohesive force on the ingroup can affect the change agent as subtly and effectively as they have the other members of the group. Further, it is easy for the change agent gradually to assimilate the vested interests of the ingroup as his own—for example, those of the teachers with respect to the administrative echelons. Also, the change agent can, like the other members in the organization, become too close to the trees to see the forest, and therefore overlook important problems.

Thus, while his status and authority can help the change agent to maintain his autonomy, he must also be sure to maintain his objectivity throughout his relationships with the staff. He must ever bear his immediate goals in mind with the perspective provided by his intermediate and long-range goals, and he must constantly engage in a process of reevaluation, both of the situation with which he is dealing, and of himself.

The change agent's basic role is a demanding one, and his sphere of activity covers an enormous area, from obtaining the funds available from the Federal government to handling the specific problems of pupils in a single classroom in a single school —and all that lies between. In this chapter, we have attempted to point to some key strategies by which the professional educator can reach and remedy the faulty process described in previous chapters, but his success depends on how he uses these strategies; in other words, on how well he puts to practice the theoretical strategies herein outlined. In the following chapter, an actual case study of how these strategies were used in one school system is presented as a further guide to the implementation of educational process change.

CHAPTER 8

IMPLEMENTING CHANGE: A CASE STUDY

This chapter presents a case study in which several of the strategies discussed in the foregoing chapter were actually used in a more or less typical urban school system in a medium-sized city. The study is based on the authors' experience in dealing with three schools—two elementary schools and one junior high—that were rapidly developing into difficult ghetto schools; that is, they served primarily disadvantaged pupils and were afflicted with most of the problems faced by schools in large urban areas—high dropout rates, a high rate of teacher turnover and a severe shortage of qualified teachers, a strong racial imbalance, a high incidence of juvenile crime, and so on.

The situation had been identified and brought to the public's attention by a university in the city: A group from the university's sociological center had conducted an investigation of the immediate communities served by these schools, and the findings were heavily publicized through the local news media. This unfavorable publicity, and the public's response to it, caused the school system's bureaucracy to join forces with the university's school of education to plan a solution. Initially, this plan was to develop an academic enrichment program for the pupils in these three schools, and the university and the school system drafted a proposal around this theme to solicit funds from a private foundation. The state department of education was also brought in on the problem. The main power sources for the project at its outset, then, were the private foundation and the state, and the project was launched on funds provided primarily from these two sources. The vehicles for initiating change—the three "ghetto" schools—were developed through an organizational need on the part of the city's educational bureaucracy.

A change agent—a professionally trained and experienced educator—was brought in for the express purpose of initiating and administering the educational enrichment program. While this program was conceived to be mainly a supplementary program with many compensatory features, it soon became clear to this change agent that if the immediate problems connected with educational disadvantage were to be remedied, a basic change in the regular school process was required. Of course, the extent

Hays, Monkmeyer

IMPLEMENTING CHANGE: A CASE STUDY

to which the change agent's efforts would ultimately be applied would not have been well received by the bureaucracy at this point; nevertheless, having recognized that relatively drastic measures would be needed to upgrade these problem schools, the school officials were receptive to a fairly wide range of experimentation, insofar as the enrichment program was concerned. The change agent thus began to plan in his own mind a broad overall strategy that would capitalize on this receptivity and flexibility.

The change agent's primary contacts were the school board, the superintendent of schools, the central office, and the principals of each of the three schools, however, leaving the change agent little time or opportunity to relate to the *teachers*. To be sure, a great deal of organizational change might occur as a result of his efforts with these administrative staff members, but this change would flow from top down, and would fail to get at the root of the problem at the instructional level. The change agent recognized that, if the real educational needs of the disadvantaged pupils were to be met, administrative policies would have to be based on a full understanding of these needs. Because teachers are the closest to pupil reality, some means for an upward flow of communication from the instructional to the administrative level would have to be established. In addition, if administrative policies which concern instructional activities were to be integrated into daily teaching practice, supervisory follow-through would be necessary. Certainly the change agent could not accomplish this follow-through in addition to his efforts with administrative personnel, and even the school principal, over whom the change agent had line authority, would not have the time to supervise the teachers' daily activities with the pupils. Thus, the need for a change agent to work with the teachers was indicated.

This is where the notion of double teaming entered into the situation, and another professionally trained educator was recruited and introduced officially as a Curriculum and After-School Activities Coordinator. This second change agent's duties were to help implement the educational enrichment program; but, as a part of these duties, he was to relate to the regular school teachers to learn from them the pupils' needs and how the enrichment program might be coordinated with their daily school program. At the same time, he was tactfully to involve the teachers in the search for an improved instructional process.

Through this teaming, the change agents were afforded maximum confrontation with the two main levels of the educational hierarchy. The administrative agent, to whom we shall refer as Agent A, and the instructional agent (Agent B) worked closely together—and on parallel levels with respect to one another—toward common objectives. Each also worked closely with the school staff members at his own level of operation. Agent A addressed his recommendations to the school board, relating these recommendations to the needs of the three schools as the board members perceived them. The backing he received from the school board increased his authority with the school superintendent, who then also endorsed his recommendations. When the recommendations were passed to the school principal, they carried much more weight than they would have otherwise. Meanwhile, Agent B worked solely with the teachers, learning the specific needs which could be met only with administrative cooperation. This information was passed upwards from Agent B to Agent A. The latter thus devoted his efforts to preparing the principals and the higher officials for changes he knew would be forthcoming from the instructional level, while the former devoted his efforts to preparing the teachers for changes he knew would be forthcoming from the administration. This "split-level" approach increased the speed with which changes were made, and served also to accomplish behavioral as well as organizational changes. Further, Agent B was in a position to see to it that more policies could be generated by the teachers, while Agent A was in a position to see that these policies were actually accepted by the higher authorities.

Creating an atmosphere of change

The first step toward achieving specific and far-reaching changes in the core process was to create an atmosphere of change. Ever since the university's sociological center had published the findings of its study, these schools and their communities had received widespread attention, and even early plans for the project had been published. One of the earliest measures undertaken on behalf of the project, therefore, was the exploitation of this news coverage to increase community support and to build an atmosphere of change. Capitalizing on the assumption that the community expected action rather than talk, the change agents kept the news media abreast of every phase of the project. Community involvement, therefore, was among the first objectives sought by the change agents, and this involvement served to lay the foundations for effecting an array of further reforms.

Since the project was known essentially as an educational enrichment program, there was a need for volunteer tutors to execute the program. In terms of the traditional status quo, this was a dramatic departure from accustomed organizational procedure, which permitted only accredited teachers to take any part in the public-school system's instructional programs. The volunteer tutoring program was accepted by the bureaucracy, however, for it was shown that, by tapping the human resources in the community, the project could gain the benefits of the valuable skills that existed among lay persons at no cost to the school system. The administrative agent assumed a major role in talking with various community groups—such as the Rotary Club and other businessmen's groups, church groups, parents' associations, and many others—about the need for volunteers and other aspects of the project. This speaking tour—and the publicity it received—helped to recruit a good many of the volunteer tutors and, at the same time, sustained community interest in the project—paving the way, also, for the acceptance of future innovations.

A school volunteer board which represented a cross section of the community power structure was quickly organized. It should be noted that this board was composed mainly of women, the wives of influential men in the community. Their responsibility was to form a partnership with the regular staff of the project schools, and to work with them to develop creative programs which could be used in the regular classrooms as well as during the after-school program. The involvement of the female power group served to elicit additional public support, and enthusiasm for and response to the program soon pervaded the entire city. This school volunteer board also kept the city's board of education and the central office up to date with progress reports of the project. Agent B's explicit duties were to work with this volunteer board and to supervise and to coordinate the volunteer tutoring staff, as well as to coordinate the supplementary instructional program with the regular instructional program. Tutoring and other clinical programs were initiated in a matter of weeks, and soon the enrichment program had become a part of the atmosphere of change without imposing a threat upon the regular school staff.

Among the innovations approved by the school board was the renovation of the school buildings. The libraries and the cafeterias were redecorated, and huge bulletin boards were constructed, painted, and installed within the first two weeks of school. The bulletin boards were kept up to date with newspaper reports, progress reports, and other publicity the project received. Huge photographs of the pupils in the schools dominated these display materials no matter what particular theme was being focused upon at any given point. While, certainly, such "innovations" are wholly spurious insofar as the educational process itself is concerned, they had the effect of building the morale and sense of importance among the pupils, parents, teachers, and other school officials connected with the project; they also created an atmosphere in which specific process changes might be accepted more readily and even eagerly by school personnel.

Meanwhile, Agent A continued his community speaking tour, and held frequent personal conferences with the mayor, various county and state officials, bank presidents, and other important persons. Most of these efforts were reported in the news media. A photographer was hired to take "before and after" photographs of the project schools, and these pictures were posted on the schools' bulletin boards as well as in the local news media. Later they were made into a slide presentation given before a public meeting of the school board, and made available also to other interested groups in the community. The aggregate effect of this widespread publicity was manifold: (1) It created a spirit of constructive reform in the community and sustained community support; (2) it developed an increasingly favorable disposition among school authorities to accept new areas of change; (3) it created a receptive attitude among teachers toward instructional changes; and (4) it enhanced the pupils' self-esteem.

The objectives of process change

The explicit goals of the educational enrichment program, as recognized and agreed upon by the public-school system and its personnel, were to increase the educational achievement levels of the pupils, reduce school dropout, lower the juvenile crime rate, and generally improve the overall conditions in the school. The general assumption underlying these objectives was that the pupils faced too many out-of-school cultural obstacles for the standard school process to cope with successfully and, thus, special supplementary instruction was necessary if these cultural obstacles were to be overcome for the benefit of pupil, school, and society.

Both change agents agreed, however, that if this educational enrichment program was to succeed in its objectives, the regular school process would have to be improved. It would be of little value to gain the pupils' interested participation in learning through the supplementary enrichment program if, during their regular classes, they were exposed to the tedious and sterile process that had failed to capture their attention and participation in the first place. Therefore, the regular school process would, at the very minimum, have to be integrated with the enrichment program. Yet if this integration were successfully achieved, the regular process itself would be educationally enriching, and ultimately there should be no need for a separate and supplementary enrichment program. To make the standard school process an enriching one in its own right, then, became the ultimate goal of the change agents; their explicit objective of fulfilling the requirements outlined in the original proposal for the project became merely the means by which the change agents could achieve this ultimate but implicit goal.

In order to reach this long-range goal, however, the change agents first would have to enmesh the regular process with the supplementary one, so that the positive effects of the latter would not offset the negative effects of the former. The main target of any change, therefore, was to reorient the regular teachers to examining and improving their own behavior, and to adapting the currriculum and instructional materials to meet realistically the individual needs of their pupils. In the conventional bureaucratic structure, there were serious obstacles in the way of this target and, thus, major organizational and behavioral changes would have to occur at the administrative level, as well.

Clearly, the change agents had to devise a means of communicating with the regular school staff, both teachers and principals. This was no easy matter; each teacher operated in the self-contained world of his or her classroom and had little opportunity to relate to others on the school staff. Instructional policy was fed from the central administration through the principal to individual teachers, but what actually occurred in the classroom was a private matter. There was virtually no way for teachers to share their classroom problems, methods of teaching, and other instructional matters. Of course the usual shop talk occurred from time to time in the hallways, lunchrooms, and teachers' lounges, but this contact was superficial, inconsistent, and, as a rule, not very constructive; the main content centered about the teachers' private grievances and complaints, rather than providing a genuine cross-pollination of classroom techniques. Principals, too, operated in relative isolation; policy directives concerning administrative and instructional matters were passed down to them from above, and each principal merely passed any relevant information on to the teachers. Rarely did individual school principals confer with one another to share their methods of administering their buildings, their methods of managing clerical and instructional staff, the teacher complaints and suggestions to which they were exposed, and other common concerns.

This isolation of principals and teachers from one another led to a good many of the schools' problems, but it also made the change agents' contact with them extremely difficult. Neither of the change agents had the time to contact each member of each school staff individually, and had they attempted to do so, it would have made the process of change exceedingly inefficient. Furthermore, the teachers' and principals' own work schedules were so overloaded with sundry tasks that even individual contact was impossible.

The obvious solution was to gather all the teachers or principals together at one time and in one place, and to do so frequently and with regularity. Such a procedure would not only afford the change agents an expedient means of communicating with the teachers or principals—ostensibly for the purpose of learning how best to operate the enrichment program so that it would be coordinated with the regular school process—but it would also yield the benefits of cross-pollination of ideas to the regular school process itself. Common problems that had heretofore remained hidden could be aired and recognized by all, whereupon steps could be taken to remedy them. Individual areas of strength or weakness could be exchanged for the edification and improved functioning of all concerned. Such meetings could also be used as team planning sessions where all in attendance could participate in the coordination of the supplementary program, and, implicitly, in the process of changing the faulty school procedures.

Team planning, then, became an even shorter-range goal of the change agents. Agent A would work with the planning team of the principals of the project schools while Agent B would work with the teachers' planning team; in this way, team planning would become the means for reaching the explicit objective of having the school implement the requirements of the enrichment and compensatory proposal, while, at the same time, implicitly changing the regular school process to become enriching.

Achieving process change

At first these team planning sessions were conducted with the teachers, and during after-school hours in direct relation to the educational enrichment program. However, teachers resented this infringement on their own time after their busy day. The problems which this resentment posed to the success of the project served as the organizational need for instituting released time for teachers' meetings. Both change agents agreed that such released time should be built into the daily school schedule, and Agent A then confronted the administration with the proposal. He demonstrated that, in light of the severity of the educational problems faced by the school, it was imperative that teachers be provided with a convenient time during their normal work day to exchange information and to plan together. This would afford teachers the opportunity for adapting the school curriculum to the needs and interests of the pupil population and, at the same time, provide a way of utilizing the strength of individual teachers as a common resource to teachers and volunteer tutors alike.

The administration found no objection to this theory, but when it was brought to the principals of each school, concern was expressed as to how it could be implemented. The schedules were already too tight as they were, and to add regular teachers' meetings to them would seem to be out of the question. Both change agents then proceeded to meet with the principal of each school to go over the school's schedule. In each case, it was shown to the principal just how, by shifting activities, released teacher time could be made possible.

Before these new schedules became final, however, the faculties of each of the schools were assembled and given the educational rationale for team planning as well as a preview of what a specific team planning schedule might look like. It was demonstrated to them that such sessions would actually involve them in the school planning process, and this promise was reinforced as the administrative change agent actually called for their suggestions and criticisms concerning the new schedule. Until now, the teachers had never been involved in any scheduling decisions, and the fact that their suggestions and criticisms were incorporated at this meeting was visible proof of how team planning sessions might work for them. There was, of course, the additional appeal of being released from teaching time each day, and thus the new idea was heartily accepted by the teachers despite its radical departure from established convention.

Shortly thereafter, Agent A established weekly team planning sessions with the schools' principals. These meetings were rotated by school, and paralleled the teachers' team planning periods. The principals had been virtually forced into accepting the released time for teachers' planning sessions, as they had been pressured from both above and below, and since it had been shown that their only reason for objecting could be overcome, they had little choice in the matter. But when it was shown to them also that they could afford some of their own normal work week for similar meetings, any misgivings they might have felt over the teachers' meetings soon gave way. The principals were encouraged to see themselves as climate setters rather than as harried managers, and to help establish an atmosphere of experimentation and innovation in their schools. Thus, with team planning sessions initiated as an integral part of the daily school routine, the main route toward effecting core process changes had been paved.

CONTACT STRATEGIES WITH TEACHERS

As the Curriculum and After-School Activities Coordinator, Agent B's explicit task was to coordinate and implement the after-school activities as well as to provide instructional aid. An important aspect of this task was to confer with the regular teachers in order to learn pupil needs, the modes of instruction pupils were typically exposed to, and so forth, ostensibly for the purpose of supplementing the regular process, rather than of changing it. Agent B's role during the first half of the first year, therefore, was essentially that of sympathetic listener. As such, of course, Agent B gained a great deal more information about the needs of *teachers* than about the needs of pupils, for teachers soon began to come to him with their annoyances and dissatisfactions about administrative and other obstacles to their work. When he was specifically asked for help, or when a particular need area became obvious, he could provide this help, and so increased the teachers' confidence in him.

For example, it became clear during early team planning sessions that a common complaint of teachers centered about the fact that they could not obtain suitable instructional materials. Agent B asked them to list those materials which they had never been able to get before, and their suggestions were acquired with lightning speed for dramatic impact. Rarely had teachers been asked what they wanted, and even when they requested certain materials or equipment, the lumbering wheels of the bureaucracy had made the process of acquisition so difficult and time-consuming, that the element of immediate reinforcement had been lost; they felt that the granting of their requests by the administration was virtually impossible. Therefore, when their suggested materials were actually delivered to them without delay, the teachers came to trust Agent B and his connections with the higher-ups as a means for getting their own needs met. More and more he became their confidant and guidance counsellor. His obvious part in gaining released time for team planning sessions served to make them even more receptive to Agent B's helpful advice.

The administrative change agent's obvious power and authority, and the instructional change agent's visibly close association with him, were thus used to increase teachers' confidence in both change agents and the reforms they initiated. The atmosphere of constructive change that had been created throughout the project so far was reinforced at their faculty meetings, where the teachers themselves indicated the areas they wished to see changed.

Agent A attended some of these meetings and stressed the need for professionalism among the teachers. Until this time, the teachers' feelings of professional worth had been extremely low, for they had come to assess their professional worth in terms of the extremely poor image which the ghetto schools had suffered prior to the launching of the project. The project schools had been consistently avoided by teaching applicants, and those on the staff awaited only a reasonable opportunity to leave. As a result of the overwhelming amount of favorable publicity that had accrued to the project since its beginning, however, the image of these schools had altered considerably for the better. Agent A pointed this out at the faculty meetings, emphasizing that by the middle of the first year there would be a waiting list of teachers trying to get jobs in the project. Thus, a sort of reverse psychology was applied; the teachers in the problem schools began to think of themselves as truly professional.

Meanwhile, in an attempt to offset the grave shortage of teachers and the high rate of teacher turnover in the ghetto schools, Agent A had initiated an appeal to all teacher-training institutions in the state, using the theme "Wanted: A New Breed of Teachers." As a result of this campaign and the widespread publicity given to the entire project, the waiting list of teachers actually materialized and created a strong competition for hiring. This turn of events enhanced further the feelings of professional worth and new-found prestige among the existing project teachers.

The net effect of these various reinforcing tactics was to heighten teachers' receptivity and even enthusiasm to changes in their accustomed status quo. The fact that the administrative agent had power and authority *and* was on *their* side put them at considerable ease. The fact that the instructional change agent was trusted friend and confidant *and* could get their needs met by the higher echelons raised their confidence even more. And their new-found feelings of professional status and self-esteem elevated their morale and spirit of cooperation still further. Thus, when, at some of the faculty meetings, Agent A pointed out that their full professional cooperation in carrying out their regular instructional activities was needed if the enrichment program was to succeed, the teachers were eager to help. These rallying talks by Agent A also elicited the teachers' help in guiding and training the volunteer tutors, who by this time had begun to help out during the normal school day, as well as in the after-school tutoring program.

Thus far we have discussed primarily organizational or structural changes. To renovate the physical plant of the school and otherwise to create an atmosphere of change, and to revise the daily school schedule, do not automatically lead to the behavioral changes which are necessary if true process change is to be effected. Most of the main difficulties which lead to educational disadvantage lie at the instructional level, and only by changing the orientation and teaching behavior of individual teachers can true process change come about. Of course, such behavioral change in teachers cannot come about without similar behavioral change among those in the higher echelons of the school network, and organizational and structural changes do serve to open up much of the closed and rigid bureaucracy. Nevertheless, providing teachers with time to meet and to plan together does not necessarily mean that they will easily transfer to a cooperative view of planning; nor does bolstering their professional self-image mean that they will automatically respond favorably to new ways of relating to their pupils. To encourage them to do so, a new role was needed, that of Instructional Leader, under whose supervision teachers could be retrained for and reoriented to a new educational process.

Agent B, of course, undertook the playing of this role as his major responsibility. At first this role was implicit, and during his team meetings he artfully raised key questions that were aimed at revealing problem areas. As the discussion proceeded, he offered suggestions which not only guided the direction of the discussion and prevented it from degenerating into an aimless conversation, but also cued the team members' thinking about what and how they were teaching. As a materials coordinator, he kept in contact with educational publishers and manufacturers, and ordered relevant instructional aids, keeping materials and equipment readily accessible to teachers. In demonstrating the value and uses of these materials, he was able subtly to reveal new teaching behaviors and attitudes as well. As a professionally trained educator, he was able to keep the team informed of the latest in educational developments and theory wherever relevant, and often introduced some of his own instructional ideas for the team to evaluate, and to use where applicable.

A particularly useful contact strategy for achieving behavioral change was for the change agent to express doubt about the techniques he had been suggesting. Periodically and with a certain suddenness, Agent B would ask something to the effect of "Is the nongraded approach really that good?" This unexpected and apparently earnest about-face caused most of the teachers to argue for the idea that the agent himself had introduced. This approach not only had the effect of reinforcing the particular teaching technique in the teacher's own mind and behavior, it also afforded the change agent an opportunity to see how well the teachers had internalized these ideas. Thus, in his implicit role as instructional leader, Agent B gradually and effectively altered the teaching environment and stimulated teachers to search for more meaningful ways of performing in the classroom, all the while maintaining and building the teachers' confidence and trust.

Gradually, however, this implicit role became more and more explicit, and Agent B began to act as a kind of demonstration or model teacher, taking over class instruction in certain areas to illustrate formally some new approaches and techniques for the teachers. As he became established as coordinator and supervisor of in-service training, he helped to set up in-service workshops, arranging for special consultants and other professional resource people to fill gaps in the abilities which existed in each of the teaching teams. As liaison between the instructional and the administrative levels, Agent B kept the administration informed as to how the instructional program was developing, and provided feedback to the principal as to the teachers' specific needs. Now known as the Instructional Specialist, Agent B had less and less need to resort to calling upon Agent A for administrative backing, and where the principal's endorsement was required for a certain innovation, he would consult directly with the principal. For example, if the teachers wished to experiment with new pupil groupings, the Instructional Specialist would try to work this out with the principal.

CONTACT STRATEGIES WITH THE HIGHER ADMINISTRATION

Because it was from the upper echelons of the administration that the change agents derived most of their power and authority, it was essential that the board members and their administrative personnel be dealt with in such a way as to maintain their support. Without the board's strong support, it would have been difficult to maintain locomotion.

The main strategy used in dealing with the board was based on its expectations of the project. Since it had been unfavorable publicity which had led to the creation of the project in the first place, achieving and maintaining favorable publicity was one important aspect of this strategy. As previously noted, photographs and slides were taken showing every important phase of the project, including pictures of the renovated buildings, of meetings with various community groups and civic and business leaders, of pupils and volunteer staff, and so forth. These appeared constantly in the local press, and good radio and TV coverage of the project was also maintained. In fact, a few outside observers criticized the project for being overpublicized. However, the strong community support gained through the efforts of the school volunteer board and of the administrative change agent also kept the board's satisfaction at a high level.

At the first public meeting of the board, Agent A gave a carefully planned and dramatic slide presentation which yielded a clear and concise picture of the entire project. The presentation conveyed, with a dynamism of purpose and direction, that the project had been successfully launched, that the board's financial investment appeared to be sound, and that the public seemed to be favorably impressed with the project. After the presentation, several of the board members commented enthusiastically about the project, and the fact that the superintendent observed these reactions reinforced Agent A's position with the superintendent as well as with the board. Agent A had arranged to have an extensive turnout for the meeting, and the fact that the presentation had been so well attended also lent strength to the future of the project. Furthermore, the news media published the proceedings, and the favorable publicity sustained for several weeks thereafter. Indeed, there was a large demand among other interested groups to be given the slide presentation, and this demand, in addition to maintaining the support of the educational administration, served also to sustain community support and aid for the project.

Once the initial progress had been demonstrated, however, means for continuing the board's interest and cooperation had to be devised. Again, favorable publicity was bound to keep the project visible, but if possible this visibility should occur on national as well as on the local level. Both change agents participated in national conferences which were also publicized, and this produced another kind of authoritative leverage. The superintendent became aware of the national reputation the local project was receiving and reported this at several board meetings. The change agents' own contacts with various nationally prominent agencies also reinforced their authority with the higher administration.

A particularly fortuitous situation existed in this school system which Agent A was able to exploit as a strategy for dealing with the higher echelons. The superintendent of schools had left and, before another could be hired, a man was appointed to act as a temporary superintendent. Seizing his opportunity, the administrative change agent moved in quickly, and offered the acting superintendent the benefits of his outside perspective. The acting superintendent began to lean on Agent A for counsel on various school problems that exceeded the boundaries of the project schools. This alliance not only served to reinforce the direct line of communication between Agent B at the instructional level of the project schools and the central administration, it also paved the way for expanding the base of process change to include other schools.

Agent A's frequent and direct personal contact with the board members and with the superintendent created in these people the image that he was a reliable and effective executive in whose hands the project, and all that was associated with it, was secure. This proximity to the higher administration was another strategy used to sustain its support. This proximity served to strengthen the personal ties between change agent and the educational administrators, and the bureaucracy's recognition of other areas of organizational need (e.g., racial imbalance, teacher shortage and turnover, etc.) and acceptance of remedial innovations were more likely to be forthcoming through this personal contact than it would have been had Agent A devoted most of his efforts to the principals and the central office. Such personal contact created the impression that the administrators still had an important say in what was going on in the project schools, and that in no way had their control been usurped. Of course this proximity with the upper echelons of the bureaucracy also communicated to those at the lower levels that Agent A was an integral part of the top level of the hierarchy.

CONTACT STRATEGIES WITH THE PRINCIPALS

In continuously reinforcing his position among those highest in the educational bureaucracy, Agent A's authority with the individual school principals became less and less questionable, and, as Agent B simultaneously strengthened his position among teachers and increasingly involved them in school decisionmaking, the principal found himself more and more squeezed between two forces. For example, fairly early in the change process, Agent B developed with a team of teachers the idea of continuous diagnosis of pupil strengths and weaknesses, and of grouping and regrouping them periodically among the teaching-team members for work on specific skill weaknesses. While the teachers responded favorably to this idea, they expressed some doubts about administrative permission to implement the notion. Agent B contacted Agent A to discuss the validity of such a practice and, assured of its merits, Agent A once again asked the superintendent of schools if, in these experimental project schools, they were really free to experiment. Of course, the superintendent agreed, and both change agents subsequently converged upon the principal with the idea. At this point, the principal found himself sandwiched, and he had no reason *not* to cooperate. Thus, this double teaming of change agents was one of the early strategies employed by the change agents in dealing with the principals of the project schools.

This sort of squeeze play is effective only in achieving *organizational* change, however; to achieve true and enduring *process* change it was necessary to change the principals' orientation and behavioral role. The accustomed role of the principals was that of manager of the status quo, and they were firmly oriented to the traditional process. In order to change this role to one of administrative innovator and to orient the principals to experimentation—indeed, merely to break down the principals' resistance to innovation and experimentation—Agent A had to deal with their needs as *they* perceived them.

Winning the support of the principals was especially important in the initial stages of the project, because the principals were actually spokesmen for the established bureaucracy. As "outsiders" invading the sanctity of the organization, the change agents needed to have "insiders" on their side. They especially needed to gain support of certain *key* insiders—those whose words carried weight. One principal became a particular help and provided the link to the formal school organization, softening the overall resistance of her school to the efforts of the change agents.

Again, it was a question first of gaining the confidence of the principals, and this had to be done as quickly as possible. As Agent B had produced with dramatic rapidity novel instructional materials for his teachers, so Agent A began by asking the principals what services they had always wanted but had never received. With some pessimism, the principals said that they wished for an extra secretary, a reading teacher, a family worker, or similar additions to the staff. These were immediately provided to the amazed delight of the principals. While these services were merely additive and in the realm of purely organizational change, they served to gratify the principals because these were the sort of "innovations" which were most familiar to them. Thus, in accommodating their wishes, Agent A was able to gain the principals' confidence and, at the same time, add something to the atmosphere of change as it affected the principals.

Actually, in this particular strategy, there was another ingredient for effecting behavioral change, although it was hidden from the principals who requested the additional staff. Both change agents would interact with the new personnel, and since new staff members were not an entrenched part of the school bureaucracy, it was easier to change *their* behavioral roles on behalf of the core process change. In a hidden sense, therefore, these new school employees became change agents also. For example, disguised as Family Worker to the regular school staff, and to herself as well, this new staff member quickly became a part of the in-service training program for both teacher and principal.

Because every individual has a complex of emotional needs, a large part of the administrative change agent's contact strategy with the principals was to identify the most obvious of their emotional needs, and then to proceed to capitalize on it. For example, one principal—a woman—felt very protective and "motherly" toward her school domain and all it contained. Agent A exploited this trait by couching his suggestions with something like, "I have a problem and I need your advice," or "Some of the observations you have been making are now being realized, so I would like to share them with you." Another method was to build on the principal's sense of professional worth: "In your absence, we made certain decisions, and I took the liberty of saying that you [the principal] are a professional person who would endorse these ideas because they are educationally sound," or, "I feel certain that these programs will have your full professional support, as you are fully familiar with their excellent educational promise." Thus, by attributing to the principals a familiarity with sound educational policy, Agent A was able to bring the principals up to date with what actually *was* sound educational policy, and at the same time to soften the severity of the particular change being wrought. Another effect of this strategy was to create in the principals a sense of their own professional worth and a confidence in the change agents.

Status was another emotional need that was utilized by Agent A in his dealings with the principals. Whenever possible, the principals were invited to participate in "status meetings." These included not only top-level school-system officials, but also prominent community and university leaders. This strategy served to instill in the principals a feeling that they belonged in the upper echelons of the educational establishment, and that they were an integral part of top-level policymaking. As a result, they offered less resistance to new proposals.

In addition to including them in these "status meetings," Agent A used the principals' own team planning sessions to reinforce their sense of status. For example, at an appropriate point during such a meeting, he would say, "So important is your role in this project, that without your help there could be no project," or, "A school could have the best teachers in the world but, if it had a poor principal, it would not be a good school; on the other hand, with a good principal leading only average teachers, a good school can result."

These team planning sessions had to be reinforced with frequent individual contacts, during which these kinds of personal diplomacy were used and adapted to the individual's particular emotional needs. Of major importance in this regard was Agent A's ability to diagnose and to utilize these emotional needs.

PERSONNEL PROBLEMS

It should be noted at this point that the process of change is never an entirely smooth one, and no matter how carefully strategies are planned in advance, there are always unexpected situations and problems which arise. These must be handled on the spot or dealt with in one way or another as well as possible with the overall objectives of the process in mind. Inevitably, there are personnel problems which cannot be solved with the foregoing strategies. This was certainly true in these three project schools.

One such problem involved the incompetent members of the school staff. Every school has its share of these, and in most urban schools, where scarcity and turnover of teachers are severe, the principal must live with the problem. Many of the most incompetent teachers thus build up tenure, and become firmly rooted in the school structure. Another problem group was composed of those who were fairly competent when judged by traditional standards, but who put up great resistance to change. These two groups posed difficulties for the change agents, and there was little they could do to remove them. Certainly it was very difficult for the principal to discharge these people.

Nevertheless, when the change agents entered the scene, a new climate was generated, and the accustomed routine on which the school staff had come to depend, despite all of its problems, was splintered. Cumbersome, burdensome, yet comfortable schedules gave way to radically new ones; informal coffee klatches were replaced by formal team meetings; and individual teachers' safe and private classroom worlds were invaded by teaching teams, volunteer teachers, and in-service instructional specialists. Subject supervisors, whose authority and domain had been inviolate, became subordinates of instructional specialists along with even the newest and least experienced teachers. As a result of all this upheaval, only the most flexible could endure the momentum; those who were the least flexible or the least competent found themselves unable to adapt and became very unhappy. Many threatened to resign, and meeting no resistance to their threats, they did; others left readily upon gentle encouragement. This loss of staff was soon recovered with replacements from among the most highly qualified of the applicants on the waiting list referred to earlier. Thus, by initiating a new environment, most of the incompetent and inflexible people were forced out through their own volition, and a sort of natural environmental selection of personnel occurred.

There is, however, a serious liability associated with rapid and drastic change. While the aim of the change agents was to utilize as much of the existing staff as possible to build momentum for the change, some were unavoidably neglected. In this project, it was the system's subject supervisors. Situated in the central office, these people had enjoyed total rule in their domains. As the teachers in each school became involved in curriculum planning, the subject supervisors' realms were obviously invaded. The change agents took the calculated risk of not involving them in the many ideas that were being developed, and administrative approval for implementing these ideas at the instructional level was gained directly through the superintendent and the principal. In going over the subject supervisors' heads, the change agents naturally incurred their alienation and criticism. Since the change agents had the endorsement of the higher authorities, these negative repercussions did not impede progress.

The change agents also encountered problems with their own project staff, the members of which had been hired to assist with the in-service training of the regular school teachers. Because this staff was composed of top professionals in different disciplines—an audiovisual specialist, a psychologist, a sociologist, a psychiatric social worker, and others—it was felt that it could work autonomously with the teacher teams, and without guidance from the change agents. These staff members were told at the outset that they would have to develop their own roles and positions in the change process in the severely confused state of affairs that the rapid change had wrought and, at the same time, they would have to help further this change process. The professionals responded heartily to this challenge and became thoroughly involved in their own staff meetings.

Unfortunately, in the process of clarifying one another's frames of reference, discussing the multitude of problems, and analyzing them, these professionals got themselves bogged down in a great deal of academic theory and sheer verbalization, at the great expense of concrete application of their knowledge. Consequently, they failed to carve out any substantive roles for themselves, and merely added to the confusion that prevailed. The community and the school board had high expectations for immediate action in the project, rather than mere theoretical verbalization—an expectation which had been encouraged in other aspects of the project. For this reason, and because the real goals of the project were being impeded, the change agents decided to step in. The number of meetings with these professionals was reduced, and each professional was dealt with individually by the agents in an attempt to develop with him a concrete role and operating direction. This jump from complete autonomy to a supervised state, and from group involvement to individual treatment, caused a great deal of resentment among the professionals.

This new approach was maintained, nevertheless, and gradually most of the professionals became much more satisfied as they acquired a clearly delineated area of responsibility and purpose. As a result of these problems, however, the change agents concluded that it cannot be assumed that such professionals are necessarily change- or action-oriented, when they are inexperienced in school settings. More likely, they have become more dependent on their specialized theory than on practice in the real and unpredictable circumstances which arise in the school. To avoid this sort of problem, it was decided that, in the future, the project should be staffed first with graduate assistants in these fields who are not likely to be as status oriented, and who are more likely to draw on their theoretical knowledge insofar as it applies to reality. Only a few full professionals should be brought in at first, and only when the new structure and process have emerged and become relatively stable should others be hired.

Expanding the base of change

The original project had been conceived as a relatively small-scale enrichment and compensatory program for the disadvantaged pupils in three particularly problematic schools; moreover, the project had been scheduled for successful completion in three years.

As already stated, the change agents realized from the beginning that the success of this specific plan could come about only if the basic educational process in these schools was revised. The difficulties these schools had been facing went far beyond the low educational achievement and high crime rate of their pupils; racial imbalance, teacher shortage and turnover, and inadequacy of teaching and curriculum were the core problems, and all of these involved the regular process. Thus, for a number of vital reasons, the change agents had to move from the enrichment program, for which they were explicitly responsible, into the regular program. It was essential that they become an integral part of this regular program, and quickly, for three years is hardly sufficient time to overhaul a fully established system.

By continually exposing and exploiting new organizational needs which were directly related to those already recognized and accepted by the educational administration, the change agents were able to infiltrate the standard process and widen the sphere of change insofar as these three schools were concerned. By the end of the first year of the project, the change agents had not only fully set up the after-school tutorial program, but had also involved the volunteers in the daytime program, established new school schedules, set up experimental teaching teams which utilized several nongraded approaches, instituted team planning among teachers and principals, initiated a revised curriculum, and started in-service training of both teachers and principals. In addition, the shortage of teachers and the high rate of teacher turnover had been reversed through the use of volunteer staff and as a result of the campaign to attract accredited teacher applicants.

Access to additional schools began when the educational administration was confronted with high teacher turnover in some other schools in the system. Agent A seized this opportunity to begin negotiations with the dean of the university's school of education and a private foundation to sponsor a joint research and action program for preservice teacher training. The result was a foundation grant of some $400,000 for urban teacher preparation. The plan was to provide a real clinical setting for student teachers and, at the same time, provide the schools with badly needed teachers at very little cost to the school system. The plan also called for professors of education from the college to spend a good portion of their time guiding and supervising their students right in the school setting. Simultaneously, of course, this provided the schools with an in-service training program for their existing teaching staff. Having initiated this program through his packaging strategy, Agent A would, of course, be integrally involved in its implementation, as would his colleague Agent B.

One of the most significant problems which remained in the

original project schools, however, was the racial imbalance that existed. The neighborhoods served by these schools were very unhappy about this state of affairs, as was much of the larger community; yet within the scope of the project thus far, there was little that could be done to remedy this situation. The solution to this problem would have to involve additional schools.

An explicit approach to the racial situation started with Agent A's collaboration with another department in the university, one which was devoted to researching the problems and behavior of youth. Together, Agent A and officials from this special department drafted a proposal for the National Institute of Mental Health which was aimed at obtaining a grant to be used to demonstrate and to study the effects of desegregation. The U.S. Office of Education was also approached and a grant was obtained.

The parlaying strategies employed up to this time had evolved from the grants obtained for the original three-school project, and that obtained for the Urban Teacher Preparation Program. This latest power backing for desegregation was then added to the change agents' credit rating to gain still additional funds from various other agencies. The state department of education, the county mental health department, the President's Committee on Delinquency and Youth Crime, and the Mayor's Commission for Youth were among those solicited for funds and endorsement for a variety of programs related to racial imbalance in the schools and to education generally—emotional disturbance among pupils, delinquency and juvenile crime, school dropout, educational deprivation and underachievement, and so forth.

The interrelationships among these programs, together with their apparent outgrowth from and dependence upon the original project, gave rise to a major administrative reorganization of the educational bureaucracy. This reorganization strengthened the roles of both change agents within the administration, and the original project was officially recognized as a laboratory and demonstration model for expanding the project. Agent A used his reinforced position within the administration to request that he be placed in charge of the entire scope of the multifaceted program, in which the additional schools and funded programs would be included. The superintendent approved all the conditions, and Agent A became officially known as Staff Director of Special Projects.

Having thus established a firm position within the bureaucracy, Agent A proceeded to identify key personnel, in addition to Agent B, on whom he could rely to mobilize change in the expanded framework. He then placed these people in strategic places within this expanded framework. Agent B was positioned so that he could coordinate the efforts of these people and train them to take over his role as instructional change agent; in other words, his new job was to work less with teachers and more with leaders of teachers.

By the time the change agents had trained a sufficient number of people to start planning for their own retirement from the project, the process of change had encompassed eight schools in the system, and had achieved both organizational and behavioral changes in the core educational process. New curricula, new arrangements of both teachers and pupils, new methods of teaching, and new kinds of personnel—for example, volunteer teachers from the community, professional consultants, business-

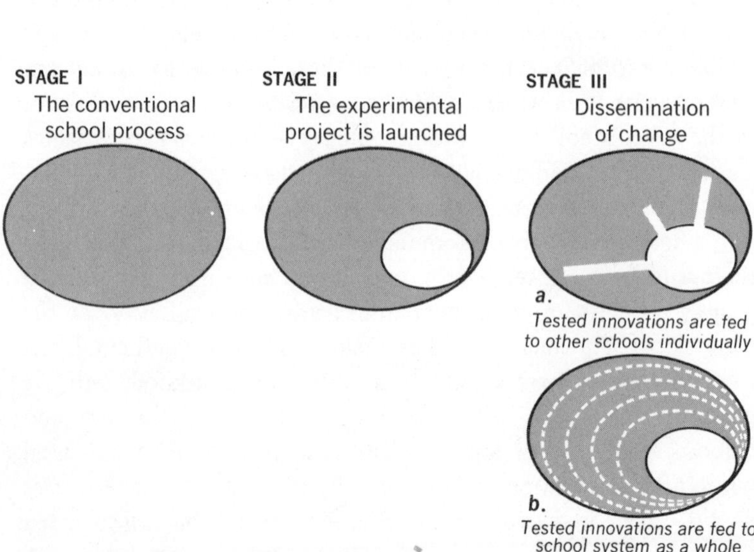

men to participate in work-study programs, and so forth—were being introduced in all of these schools. Eventually, and as an outcome of the desegregation study, the original three project schools were closed so that a better racial balance could be maintained in the city's schools as a whole, but many of the programs which began in these three schools followed their pupils to their new schools.

Thus, the original educational enrichment and compensatory program for pupils in three especially blighted schools was, through the effective use of change strategies, transformed into a citywide educational process change. It may be helpful to diagram just how this transformation takes place (Fig. 8.1). Stage I represents the bureaucratic public-school system and its outmoded conventional process before any change has occurred. Stage II represents the vehicles for change—in this case, the three project schools—which comprise a kind of laboratory in which innovations are initiated and tested. Once innovations are proved successful, they may be fed out to the larger system as shown in Stage III—perhaps to one school at a time (A), perhaps as a package program to several schools at once (B). For example, having found that preparation of urban teachers through the clinical setting of the schools is a useful way of offsetting a teacher shortage, many or all schools in the system may become clinical training centers for student teachers, while other innovations remain restricted to the laboratory school until their value is proven. Stage IV shows how the original laboratory project is expanded to include additional schools until, in Stage V, virtually all the schools in the system are modified. However, lest this

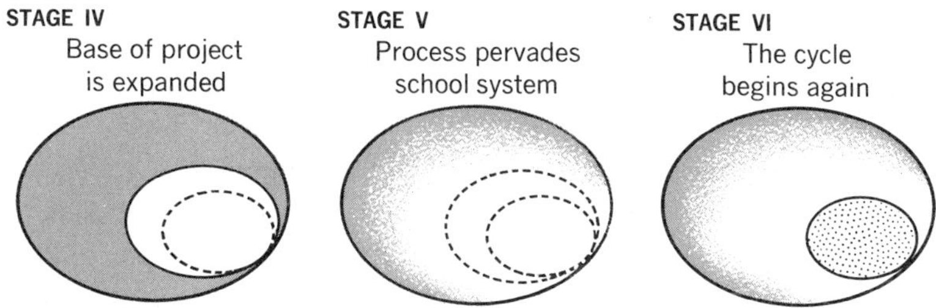

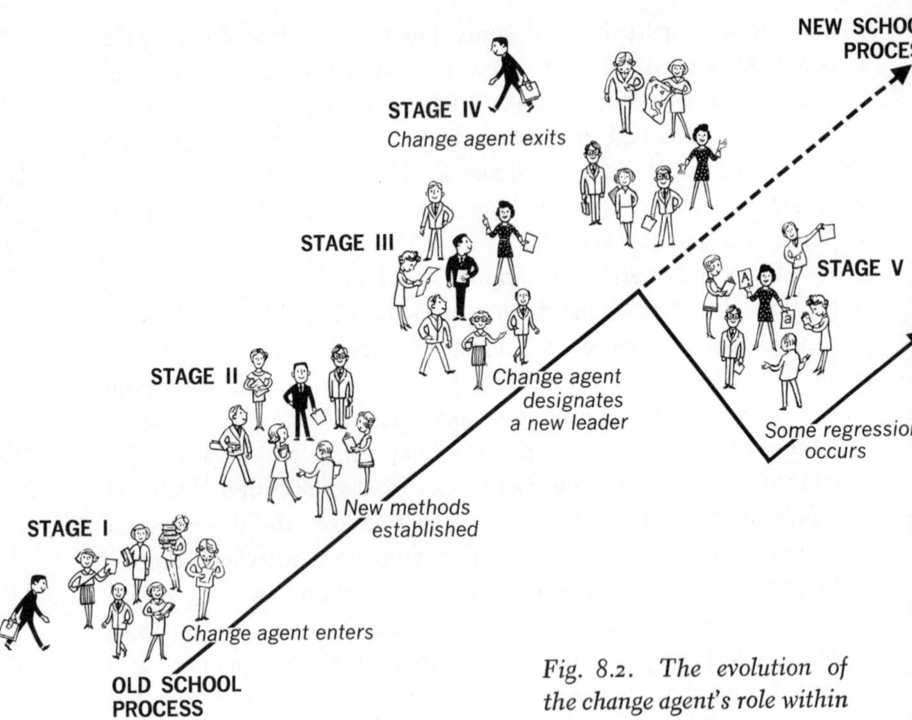

Fig. 8.2. The evolution of the change agent's role within the change process.

new process, in turn, become stagnant—and to keep the school institution self-revitalizing—a new cycle should begin, as shown in Stage VI.

During this process, the change agents' own roles must evolve to encompass wider and wider spheres in the school system. This evolution can take place only as each change agent prepares other individuals to take over his previous roles. This is essential to true and sweeping process change for, as the project expands, the number of teachers, principals, professional consultants, and others who must be dealt with also grows, and the facets which must be manipulated and coordinated burgeon. For this reason, it would be quite impossible for any one or more change agents to continue in their original roles and to supervise the larger process change as well. Further, if the process change has truly been effective, it should be capable of sustaining itself; it cannot do so if it must always rely on the original change agents.

When the change agent leaves any part of the change process, however, the progress achieved under his influence is likely to halt—even to regress to some previous stage—at least temporarily. This is shown in Fig. 8.2, where, for example, team planning is a part of the changes being instituted. As this innovation and others are progressing toward the new school process, the change agent singles out the most promising of the regular team members to become a replacement for himself. After preparing this individual to assume his own role as team planning coordinator, the change agent then moves to other spheres. Because the team members and others in the bureaucracy have become accustomed to the change agent's own brand of dynamism, some breakdown in progress is likely to occur while the school personnel readjust to the behavioral mode of the new team planning coordinator. Whether or not the same level of progress originally achieved by the change agent will be regained is largely a question of the ability of the replacement and of how well he has been prepared to continue change. It should be stressed that, at the very minimum, the state of affairs should remain *above* the level of Stage I; that is, where the original and inadequate status quo was perpetuating itself.

Thus, to lead the bureaucracy toward behavioral change in each of its members is the real aim of the change agents. The question still remains of just what specific behavioral changes should occur among these staff members, however. Certainly all school personnel, and particularly those who administer the educational process—the school board, the superintendent, the curriculum planners, and the principal—should be flexible and alert to the real educational needs of pupils. But it is the teacher who must ultimately meet these needs, and thus it is the teacher's behavior which is the most important in the educational process. In Chapter 9 we examine in some detail the teacher's role in educating pupils, and particularly disadvantaged pupils.

CHAPTER 9

THE TEACHER: STRENGTH WITH SENSITIVITY

The question of who is a good teacher of the disadvantaged has been answered most frequently by the statement "A good teacher is a good teacher no matter whom she may have to teach." The assumption has been that a good teacher—that is, one who is effective with advantaged children—would be effective with children who were disadvantaged. This assumption has been coupled with another which implies that the "experienced" teacher is an effective one. These two assumptions are illustrated in various educational policy statements such as one in New York City where an intensive program was announced to get the "better and more experienced" teachers into the disadvantaged schools. A major catalyst for such an effort was the Civil-Rights organizations who pointed out the number of substitutes and uncertified teachers who were presently staffing the inner-city schools. As far as one could tell, the major criteria for improved education in these schools were experience and certification. While the authors wholeheartedly concur that, on the whole, disadvantaged schools have historically held the least status for teachers, and many teachers avoided or moved from them at the first opportunity, there is a possible danger in merely asking that "better, experienced" teachers staff these schools.

Although in the Chapter 6 it was explained where and how the teacher is developed, a few points bear iteration. More teachers appear to be "good" when there is a congruence between the teacher, the schools' program she represents, and the learners; that is, in those schools where the pupils have been taught by their hidden curriculum to buy whatever the school is selling, there are more "good" teachers. In this situation, "good" is only being tested on a few dimensions. When teachers, who are trained to be good in advantaged schools, teach in schools in the inner city, the cultural shock may be such that in this new context it is difficult to recognize them as good.

A major reason for this difficulty is that many teachers, and those who have trained them, have accepted one educational process as appropriate for all learners. When "good" pupils come to them, pupils who have learned in their hidden curriculum that "teacher is right," the process continues unquestioned and

Bob Adelman, Center for Urban Education

THE TEACHER: STRENGTH WITH SENSITIVITY

serves to reinforce the teacher. In a setting where the pupils have not learned that "teacher is right," hostility and lack of response to what has usually worked for this teacher arises. The reaction to these challenges is to view the pupil as misguided or deficient in relation to the accepted process. The teacher, in other words, confronts a more divergent view with a convergent frame of reference. Real diversity is viewed with alarm because real diversity, when viewed through a personal construct that is too narrow, becomes a handicap.

Teacher training institutions have, more often than not, been most concerned with the "good" schools, "good" pupils, and the "good" teachers. Their training programs have used the "good" models to train by. When this kind of training is juxtaposed against a depressed urban area, the faultiness begins to show itself. This is most dramatically illustrated by the problem of discipline or classroom control as treated by teacher trainers in relation to cultural disparity.

Control

Of all the variables which make it difficult for urban teacher trainees to succeed, discipline problems loom largest. Of all the variables which drive any teacher from the urban classroom during the first year of teaching, discipline problems are strongest. Ask any first-year teacher in an urban disadvantaged setting what her most critical problems are and they will be discipline centered.

In most teacher-education programs, the emphasis is on understanding the child, understanding his needs, and generally developing a nonauthoritarian role for the teacher. As trainees are thus indoctrinated, they vow never to treat children the way they themselves were treated in school. All they have to do is walk into the classroom, demonstrate how "friendly" and "understanding" they are, and let the pupils know that from now on they will be like no other teacher they ever had before . . . *they* are going to be "buddies."

What happens is traumatic. The reality shock of the urban

classroom is so great than many teachers stop eating, suffer insomnia, and return home from school each day to cry. Typical comments are:

> Why didn't someone tell us it would be like that?" "Why weren't we prepared?"
>
> I had these beautiful lesson plans all set. I might as well have thrown them in the basket. They weren't quiet long enough for me to even start teaching.
>
> All I am is a policeman, and a lousy one at that.
>
> I really wanted to make school happier for them but they wouldn't even give me a chance.

Or, even more poignant are these excerpts from the journals of two urban teaching trainees in Syracuse.

> The class got so out of hand that I could not get them to line up to go to gym or music. It was at this point that I began to lose confidence in my ability to handle this group. Every day at about 9:30 it would start, then get bigger and bigger. The afternoons were quite bad, but the worst was yet to come. Sue [roomate] and I would meet every night to try to plan. We were lost. We would stay up until 12 or 1 o'clock and then I would have to get up at 6. By Friday I was really beginning to feel it. I was sarcastic with my family. I could not eat anymore, and every morning that I woke up, my stomach would tighten up and my pulse would quicken. I would get scared and nervous—I hated to go in that Friday. I had not done anything with that class since they came in on Wednesday afternoon and I wanted so badly to accomplish something today. But the situation was getting worse. I could not get the group quiet after 9:30, so the children who wanted to go along with me would wait as long as they could, but finally they would give in to the children around them. The first problem was the airplanes—I had so many it looked like it was snowing. Then I had poppers—then others would run into the back closet and close the door. Some children on my left-hand side would take chalk and write on the board. The children

on my right near the windows would pull the cords. About this time I had several serious fights—fist fights. One boy in the class would tighten up, clench his hands and would tear across the room to beat up someone. He would be in a rage. I would be in a rage. I would try to tear them apart and then quietly talk to Tommie trying to calm him down. One time he started chasing a girl around the room violently —I couldn't get to them—I stationed myself at a point where they would pass me—I grabbed Tom and told Dorothy to leave the room and come back in a few minutes. It was after this that I began to "drift out" of the situation and what was going on. I could not think as quickly as I should be. I wasn't seeing half of the things going on around me. I was staying up late every night and was so tired by 11 a.m. I remember yawning one time on Friday afternoon, right at a time when I should have been disciplining and directing and guiding. It was like I was not there, that was how much effect I was having on the children.

Today was quite something! I can distinctly remember being one of the people who thought the discipline role-playing of seminars were too extreme. Well, today I lost control for the major part of the morning. I could feel a tenseness in myself which carried over to the kids. . . . I took the whole thing pretty emotionally and was really upset that the whole thing happened.

I'm not too much in the mood for writing because I'm tired and it's late, but I feel that there is so much to be said and it's got to be let out. I cried over what happened today and this made things better. Perhaps I am able to write because I'm not facing school tomorrow. . . . I walked into class feeling well-prepared this morning and later I walked out of it feeling that I'd never go back. There was about one hour of peace in my room today and then hell broke loose. No books went flying or anything but the atmosphere of the room became "I dare you." . . . Even the good ones succumbed to group pressure and chaos broke out. I sent people out of the room but it didn't get better.

> Actually I'm not going to write about what happened because it's upsetting me. I do know, though, that something has got to change because my depressed attitude right now is going to ruin everything.

For any of us who have been in supervisory situations and been in classrooms where our trainees were confronting unruly, and at times, chaotic conditions, one shares the feeling of intense helplessness. How is it possible to help someone in a situation like this? Certainly, we had gone over the usual prescriptions for getting off to a good start with a new class. We had carefully documented the need for consistency, routines, basic rules, procedures for dismissal, change of activity, passing out and collecting materials; and yet, here are trainees that appear helpless before a class of acting-out youngsters. We meet privately with the distraught trainee and confront him with some of the things he neglected to do.

"You remember we talked about being consistent and yet you let some children call out answers while you told others to raise their hands first."

"Yes, I know," comes the reply, but I just can't keep everything straight. When I pay attention to one thing something new comes up and I don't know where to spend my energy—so usually I just float along."

And so goes the dialogue. The longer the situation continues, the less helpful the supervisor becomes, because the less objective the situation becomes for the trainee.

When pupils in these schools are interviewed and asked whom they consider to be the good teachers, the frequent response is, "Mr. So-and-So—he doesn't let us get away with anything." The children seem to respect those teachers who can dominate them, those teachers who display enough strength to keep a class moving without constant disruption. In urban disadvantaged communities in particular, strength is seen as the overriding value. It is seen as control—mainly through physical dominance, but in a few other ways as well. The "con" artist is also seen as strong, for he is the one who can control a situation through his "style" of walk and talk. But, whatever form it takes, strength is the virtue. The children, because of their hidden curriculum, regard as weak anyone who is small physically, backs down in the face of a challenge, is wordy without style, who is easily intimidated, who is sentimental and trite, who gets flustered, or who is too "goody-goody" or "phoney."

Understandably, strength is, in a way, what education has been trying to get rid of. The authoritarianism and repressiveness of traditional schools deserved to be eliminated and the emphasis became the release of children rather than their coercion. However, in the process, many issues became confused. Polarization has set in so that "understanding" and permissiveness have become the opposites of authoritarian control. When a teacher so trained moves into a protected environment, the release philosophy usually does not produce chaos. But not so in a less protected environment. Nothing less than shock is the result.

The Syracuse trainees experienced this shock. It was found that those trainees who appeared to have the most insight, understanding, and sensitivity toward children, and the disadvantaged in particular, had the most trouble in initiating enough structure in the classroom for their sensitivity to become operative. They couldn't bring themselves to "coerce," as they termed it, pupil behavior. It seemed to oppose everything they believed in. Their ability to handle this "conflict" diminished the longer they stayed in a classroom.

In preparing teachers for the disadvantaged schools two main problems emerge:

1. Is there a way to assess dispositional qualities of teachers that allow for strength?
2. What can be said about strength training?

Before we begin to tackle these two issues, however, we shall define our use of the term *strength*. Briefly, *strength* includes the ability to initiate an identifiable structure, and to maintain that structure with a certain degree of compellingness and persistence even under exasperating circumstances.

THE CLASS CONTROL TASK

In an effort to determine at the outset of one teacher training program the strength component of the candidates, a situational performance task was devised through which each applicant for the program was required to demonstrate his ability to "control" a class. Briefly, the task consisted of some minimal instructions to the candidate in which he was told he would face a class on the first day of school and must fulfill a few "simple" objectives. The "class" he actually faced was three trained staff members who role-played disadvantaged youngsters displaying typical behavior problems. As the applicant proceeded through the task, certain planned interjections were made by the role-players and the applicant was coded on the responses he made to these interjections.

Among the 73 candidates who were observed in this situation, the degree of strength exhibited ran the gamut from those who were so strong that the role-players felt they were in a concentration camp, to those who were so weak that they actually gave up in the middle of the ten-minute task. One girl, after about five minutes in the "classroom," sat down, lit up a cigarette, and refused to continue. Strength was exhibited in a variety of ways. One could easily assume the strongest people were aggressive, loud, domineering, etc. But one of the strongest candidates demonstrated strength without any of the aforementioned behaviors. She was soft-spoken, supportive, relaxed, but all the while in control of the situation. In fact, the role-players, after her session, said that they hardly realized that they were being controlled, but, as they looked back on it, realized that she had conducted the "line of march" throughout.

The hypothesis was that from this task one might predict how a candidate would establish order when given full responsibility for a class. In other words, it was a kind of diagnosis of a trainee in reference to strength. But once the diagnosis is made, the real problem becomes, can one be trained to become stronger?

This is still in the elementary stage of investigation and is presently being pursued.

Strategies of discipline

While there are no precise formulas that work for all teachers in discipline, strategies do emerge which warrant reporting. Please bear in mind that the following strategies are initiatory and are especially important for the new teacher. The dictum "the stronger the start the easier the year" is a good one.

One of the most interesting social phenomena operating within school involves the pupils' perception of teacher expectation and conformity to these expectations. All of us who have gone to school can remember receiving report cards and being promoted to new grades and new teachers. The responses to this are often "Did you get promoted?" "Yes." "Who's your new teacher?" "Mr. ———." "Wow, he's tough. He's strict. You don't get away with much in that room." "Yeh, I know; I gotta watch my step there."

This sort of dialogue reveals the typical teacher visibility in the student culture and the reputations which follow the teacher. How many teachers realize the parts they play in student conversation and how deeply in neighborhood schools they may actually permeate the neighborhood itself? In informal situations, ranging from parties to the street-corner society itself, the image of the teacher is reinforced as "tough or easy," "swinging or dull." Students take delight in talking about their teacher as tough and do so with a great deal of respect. On the other hand, they also boast about the easy teacher and what they are able to get away with.

How does one go about establishing a suitable image with the students? This image has nothing to do with age and sex; it deals exclusively with the perceptions of the student of the expectations of the teacher and the ability to enforce his or her expectations. Once a positive image is established firmly within the student culture, many of the so-called "problems" are reduced or eliminated. Students become conditioned to the teacher's expectation and tend to conform to the teacher's reputation which the students themselves have disseminated.

Repeatedly, overseers have related witnessing students, described as wild and boisterous in one class, proceed to another classroom with another teacher where they behave "beautifully." School administrators often cite students who run and then freeze suddenly at the sight of a certain teacher. Many of them find it difficult to understand exactly how or why this happens. Many say that teacher X is "good" or a "kind" teacher, and yet students get away with misbehavior in her room. At the same time Y, a stricter teacher who makes demands on students, finds that students obey with little or no rebellion. Certain teachers find students easy to cope with while other teachers find them wild. Perhaps the following case study can shed some light on one teacher's ways of establishing an image, and the effect this has on producing orderly student behavior:

> It was the first day of school. Staff and students were assembled in the auditorium early in the morning, with the principal presiding. After several words of greeting, the principal began to call out the pupils' names alphabetically to meet with particular teachers who were standing in various parts of the auditorium. He told the groups to file out and to meet with their teachers who, in turn, would take them to their classrooms.
>
> As happens sometimes in schools, new teachers are occasionally assigned the most difficult classes. A5 had this reputation, and was assigned to Miss Tyler, a young, new teacher. Miss Tyler was unaware of the reputation that followed this group and, as they filed close to her at the far end of the auditorium, she remained motionless and erect, looking each student squarely in the eye. Not saying a word but using gestures, she indicated where they should line up. Still without words, she grouped the girls before the boys and indicated by means of example that she wanted them to line up according to height. This was accomplished. The teacher remained silent and calm; her face remained expressionless with the exception of long hard

stares at the students who, in turn, were attempting to interpret what the teacher was communicating. She motioned to one boy with her index finger to move back into line. He looked at her for a long time and then responded accordingly. The teacher moved to the front of the line and looked over the heads of the students.

Again, through her eyes, she motioned to the students to proceed through the hall. She uttered only one command: "Stop at the edge of Room 2." The students proceeded through the hall to the designated spot, which was only about 20 feet from where they had lined up, and the teacher began to walk along the line almost as an officer would inspecting his troops, occasionally stopping and focusing squarely on a particular individual who was either moving or poking the person in front. The first girl began to move and the teacher said, "Stop, move back." This seemed to puzzle the group, who began to look at her and she looked at the leader. "I don't remember giving you permission to move," she said. After repeating her instructions she paused for what seemed to be a full minute and then said, "Proceed," and the group walked toward the end of the hall.

Before the pupils reached the end of the hall, the teacher said, "Stop." Everyone seemed to freeze in place. The teacher again walked by and said, "One person was not in order." She did not indicate who this was, but expressed shock through her voice as she looked at each person. Again, mainly through her eyes, and after what seemed to be another very long pause, she said, "Proceed" and the group marched very quietly to the end of the hall. The teacher remained near the middle of the hall looking very closely at the marching group and, when the group had halted at the designated spot, the teacher very quietly walked by again to the front of the line. Once more she reviewed the posture of each student and gave another set of instructions. "This time proceed to the stairwell and stop at the bottom." The first student was about to begin walking, when the student behind said, "Don't—don't move, she didn't say go ahead." The teacher, again pausing and looking over what seemed to be each and every student, finally indicated that they were to proceed.

Doors, however, blocked entry to the stairwell and, while passing through them, each student allowed the doors to swing back into the path of the student behind. Once more, Miss Tyler indicated halt and directed them back to their original positions in the hall. Motioning with her hands and meeting each students' eyes, she said, "When you walk through the door leading to the stairway, I want [pointing to a boy] you to go over to hold that door. Now let us proceed. Whenever we pass in the future, someone should always hold the door."

The designated boy moved out of line and passed directly in front of Miss Tyler on his way to the door. He was within a few inches past her when she threw out her right arm. The boy stopped suddenly, looked at her, and remained almost motionless while the rest of the class observed the episode. Miss Tyler asked him to return to the line, which he did. Then she signaled him to proceed toward the door, but again, moving in front of Miss Tyler, he found she had extended her arm. This time, Miss Tyler said, "What do you say when you pass by?" The little boy immediately said, "Excuse me; excuse me, Miss Tyler," and with that, Miss Tyler nodded and he assumed his responsibility at the door. Then she signaled to the rest of the class to proceed.

After the first three pupils had passed the boy who was holding the door, Miss Tyler signaled the class to stop immediately and to move back to their earlier positions. The first one in line was asked what the custom was when passing by someone—and she said, "I would say, 'Excuse me.' " With this, the little girl walked by the boy holding the door and said, "Excuse me." Then the teacher nodded to the rest of the group to proceed and each and every child passing by said, "Excuse me."

The first day continued with very small steps, highly structured, that gradually introduced the pupils to the "rules of the game." It was mainly nonverbal, with much use of eyes and gestures. What was verbalized was brief, crisp, and clear. Each situation was utilized as a teaching one.

During the course of the year, Miss Tyler was able to move from this exaggerated external control to a much more relaxed situation, still with clearly defined limits.

Contrast this with the following, admittedly hard to believe, opening day exchange of a new teacher and her class:

TEACHER: Hello (embarrassed laugh). . . . I guess we're all in here together and . . . um . . . I wonder why . . . we are in here. . . . What we're doing here . . . um . . . Perhaps we should begin so we can talk to each other by telling everybody our names. I'm Mary Miller and you are. . . .

BILL: Bill Brown.

TEACHER: Bill Brown? And you are. . . . [Prolonged pause]

JANE: Oh . . . us . . . Jane. Jane Williams.

TEACHER: Jane Williams? And you are. . . ?

BOB: Who'm I?

TEACHER: Yes.

BOB: Bob.

TEACHER: Bob? Now Bill, do you know Bob . . . did you know each other before? And . . . Jane—is that right?

JANE: Um-hmmmmmmmmm.

TEACHER: Did you know each other?

BOB: Naw . . . I don't know them.

TEACHER: You don't know them? I guess you're going to get to know them, and I guess we're all going to get to know each other. If you remember my name, like I try to remember yours . . . I—I'll try pretty hard . . . I'm pretty dumb on names . . . [Class doesn't seem to be listening]
Well, I think . . . we're all here together. . . .

BILL: Can I get a drink?

TEACHER: Um—wait a second to discuss that.

BILL: Well, can't I get a drink and not discuss it?

TEACHER: I think maybe it might be a little more fun if we all talked about it.

BILL: (with exaggerated desperation) I'm thirsty.

TEACHER: You're thirsty? Do you (hesitantly) . . . are there any rules in this school about drinks and stuff?

JANE: Don't you know the rules?
[Teacher suffers ridicule from students because she doesn't know rules]

TEACHER: Wha . . . Wh-who is the school for? Who makes the rules for you?
JANE: The principal.
TEACHER: Why does he make them?
BILL: I'll be right back.
TEACHER: O. K.
[Bill leaves]

In less than fifteen minutes, this teacher had no class. Both of these teachers had very similar attitudes toward children, attitudes that we would regard as positive, but only one would eventually be able to develop something constructive and consonant with those attitudes in a classroom. In a study of class managerial techniques and their effectiveness with deviant behavior, Kounin, Friesen, and Norton found the most significant variables to be "Overlappingness" and "With-it-ness":

> Overlappingness refers to the degree to which a teacher overtly manifests signs of attention to two aspects of a classroom simultaneously. When two issues are confronted, does she attend to both or drop one completely and go "all out" to the other? For example, she may be working with a reading group when a deviancy occurs in the seatwork group. She may issue a Desist order to the child in the seatwork group while simultaneously attending to the reading group. . . . Or, she may immerse herself in the deviant and completely drop the reading group for the time. . . .
>
> With-it-ness refers to the degree to which the teacher *communicates* to the class the impression that she does or does not know what is going on (has the proverbial "eyes in back of her head"). In desisting, the teacher communicates that she is not "with it" by (*a*) desisting a minor deviancy while a major one is not acted upon (desisting two children for whispering while two others are throwing paper airplanes or chasing each other), or (*b*) desisting too late (after a deviancy has increased in seriousness or has begun to spread to other children).[1]

[1]J. S. Kounin, W. V. Friesen, and A. E. Norton, "Managing Emotionally Disturbed Children," *Journal of Educational Psychology*, **57:1**, 6.

Kounin, Friesen, and Norton also point out that the way a teacher initiates and maintains movement in classroom activities has a strong effect on pupil behavior or misbehavior. If, in moving from one activity to another, the teacher's transition points include a high degree of "antiresolution properties," the work involvement of the pupils is likely to be minimal and classroom deviancy high; conversely, if the degree of antiresolution properties is low, classroom control is likely to be maintained. These antiresolution properties—or teacher behaviors which oppose the teacher's overt intent to stop one activity and to start another—are:

1. Providing contrary props, or passing out props that were judged to lure the children away from the teacher-designated official new activity—for example, passing out spelling tests the children had previously taken while telling the children to start their arithmetic.

2. Returning to old activity, or designating a new activity and then initiating an issue pertaining to the old—for example, asking how many children had all their spelling words right after having told them to stop spelling and start arithmetic.

3. Dangling, or signaling the pupils to start a new activity, and then dropping it in midair, so to speak, leaving the children with nothing to do.

4. Thrusting, or injecting a transition order at a time or in a manner indicating the teacher's unawareness of the children's receptivity to this message. For example, a teacher had been working with a reading group while the Robins were doing arithmetic seatwork. Suddenly, and in a manner indicating that her own intent was the only determinant of the timing—she had not looked up to see what the Robins were doing nor given verbal warning—the teacher thrust the order: "Robins, take out your reading books." A thrust is similar to a person butting in on the conversation of two other persons without either waiting for them to notice his presence or easing in by listening to what they are talking about.

5. Giving conflicting, confusing directions, or giving too

many orders or contradictory things for the children to get with.[2]

One approach to discipline is what may be called the tactic of reverse psychology. It has its roots in the process of conditioning the student culture to reward and punishment. For example, "If you don't behave, class, you'll have to read another chapter for homework tonight," or "All right, Jane, for talking out so often today, I want you to write 50 more spelling words from the list for tonight." This punishment in the form of more work has become so common a theme that the association of learning with work and punishment is constantly reinforced at every grade level. A *negative* image of learning and undertaking work thus becomes inculcated. Where, in this conventional disciplining technique, is the notion that learning is desirable?

The employment of a strategy of reverse psychology would in a sense tamper with this conventional framework. In essence, this strategy will say to the learner that being *deprived* of doing schoolwork will be the highest form of punishment. The authors have seen a misbehaving child ordered to clear everything from his desk and sit silently while the rest of the class proceeded with the lesson. In no way would the child be recognized or called upon during the lesson. He would gently yet firmly and convincingly be made a temporary pariah.

As the pupil clears his desk, the teacher might focus and limit the situation by saying, "You're going to have to miss your arithmetic [or spelling or reading] lesson today" (Rather than allowing him a complete holiday from *all* class work,) the teacher might say, "I hate to do this to you; maybe if you're interested, you can do the lesson with us tomorrow or the next day." A slightly different twist could be given the episode if the teacher were to merely take his book away; for example, "I'm sorry, but you can't have your reading book today" and make him sit quietly with nothing on his desk. This tactic of excluding the pupil from the group work usually makes the child eager to gain admission again. At the same time, it promotes the feeling

[2] *Ibid.*, 8.

that being *denied* work is far worse than being given extra work. Imagine a situation where a teacher says, "John, I think you have earned the right to get a homework assignment"!

Once her image of strength and firmness has been established by the teacher, what other control or discipline techniques can be used uniquely and effectively? Once the boundaries have been set and student expectations have been molded, what types of less militant, more creative, more subtle, yet still calm devices might be employed to harness an habitually or occasionally unruly class? An episode of a distraught sixth-grade teacher is perhaps pertinent as an example:

> Nervous, frantic and concerned with the disorder and chaos in her classroom, a beginning teacher was unnerved by the apparent lack of progress of the class and by her own inability to see any sort of organization within each student. Her supervisor was reminded of a personal experience in the first few months after his daughter was born. He was, in his own words, "going nuts." After only a few weeks, he had become convinced that the baby was planning to spend the rest of her life screaming, helpless, and showing no progress in any kind of mature development. The thing that kept him "sane" during this period was initiated when he recalled the charts he'd seen in a child-development book. At this point, he decided to chart his daughter's behavior and progress and proceeded to draw up a plethora of charts and graphs which kept him busy and helped him to see that within the chaos there was actual learning taking place.
>
> "Why don't you try this with your class?" he suggested to the distraught teacher. "But, instead of doing all the work yourself, let the kids make the charts, since they're going to be working on graphing in arithmetic, anyway. You can set up two or three things to watch for, such as How many times did the teacher pay the class a compliment? How many times did someone leave his seat without permission? How much teaching and learning time did we have for social studies?"
>
> The young teacher decided to try it, and the next day

> delegated to various pupils, especially to the discipline problem students, the responsibility for keeping score on a particular question. At the end of the day, they compiled the data on line or bar graphs and put them on display. The progress through the entire week was handled this way so that the class and the teacher could see it.

This control technique pinpointed the goals and gave teacher and students more of a feeling of security. It's a possible way to structure discussions. For example, a teacher might raise the question: "Why do we have problems with our discussions?" The class could then make a list of factors that disturb and hinder discussion. This could be translated into questions to chart, such as: How many people didn't call out today? How many times did the teacher have to remind the class of discussion rules? How long were we able to discuss today? In this way, too, the students can be made aware of their own behavioral progress while simultaneously learning the skills of graphing.

Eric Berne's popular book *Games People Play* suggests another possibility for imaginative control strategies.[3] *Games* here refers to social interaction games between people rather than the various sports. If the game is named, it loses much of its excitement and reward. For example, "Get the Substitute"—often played to destruction of class and teacher in different schools—contains several easily identified games: "We can't do this work," "We have never done this before," "Mr. X never collects our arithmetic papers, we correct them ourselves," "I always go to dance in Mrs. Smith's room on Thursday mornings," or "Mr. X lets us play dodgeball *every* Thursday afternoon."

If the substitute teacher can name and analyze these games with the class, his chances for survival with the class will be increased. Since the days when a substitute teaches are often seen by the regular teacher, the principal, the children, and even the substitute as a time when nothing is accomplished no matter how hard the substitute tries to carry out the lesson plans, this may be one of the best times for experimentation. Once the process of

[3] E. Berne, *Games People Play*, New York, Grove, 1964.

"Name the Game" is carefuly worked out with the *help of skilled personnel,* this strategy for controlling behavior can be most helpful to the regular teacher.

The progress from strong external control to more internalized controls on the part of learners, as well as to programs in which control becomes incidental to the instruction, is analogous to the contact and developmental patterns discussed in Chapter 10. The strong external measures suggested for discipline are the contact phase. It is the developmental phase that makes the difference between a regimented, mechanical, extrinsically motivated classroom, and one in which true growth on the part of the learner can be effected. Too many teachers, once strength and control have been exhibited, remain arrested at the contact stage. They have worked out certain procedures and understandings with their class in which order was achieved, but have maintained a rigidity that is hardly productive for pupil growth. In difficult schools especially, the "don't rock the boat" attitude is understandable. In such schools, the teachers might very well say, "It took so much finally to get my classes in order—and I almost didn't make it—that I'm not going to try anything that has the slightest potential for shifting the balance of power in my room."

Sensitivity

In the authors' view, the key factor which makes it possible for teachers to move progressively from stage to stage with a group of learners is sensitivity. Realizing that this has been an overworked term that rarely becomes identified operationally, we will attempt to clarify our view of this dimension. Since those of us who are searching for better educational processes are still scrambling in the dark for what might replace programs that are obviously ineffective, the major source of ideas must come from innovative practices that are derived in the teaching situation. This emerging and derived program, the strategies, if not the content also, should emerge from a sensitivity to the unique needs of children—from the seeking of cues from the learner, "reading" or interpreting the cues, seeking more information to clarify cues, and adapting instruction to the cues. These components may best be illustrated by an assessment procedure which we will now describe.

THE COMMUNICATION TASK

This task was originally developed by David Hunt to assess Peace Corps trainees.[4] It consists simply of obtaining a fifteen-minute behavior sample of the way in which the trainee communicated some information (in this case, the concept of the balance of power in the federal government) to a specified person (a not-too-articulate Venezuelan immigrant who hopes to become a citizen) with the purpose of increasing his understanding of the concept of checks and balances. Each trainee was given information on the topic, information about the person, and the instructions to prepare a brief lesson plan or strategy to attempt to communicate the concept to a person who played the role of the Venezuelan immigrant. During the 15-minute presentation, the role-players systematically presented obstacles to effective communication in the form of misunderstanding, impatience, confusion, and the like. The trainees' behavior was coded along several dimensions to assess how effectively they took cognizance of the person's frame of reference, modulated to this frame of reference, and how effectively they dealt with the various obstacles.

George Lopez was the name of the "Venezuelan" and he was taught by about 400 different people. "Poor George"—as he was affectionately termed by the trainees—was "steamrollered" by the trainees. Not many cared about what he thought or how he thought; they were more interested in completing their lesson plan. One trainee started out with "Now George, don't ask me any questions until I finish my presentation"! She was so determined in this that it was almost impossible for the role-player

[4]D. E. Hunt, "A Behavioral Model for Assessing Effectiveness in Interpersonal Communication Derived from a Training Model," Unpublished Report, Syracuse, N. Y., Syracuse Univ., 1965.

to present his prescribed interjections. Some trainees sought feedback from George, but made no attempt to utilize it: "What kind of work do you do, George?" "I'm a waiter." "Oh . . . okay; now let's get back to the three branches of government."

In this task, the language difficulties of George, the assumptions the trainees made and took for granted, the avoidance of modulating strategies to suit the situation, and finally the belief on the part of the trainees that, since George had been given the information one could assume he had learned it, illustrated dramatically some problems and faults of the urban teacher. The ramifications for the teaching of the disadvantaged should be obvious. These are exactly the conditions which negate the communication between teachers and pupils.

Considering the above, we may have a way of determining which teachers and trainees are disposed to sensitivity toward the learner. It is interesting to note that there is a positive correlation between sensitivity as measured in the Communication Task and sensitivity as measured by the Class Control Task. On the other hand, the authors see a negative correlation between strength and sensitivity. From these two tasks we have developed a four category system for assessment:

1. *Strong-sensitive:* This person can maintain a consistent orderly structure in which learners can operate and, at the same time, indicate that he is constantly aware of what is going on with the pupils. The pupils are treated as important and respected persons with feelings, attitudes, and experiences that are worthy of attention.

2. *Strong-insensitive:* The person can keep a class in order and maintain his authority, but he never can really see, hear, or experience the pupils. It is pretty much a case of him against the pupils, and the stronger will win.

3. *Weak-sensitive:* This person holds the interests and needs of the child foremost in his mind, but is unable to establish the degree of order which would allow him to capitalize on his sensitivity.

4. *Weak-insensitive:* This category obviously speaks for itself.

Ideally, the strong-sensitives would appear to be the most desirable trainees. According to the authors's findings, they are in the distinct minority. In one group considered, 5 out of 73 were given that rating. The largest number of people fell in the categories of strong-insensitives and weak-sensitives. Obviously, much more investigation is required; this is only a beginning.

What kinds of training can help people become more sensitive and yet stronger? Perhaps it would be useful to use the assessment tasks themselves as training vehicles. Perhaps in giving immediate feedback and criticism to trainees, and allowing the trainees to repeat their performances while other trainees observe, evaluate, analyze, and recommend alternatives, would be helpful. New tasks could be developed for training purposes.

Having trainees live in the area from which their pupils come, with no other instructions or objectives other than to make friends with their neighbors, is a practice the authors have experimented with and which seems promising for developing sensitivity and more effective communication. Developing strength is a stickier type of problem. The authors have, up to now, relied mainly on constant role-playing in which they asked trainees to assume a variety of attitudes toward a class of pupils. Perhaps one possibility might be an intensive training in dramatics with "weak" trainees assuming "strong" roles in scenes from various plays.

Whatever training device we come up with, it is secondary. Primarily, we must concern ourselves with diagnosing weaknesses, as well as strengths, for certain job settings. We must then individualize training programs on the basis of this diagnosis. It is necessary to give up the notion of all trainees going through the same mill regardless of needs. This is exactly what we ask the public schools to do, so why shouldn't the teacher-educating college?

The most obvious demonstration of sensitivity is the way the teacher interacts with the pupils. Most discussions on sensitivity have focused on the attitudes, understandings, and respectfulness of the teacher with the pupils. But, as important as they may be, sensitivity is also related to another, more long-ranged, type of planning, usually termed *diagnosis*. Because of the kinds of diagnosis which are usually carried on in a school based on scores on the Iowa Test of Basic Achievement or similar tests, the relationship of diagnosis to sensitivity has not been important. How much sensitivity do you need to group children on the basis of a test score? If we can see diagnosis as involving a broader range of teacher activities than looking at test scores, the relationship between sensitivity and diagnosis we hope can be made clear.

The teacher as diagnostic analyst

The literature of education has been laden for many years with the notion of diagnosis as a major task of the teacher. But, because a body of professional literature contains such concerns, that does not mean that the idea becomes operational. If it has become operational, it is usually only in a restricted sense. There seem to be at least three major obstacles to the achievement of an expanded view of diagnosis for the teacher:

1. We have rarely clarified the meaning of diagnosis in its most generative sense.
2. We have rarely trained teachers to diagnose at a variety of levels—and if we have, we have rarely helped them decide how to work with their findings.
3. The teachers are placed in school organizations that restrict diagnosis to a bare conventional minimum.

TOWARD A LESS-RESTRICTED VIEW OF DIAGNOSIS

Our views of diagnosis are restricted in a number of ways. An important example is that diagnosis is conventionally used to evaluate the learner rather than to initiate a process that makes a better match between him and the programing. In a way, diagnosis is used more to find out what's wrong with a child than what is wrong or right with the program. Rather than using diagnostic data for making decisions about what the program should be, we use it simply to determine how far behind or ahead the child is. Testing, the major diagnostic tool, leads to judgment of the child rather than of the program.

Another restricted view is demonstrated by the preponderant focus of diagnosis on academic achievement. The major portion of the schools' efforts in diagnosis is geared toward "skills" acquisition, cognitive deficits. "What grade level is he reading on?" "What usage skills is he lacking?" These are the most often heard diagnostic questions. The assumption is that if achievement deficits are plugged, we will turn out the kinds of people we want. Most of our nationally used texts are aimed at this objective. With this emphasis we have avoided confrontation with the most relevant aspects of the learner himself.

In order to review a more extended role of diagnosis, we would like to refer to the model developed in Chapter 10. Our basic contention, it should be emphasized, is that *diagnosis must be used to decide what the program will be and not for determining the success or failure of the learner*. The model itself exemplifies this contention. It was conceived as a decisionmaking organizer in which different kinds of diagnoses are to be utilized with their main goal being more pupil-relevant programing. Almost every component of the model requires certain diagnostic procedures. Recognizing cues and interpreting their relationship to patterns of concern to certain groups of youngsters is crucial if one is to utilize the model as something generative. To know how to observe and what to observe requires skill. In addition, to be able to identify the concerns of groups, one must understand how and why certain patterns emerge from the groups.

The next component of the model that requires diagnosis is concerned with finding out what the learner's reality and content are. This requires some of the anthropologist's concepts and skills for what we are after is some direct feedback on the cultural artifacts, mores, and activity of the learner. A migrant worker once said that people who are professionaly interested in the disadvantaged would never be able to find out "what's going on with them" because they wouldn't be told the truth. Very few of us have the skills required for getting honest feed-back, but if anthropologists can be trained to do it, why not educators?

The next diagnostic area is concerned with the learning style of the youngster. How has the child been taught and which teaching styles make the best contact?

Finally, and this is where school efforts have been traditionally directed, *where* is the child in relation to various academic skills progression? We repeat, the use of this diagnosis should not be the traditional use, the difference being that we should *plan our programs* around the feed-back collected, rather than use it for report-card marks or for placement of pupils in slow or fast groups.

DIAGNOSTIC STRATEGIES

The cognitive level of the learners is only one area for diagnosis; the emotional level must also be diagnosed. In the following suggestion, we will highlight those procedures which attempt to get at the child's total reality, his experiences, values, and concerns. Some of these suggestions are not new, but they have rarely been used to determine what the nature of the instructional program should be.

Suppose for example, after explaining to the class what a time capsule is, the teacher allows the class to construct its own. The class's time capsule would be a small one, and would state on its outside, "Do not open until 5066." The pupils would put things into the capsule that would allow whoever opened it in the year 5066 to get the best idea possible of what the pupils in this class were like. There are a number of possibilities for proceeding. A few cameras could be given to the pupils with the following instructions: "You can shoot 2 rolls of film each and then select 3 pictures that will go into the time capsule. You may take a picture of anything that will best show us as we are." Or the class might decide upon one popular song to go into the capsule. By having the class arrive at a consensus, the teacher might hear throughout their discussion *their* reasons for priority of some songs over others. In this way, a variety of raw data could become available for the teacher's analysis. What would the class put on a tape? What would they say and how would they say it? Would this not be good data for analysis?

This is only one sample of the type of lessons which allow pupils to express themselves. Other situations might be "Draw nervousness," "How would you feel if you were an ant and saw a lawn mower coming toward you?" Or perhaps, "If You Had Three Wishes . . ." or "Suppose you suddenly got $10,000, what would you do?" Almost every teacher of writing has at some time or other had his pupils write their autobiographies, but all that usually happens to these materials is that they are read, regarded as interesting, and, possibly, the better ones are hung on the bulletin boards. Perhaps, if the teacher were given some help, he might find some specific cues in these materials which might serve as a basis for curriculum decisionmaking, for it is the utilization of this feedback which is the central issue.

Children's drawings have for many years been used by psychological researchers as a way of getting feedback from pupils. The book *Group Values Through Children's Drawings* demonstrates this.[5] Drawings that indicate self-concept have been in use in getting at the real concerns of learners. Along this line, Bruce Joyce at Columbia University has been culling diagnostic instruments and strategies used in these areas to see if they can be utilized not only as diagnostic strategies for teachers, but also for teaching strategies as well. Can we teach teachers to interpret feedback in a consistent, accurate, and useful manner? This, if we want teaching to go beyond the superficial, must be another major priority for teacher training.

In the writings about teachers of the disadvantaged, phrases such as "exhibiting a love for children," "interest and enthusiasm for teaching," or "love, warmth and understanding" seem to predominate. The teachers described are sound, mentally healthy people. But who is mentally healthy? And how do you get people to become mentally healthy? The essays sound as though a complete personality restructuring is being called for. But, in light

[5]W. Dennis, *Group Values Through Children's Drawings*, New York, Wiley, 1966.

of present demands, no one has time for giving therapy (assuming therapy produces mentally healthy people) to all the people needed in classrooms. This notion is unrealistic and it reinforces those who continually say, "It all boils down to the teacher's personality and the art of teaching." If it all boils down to the personal ingredient, then teacher training is an anomaly, for how does one go about training personalities? We should be more interested in respect for the children than we are with love. We should be more interested in developing specific skills in which that respect becomes manifest. To the extent that it is possible, we wish to objectify attitudes into specific behaviors that are based on those attitudes. In other words, it seems more helpful to show teachers how to recognize concerns of pupils, and match content and procedures to those concerns, than it is to talk to them about love and understanding.

A behavioral training program

What constitutes the teaching act? Is it not a person interacting in a variety of ways with learners so as to produce change on the part of those learners? Obviously there are many ways of interacting, certain ways being more effective for certain purposes than others. But interacting is behaving, and the result of teacher training must be a person who possesses a repertoire of behaviors.

That one can, to any extent, develop a repertoire of behaviors without behaving is highly questionable. One cannot imagine an actor being trained to act by attending lectures and reading books for three and one-half years, then for a part of the fourth year being given a small part in a play with an acting supervisor writing a critique of the performance once a week. Yet this parallels to a great extent the teacher-training process. If one is to be a teacher, he must learn to use his body and mind as instruments in a variety of ways, as an actor does; trainees must be given sufficient opportunity to develop that instrument directly.

The most that a conventional teacher-training process can

accomplish is the development of analytic personnel who can expound profusely *about* teaching. If some of these actually perform effectively, we cannot be sure that the teacher's training had anything to do with that result. Teacher-training, to be effective, must provide a wide range of opportunities for experimenting with new behaviors, examination of the range of roles in teaching, and time to practice as many of these as possible. Once the roles become comfortable, the next step should be to determine which roles are most effective for certain purposes and with certain learners.

The opportunities for experimenting with new behaviors in a public school can be extremely limited. This is true especially for new teachers in disadvantaged schools, where the administration is usually under severe pressures from the community and the current political climate. Under such conditions rigidity becomes the rule rather than the exception, and any sign of deviance on the part of teachers is regarded as threatening. Teachers are kept in line by a variety of techniques. One such was the use of a memo to all teachers of a large city system, "All teachers are encouraged to experiment, but not to initiate anything new without explicit permission from the district superintendent." This exemplifies the setting in which teacher trainers expect to have their trainees experiment with new behaviors.

Teacher training, then, must be largely constituted of behavioral training, in settings where there is a wide latitude for practicing behaviors in real situations. David Hunt, of Syracuse University, has developed a training model which suggests a scope and sequence of strategy development that will serve us as an example.[6]

Before one can learn to generate a variety of behaviors aimed at producing some desired outcome, he must become aware of what classroom behaviors are possible. Hunt suggests as the first step in the training of teachers the development of discrimination skills in identifying various class-room environments.

[6]D. E. Hunt, "A Model for Analyzing the Training of Training Agents," *Merrill-Palmer Quarterly*, **12**:2 (April, 1966), 141.

> Before a trainee can learn to radiate a variety of environments he must be aware of the differences between these environments and be capable of accurately classifying them. For example, consider the following teacher comments-which may be viewed as environmental stimuli to be classified:
>
> 1. "I'm disappointed in you."
> 2. "That's right."
> 3. "That's interesting—any other ideas?"
> 4. "How could you go about checking on your ideas?"
>
> Teacher comments 1 and 2 might be classified together as representing teacher-centered reactions and thus discriminably different from 3 and 4 which might be classified as being reflective or student-centered.[7]

The second kind of discriminatory skill needed by the trainee is that of identifying what pupil behaviors are being sought for in various teaching situations. Are they skill behaviors, as, for example, adding up a row of figures? Are they informational as in where was the first battle of the Civil War fought? Are they understandings, for example, Why do we act as we do? Are they thinking, analytic, and divergent behaviors? Are they behaviors that indicate greater coping skills for the pupil with his environment? Discriminating between outcomes is necessary for determining which strategies are best suited for which outcomes.

The third discrimination skill involves ways of looking at who the learners are. What are their particular distinctions? Again, we refer the reader to the model in Chapter 10 as it illustrates the various ways in which the learner can be viewed.

The first step in the teacher-training program, then, is the learning to discriminate between various strategies, outcomes, and learners and the relationships among the three.

The next major training step is the development of teaching skills for radiating a variety of environments.

> Once the trainee has learned to discriminate between environments radiated by others, he needs to learn to radiate these environments himself. Trainees initially vary con-

[7] *Ibid.*, 145.

> siderably in their preferred environmental style, or teaching style . . . and it is important to measure this preferred style or styles at the beginning of training. Teacher trainees entering training may exhibit preferred styles ranging from directive to supportive to reflective. The trainee who is primarily supportive will therefore need to learn to radiate directive and reflective environments. Ideally he should be able to convey the same lesson topic through different environmental contexts when needed."[8]

One of the training techniques used in the Urban Teacher Training Program at Syracuse was to have the trainees develop three or four scripts all based on the teaching of the same subject concept; for example, the difference between rotation and revolution of the earth. Each script had to represent a different approach, however. Trainees were given the opportunity to try them on groups of pupils and each was videotaped so the trainees could see themselves. At this point, effectiveness of the approach was not emphasized, but rather the degree to which a trainee could do the same thing in different ways. The goal was to have the trainee perform a role on command.

Once a variety of teaching environments can be radiated by the trainee, the question becomes which environment is most likely to produce the desired outcome? If someone were trying to teach consonant blends to children, would a more directive and less reflective approach (to mention only two) be most efficient? Would a more reflective method of teaching be appropriate for instruction aimed at having the pupils develop new problem-solving strategies? Whether or not the above can be examined without a specific learner in mind is something that Hunt says should be investigated.

The final step in this process requires that, based on his skill for discriminating between pupil behaviors, the trainee must ascertain which environments and outcomes match the learners. Here is where sensitivity and diagnosis becomes crucial again. If this task is approached as an action-research type of procedure, more objectified for the trainee, probably more can be gained

[8]*Ibid.*

than by putting a trainee on the spot by requiring him to teach an effective lesson. The more this procedure is developed as a trainee-group undertaking, the less personalized it is likely to become. If a group of trainees helps to plan the strategies and sends one of themselves as a representative to test what the group has planned, the classroom evaluation of the outcomes and establishment of criteria becomes a shared responsibility.

Some teacher-training programs are beginning to experiment with simulation devices through films and videotapes. Role-playing is another device which may be most important for establishing initial frames of reference for the trainees, but contact with reality must be early and extensive in a training program. Reality training must begin earlier than the fourth year of a preservice program. By that time, the trainee should be ready for internship in the classroom, with no master teacher to shield him from reality. Once the teacher gets through the first year, his chances of success are pretty good. We should provide the neophyte teacher with an opportunity to get through that difficult first year with the support of the teacher-training institution, instead of turning out graduates who must go it alone.

Content

A teacher must know his subject. Very few people can become expert in their fields, however, especially when knowledge is developing at the rate it is today. It has been assumed that, if each subject area has its own structure, generalizations, concepts, and processes, the teacher's familiarity with these will best prepare him to teach. And yet, most professors do not emphasize the structure of knowledge in their own teaching. Usually a university specialist has become more enmeshed in the intricacies of that discipline than with that which would be most useful to a teacher. It is only recently that scholars have begun to meet and to work with classroom teachers to define, clarify, and organize knowledge to make it more communicable and relevant to the learner. Those teachers, who have had the benefit of this cooperation are probably the ones who would qualify as knowing their subject.

If grounded in the *structure* of knowledge rather than in a mass of facts, the liberally educated teacher has more to offer children. The more broadly educated the teacher is, the more familiar with a variety of subject areas he will be, and the more useful he will be to children, especially below the tenth grade. Those who claim that the liberal-arts graduate makes the best teacher hold this view because they think that this kind of person has the best command of knowledge. More important, however, the liberally educated person can use a greater variety of knowledge to help children find *better ways of coping* with their social dilemmas. The teacher's knowledge can make available a broader range of resources which can help children manage their own destinies more constructively. As will be shown in the next chapter, the teacher's command of subject matter *per se* is far less important than the way he *structures* it for his pupils, and relates it to the learners' own reality.

CHAPTER 10

TOWARD A RELEVANT CURRICULUM

Harmin and Simon, in the *Harvard Educational Review*, have described what could happen when a school superintendent decrees that all seventh-grade social-studies classes will learn the local telephone directory: After the directories are distributed, teachers use a variety of strategies to motivate their classes.[1]

The "human relations" type: "Boys and girls, we are going to have an exciting new unit this term. As a way of studying our city, we're going to learn this amazing collection of information which tells us about the melting pot our city has been."

A more traditional type: "There will be an examination on this material in February, so you had better learn it."

The "personalizing" teacher: "You wouldn't want to hurt my feelings by not memorizing these few names and numbers, would you, children?"

Various homework assignments, teaching aids, objectives, and activities were developed during the term to make the directory "come alive." The project was so successful that it was extended to other grade levels and subject areas.

To extend the fiction a bit: Publishers became interested in the project and textbooks, with teaching manuals, appeared on the market. Meanwhile, someone had applied to a foundation for a general school-improvement grant, which was given after extended negotiations. The extra money was promptly used to establish team-teaching; the teachers with the best background in telephone-directory subject matter were given responsibility for large-group instruction, while other teachers provided individual attention in small groups. A teaching machine corporation constructed programed materials to help the pupils learn names and addresses in small, carefully sequenced steps with immediate reinforcement. Educational television brought some of the most dynamic teachers into all of the classrooms.

When the national government officially declared its war on poverty, disadvantaged pupils were discovered within the

[1]M. Harmin and S. Simon, "The Year the Schools Began Teaching the Telephone Directory," *Harvard Educational Review*, **35**:3 (Summer, 1965), 326–331.

Bob Adelman

school system. While most children were able to get through the *H*s by fifth grade, the disadvantaged child was still on the *C*s and was about five letters behind in his directory work. The school began to focus on this problem. A variety of programs was instituted to compensate for deficiencies of experience in "deprived" children.

Field trips were instituted so disadvantaged children could experience the real streets and associate them with their abstract symbols. Parents of the disadvantaged were asked to read a few pages of the directory to their children each night at bedtime. Attempts were made to show, in the yellow pages, city scenes and people of all races so that greater identification could take place.

Yet this curriculum may not seem quite so absurd when we consider that much of what is taught in schools today has about as much rationale in the curriculum as the contents of the telephone directory. Most conversation in education today concerns innovations and hardware aimed at increasing the efficiency of "directory-type" teaching and curriculum. The majority of teaching energies are devoted to developing a technology to get pupils to learn things for which they have little use or concern.

> To reach the dropouts and give them a reason for staying, the school would have to start by accepting their *raison d'etre*. It would have to take lower class life seriously as a condition and a pattern of experience, not just as a contemptible and humiliating set of circumstances from which every decent boy or girl is anxious to escape. It would have to accept their language, their dress, and their values as a *point of departure* for disciplined exploration to be understood not as a trick for luring them into the middle class, but as a way of helping them to explore the meaning of their own lives. This is the way to encourage and nurture potentialities from *any* social class.[2]

The true test of relevance is the correspondence of the curriculum to the "condition and pattern of experience" of the learner. The closer they are, the more relevant the curriculum. However, because the national population is so diverse, the conditions and patterns of learner experience are also diverse. It becomes necessary to break the bonds of uniform curriculum to the extent that the match can be made. The first step in exchanging the uniform curriculum for one which matches pupil reality is to move from a prepackaged, rigidly scheduled, and uniform curriculum to one flexible enough to be geared to the unique needs of individual schools within a system.

[2]E. Friedenburg, "An Ideology of School Withdrawal," in D. Schreiber (Ed.), *The School Dropout*, Washington, D.C., National Education Association, 1964, p. 38.

From a uniform to a diversified curriculum

The standard curriculum is usually the product of a committee of a few teachers and a supervisor who propose what will take place in every classroom in their city at their pupils' grade level. The material to be taught is arranged in standard form with objectives, content outlines, activities, resources to be used, and a "suggested" time allotment for each division of the content outline.

Contrary to everything known about human behavior, individual differences in abilities, learning styles, and interests, this document proclaims that every child in the same grade will learn the same thing at the same time within the same length of time. Small wonder that teachers are anxious about how much of the material they are "covering." The standard cry in social studies is, "I simply must get to 1890 before the end of the term!" Usually, 1890 is never reached. Few teachers get further than the American Revolution or the Civil War during the entire year. World War I, the great Depression, and World War II and after are, to many students, only pages in the end of their history texts.

To assume that a few people who are basically unaware of the peculiar needs of schools other than their own should direct what is taught, and for what lengths of time, is fallacious and dangerous. It is hard on teachers and unrealistic for children, especially the underprivileged ones. It is inconsistent to ask teachers of the disadvantaged to read, to study, and to try to understand their pupils as much as possible while they, as teachers, are limited by curricular mandates in putting such knowledge to use. The resulting curriculum is geared to uniformity rather than to diversity.

One alternative would be for each school in the system to make its own curriculum decisions within certain broad limits set up by the central administration. It would then be the responsibility of the central office to outline the most crucial concepts for each discipline, as well as those that cut across subject lines, and have these serve as a flexible guide for each school. The school's responsibility would be to redefine and to clarify these concepts, to add any that seem crucial for its particular population, to determine which content will create understanding of the concepts and be most relevant to its pupils, and to make decisions regarding time and sequence of teaching.

We predict the immediate reaction of a teacher reading this recommendation: "Oh, sure, I agree with you. It's all well and good; but meanwhile, I can barely get through a week with all I have to do now just planning for each day, let alone find time to make all those decisions you outlined. It doesn't seem realistic, and you're the ones criticizing the school's inconsistency with reality. All your remarks assume that the central administration will change its policies. You know they aren't about to do that in any big hurry; meanwhile, I've got kids to face tomorrow, next week, next year. What do I do *now?*"

It is necessary to confront each of these issues squarely. Given present conventional scheduling, teachers cannot be expected to make any meaningful curricular decisions. After-school meetings are deadly, and the law of diminishing returns takes a sharp toll on teachers' creativity and energy as soon as the last bell rings. What is needed is a channel for teacher communication: Team planning, with time set aside each day during regular school hours, would enable teachers with similar interests to meet together for planning purposes. This is more feasible now than at any other time in our history because of the advent of team *teaching*. Until such planning is arranged, a curriculum committee for each school could meet on a regular basis and begin making some of these necessary decisions, working on one area at a time.

The problem facing the proposed committee could be formulated as follows: to choose one of four possible alternatives, listed in ascending order of deviation from the conventional course of study.

1. Take the course of study as it stands and try to "cover" as much of it as possible, making the content as dynamic as possible, using many techniques to makes it appealing to youngsters. We will attempt to use field trips, audiovisual aids, interesting and related materials, and try to be flexible concerning time allotments for each unit.
2. Survey the content in a particular subject area and, based on the general needs and interests of the school population, select only those sections that are most relevant and that would have the best chance of making contact with the pupils. For example, spend more of science time on the human body and its care than on the earth's crust. In history, spend more time on the Constitution and its relation to Civil Rights, the Civil War and its aftermath as a key to some of today's racial difficulties, and the rise of industry, automation, and job opportunities.
3. Ignore the prescribed units, but not the general subject area, and within those subject limits create and develop *original* units of study, with sequence and time allotments determined individually. For example:

History	The Civil Rights Movement
	The Roots of Conflict
Math	What is "good" money?
Science	How can we make work easier?
	What is race?
Language Arts	How can advertisements fool us?
	Words and what they do to you
Social Studies	What part can we play in politics?
	Why are rules necessary?[3]

4. Isolate a problem, perhaps in social studies, to create an interdisciplinary problem-solving unit, and then ask how each subject or one single subject might contribute toward the solution of that problem. Only the content relevant to the problem

[3]Some of these units will be described in greater detail in chapter 11.

would be included. Many of the units suggested above could easily be developed across disciplinary lines.

All these suggestions for deviation are, however, still abstract, symbolic, and merely theoretical. What a teacher does with them is the crucial issue, as summarized by John Holt:

> We have to think about that Miss or Mrs. X who is running the class that we want to reform. How does she see her job? She sees, on the one hand, all those pupils; on the other hand, all that material she is supposed to teach them. She wants to be sure that at the end of the year she can convince her bosses either that the children do know all that material, or if they don't, *that it is not her fault*, that she did everything she could, or even better yet, all that she was told to do.
>
> This is . . . perhaps the main reason, why many teachers like detailed teaching instructions, workbooks, manuals, day to day lesson plans and assignments. It saves them from having to think about all these things, which is good; but better still, it protects them from the possibility of blame if things go wrong. If a teacher has decided herself most of what goes on in her class, she can be blamed if later the kids seem not to know what they were supposed to know. But if she has not decided anything, if it was all decided for her by the curriculum, book, and manual, then how can she be blamed? Someone or something else was at fault.
>
> We can't blame teachers for feeling this way. Miss X, facing her class at the start of the year, knows very well that a good many of them, no matter what she does or how hard she works, are *not* going to know, by the end of the year, all they are supposed to know. Furthermore, she knows very well that many of them do not know what they were supposed to know at the end of the previous year, and that she is going to have to take some, perhaps a great deal, of her precious time reteaching them what they should have learned before. Every school is full of these recriminations, expressed or unexpressed. "Why don't you people down there teach these kids what they're supposed to know?"
>
> The least a teacher can do, in such a spot, if she can't

get the kids to know what they are supposed to know, is make it clear to all that she didn't waste a lot of time fooling around with something else. If she takes any of these excursions into useless—i.e., untestable—learning, she is sure to be asked by parents and superiors, "How is it that you found time for all this fooling around when these pupils can't add, multiply, spell, etc., etc.?" I have often been asked just this question. The safe answer is to say that 100% of your class time was spent on the required curriculum. If the authorities want, officially, to waste time on frills like Music, Art, and so on, then let them take the blame, if there is blame to take. But the teacher is not going to stick her neck out.

It seems to me obvious that we have to lift the burden of the required curriculum and minimum standards off the teacher's back, if we want her to allow classroom time for genuine exploration and discovery. We have to create a situation in which she is not going to be held responsible for seeing that children learn this or that, and blamed if they don't. Otherwise, as has so often happened, the most powerful materials and ideas will be converted, like everything else, into little, tiny, prechewed and digested bits of one-bite-at-a-time rote learning.[4]

From a symbolistic to experiential curriculum

The disadvantaged child is really experientially disadvantaged. Although his hidden curriculum has provided him with a great many experiences, some of them quite rich, they are not the ones which prepare him to deal with the multitude of abstract symbols and their manipulations confronting him in the school curriculum. These symbols are constantly tossed at him from every direction on the assumption that there is something in the child's experience which he can relate to teacher-talk and printed words.

All the kinds of experiences possible for a child in school, as

[4] J. Holt, "Curriculum Reform; Some Questions," *Elementary Science Study Newsletter*, December, 1964, pp. 4–5.

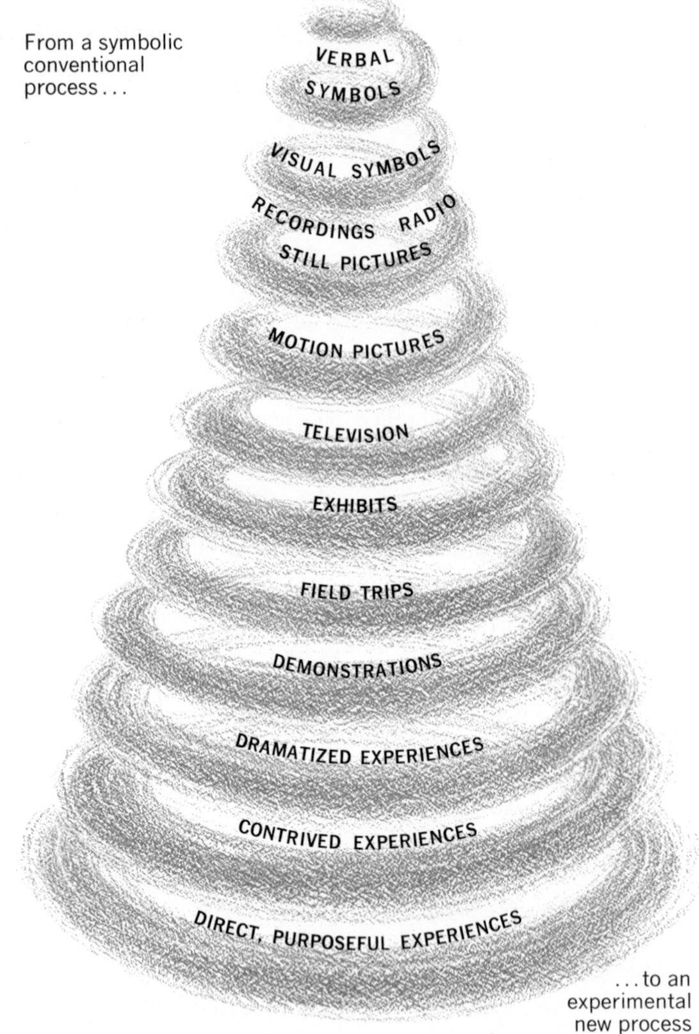

Fig. 10.1 The cone of experiences. (Adapted from E. Dale, Audio-Visual Methods in Teaching *(rev. ed.), New York, Holt, Rinehart and Winston, 1954, p. 43.)*

illustrated in the Cone of Experiences (Fig. 10.1), range from the most concrete to the most abstract. Yet, in the majority of schools by far the major teaching approach is located at the apex—at the position farthest from concrete experiences, via talk and the printed word. In middle-class schools, teachers to some extent succeed this way, although much of their real effectiveness is questionable. In lower-class schools, such tactics will not work—and for good reason:

> . . . No one ever tells slum children much about anything. Conversation is not a highly developed art in their families. Suddenly the child, accustomed to learning through his senses, is obliged to sit still all day before a talkative teacher—she can talk for hours without stopping. Moreover, she seems to think the most important thing in the world is to make out printed words on a page.[5]

Obviously, the abstract is crucial, but not as a starting point for instruction. A curriculum for the disadvantaged must begin as closely as possible to the pupils' direct experience; without such an approach, the abstract cannot be attained. By definition, *to abstract* means to *represent* something that is real, and the basis for abstraction must be based on the concrete reality of the individual to have any meaning for him. Too often teachers assume that the words they use are related to the child's world, when, in truth, they have little or no relationship to him. Many problems in disadvantaged schools stem from this discrepancy. The cardinal rule could be "Experience first; we'll talk later."

In approaching any unit of study, the teacher must ask what could be pulled from the *bottom* of the cone of experiences to serve as a concrete base for what is to be taught. If there is no direct relation, then a contrived one must be developed. It is here that role-playing and dramatic activities make their important contribution.

All this is a departure from current practice, and gives the curriculum guide for the disadvantaged a new character. Instead of just content outlines, the guide should suggest a series of direct or contrived experiences with possible concept outlines to be developed from each, in sequential experiences, beginning in the immediate neighborhood area and expanding outward. The focus should expand each year from simple concepts to more complex ones.

[5]B. Asbell, *The New Improved American*, New York, McGraw-Hill, 1965, p. 91.

From horizontal to vertical skill sequences

Most school skill-development programs place the child in a maze-like situation. At each turn, he must master a new skill before he can proceed, although he is uncertain of the direction he should take or the new skill he will need at the next turn. He has no overall conception of the maze, which would make it easier for him to master future skills, nor has he much recall of how previous skills had enabled him to reach his present position within the maze.

The middle-class child more easily masters this trial-and-error process of mastering the disjointed sequence of skills because he often derives, through his home experiences, the missing links for the overall picture. For the slum child, this overall picture is seriously obstructed. It would be much easier, however, for *all* children to acquire skills on the basis of a vertically programmed, small-step sequence.

In this sequence, the child would have the pattern for the school year laid out before him so that he knows where he is, where he is going, and where he's been. As it now stands, only the teacher has this master plan. In addition to realizing exactly his position in the scheme of things, the child would also find it easier to learn if his mastery of skills progresses in small logical steps from the simplest to the more complicated. Because such steps are small and easy to master, the pupil would have a greater opportunity for immediate positive reinforcement, and will sense a continuous progression rather than a continuous failure. The skill area might be seen as a ladder, with each rung the equivalent of one skill concept.

The ungraded school is an organizational vehicle that, potentially at least, accommodates such a vertical sequence. When well run, multiple ladders for each subject reach continuously from the primary grades through high school, and even through college. The child would be allowed to climb the ladder at his own pace in each subject, and he would be at different levels of achievement for each skill in each subject area.

But even without an ungraded organization, teachers can develop small-step skill sequences. In programming vowel sounds, for example, the teacher might begin by limiting the focus to long-sounding vowels. He should then review in his own mind the prerequisites to this particular skill by asking: What does the child have to know before he can learn the long vowel sounds? He must be able to recognize vowels. What must he know before this? He must be able to distinguish vowels from consonants. Before this? He must know the alphabet. Before this? He must be able to distinguish perceptual shapes of figures. In this way, he determines the small step-by-step sequence of the particular skill area.

The next step is to diagnose the child's present place in the sequence, and to let him know where he is on the ladder so that he can chart his own progress and score. To avoid the impossible task of working individually with perhaps thirty pupils, the teacher must organize the class on the basis of one of three alternatives: (1) begin where most of the pupils are and try to give as much individual help as possible; (2) form two or three groups in the class, letting each group work on its particular level; (3) arrange with several other teachers of the same subject to regroup the classes for this skill.

When the class is organized and the desirable skill sequence determined, the teacher must develop strategies which will enable the child to progress from the concrete to the abstract, and those which will help the child at each level.

Sequences to develop specific skills are already available in outline form. The *Teacher's Manual of the Iowa Test of Basic Skills* is useful for this, as it not only breaks down each sequence, but also gives suggestions for many activities which are related to developing each area. Map reading is an example of a skill in the social-studies skill area:

MAP READING

1. Orient the map and note directions.
2. Use cardinal and intermediate directions in the classroom, neighborhood, and in working with maps.

3. Understand that north is toward the North Pole, south is toward the South Pole.
4. Use the north arrow on the map.
5. Construct simple maps which are properly oriented as to cardinal direction.
6. Recognize the home state and city on the map of the United States and on a globe.
7. Recognize land and water masses on a variety of maps and globes.
8. Identify on a globe and on a map of the world the equator, tropics, circles, continents, oceans, large islands.
9. Use map vocabulary and key accurately.
10. Make simple large-scale maps of a familiar area such as school or neighborhood.
11. Develop the habit of checking the scale on all maps.
12. Understand that real objects can be represented by pictures or symbols on a map.
13. Learn to use different types of keys on different types of maps.[6]

The development here is from the simple to the complex, and it conscientiously covers all the steps necessary to accurate reading of any map.

An especially good example of a vertical-skill sequence, one which expresses each step behaviorally, was developed by the Oakleaf Schools, near Pittsburgh, Pennsylvania:

LEVEL A

Numeration

1. Counts orally from one to ten.
2. Presented with numerals, 1 to 10 in order, reads them orally from left to right.
3. Responds to questions related to the number sequence, 1 to 10, e.g., tells what number comes before, after a given number, or in-between two numbers.
4. Identifies (orally or in writing) the cardinal number of a structured group to 10. Selects a set, or constructs a

[6]Yearbook, Washington, D.C., *Skill Development in the Social Studies*, 33rd Yearbook, National Council for the Social Studies, 1963, p. 161.

set, which contains as many objects as a given numeral. Child uses term "set" to mean a group of objects.

5. Counts orally a set of from one to ten objects by pointing to each object and saying a number.
6. Writes numerals from 1 to 10.
7. Writes numerals, 1 to 10, from left to right on an ordered set of pictures.
8. Takes away all the objects in a given set and says that there are "zero" left.
9. Identifies the correct object or objects for the following relationships: before, after; smaller, larger; more, fewer; smallest, largest; greater, lesser.[7]

From a remote to an immediate curriculum

Almost everything taught in schools is future- or past-oriented; content focused on the here-and-now is the exception. The child who cannot make a specific connection between present events or activities and future goals is discriminated against by a process which emphasizes long-term goals. Such a child is a kind of existentialist—to him, the present moment is absolute and relevant, all else is meaningless.

A functional curriculum, therefore, must use the present as a starting point for learning. Units should consist of projects the end results of which are concrete and tangible—for example, making a model of the pupil's community, a special trip, compiling a short-story anthology, producing a newspaper, or writing and producing a play. Units in social studies should start with the present, with topics such as Civil Rights; studies of the neighborhood and community, or current political campaigns. Some units might deal with present social problems such as juvenile delinquency; prejudice, sex, or school dropout. Other units might begin with an analysis of the students' present interests in music or literature, or even with comic-book analysis, if that is where

[7]"Revised Mathematics Curriculum for September, 1965," Oakleaf Project, Baldwin-Whitehall Public Schools, Pittsburgh, Pa.

the pupils' interests lie. Units can also concern advertising analysis, analysis of payment plans and discounts, propaganda devices.

From a what to a why curriculum

Consider the statements: "New York City is the largest city in the world" and "Most, if not all, of man's behavior is aimed at satisfying his needs." Which of these facts is the more useful? Which has the broader range of application?

The first has limited value and can easily be looked up in a reference book; its application to other situations is restricted. The second statement is general and not as easily arrived at, but it has possibilities for application in a wide variety of contexts. Thus, the latter statement comprises a concept, whereas the first is but a small and specific piece of information. When added to other pieces of information, a concept might be built, but, in the conventional curriculum rarely proceeds toward broad and widely applicable concepts. Usually, the fact remains isolated, important only for itself, and indicative of hundreds of similar tidbits of knowledge. The emphasis is placed on such bits and pieces of information, which the psychologists tell us are the kinds of information the human mind is most likely to forget unless they have some relevance for the learner. Such information becomes relevant only when, in combination, they weave the pattern of an important idea or concept which has frequent application to everyday life. Examine almost any subject-matter test a school gives children, and it is probable that almost 100 percent of the questions require "what" answers. Not a "why" question in the lot.

Specific information has value, but not as isolated facts. Each "what" question must eventually lead to a "why" answer. Ironically, this fast-learning process becomes more and more archaic and impossible to cope with because, with each moment, millions of new pieces of information are being added to the storehouses of human knowledge. New processes of information retrieval bear witness to the fact that we are running farther and farther behind in categorizing and coping with this avalanche of information.

Bruner advocates a curriculum of spiral concepts around which factual information becomes a means of understanding concepts rather than an end in itself.[8] It has been said that the disadvantaged child is too oriented to the concrete to deal with concepts involving a high degree of abstraction. Such an assumption obscures the issue, for disadvantaged children *do* conceptualize—sometimes very poetically—but they do so in their own style and from their own experience. When the school fails to provide concrete experiences, the child has difficulty in forming concepts. There are many levels of conceptualization, from simple to complex, which can, in a sense, be programed by starting slowly and gradually broadening so that both the process as well as the concept itself become more elaborate.

A curriculum for the disadvantaged which is based on generalization must determine which concepts have priority. Selection of concepts should be based as much as possible on the needs of the learner; given the choice of a concept which deals with the organization of national sovereignty within the community of nations, or one that deals with the origin, expression, and resolution of international conflicts, the teacher most assuredly should choose the latter for connections with the pupils' own interpersonal conflicts can be made. For example, one report on major concepts for the social studies sets forth all children's need to study human conflict; this is especially true for the disadvantaged child, whose real world offers less protection from constant human conflict:

> Conflict is characteristic of the growth and development of individuals and to civilization as a whole. Society is constantly pressured to respond to conflicting forces. Rather than to minimize conflicts or shield young students from the fact of its existence, we should make them aware of the origins of conflict, and help them to develop healthy attitudes toward conflict as an aspect of reality with which they must learn to cope.
>
> Most important, the child should learn that for all the varieties of conflict there are culturally approved and dis-

[8] J. S. Bruner, *The Process of Education*, New York, Vintage, 1960.

> approved means for resolving them. In contrast, the student must understand what happens when conflict is unresolved or resolved through means that are not considered legitimate by society. This concept is developed to assist the student to acquire satisfactory patterns of conflict resolution, whether with classmates, between individuals and the state, or between nations, to be used throughout life.[9]

The advantage of utilizing conflict as a conceptual theme is that it can easily become cross-disciplinary. It can be used in the study of literature, for almost any literary work—fiction or nonfiction—deals with some aspect of conflict; if it is simultaneously used in social studies, music, art, or science, a real integration of the ideas in various subject matter fields can be accomplished.

From an academic to a participating curriculum

An article about the involvement of youngsters in the southern Civil Rights movement reported the reasons, feelings, and experiences of the participating children, and reflected the intense sense of pride and purpose the children gained from this involvement. The children spoke as if, for the first time in their lives, they had found and accepted themselves, and liked very much what they accepted. One child said, "I used to wish I was white, but now I wish that I was blacker."[10]

Almost every project working with disadvantaged youngsters has, as one of its major objectives, the improvement of their self-image. The objective can be reached by a variety of means, but the situation depicted above demonstrates a dramatic achievement of a positive self-concept. What elements in the Civil Rights movement had such an impact?

[9]R. Price, G. Smith, and W. Hickman, "Major Concepts for the Social Studies," Social Studies Curriculum Center, the Maxwell Graduate School of Citizenship and Public Affairs in cooperation with the School of Education, unpublished report, Syracuse, N. Y., Syracuse Univ., 1965, pp. 11–12.
[10]Pat Watters, "Why the Negro Children March," *The New York Times Magazine*, March 21, 1965, p. 29.

1. *Action involvement:* The children were placed in action roles through marches, demonstrations, going to jail, and even being beaten or molested by the police.
2. *Sense of power in numbers:* They belonged to a massive power movement, and those in traditional power roles (the white political structure) were forced to bargain and compromise. The children were acting on rather than being acted upon.
3. *Creative expression of discontent:* For a people who have had to keep so much resentment and frustration to themselves, the movement provided an outlet with support and channels through which discontent could be utilized for bettering existing conditions.
4. *Recognition:* They see themselves through the news media as heroes, as people who are battling to right a wrong and who are being celebrated.
5. *Clarity of goals:* Almost every child interviewed was able to articulate the immediate and long-term goals of the movement: "I want my mom to get paid the same as whites for the same work"; "I want to be able to vote"; "I don't want my children to be in the same mess"; "Freedom: better jobs and better homes."

These were goals they really believed in—"God knows we're right"—and goals aimed at the reality of their situation. To what extent can a school curriculum include the same elements to insure such positive self-acceptance?

This should be an objective for all children in our society, as the following statements, by a commission of teachers in California, indicates: ". . . the individual who has benefited by excellent education will have come to know himself and to accept both his strengths and his weaknesses. [Then] he will see himself as a part of a society in which he shares responsibilities. He will have discovered and retained a concern for the social community and will possess the capacity for effective action within the group."[11]

The objectives of positive self-concept and participation in

[11]Statement by California Teachers Associations. Commission on Educational Policy, *Education, U.S.A.*, December 24, 1964.

a democratic society can be reached *through* a school process which utilizes *social action*. Involvement in such action, as demonstrated by the Civil Rights movement, has produced the self-concept and participation we say are our educational goals. Recent surveys have shown that Negro violence, crime, and delinquency in the South have decreased dramatically since the movement began.

If it is true that the disadvantaged are most likely to learn within the context of social movement and that they must act before they learn, then a prime learning principle is also established: The environment must stimulate the need for learning, and ideals and ideas must be employed as guides to action to take education beyond the classroom. Neither the ideas nor the action come first. Children with only a minimum of information can take no constructive action; therefore, action and ideas must interact from the start, each building on the other.

Bruner's spiral curriculum can be used as a frame of reference to see how a social-action curriculum could take form. Bruner insists that "any subject can be taught to anybody at any age in some form that is honest."[12] A spiral could be established of social-action projects, beginning at the elementary-school level and continuing through high school, with each year's project increasingly expanded and complex. Projects in the elementary school might focus on classroom needs, such as development of a class library, and might involve the pupils in raising money or canvassing neighborhoods for second-hand books. Such approaches offer staging points for skill development, decisionmaking, and role transposition.

Another project could evolve around a school procedure the class would like to have changed. Development of skills in negotiating with others would be acquired, and the pupils would also learn to determine channels through which to move. Later, the evaluation of old and the planning of new strategies would create an atmosphere of growing involvement in the school itself. As the child progresses to later grades, the problem might move from

[12] J. S. Bruner, *op. cit.*, p. 33.

the school to the neighborhood. A neighborhood survey of particular needs—stop signs, street lights, playground improvement—and determination of remedies for change could now take place, as well as learning how to contact proper authorities, and what strategy to use in preparation of a case. All these take the children inside the real workings of government in a way that the conventional curriculum has not begun to approach.

Ironically, one source for this curriculum is in the conservative argument leveled against welfare programs for the poor: The more you give to the poor, the more dependent they become; we stifle their initiative by keeping them on the dole; they should be encouraged to assume responsibility and pull themselves up by their own bootstraps. It is agreed that the major institutions which deal with the poor have had the historical pattern of keeping their clients dependent, and that the poor should have responsibility in the solution of their problems. The logical follow-through to have the poor solve their own problems is to teach them to do so with problems they *must* solve. What could be more direct and appropriate? They must work for themselves; no handicapped person ever learned to walk by always using his crutches. The school has an important role to play in developing a product who is a problem-solver, and the problems must be real for the same reasons that the children quoted earlier perceived their Civil-Rights involvement to be real. The process, in effect, must aim at social reconstruction, and the present state of society makes the reconstructionist point of view more relevant than ever.

The real difference between this approach and older ones is that in a social-action curriculum actual participation—rather than mere awareness—is the key. It is the difference between the person who talks about the problems of mankind and the Peace Corps volunteer who moves in and does something about them. It is the difference between the person who says, "Every Negro should have his rights . . . but I wouldn't want one living next door," and the person who organizes his neighborhood to encourage integration.

"Communication," listed as an objective in countless curriculum guides, often fails because the pupils find that the things they are asked to communicate about are those things they do not care about. Teacher training is really a high-level form of communication training. Trained teachers know that the more they learned about behavior—their own and others'—the better they understood the problems and strategies of communication. If part of the school curriculum utilized older children to teach younger pupils the older pupils would learn to observe and to diagnose behaviors, and to develop appropriate strategies and would learn about themselves in the process. All the children would thus be better educated as future parents, participants in a service economy, future teachers, social workers, and as more complete individuals.

To some extent, such attempts exist in a variety of forms across the country today. Its most direct form is in projects initiated by Ronald Lippitt at the University of Michigan. Peggy Lippitt points out some assumptions underlying projects aimed at training children for roles as socialization agents:

> Five Assumptions
>
> One assumption underlying our pilot projects has been that much of the process of socialization involves use by younger children of the behavior and attitudes of older children as models for their own behavior. This process has great potentiality for planned development as an effective educational force, provided that children are trained appropriately for their roles as socialization agents.
>
> Some of the important natural components of this cross-age modeling process include: an older child's ability to communicate more effectively than adults at the younger child's level; the fact that an older child is less likely to be regarded as an "authority figure" than an adult would be; the younger child's greater willingness to accept influence attempts when he perceives a greater opportunity for reciprocal influence; and the fact that a slightly older child provides a more realistic level of aspiration for the younger child than an adult would.
>
> A second assumption of our projects has been that involvement of older children in a collaborative program with

> adults to help younger children will have a significant socialization impact on the older children because of (1) the important motivational value of a trust- and responsibility-taking relationship with adults around a significant task, and (2) the opportunity to work through—with awareness but at a safe emotional distance—some of their own problems of relationships with their siblings and peers.
>
> A third assumption has been that assisting in a teaching function will help the "teaching students" to test and develop their own knowledge, and also help them discover the significance of that knowledge.
>
> A fourth assumption has been that both younger learners and their adult teachers will be significantly helped in "academic" learning activities through the utilization of trained older children available for tutoring, drilling, listening and correcting, and other teaching functions.
>
> A final assumption has been that a child will develop a more realistic image of his own ability and present state of development, and will gain a greater appreciation of his own abilities and skills, if he has an opportunity to help children younger than himself to acquire skills which he already possesses and to develop positive relationships with children older than himself.[13]

Other programs are developing around the concepts outlined in Riessman and Pearl's book, *New Careers for the Poor,* where new kinds of teaching roles are suggested, each requiring different levels of training for a greater variety of people.[14]

Fred Strodtbeck of the University of Chicago, in his research into patterns of family interaction in the lower class, found that children who experience the feeling of power within the family circle usually develop into socially desirable products. Such an experience for a lower-class child is likely to be exceptional. Strodtbeck recommends decisionmaking activities in the classroom to help pupils become more responsible for their own acts.

[13]Peggy Lippitt and J. E. Lohman, "Cross-age Relationships—an Educational Resource," from *Children* **12**:3, 1965.

[14]A. Pearl and F. Riessman, *New Careers for the Poor,* New York, Free Press, 1965.

From an antiseptic to a reality-oriented curriculum

> The truth is that life is hazardous, full of risks, offering only special types of security, and, these not the types usually talked about. We must find some way of facing this fact without becoming morbid about it. We must also find a way of presenting it to our students without blunting the keenness of their desires or interfering with the buoyancy of their hope. But can we impress on them that the battle is worthwhile unless we ourselves know what we are fighting for?[15]

What are study units on the "People of the Tropical Rain Forest," or "People of Brazil," often inclusive of no more than the quaint clothes worn, the little houses lived in, the little jobs done, the cute games played? Rarely, if ever, are the realities of the social situation studied. Are the smiling little South American boy and his burro realy so happy? If the South American boy's life is so pleasant and quaint, why do we have an Alliance for Progress, or ship millions of dollars worth of food to the area? Why do we have a Peace Corps? The conventional educational process seems to operate on the assumption that, if evil is ignored, it will go away, when the truth is that to ignore evil is to encourage it.

This antiseptic curriculum not only fails to help pupils to investigate the broader social facts of life, but it also denies the personal and emotional facts of life of the learner himself. The curriculum must help the child, especially the disadvantaged, to answer two major questions:

1. How has society been a major contributing factor to the more negative conditions of all of the people in this country and to certain groups of people in particular?
2. How have these social factors led to ways in which we define ourselves as individuals?

These questions take on special significance when considered

[15] J. S. Bixler, *Education for Adversity*, Cambridge, Mass., Harvard Univ. Press, 1962, pp. 5–6.

in relation to the Negro child. A report entitled "Black Belt Schools: Beyond Desegregation," stated: "The most pernicious psychological consequence of a caste system must surely be the tendency for individuals to accept as accurate for themselves the social definitions of inferiority inherent in the system."[16]

Society has made the major contribution to the difficult situation in which the Negro finds himself; as a result, the Negro may define his social worth by the criteria established by society. The negative connection between dark skin and personal worth results in self-rejection by too many with dark skins. As one of Miller's characters says in the novel *The Cool World*:

> WHO AM I?
> Man—you ask why should I be me—how I get to be me—why am I here and not someplace else—and you just end up scared like you was walkin' down a empty street at night. So scared it running out you ears.[17]

Some other comments which children have been overhead to say are:

> The people that are white, they can go up. The people that are brown, they have to go down . . . black people—I hate 'em.
>
> 4½-YEAR-OLD-NEGRO GIRL

> I don't like that father. He's got a black head.
>
> 4½-YEAR-OLD-NEGRO BOY

> I don't *want* to be colored.
>
> PRESCHOOL NEGRO GIRL

> He's black! He's a stinky little boy. He's a stinker—he sh—! Take it away . . . I don't like colored boys.
>
> PRESCHOOL NEGRO BOY

> She stood up, looked right through me at Wilson, and

[16]"Black Belt Schools: Beyond Desegregation," *The New York Times*, December 12, 1965, p. 75.
[17]W. Miller, *The Cool World*, New York, Little, Brown, 1959.

> shouted, "That black thing—he's blacker than I am!" Wilson jumped from his chair and yelled back, "That's what you think, you black bitch!"
>
> FOURTH-GRADERS IN HARLEM

The excellent study, *Race Awareness in Young Children*, by Mary Ellen Goodman, contains a wealth of evidence on how very young children evaluate themselves and each other in terms of color and race.[18] The tragic conclusion is that, even before many Negro youngsters start school, they are seriously contaminated by the white society's evaluation of the Negro. Self-hate and self-rejection come through in the quotations cited above.

According to Ausubel:

> The Negro child inherits an inferior caste status and almost inevitably acquires the negative self-esteem that is a realistic ego reflection. . . . The Negro child becomes confused in regard to his feelings about himself and his group. He would like to think well of himself, but often tends to evaluate himself according to standards used by the other group. These mixed feelings lead to self-hatred and rejection of his group, hostility toward other groups, and a generalized pattern of personality difficulties.[19]

These children also acquire confused feelings about themselves and the color of their skins:

> . . . Children become aware almost from infancy of the opprobrium Americans attach to color. They feel it in their parents' voices as they are warned to behave when they stray beyond the ghetto's wall. They become aware of it as they begin to watch television, or go to the movies, or read the mass-circulation magazines; beauty, success, and status all wear a white skin.[20]

The connection between this self-contempt of failure and achieve-

[18]Mary Ellen Goodman, *Race Awareness in Young Children*, New York, Collier Books, 1964.

[19]D. and Pearl Ausubel, "Ego Development Among Segregated Negro Children," in Harry Passow (Ed.), *Education in Depressed Areas*, New York, Teachers College, Columbia University, 1963.

[20]C. E. Silberman, *Crisis in Black and White*, New York, Vintage, 1965, pp. 49–50.

ment in school, as educational psychologists report, "instills a sense of unworthiness that eliminates trying."[21] The child who is a failure because of his color has greatly reduced motivation for school achievement. A positive self-concept is essential for achievement in school.

If the child acquires the specific skills required for achievement, his self-image may be improved, for success experiences can have a positive effect on school achievement. But children must *want* to achieve, and a damaged ego structure because of a caste system must be considered in the school's planning. As Ausubel states:

> Before Negroes can assume their rightful place in American culture important changes in the ego structure of Negro children must first take place. They must shed feelings of inferiority and self-derogation, acquire feelings of self-confidence and racial pride, develop realistic aspirations for occupations requiring greater education and training, and develop the personality traits for implementing those aspirations.[22]

There is the problem, accompanied by a fairly comprehensive diagnosis. Once again, the almost futile question: Where does the antiseptic curriculum confront this issue? Race, color, and sex all assume equal status in the antiseptic curriculum—they are all equally taboo. As Goodman notes:

> There is a general feeling among the nursery school teachers and directors that it is rather shocking to mention race publicly, just as one does not talk openly about sex (in these or other schools with "nice" teachers who are creating a "nice" middle-class atmosphere). Racial identity is deliberately and consistently ignored; racial differences are dealt with by behaving as though they did not exist. This is the official policy, and departures from it are rare, private (as in conversation between teachers), or instigated by the parents or children themselves.[23]

[21]L. Cronbach, *Educational Psychology* (2nd ed.), New York, Harcourt, Brace & World, 1963, p. 127.
[22]D. and Pearl Ausubel, *op. cit.*, p. 130.
[23]Mary Ellen Goodman, *op. cit.*, p. 159.

This is truly a legitimate area for curriculum development. Continued avoidance of the real concerns of the child can only add to his confusion and lack of understanding.

Toward a more affective curriculum

The search for model curriculum development can begin here. There is still a great distance to go, but a general discussion may illuminate an avenue of approach. The term *affective* can be used in a broader sense than its traditional definition for education to mean emotional concerns—feelings about oneself, others, experiences, and objects that press upon the learner—and patterns which affect specific groups in our society. Most descriptions of the disadvantaged child are in terms of his feelings—negative self-concept, passivity, alienation, emotional style, lack of motivation—but programs planned for such children are aimed for the most part at his "cognitive" rather than emotional needs.

Man is born with basic needs, psychological and emotional, and his life is a series of activities aimed at satisfying these needs. Cognitive needs are not basic and become needs only when they can be utilized to satisfy basic ones. They are, then, the tools with which one attempts to satisfy one's physical and emotional needs. Educational programs must be developed to reverse the current practice and to determine that there is a connection between what the child *needs* to know and what he is actually taught.

The school must consider the emotional concerns of its pupils and help them work with those concerns. In this way, emotional and social concerns can become the core around which the curriculum is organized. For example, Joseph Golden, of the Syracuse University drama department, has successfully established a relationship between the theater and teaching the disadvantaged. The disadvantaged have been the prime audience for drama; from the time of the Greeks, and especially during the Elizabethan period, drama has appealed to the common man. Hamlet, in spite of elaborate Shakespearean language, was able to maintain contact with such diverse audiences as the lords and ladies in the boxes and the common people in the pit, for there was something classless and elemental in the play. The major point of contact in these dramas was their common emotional concern—Hamlet's desire for revenge to right a wrong. When such a common concern is the central issue, the drama establishes a meeting ground for all people regardless of background.

As an illustration of how this common concern can be utilized in teaching, one teacher was experiencing difficulty in teaching the Declaration of Independence to a recalcitrant class. No one cared to learn about it, and she tried every trick of motivation in the book but succeeded only in losing the class each time. She asked himself, "What in the Declaration of Independence is most like an emotional concern of the pupils?" The answer "Defiance!" Is not the whole emotional context of the Declaration one of defiance? What child has had no experience with defiance? Indeed, much of daily classroom activity is occupied with just that defiance. The teacher then began to explore the notion of defiance and the children's experiences with and feelings about it; then, when she reintroduced the study of the Declaration of Independence, it became a vital issue. Thus, there are possibilities for organizing a whole curriculum around areas of emotional concern, with especially significant implications for integrated schools. Groups of pupils from a variety of backgrounds can work together around common centers of emotional experience that are relevant to them as people.

Concerns should not be confused with interests. Much of the progressive education movement was dedicated to building curriculum around the interests of students. Teachers had found it difficult to motivate learners because the learners were not really *interested*. Therefore, it was decided that if pupil interests could be assessed, and programs built from them, pupils would become motivated. In other words, if children were interested in space, space is what they studied; if they were interested in animals, they studied animals. Curriculum building based on whole interests is clearly limited; we don't always know what we are now or could be interested in, and what we say we are interested in may not *really* be what concerns us in the final analysis. For example, one teacher found that her class had an almost compulsive interest in science. "What aspect of science?" she was asked. "Evaporation—the children seemed utterly intrigued by evaporating water." After a further investigation, however, it was discovered that it wasn't so much *evaporation* which intrigued the class as it was a concern for change, permanence, and absence. As the children phrased it, "If water can disappear, can we?"

Similarly, boys who express an interest in strong men may be really concerned with power and potency. Girls who express an interest in "dating" may be concerned about sex and popularity and their role in society. Therefore, it is *concern* rather than interest that contains more durable potential for a relevant curriculum. Concerns are feelings of uneasiness. A person may have interests and yet not be concerned or, on the other hand, interests may reflect concerns.

"What," a teacher may ask, "are the concerns of a group of youngsters in my school, my class? By what cues can I recognize them?" The professional literature is one source of such cues, given the fact that the disadvantaged have been described and evaluated by a great variety of professional observers in a number of fields. However, these areas are the least direct and most general. Another source of cues to concerns lies in the normal give-and-take discussion among colleagues within the school, particularly the descriptions of incidents as they occur. A third source is, clearly, one's own direct observation. Obviously, the same cues observed by different people will lead to a variety of interpretations. What is needed are some ways to refine *what* cues stand for *what* concerns. This we intend to pursue.

Should concerns become a more intrinsic part of the school's programing? The answer lies in our hypothesis that the greater the degree of relevance teaching contains, the better the chance for making contact with the disadvantaged learner, and the greater the potential for learning to become consonant with action and feeling. So oriented, we will now explore the model as a way of generating an instructional program from the concerns of youngsters.

A model for developing a relevant curriculum[24]

To develop a curriculum which is suitable to the particular needs of a particular class requires decisionmaking. Appropriate decisions must be made at several levels, and thus, it is necessary to break the process into easy steps (Fig. 10.2):

1. *What is the learning group?* The first of these steps is to define the class as a whole. What kinds of pupils make up the group? What is their age level? At what stage of human development are they? Do they come from impoverished or wealthy homes? For example:

Developmental	12-year-olds
Economic	poor (or middle, upper class)
Geographic	rural (or urban, suburban)
Cultural, Racial, Ethnic	Negro (or Indian tribe, Mexican-American, etc.)

2. *What cues indicate patterns of emotional concern among the group?* Once the broad description of the group has been made, the next step is to assess what apprehensions the pupils may implicitly be dealing with. To discover these, the teacher must be able to recognize cues given through the pupils' overt behavior which point to the areas of pupil concern; he must also be able to evaluate their meaning. An examination of the pupils' expressed observations and reports will reveal that their hidden concerns probably fall into one or more of the following categories:

Self-rejection reflects a need for a positive self-image; sample cues are:

"Why do I live in the slums?"
"I may be brown, but I'm not black!"

[24]For a more detailed version, see G. Weinstein and M. Fantini, *A Model for Developing A Relevant Curriculum*, New York, The Ford Foundation, 1967.

"How can you like me when I don't like myself?"
"We're the dumb-class special!"

Disconnectedness from the rest of society or from one another reflects a need to establish connection with each other or with society at large; sample cues are:

"Whenever I leave Harlem I feel like a fish out of water."
"Why should I listen to my parents? Look at the way they live!"
"In order for me to get educated, I gotta be like you. What about me?"
"You can't trust nobody, white or Negro."

Powerlessness reflects a need for pupils to acquire greater control over their lives; sample cues are:

"It's no use trying; there's nothing you can do."
"I'm Hercules; I can do anything!"
"What the hell can I do? This is the attitude; that we can do nothing, so leave it alone. People think you're always going to be under pressure from the white man and he owns and runs everything, and we are so dependent on him that there's nothing I can do. This is the general impression I've gotten from most of the adults in Harlem."

3. *How and why have the distinctive manifestations of concern patterns emerged for the identified learning group?* While many patterns of concern may be common to most humans in our society, their manifestations may be different in different sub-

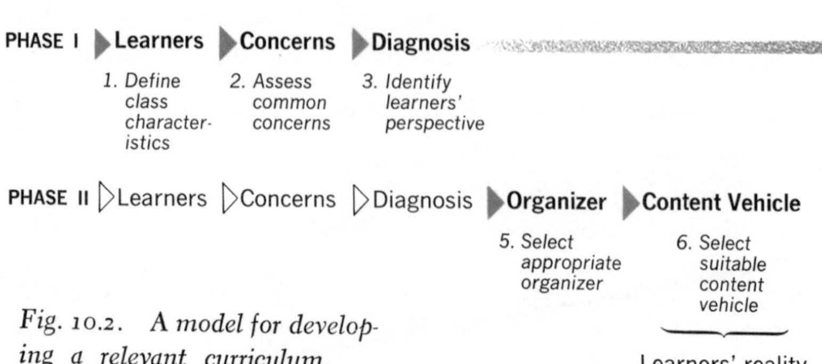

Fig. 10.2. A model for developing a relevant curriculum.

cultures. Thus, while a disadvantaged child may be struggling for greater control because he has had very little support from his social milieu, an advantaged child may be struggling for greater control because he has been given too much protection. Or, while the disadvantaged child may indicate his need for power by saying, "So what if I graduate from high school; I won't get a good job anyway," the advantaged might show his need for power by saying, "Sure I'm glad I finally got my own car. When I'm winging along in it I feel free as a bird. It's the only time I'm really in control."

4. *What would we like to see occur in the learner's behavior that would be different from what we observe now?* Once we diagnose the reasons for the feelings of powerlessness among the disadvantaged, we can begin to consider desired outcomes. If feelings of powerlessness are evident, for example, it is not enough to aim at making the learner feel more powerful. We must go on to ask, "If he felt more powerful, what would a child *do* that he isn't doing now?" In other words, we have to describe those behaviors which indicate increased feelings of potency.

A person who feels potent is able to plan and to develop a variety of strategies for getting over obstacles to attain his ends. He knows a variety of resources he can tap, reorganize, and manipulate in different ways to get things done. He demonstrates feelings of potency by *trying* to do things and persisting through alternate routes. Such a child might say, "Let's try it this way," "Let's figure out how to do it," rather than "It's no use, nobody

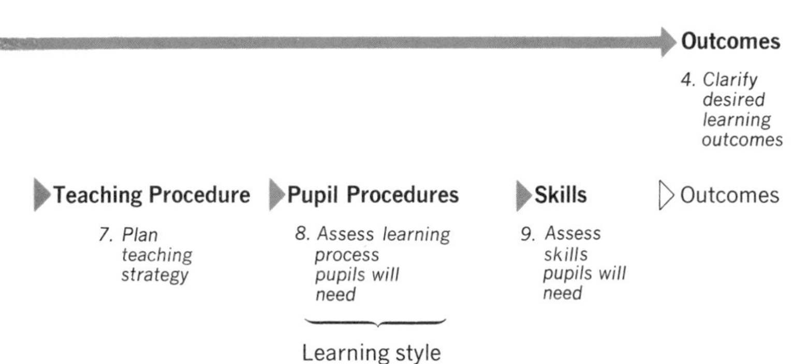

can do anything." He is able to be realistic as to what is achievable —alone, or with groups.

5. *What organizers can be used to integrate the concerns, desired outcomes, and the instructional program?* Thus far we have identified the learner and some significant cues, their diagnosis and the outcomes. Now let us move to a consideration of the school program. There are at least three types of organizers that are useful:

Generalizations are the fundamental ideas, principles, and concepts—that is, the main themes—around which the specific content and teaching-learning procedures will be structured. For example, specific school subject matter in English or the social studies might be structured around the theme sequence:

a. The way we see ourselves is learned.
b. What we learn about ourselves depends upon where we live and whom we live with.
c. What we learn may be inaccurate.

Procedural Organizers are a set of procedures which the learners might acquire to improve their coping or controlling of problem situations as indicated in their cues of concern; there may be new ways of thinking about and acting upon these situations. Examples of some procedural organizers might be:

Analyzing a problem to find out what it is and its possible causes.

Learning how to negotiate with someone with a different point of view.

Generating alternatives to a situation, trying them, and evaluating the outcomes.

Procedural organizers used without accompanying generalizations may not aid the learners in understanding these situations any better, but it offers a more instrumental kind of help through new strategies and experimenting with new behaviors.

Questions that facilitate inquiry by both the teacher and the learners into the problem area can serve as a way of organizing instructional experiences.

Each of these organizers can be used alone or in combination. But, regardless of which organizers are used, it is essential that some relevant organizer is required for sustaining an instructional program.

6. *What content vehicles can be utilized to tap into the organizer we have established?* A content vehicle is a subject-matter unit which can serve as a staging point for instruction, such as prescribed units within English, social studies, math, science, etc.: Colonial Times, Our Community, Matter and Energy, Communication. Other disciplines not standard to the school curriculum can be drawn upon, too, however. For example, psychology, sociology, anthropology, philosophy, education can be integrated into the subject-matter. Content vehicles can also include the media, such as films, books, pictures, and field trips; classroom incidents, episodes, and problems; pupils' experience—in and out of school; and the children themselves.

As previously stated, that content which is most closely connected to the learner's reality will have the best possibility for engaging the learner, especially those who are disadvantaged. Therefore, we suggest that the initial series of content vehicles selected be close to the learners themselves—*their* content. What content does the child bring to school? What does he already know? What can he teach the teacher? What does he talk about when no one is structuring his talk? The answers to these questions may lead to the initial content vehicles used to tap into the organizers.

7. *What teaching procedures, strategies, or methods are most appropriate to the learners' style and for developing the desired outcomes?* It is possible, even if one matches teaching and learning styles, that the methods used might not enhance the desired outcomes and, in fact, might even be contradictory to those outcomes. For example, if the desired outcomes were related to having the learners feel greater potency, and the teaching pro-

cedures were such that the learners were in dependent learning roles, it is difficult to see how the outcomes would be achieved. It is one thing to talk about power, but perhaps even more essential to the experiencing of power—with its responsibilities and problems—teaching procedures should allow for this kind of experience. Some excellent examples of procedures which allow the learners to experiment with power roles have been mentioned, that is, social action and cross-age teaching.

Here again, material which describes the learning patterns of the disadvantaged comes into play. The task is to match teaching procedures with the learning style of the youngster. Training teachers to develop interaction systems with the learners which give the learners emotional support and feelings of worthwhileness are important here. Most of the work on changing teachers' attitudes towards the learner so that a climate of mutual respect is developed, when placed in this broader context, adds to the meaning of this kind of training.

8. *What procedures, ways of thinking, examining, behaving, would the learners need in order to attain the desired outcomes?* Again, if power were the central issue, procedures involving the generation of real alternatives to action—planning change steps, mapping out of strategies, experimenting with new behaviors, and evaluating outcomes—become the most crucial.

9. *What skills does the learner have and/or need in order to expand his base of resources for attaining the concepts, procedures and outcomes?* The acquisition of a great many of the pupil procedures depends on the degree to which the learner can utilize skills, especially language skills. It would be hard to imagine pupils engaging in an analysis of their experience without at the same time developing more elaborate speaking, listening, reading, and perhaps writing skills.

10. *To what extent were the desired outcomes attained?* This step represents the evaluation of the learning situation. If not all outcomes were achieved, why not? In which areas did the programing seem weak or strong—diagnosis, content, or procedures used? If the outcomes were achieved, to what extent? What is the next step? If behaviors were changed, what new strategies or

content are suggested? Is there a different learner reality, learning style, or learning-readiness evident? How much more elaborate in dealing with his concerns do we want the learner to be? How much time do we have to spend?

Such questions lead to a movement through the model again —in ever-increasing spheres of complexity and elaboration. However, even when the curriculum has been ideally structured according to these questions, its effectiveness with the learners will depend on the way the teacher presents it in the classroom. It is to this area that we turn next.

CHAPTER 11

TOWARD CONTACT CLASSROOM METHODS

The ultimate testing ground for contact with the pupil is the classroom. Regardless of what curriculum, school organization, or theories have been developed, the final test remains: Can the teacher meet the pupil as the pupil really is and establish a dialogue for learning? Is he willing, and does he have the skill, to search out those connections which can link the child's nature and interests to a more elaborate perception of the world, and utilize those connections as learning vehicles?

Since we communicate chiefly through verbal language, this must serve as the main entrance to the world of the child. However, if the teacher perceives language narrowly, as simply a mechanical skill which is valid only if it matches his own language skill, he has lost the opportunity for contact. If language is to help to bridge the gap between the hidden curriculum of the child and the formal curriculum of the school, it must be used not only to diagnose the pupils' verbal limitations or richness, but also to discover and to diagnose the child's particular perception of the world, his concerns, problems, and realities. When we consider language as behavior, we move it from the merely cognitive to the emotional life of the learner. It is not enough to know, for example, that the term "cool" means indifference. One must be aware that the affectation of "coolness" is a protective device for not exposing to the public all of the hurts or feelings of inadequacy that a disadvantaged child might harbor. Thus, the heart of teaching lies in reaching for the *child's* content, understanding its significance, and building upon it so that it becomes larger, and expands the child's frame of reference.

This goal cannot be reached unless the teacher learns the language of the child. In practice, the rule is more often that the child is obliged to learn the teacher's language, and that is where it ends. It is here that the school's phoniness becomes reinforced.

But language is only the beginning, and an astute teacher can proceed to make familiarity with pupil reality work for him and his teaching purpose. It is true that much of what is *supposed* to be taught is so utterly remote from the pupils' reality that it seems the two can never mesh. Yet, if we look long and hard enough at the standard curriculum, we find that there are ways

Bob Adelman, Center for Urban Education

TOWARD CONTACT CLASSROOM METHODS

of manipulating it to fit more closely the living world of pupil reality. Significantly, when this is done, the subject matter takes on a more vital relevance for the teacher as well as for the pupil, as opposed to its present "dry as dust" character.

Contact through language

A teacher can become familiar with the language of his pupils by *listening* to that language, rather than merely hearing it. The natural speech of children occurs during informal play, for it is in play that children lose their self-consciousness and their language is most natural; this is especially true if the play is not under the auspices of the school or other adult supervision. For example, the Saturday baseball game, for which the children have their own rules and procedures, on the neighborhood sandlot or playground is rich in potential for gaining language insight. How do the children organize a game? How do they choose sides? On what basis do they select their leaders? What words or phrases do they use to tease or to encourage each other? How do they resolve their disputes, handle each other's errors and triumphs? Here is language that is alive. From this language, one can learn the rhythms, unique phraseology, colloquialisms, and usage within the pupil's social context. Proper diagnosis of the cultural and social values, attitudes, and interests from this living language is an important prerequisite to the preparation of original teaching materials that are less phoney to the pupils.

One of the first assignments given to a group of urban teaching trainees was a "Pupils' Culture Survey." As part of this assignment, each trainee was to list some of his pupil's most often used slang expressions with illustrations of their usage. One trainee listed "bustin' suds," which, when translated, means "washing dishes." Such esoteric knowledge can often be utilized later, as illustrated by the following report from this trainee:

> The sixth-grade class had just returned from lunch, and the teacher expended a considerable amount of energy in getting

> the pupils settled down. Then, one of her "troublemakers" walked in late.
>
> "Why are you late for class?" she asked.
>
> "I was bustin' suds," was the reply from the latecomer.
>
> The rest of the class became interested in the outcome of this exchange.
>
> "Well," the trainee said, "I'm sorry you had to wash the dishes but still that's no excuse for coming to class late. Now sit down and start your work."
>
> The boy's expression changed from amusement to surprise. "How did you know what 'bustin' suds' meant?"
>
> "Oh, I get around," she replied smugly. "Now take your seat."
>
> He did and the class continued its work.

It was a small victory for the trainee, but every new teacher will testify to the importance of such victories in developing control of a new class.

Another teacher effectively utilized "Teach-Me" time. One period a week was set aside when the pupils were required to teach the teacher something they knew that he didn't. They would begin these periods by asking the teacher a series of "Have-you-ever-heard-abouts." Whenever he pleaded ignorance, they would explain it to him. The topics ranged from the latest dance-step, to a street game, to pupil expression. This was not only an effective way for the teacher to learn his pupils' language and culture, but it also afforded him an opportunity to teach the pupils how to articulate more clearly their own experiences which they had taken for granted in more generalized form. Since the pupils tended to explain nonverbally, through facial expressions and gestures, the pupils were missing the value of explicit experiences. As the teacher gently and consistently prodded them to use words, they discovered that it was one thing to *play* stick-ball but quite another to tell someone *how*. Thus, both the teacher and his pupils learned from each other.

Frank Riessman tells of another strategy for making contact through language—using a "hiptionary," a dictionary of "hip" terms and their formal definitions.[1] If pupils with low verbal ability study through games and exercises such terms as "bug" (to disturb, bother, annoy) and "cop-out" (to avoid conflict by running away), they become familiar with the new vocabulary and begin to substitute accepted words.

Teachers can easily have their pupils compile "hiptionaries" of their own and practice writing short paragraphs in both informal and formal language. The difficulty is in *how* the teacher pulls the meanings from the pupils. They must be asked to supply as many sentences as possible using the "hip" term so the teacher can decipher the meanings from context. In addition, the teacher must be constantly aware of the multiple meanings for many of the terms. This teaching procedure is illustrated in the "Dig All Jive" poetry lesson on page 382.

We have often found the language of the urban Negro youngster to be rich in metaphor. The concept of metaphorical language can easily be taught by utilizing their language. Riessman mentions, for example, the "hip" terms for someone who is bisexual: "AC-DC" or "switch-hitter" or "swings from both sides of the fence." Another concept is that of being "far out"—not of the mainstream, strange, weird, atypical. When the pupils examine their own use of metaphor and recognize how others use it, a cross-cultural connection can be established.

Utilization of pupil language for the improvement of writing skills was demonstrated by a teacher who, after learning that language, developed the following exercise:

> The paragraph you are about to read was written by a typical teenager. The language is all right at times, but this boy has fallen into the habit of talking this way all the time; therefore, he can't seem to get a job. Would you kindly help him translate this into understandable language so that he might get a job. Thank you.
>
> I were on the stone one day when along came my pal who had recently got busted for boostering a set of threads. The fuzz caught him making the hit and he took a trip to In-

[1] F. Riessman, *Hip Word Game Workbook*, Chicago, Follett, 1967.

dustry. He did his trick and they turned him loose last week.

Mr. Charlie ain't about to come on no job for me or him so we mainly catch the breeze most of the day. Along came an old pal of mine in a '64 chine—a ragtop at that. He was long on coin but short on smarts but he was making it big. He told us that he has cut Mr. Hard Times loose and no laying down the numbers around the street.

He says, "Why don't you get in the wind and come on some bread?" We said we didn't have a contact but if he had anything on the line to clue us in. He cut out.

About five days later my man in the ragtop plowed his wheels into a bridge and the minister will lay a few words on him today just before they drop him. Seems he got aholt of some cheap wine and he thought he was going under the bridge.

Well I'm still on the bricks and if I don't come on something soon I have to hit the line at the armory to get me some welfare greens.

You think them people would come on a job for an intelligent drop-out like me. Some cats are always screaming on you. Well I gotta get me a new earring because I going to get me a job Friday and I want to come on like a dude. Well I catch you clowns playing the school games later. I got no time for that jazz. Who knows if I start booking skin or get into the Cuban I can get me a set of bolts and get my head busted like the ragtop man. I think I'll hit the park when the boys bust out the cage at 3 o'clock. I gotta give them that talk on the value of dropping-out of school. Cool it—I'll catch your act later.

(Signed)
WILLIE FINK

P.S. I writ this by hand.

This particular exercise was given to a group of ninth-graders in Syracuse who were extremely reluctant to become involved in anything resembling typical academic work. However, they attacked this assignment with relish. They worked on writing skills and vocabulary development and developed a very interesting discussion around such questions as: Was Willie really "hip?" What was "hipness?" Was it the same for all situations? These questions led to controlled verbal disputes that provided an excellent stage for the examination of these very important concepts.

The following lesson serves to summarize some of the major concepts we have attempted to develop in this book; here, "Do You Dig All Jive?" utilizes contact through the child's language. It also illustrates an approach to nonstandard dialect in such a way that the pupils feel that learning standard English dialect doesn't mean they must discard their own. It exposes children to the idea that poetry can "swing" and that some of the "swingingest" has been written by Negro authors. Its methodology is the inductive approach through questioning to challenge the imagination. Finally, it shows the way to vocabulary development through role-playing.

In order to aid a teacher who asked how she might get her eighth-grade class interested in poetry, one of the present authors related his experience:

> Some time after I had been asked for aid, I was looking through my materials when I came across an anthology of Langston Hughes' poetry. I noted a poem entitled "Motto:"
>
> I play it cool,
> And dig all jive.
> That's the reason I stay alive.
> My motto, as I live and learn,
> Is: To dig and be dug
> In return.[2]
>
> I made about thirty copies and, with the permission of the English teacher, took them into her classroom. The children stared at me, probably wondering what I was up to. Without saying a word, I distributed the copies of the poem so each child had one.
>
> There was a moment or two of silence while they read the poem. Finally, I heard someone mumble, "Tough!" followed by, "Hey now, this is really tough, man!"
>
> Being familiar with their jargon, I realized they had paid

[2]L. Hughes, *Langston Hughes Reader*, New York, Braziller, 1958, p. 98. Reprinted by permission of George Braziller, Inc.

the poem a supreme compliment, although it probably didn't appear that way to the other teacher.

"Hey now . . . this cat's pretty cool. Who wrote it?"

"Langston Hughes," I answered.

"Who's he?"

"He's a very famous Negro author, poet, and playwright." I saw that most of the class hadn't heard of him. "Do you know what this poem is talking about?" I asked them.

"Sure," they said.

"How come?"

"Well, it's written in our talk."

"Oh! Then you understand everything this is saying?"

"Sure," they said.

"That's good. Maybe you can tell me then what the first line means by 'playing it cool.' They had great difficulty in verbalizing the concept of coolness. "Are there any brave souls in here who would try something with me?" A boy's hand shot up. "Good! come up here. Now I'm a teacher standing in the middle of the hallway. You're coming toward me down the hall, but you're walking on the wrong side. I'm going to tell you something, and when I do, I want you to play it cool. Okay?"

"Yeah," he said.

The boy started walking toward me, and I said in a very fierce manner, "Hey you! You're walking on the wrong side of the hallway. Get over where you belong!"

The boy, very calmly and without raising his head, moved with deliberate slowness to the other side of the hall and sauntered on as if I did not exist.

"Is that playing it cool?" I asked.

The class agreed that it was.

"I'll tell you what," I said to my volunteer. "Let's do the same thing, only this time show us what would happen if you didn't play it cool." Our little scene began again. But this time, after I had ordered him to move to the proper side of the hall he stopped angrily and said, "Who you talkin' to?"

"To you," I said.

"I ain't doin' nothin!"

He became very belligerent and a hot verbal battle ensued.

I stopped the scene before it got any hotter, and said to the class, "Well, what's the difference between playing it cool and not playing it cool?"

Finally, one pupil came up with, "When you're cool, you're calm and collected."

"Very good," I said, writing *calm* and *collected* on the board. "Anyone else?"

They were able to supply a few more words. I then gave them a few, such as *indifferent* and *nonchalant*. They were especially intrigued by *nonchalant*, and kept repeating it aloud to themselves.

"Now, how about this word 'jive' in the second line: 'And dig all jive'?"

One pupil said, "It means jazz."

Another told how jive meant "teasing" in the expression "stop jivin' me."

Then, a third boy chimed in with this incident: "I was in another city once, walkin' through a strange neighborhood. These guys were standing on the corner and one of them, he yells to me, 'Hey man, *cut that stroll.*' Now I never heard that before, so I turned and said, 'What?' That's all I had to do. If there wasn't a cop on the corner I might have been messed up good."

"Do you know what *stroll* means now?" I asked.

"Oh yeah. It's when you're walkin' like this." He proceeded to demonstrate. It was a walk with a limping gait or strut that I have seen our children use many times. It seemed to generate a "devil-may-care," or "watch out, it's me," attitude.

"It's like they were tellin' me," the boy continued, "that I was walkin' too big to suit them!"

"How does all this show what the word *jive* means?"

"Well, I just didn't dig their jive and almost got messed up."

"Then what's another word for jive as you have just used it?"

"I guess . . . talk, a kind of talk," he answered. "This here poem is written in jive talk."

"Do you think that 'all jive' in this poem could mean 'all kind of talk'?"

They nodded in agreement.

"What does *dig* mean?" Again we compiled our multiple meanings on the board. To dig someone is to like him; to dig someone later is to see him later; and to dig something is to understand it. When I asked which of the three meanings fit best with "dig all jive," they readily agreed that "to understand" was it.

We continued similarly to the end of the poem. The final interpretation was that "to understand and be understood in return" was the poet's rule for life.

"How many kinds of jive do you understand?" I asked them.

"Oh, we understand all of it."

"Well, let's see if you can understand my kind of jive. Okay?"

"Go ahead," they said.

I then proceeded to give an elaborate oral essay on the nature of truth, using some of the most complicated words I could think of. At the conclusion, I said, "Did you dig my jive?"

They looked at me blankly.

Then I said, "Now let's see if I can dig yours. Would you like to test me?"

They responded eagerly. Expressions were thrown at me. I was able to get five out of six, which impressed them greatly.

"According to Langston Hughes, who has a better chance of staying alive, you or I?"

"You."

"Why?"

"You dig more than one kind of jive."

"All right," I said, "I think I agree with Mr. Hughes, and I feel very lucky that I do understand many kinds of talk. In certain situations I'm able to use one kind of jive and in others, another kind. But you sitting in this class have, up to this point, mastered only one kind, and one that I think is very beautiful. But it still is only *one*. You've got to dig the

> school jive as well as your own, and also jive that might be needed in other situations. School helps you dig all jive and helps you stay alive."

Mrs. Baker, the English teacher, commented afterwards that it was the first time she had seen the class so involved in a lesson. "I couldn't believe my ears. I saw some pupils participate today who haven't opened their mouths since the beginning of the term."

Shortly after that, various pupils asked me where they could find more of Langston Hughes' poetry. I allowed the anthology to circulate, and circulate it did. It was difficult for me to get the book back.

Mrs. Baker and I developed a unit on Langston Hughes' poetry. Her pupils read and discussed some of his other poems that had a high interest level but were written in more conventional language, and they found that poetry could be an enjoyable experience.

Ralph Ellison, the famous Negro author, is reported to have made the following pertinent points concerning the culturally different:

> One uses the language which helps to preserve one's life, which helps to make one at peace with the world, and which screens out the greatest amount of chaos. *All* human beings do this. And if you have one body of people that have been sewn together by a common experience . . . and you plant this people in a highly pressurized situation, and if they survive, they're surviving with all of those motivations and with all of the basic ingenuity which any group develops in order to remain alive.
>
> . . . within the bounds of their rich oral culture they possess a great virtuosity with the music, the poetry, of words. The question is, how can you get this skill into the mainstream of the language, because it is, without a doubt, there. . . .
>
> If you can show me how I can cling to that which is real to me, while teaching me a way into the larger society, then I will not only drop my defenses and my hostility, but I will

sing your praises and I will help you to make the desert bear fruit.[3]

Ellison makes two important points: (1) human beings cling to the language which makes it possible for them to control chaos and to survive in the situations in which they find themselves; (2) the way to teach new forms or varieties or patterns of language is not to attempt to eliminate the old forms but to build upon them while at the same time valuing them in a way which is consonant with the desire for dignity which lies in each of us.[4] "Dig All Jive" can serve as a beginning step toward such goals.

We learned recently of a teacher tutoring a group of disadvantaged youngsters between the ages of 9 and 12 who reported their reaction when she offered them some books about a boy and his horse: "We don't wanna read about 'whitey' boys and their ponies." Stimulated rather than dejected by this response, she developed some materials with and for them that are reminiscent of Sylvia Ashton-Warner's approach in *Teacher*.[5] She asked each child to give her his most important words that he couldn't read or spell. As the words were dictated, she wrote each on a card. The children were given the cards and asked to study them; when they learned to recognize their words, they were allowed more. It was thus a *privilege* to have words and to see how many more they could learn.

The following are some of the words offered by that group:

creature	important	Ulysses
Samson	answer	Al Capone
second-hand-store	Hercules	Superman

It is interesting to note that all of the proper names on the list were given by boys, and represented "power" figures with whom they identified. Each day, the tutor held up the cards for the

[3]R. Ellison, quoted in T. J. Creswell, *The "Twenty Billion Dollar Misunderstanding,"* in R. W. Shuy (Ed.), *Social Dialects and Language Learning*, Report of a Conference sponsored by Illinois Institute of Technology and the National Council of Teachers of English, Champaign, Ill., Cooperative Research project No. OE 5-10-148, 1964.
[4]*Ibid.*
[5]Sylvia Ashton-Warner, *Teacher*, New York, Simon and Schuster, 1963.

pupils to read. When they had learned to recognize their words, they were given the card and permitted to dictate more.

As a reinforcement to this word study, and as a substitute for typical reading materials, this tutor developed very simple story exercises, made up of his own words, for each child. The stories were enclosed in a sheet of colorful construction paper and the cover was illustrated with a magazine picture related to the story inside. Each pupil was to fill in the blanks with an appropriate word from his life. For example:

> One day a terrible thing happened to this ship. During a bad _____ a gigantic _____ started to attack. Luckily, two _____ men were on the ship, They were _____ and _____. They killed the _____ and saved the people who were very _____.

My Word List

creature (2 times)	Superman
important	storm
Samson	happy

> There is a new rock and _____ group called The _____. They sing and play _____, piano, and drums. Why are they called the _____? Can you tell me the _____?

My Word List

Creatures (2 times)	roll
guitars	answer

One of the most consistent patterns of emotional concern expressed by the disadvantaged child is for potency or power. His heroes are the strong, invincible men, such as Hercules or Superman. We could speculate that the interest in Greek mythology expressed by disadvantaged pupils is also related to this concern. As a result, we would like to see the schools investigate, with the children, the power concept. This is a possible study topic for even the earliest grades. Can people be strong in ways other than physical strength? The teacher might begin by asking the youngsters who their neighborhood heroes are—who are the "top cats" on their block—and then asking why they are so. We would guess that the responses will probably be in terms of physical strength. The objective then, would be to help the class begin to explore other routes of power. Staging points for such discussions might be derived from reading excerpts from the powerful autobiography of Claude Brown, *Manchild in the Promised Land,* the author's experiences growing up in Harlem.[6] The most direct method, however, to help children *feel* greater potency is to let them experience it. A way that combines such experience with the improvement of writing skills was demonstrated by one of our teaching interns. In a seventh-grade English class, required by the curriculum guide to study paragraph skills, the teaching intern asked the class, "How many of you can remember any of the things you had to read in school when you were in the third grade?" Some hands went up, and names of books were reported. "How did you like them?"

"Terrible!" was the unanimous reaction of the class.

"Do you think the kids in the third grade in your old school feel the same way you do?" Some evidence was offered regarding the younger children's comments on the "bad stuff" they had to read.

"Suppose we find out," the teacher offered. "I think I can arrange to have you visit a third-grade class so that we might really find out how they are thinking." The teacher went on to discuss with them how one proceeds to find out what people are thinking. The pupils made up informal questionnaires and than practiced interviewing through the use of role-playing with their peers. Finally, the entire class spent an hour in a third-grade classroom, with each member interviewing a younger child. The third-graders, by the way, were quite pleased with all the attention from the older kids.

Armed with their findings, the seventh-graders returned to their own school and analyzed them in the next week's English periods. They were asked if they thought they could develop reading materials that would be better for the third-graders. Of course, the response was, "Who couldn't?" And so, using their interviews as a basis for something better, they spent the next month developing those better reading materials. The children

[6]C. Brown, *Manchild in the Promised Land,* New York, Macmillan, 1965.

now saw the necessity of language-arts skills in writing such materials. They received instruction in paragraphing and attacked their work with relish. When the third-graders had evaluated the completed materials, their criticisms were used for final revisions by the older children.

Whether or not there was any real benefit to the younger children is hard to say, but certainly there was involvement on the part of the older pupils. They were given a real task and a real responsibility—the essential ingredients for experiencing potency, however limited.

Contact through pupil content

Unfortunately, many good teaching practices are dropped after the elementary level. One of these is the experience chart, or story, in which the children's experiences are compiled by the teacher and used as a reading lesson. For example, when children tell their teacher what they did, said, and felt on a trip, the teacher writes these comments on a chart and, with the class, organizes it into an "experience story." Tape recorders if used at this time can be crucial in developing listening and speaking as well as reading skills. In fact, we have concluded that the language-arts program for disadvantaged children for the first two years of school should emphasize not reading but speaking and listening skills based on a variety of direct experiences. These are the skills that precede reading. If the children record their reactions to the trip directly on tape, listen to it, correct unclear comments, practice the corrections, and then retape, these important skills could be developed. A story for reading practice could then be written from the tape.

In the upper grades, one sure way to invite failure is to ask a 14-year-old boy who reads at the third-grade level to read a third-grade book. "I ain't gonna read no baby book!" is a frequent reaction. We have, however, seen experience stories work remarkably well for these older pupils. Here is an example of how one was introduced and used.

In this particular situation, Peace Corps trainees were observing the teacher, whose lesson plan listed the following procedures:

1. Ask pupils to tell about city activities.
2. Write these on the board (pupils responded with: football, baseball, pool, record playing, baby sitting, movies).
3. Tell pupils they will each have a private secretary.
4. Ask pupils to take one city activity and tell how it's done.
5. Pair each pupil with a Peace Corps trainee.
6. Have pupils dictate activity to Peace Corps trainee.

After class, some of the dictated material was selected for use the next day. Here is one pupil's essay:

ROTATION POOL
by *Willie Harris*

You can use two players. First you get the one ball in. After the one ball you get the two ball in, after the two, try to get the three ball—all in a row to fifteen.

After you get all the balls in, you count up the balls. If you've got a three and a four ball, then you have seven.

Then after you are through counting them, the one with the most points wins.

Like you are on the eight ball and knock the nine ball in by mistake, you spot the nine ball in the middle of the table. And after you get the eight ball in, you knock your nine ball in your pocket where the rest of the balls are.

You can have one up to six players. They put the eight ball on the spot and the first one to knock it in gets the first shot, or the one that won the last game gets the bust. The bust is when you have all the balls from one to fifteen and you bust and whatever ball goes in is your ball. When you miss or knock the wrong ball in, it's the other person's turn. Then after you've won the game, you have one or two more players to play.

The essay was then dittoed and distributed to the class. Following is a portion from the lesson plan:

1. Ask the pupils if they've ever played pool. How many

have? What kinds of pool are there? What do you have to know in order to be able to play pool? (Pupils mentioned number of players, rules, etc.)

2. Ask the pupils to look for the answers to these questions as I read Willie Harris' essay on "Rotation Pool."
3. Read Willie Harris' paper.
4. Give pupils written test on Willie's essay.

How well did you read Willie Harris' essay?

Your Name ____________________

1. What type of pool is Willie describing?
2. *Direction:* Circle the letter of the right answer. According to Willie, the largest number of people who can play this game is:
   A. two
   B. four
   C. six
   D. As many as you want
3. The person who wins the game is the one:
   A. Who hits the most balls in the pocket.
   B. Who has the most balls at the end of the game.
   C. Whose numbers on the balls add up to the highest number.
   D. Who goes out first.
4. If you hit the wrong ball in the pocket:
   A. You leave it in the pocket and lose a turn.
   B. You put the ball back on the table and lose a turn.
   C. You put the ball back on the table and continue to play.
   D. You leave it in the pocket and continue to play.
5. What does "spot a ball" mean?
6. If the player before you has just shot at the four ball and missed it, what ball should you try to get in the pocket?
7. How many ways of deciding who will get the first shot does Willie mention?
8. According to Willie, what is one way of deciding who will get the first shot?
9. What is "the bust?"
10. How many balls do you play with in this game? Why?

If you, as a teacher, could develop one experience story a week, you would be making an important start. Offer yourself as the pupil's secretary and have him dictate to you. Develop and reproduce his experience and see how his motivation increases.

If any faculty members of your school have a flair for writing, we have found that a group of writers can develop a series of vignettes to be illustrated either by photographs or drawings. They should make use of pupil language and experiences. Here is an example:

THE DANCE

Jimmy had spent about an hour in front of the mirror getting ready for this dance. He was wearing his best suit, a smart three-buttoned slim job. Even so, he still didn't feel right. He was kind of jumpy.

The auditorium wasn't too crowded, but Mary Ann was there. She looked real great with that pink lace dress and those pink high heels.

All of the boys were standing together at one end and the girls were at the other.

"Hey, Jimmy!" Frank shouted. "You're looking pretty cool. Why don't you grab a chick and start swinging?"

"I would, man, but I don't want to wear out my dancin' shoes."

"Well, why do you have dancin' shoes if you're not going to use them?"

"Look who's talking. I don't see you spinning around the floor with anyone."

"Oh, man, I wouldn't waste my time with any of these babes. They're from nowhere."

"Sure, sure, I know."

While he was talking, Jimmy was watching Mary Ann out of the corner of his eyes. She was dancing with another girl.

The boys were still gathered in one corner, laughing and shouting wise remarks to the girls across the floor. Not one was dancing with a girl.

"If I only had enough guts to ask her to dance," Jimmy said to himself. "But it would be real tough. I'd have to walk across that big floor with everybody looking bug-eyed at me. The guys would sure make some fuss about it. And then suppose she didn't want to dance with me after I asked her? I'd feel so low-down I'd have to crawl out of here. Darn, I don't know what to do!"

He thought of himself dancing with her . . . holding her real close in his arms. He became more shaky than ever.

"Maybe," he thought, "if I just walked over real cool and said, 'Let's dance, baby,' she wouldn't have a chance to say no."

Before he had a chance to move, Tommy and Neil grabbed him by the arms. They pulled him over to the rest of the boys.

"C'mon, Jimmy, we're all going over to Marshall Street. . . . This thing here is just too square, man."

Jimmy found himself strolling out of the school with the boys. "Whew," he told himself, "where am I going? I didn't get all dressed up just to hang on the corner. But . . . I guess I can't go back now. Mary Ann, you're a doll. We . . . maybe next time."

Questions for Discussion

1. Why didn't Jimmy dance with Mary Ann?
2. If Jimmy wanted to stay at the dance, why did he leave with the boys?
3. Do you believe that Frank really didn't want to waste his time with the girls?
4. Where do you think this dance took place? In an elementary, junior high, or high school? Why?
5. Do you think Jimmy will dance with Mary Ann next time? Why?

Vocabulary Development

1. Find synonyms for the following:
   cool + (2 uses in story: nonchalant, indifferent, calm; fine, smart, as in "looking cool")
   square
2. Have the class decide whether the conversation was *formal* or *informal.*
3. How could conversation be written in formal language?

4. Have the class write about the same situation written from Mary Ann's or Frank's point of view.
5. Have the class stop at the end of the line "she wouldn't have a chance to say no," and predict the ending.

In Chapter 4, we reported a dialogue between a teacher and a class on phoniness in literature. Because that particular episode illustrates some of the problems and their solutions in working with disadvantaged children, we would like to repeat it at this time with a line-by-line analysis. As you recall, the class had refused to read the literature books presented them by the teacher, and thus the sequence began:

QUESTION: Why don't you want to read?

[The goal here was to get feedback leading to an alternate strategy. Too many teachers assume that pupil negativism is an impassable roadblock and meet negativism with negativism, which leads nowhere. If, however, teachers assume the stance of inquirers, some very hostile moments in the classroom can lead to very productive learning. This first question then represents a teacher's search for the "hidden content" of the children. The class is almost certain to respond because the question itself recognizes the pupils' conflict of not wanting to read. Thus, we might generalize that one of the key ingredients for motivation is to begin with an area of tension. Most of what we teach has no tension in and of itself, forcing us to rely on punishment or extrinsic reward to produce results.]

ANSWER: Phoney

[This is a typically flat answer. "Phoney" is offered as though it might be the be-all and end-all summary. Again, this is a spot at which teachers are ready to call the whole thing off, especially when the answer is given in a style or inflection that seems to say, "Baby, if you don't understand *that*, give up!" And again we urge you to remember that as educators we cannot afford to be put off.]

QUESTION: What do you mean, "phoney"?

[The teacher continues to push the class for some abstractions. There are two reasons: First, he wants more feedback to help him understand what the perceptions of the pupils are; and, second, he wants them to isolate some of the components of phoniness to see how they relate to each other in order to clarify their own concept of phoniness and perhaps to have it become more useful.]

ANSWER: Corny.

[Again, a typical flat response that adds no dimension, and thus a circular pattern of definition is started wherein phoney is corny, corny is phoney. It is as though they were saying, "A chair is a chair, nice is nice, and that is that, period."]

QUESTION: What does corny mean?

[The teacher is still trying to get beneath the concept.]

ANSWER: [No response.]

[The pupils and the teacher clearly reach an impass which is frustrating to both. It must be understood that the class is responding this way not because they do not *want* to respond more appropriately, but because they don't *know how* to respond. Their experience has not prepared them to examine the abstract qualities of a concept, and thus they are in strange territory when asked to do so. They have a feeling for phoniness but have rarely articulated it. It is obvious that the teacher can go no further along this route. Some of the alternatives are:

1. Give up right here and move on to another activity.
2. Give a lecture on the importance of reading.
3. Give the class a definition of phoniness and see if they agree or would care to amend it, or have them look it up in the dictionary.
4. Or, continue as this teacher did.]

QUESTION: Do you know a TV program that isn't corny or phoney?

[We label this phase of the procedure "Collecting Appropriate Pupil Content." The question the teacher asks of himself at this junction is "What are the children familiar with that can serve as a connection between the concept and its characteristics?" The crucial strategy here is to take the opposite tack with something in their experience. The question is no longer "What is phoney?" or "Can you give me other examples of what is phoney?" but, "What is something with which you are familiar that is not phoney?" This shift of emphasis sets up a fresh contrast and tension that allows the group to tackle the same problem from a new vantage point and encourages the pupils to shift and reshuffle their ideas.]

ANSWER: "Naked City."

["Naked City" is an old TV series of fictionalized accounts of urban problems.]

QUESTION: Why isn't "Naked City" corny or phoney?

[This is a much easier question for the class to answer than the first, because their own experiences can be brought to bear.]

ANSWER: Because one day a kid goes to church with his mother and the next day he robs a store.

[The class continues to respond simply and with no elaboration. Here again, many teachers might make a mental leap to, "Fine, that *is* an example of something phoney," and assume that the pupils, by supplying an example, have made a connection between that example and the concept. However, unless they have articulated the connection, we cannot assume that they have made it. Therefore, the next question is the most significant in the series, for it is when the learning starts.]

QUESTION: Why isn't that phoney?

[Now the class is forced to connect the boy's behavior in their example with "un-phoniness."]

ANSWER: He isn't one-way. Sometimes he's good and sometimes he's bad.

[Ostensibly, the objective of the question period has been met. The pupils have identified one-way characterization as a dimension of phoniness. The rest of the dialogue can retrace the last few questions in order to isolate more components and may be summarized as: Encouraging pupils to supply an example, from their own reference of the concept or its opposite, and helping pupils to articulate the connection, in their own words, between the concept and the example. This kind of teaching requires great self-control on the part of the teacher: to forge ahead against what appear to be obstacles that crop up at each moment and not respond to seemingly conventional cues.]

How many readers could come up with a better way of describing a component of phoniness than "one-way," which is so poignant, complete, and to the point. If we, as teachers, are willing to allow the child to express certain abstractions in his own way, we may find them to be a great improvement over ours.

Thus far, our discussion has centered around the language of the pupil and the language arts. We would now like to develop some other generalizations concerning teaching methods in which other subject areas serve as illustrative vehicles. Chapter 10, "Toward A Relevant Curriculum," outlines the importance of the movement in teaching from the concrete to the abstract. At first glance, the social-studies curriculum, as traditionally conceived—and American history in particular—appears to defy concreteness. How can one be concrete about something that happened in the past? The next few examples serve as suggested approaches.

Contact through direct experience

In planning an American history unit for the eighth grade, a team of social-studies teachers reached the section in the curriculum guide entitled "The Role of American Industry." The question was how to provide as direct an experience as possible for the pupils. In other words, what could be pulled from the bottom of the "cone of experiences" (see Fig. 10.1) that would serve as a concrete base for what was to be taught? According to the guide, the content was outlined chronologically, going back to the McCormick reaper, the steam engine, and the early automobile. This was the traditional way. This group, however, was willing to depart from the past.

The question was raised as to what meaning the term *industry* would have for the pupils. In order not to take any chances, it was decided to show the classes an industry *first* and talk about it afterwards. Arrangements were made for a tour of a local shoe factory, one that contained under one roof the manufacturing process from raw materials to finished shoes. The entire eighth grade would visit it *before* any formal instruction began on the topic. Essentially, the classes were given only this preparation: "We are going to study something about industries for the next few weeks, and we've arranged a trip to the local shoe factory. All we want you to do is jot down or tell us anything that comes to your mind about what you see or hear."

During their visit, the children were exposed to the basic processes of shoe manufacturing, to the working conditions in a factory, to the work people did by hand, to the machines which replaced people.

When they returned, each class and its teacher compiled the questions and comments which were to become the content basis for the unit. It was necessary to return to the factory in order to obtain specific information and also to correspond with the factory management. Words achieved a basis in a physical reality; the teachers did not have to assume as much and could be certain that the symbols they were using were connected with the reality of the pupils.

In addition to making pupil contact through physical reality, this experience illustrates the value of field trips to initiate units of study rather than, as is the current practice, to culminate a unit of study.

Contact through contrived experiences

Since a direct experience, in certain areas of the curriculum, is not always possible, the next best solution is to provide a contrived experience. As a group of teachers planned a unit on government, the teachers were asked why they were interested in teaching such a unit.

"It's the course of study," they replied.

"But, if it were not the course of study would you still teach it?" A short pause followed. "Yes," they replied with less certainty.

"Why?" An even longer pause followed.

"Well, these kids have to live in a world that's organized

by and through government. It's a world of rules, and if anybody needs to know about rules, it's our kids! So we're really teaching government to show our classes that men must organize and make rules in order to make life easier for all of us."

It was suggested that they begin their unit on government with the question: "Are rules necessary?" The next problem was to relate the unit to personal experience. Could they provide a direct or contrived experience that would make contact with the pupils? Each teacher decided to introduce the unit to his class as follows:

"You are to imagine yourselves on a desert island on which there is sufficient food, clothing, and materials for shelter. You may live there for as long as you like. There is, however, only one important rule: you are not permitted to make up *any* rules. Think about it and then tell me what it's like."

Most of the classes responded with joy at the prospect of no rules. For three class sessions, pupils discussed what life was like in such a place. The teachers were to play an unconventional role—they were to be against rules! But early in the discussions, difficulties arose.

"Mrs. Blake," a pupil said, "James wants to put his house under my tree and *I* was there first! Tell him he can't, will you?"

"Oh, I can't tell him that," Mrs. Blake said. "That would mean making a rule, and we're not allowed to. Now I'm sure you two can work out an answer."

Each time problems arose the teachers insisted the pupils could get along without rules if they really tried to. Finally the classes gave up. "We can't get along without any rules: it's too much trouble." The pupils found themselves in the very unique situation of trying to persuade a teacher to let them *have* rules! The teacher held her position as long as possible before relenting, and then proposed: "Let's leave our island and move to a new location. This time we'll set up a village in the United States. You say you need rules? You decide which ones you need."

The pupils then developed basic rules for their villages and decided who would be responsible for their administration. In a very short time, they evolved their own village governments.

When asked if they would like to compare their governments with that of a real village, they were very eager. Letters were written to nearby towns and field trips were arranged. Pupils interviewed town officials, then contrasted and compared that information with their own. Only in the final stage of the unit did they turn to their books for further material. The printed word was last in the sequence, the contrived experience first. Content was relevant to experience; if experience had been lacking, the content would have been received in a vacuum, precluding significant learning.

All this means a departure from most current teaching practices. Trips must serve as unit *initiators*, not culminators. Curriculum guides for the disadvantaged must develop a new character. Instead of only content outlines, the guides should suggest a series of direct or contrived experiences listing the outlines of possible concepts that might be developed from each. The experiences would be sequential and developmental, from preschool through grade 12. Ideally, they would begin in the immediate neighborhood of the school and expand outward, focusing on simpler concepts at first and becoming more complex each year. Often the same experiences could be used, achieving a more elaborate focus in the sequence progression.

Closely related to the concept of rules is a unit based on the idea, "Man needs some kind of organization in order to survive." To put this into practice, the teachers discussed the plan in detail so that they understood all its implications. The question of how to get the pupils to acknowledge and understand the concept was rephrased to, "What experiences will help our pupils to comprehend the idea of organization?" Some suggestions that were offered:

1. Draw 12 scattered Xs on the blackboard, then cover them. Tell the pupils they will have three seconds to look at the board before it is covered again. They must then say how many Xs are there. Only a few will get the answer right. Then using the same number, write the Xs in patterns, such as *XXXX XXXX XXXX*, or *XXX XXX XXX XXX*. Cover them again and repeat your instructions. There will

now be more correct answers. The next question is: "Why did you make so many mistakes the first time and not the second?" Maybe they will use the word "organizing" in their answer; maybe they won't. The word is unimportant; the expression of the concept or idea regardless of terminology is. "Putting things in a pattern makes them easier to count" would be an excellent response.

2. To the question, "What would happen if, during the night, someone were to remove all traffic lights and road signs from our city?" the response might be, "There'd be all kinds of accidents and car crashes." The teacher would ask why. "Because no one would know when to cross a street or stop at a corner." The teacher would continue, "Oh, but you're only saying that because you're used to these things. They've been around for such a long time. Couldn't you learn to live without traffic signals if you really tried? We'd just have to be a lot more careful, that's all." The ideal final response would be, "Well, maybe we could learn, but it would be a lot harder."

3. A teacher (one with good class control) might one day move the pupils' desks into a helter-skelter pattern. When the pupils entered the room, they would be told to occupy any empty seat. Naturally, they would be surprised, but the teacher would answer no questions until everyone was seated without having moved the desks. The pupils would, naturally, be disturbed by the unexpected change, and the teacher could question them as to why they felt that way. They might answer, "Well, some of us can't see you. The children could be allowed to turn in their seats enough to see the teacher but without changing their location, just their direction. "Why can't we put the desks in rows?" ask the pupils. "Why should we?" is the teacher's reply. And thus they explore the advantages and disadvantages of organizing the furniture in their classroom.

The similarity of these three activities—the Xs, the traffic signals, and the mixed-up classroom furniture—in the pupils' demonstration of the usefulness of organization, shows the "why" we need organization in our lives.

Contact through social action

An eighth-grade class studying government complained to its teacher that the topic was "so boring." The teacher gave the pupils the conventional response: "It's important that we understand as much as possible about our representatives who constantly make decisions affecting our lives."

The children felt that understanding was of no use because, "There's nothing we can do about it anyway—we're too young."

"Are you sure there's nothing you can do about it?" they were asked.

"But, of course, you can't vote until you're twenty-one, and if you can't vote, you can't do anything," said the pupil.

When challenged, they agreed to see if 12- or 13-year-olds could play any part in politics, for, as they said, "Anything would be better than just studying city government the same old way." And so the unit on government became "Can we play any part in politics?" The best source of information seemed to be their most immediate representative, their local committeeman. Alternative ways of setting up contacts were considered. Most of the pupils had heard of committeemen, but had no notion of their functions. In addition, perhaps the committeeman would suggest some ways in which children might help in politics.

The pupils' reports to the class contained some very enlightening information. Many were shocked at how little the committeeman knew: "All he does is fix tickets!" Other commented that: "The only time anybody sees him is on election day," or, "His main job is to make sure everybody in his neighborhood votes for his party."

Pupils also arranged contacts and interviews with the ward leader, who gave them more information on the structure of local politics.

All of this coincided with the local mayoralty election, and ward leaders told the pupils they could be of help in two ways.

First was to help get all eligible voters to register and then to vote. The second was to decide carefully on the party of their choice and try to influence voters for that choice.

Unit action culminated on Election Day. The pupils had organized a small political campaign and canvassed their neighborhood to present their argument for voting for one candidate over another. On election night, they volunteered their services as runners or messengers to help get out the vote for the party of their choice.

Another learning situation developed from the fact that pupils were disgruntled by the operation of the school cafeteria. They disliked some of the menu offerings and the idea of separating the girls from the boys. Their teacher utilized the situation to teach constructive ways of civic action. A one-day "boycott" of the lunchroom was advocated, and on a designated day, no child bought a school lunch. The problem was analyzed, a case was drawn up which represented the children's position, and a special conference was arranged with the principal. The most effective ways of handling the confrontation were explored. Petitions were prepared and distributed; later, actual negotiation took place. Compromises were offered, suggestions were made, and a mutually agreeable solution was reached. A crucial factor to the success of the project was the attitude of the administrator who encouraged constructive social action.

By utilizing social action, pupils not only learn to cope with varying experiences, but are also prepared for realistic participation in our society. This is citizenship training, not from the divorced-from-reality book, but from experiences with *real* problems and *real* people. Here the children experience and *feel* the problems rather than merely talk about them.

Contact through practical reality

In conversations with teachers, those in the field of mathematics have most consistently made the comment: "What you say is all very interesting, but we don't see how any of it applies to math." The main problem here is the manner in which mathematics is taught. As long as it is defined as the way to teach math to children, we draw a blank. If, however, the task were redefined as the best way to utilize mathematics instruction in helping children better to understand and to cope with their world, more alternatives would be available. Is it not true that mathematics is a tool by which we can clarify, sharpen, and relate various elements of our existence so as to manipulate them more constructively? The problem is that we have become so enmeshed in the intricacies of the discipline that we have forgotten its original use.

A useful lesson plan can be that which is developed around the practical uses of money.

One unique and practical eighth-grade unit developed after a teacher had overheard a group of his students discussing salaries and the desire to make "good money." He was startled by the naive over- and under-estimates of what a substantial salary was, and yet the pupils kept saying, "We want to quit school as soon as we can so we can make some good money."

"What do you call 'good money'?" they were asked by the teacher.

"A dollar-twenty an hour," "Forty bucks a week," they replied.

The next day, the teacher related the incident to his math class. "How many of you think that $40 a week is good money?" Many hands were raised. "How many of you would feel pretty good about making $1.20 an hour?" Again, many hands.

The teacher then developed a working definition with the class as to what good money was: the amount of money you need to support yourself for a year, just for the basic necessities —food, clothing, and shelter.

The class was asked to write a paragraph giving personal estimates of good money and its possible uses. This excerpt was typical of the students' papers: "I think good money is getting around $200 a month and I'd take at least $25 out of that for food and $50 to my mother and around $15 in the bank."

The next step in the discussion was for the class to specify the necessities under each of the three main categories: food, clothing, and shelter. How much would it cost a month for a furnished room? Newspapers were consulted and, using the classified ads, the class determined the average monthly cost for a furnished room.

Next, they worked out a food budget. How much would it cost each month to feed themselves? Again, the newspapers supplied answers. The same procedure followed for clothing and extras.

A film, *The Most for Your Money*, was shown, followed by discussion.[7] Then the class visited a large local department store to find out other costs, to "discover" new items for their "budgets," and to reinforce some of the ideas learned from the film.

Some comments recorded by the pupils on a post-trip evaluation form follow:

> I learned that the prices of living are going up every year.
>
> I learned that the price of living was more than I thought.
>
> I learned that household appliances cost about $10.00 more than I thought.
>
> Some of the things that I thought cost less, costed more than I expected.
>
> I learned what I would like to have and how much money I would need.
>
> I found out that such little things as a coffee pot, and a toaster, and a tablecloth were very costly.

After the trip, and on the basis of that experience, the students added to their lists of wants and adjusted costs connected with them. They worked out their complete costs on a yearly, monthly, and weekly basis. These results were compared to the original estimates and the discrepancies were discussed.

The major teaching objective to this point was to help the children clarify their concepts of a minimum living wage. The next problem presented to the class was: Where can you make your good money? Once again, newspapers were consulted;

[7] *The Most for Your Money*, McGraw-Hill Films, 1955.

students checked the want ads to see what jobs were available, and at what salaries. After such jobs were located, the class was asked, "What are the requirements for those jobs that offer you 'good money'? Almost without exception, the jobs required special training and *at least* a high-school diploma. With this fact clearly in mind, the students were asked to review the statement that had prompted the four-week unit: "I'm going to quit school to make some 'good money.'" The contradiction had by now become obvious to them.

This unit developed from the teacher's perception of the pupils' needs and interests. It moved in an inductive sequence, in which various math skills (computation, percentages, graphing) were used to solve problems and in which a variety of activities (trips, discussions, films) occurred, and terminated with the conclusion "discovered" by the students that dropping out of school is *not* the first step toward making "good money."

Another interesting problem to pose to a class would be, "In how many ways do mathematics describe us?" The students could begin with simple physical characteristics of themselves and gradually work out patterns to display on charts and graphs. When they have established and described ways of looking at their own patterns of behavior, they are encouraged to go on to the next step, analysis: If such and such is a pattern of behavior, why and where did it come from? The learning of math skills in such a relevant context may then be much more efficient and rapid.

Handling color and race

Not long ago, the authors were handed a note by a Negro fifth-grader. The note was very crinkled, as though it had passed through many hands. The large, scrawled writing asked, "Are Negroes dirtier than whites?"

We were uncertain as to what to do with such a question, and assembled some teachers, Negro and white, from the school's staff as a panel before the fifth-grade class. One of the teachers said to the class, "Now look up here. Here's Mr. Shore. He's white. And here's Mr. Lind. He's Negro. Now, who do you think is cleaner?"

Most of the class chose Mr. Lind because, they said, "He has his shoes polished, and Mr. Shore doesn't." When questioned, "Does that mean that whites are dirtier than Negroes?" the class began to differentiate the relative cleanliness of the panel members and reached the conclusion that one cannot tell which *group* of people is cleaner but can tell which *persons* are cleaner.

A similar situation was described by a white fourth-grade teacher in Harlem. Shocked at the racial epithets directed by Negro pupils at Negro pupils (the same name-calling of Negroes that is done by many whites), and pushed to his emotional limits, the teacher forced a showdown in his classroom when the phrase, "You black monkey!" was flung at one of the children. The episode follows:[8]

> "You used 'black' like it was a curse. Do you think 'black' is something terrible?" I pointed to the child who happened to be nearest. "Well, Louis, is it something terrible?" He looked at me numbly and shrugged his shoulders. "What do you think?" I asked Betty. As usual, she betrayed nothing. And neither would the others.
>
> I knew there was no retreating now, and turned to Wilson; he wasn't the type to hold back from what he felt was the truth. "Wilson, you answer me." When he sat there wide-eyed and pouting, I realized I was asking the question in the wrong way. "Is black bad, Wilson? Is it mean? Is it ugly?" At ugly, he stirred. "What's ugly about black, Wilson?" He lowered his head and glowered at me. "Are white people prettier than black people?"
>
> "Yeah," he said, looking straight at me. "White people are prettier." I was stunned. I couldn't believe that he meant what he said. Maybe it was only Wilson, only this one angry little boy. I turned to Lena with the same question. She wouldn't answer me, nor would Betty nor Louis. When I asked Carmela, who was neither black nor white, she looked

[8]B. Kremen, "A Fourth-Grade Course in Color," *Holiday*, March, 1965, p. 24.

up at me, her eyes blinking in confusion. Then I came to Sarah. "Are white people prettier, Sarah?" She answered with a slow, forlorn nod of her head and turned from me with her mouth twitching.

I searched the room, not sure of what I was looking for, until I spotted Louis's delicate face. The beauty of his smooth, rich skin would be lost on no one. I picked him up out of his seat, stood him on a chair next to me and pointed to him. "Isn't his face pretty?" I moved my face closer to Louis's to sharpen the contrast between us. The pride he felt standing there before the class, shoulder high with his teacher who was publicly praising him showed itself in a flashing smile. Seeing that smile light his beautiful face, I was struck with the absurdity of having to make a point of the obvious. It filled me with a shame that made my face feel like a pasty mask next to his. I wanted all of my children to see me through my own eyes.

"Don't you think his face, his color, is prettier than mine is? Don't I look pale?" At first they hardly listened. But I repeated what I had said, half pleading with them this time, almost angry that they needed so much convincing.

Finally a voice called out, "Yeah, teacher, he's prettier than you!"

A similar situation arose during a human relations discussion with a group of Negro junior-high-school girls in which this notion of a negative self-image was poignantly expressed. The entire discussion was prompted by a statement from one of the girl: "Vivian has nice skin." The dialogue follows:

TEACHER: What *is* nice skin?
PUPIL: Lighter.
TEACHER: Why is light skin nicer?
[No answer.]
Where did you get the idea that light skin is nicer?
[No answer.]
Does *Ebony* magazine in any way tell you that light skin is nicer?
PUPILS: Yeah, it has ads for skin lighteners and most of the models are pretty light skinned.

TEACHER: What group of people, what profession has the most beautiful people in the United States?

PUPILS: Movie stars.

TEACHERS: And what color are most of the movie stars?

PUPILS: White.

TEACHER: O.K., we're being told in two ways then. But, suppose there was a country with all Negroes and they'd never seen a white person. Then, one day in walks one of these very light models or Debbie Reynolds. Do you think the people there would think Debbie Reynolds was very beautiful? Is Debbie Reynolds beautiful everywhere?

PUPILS: No, only where there were people who were used to her.

TEACHER: Are you telling me then that just because you're beautiful in one place you're not beautiful in another—that it depends on where you live and who you live with? This reminds me of the old theory the Chinese had about how the races began. They said that God had three lumps of clay and put them in three different ovens to bake. He took one out too soon and it wasn't done enough—this was the beginning of the white race. He left one in too long and it got overbaked and this was the beginning of the Negroes. But, the one he took out at the right time and that was done just beautifully was the beginning of the Chinese race—the most beautiful ones. But, if white is so beautiful, why do so many whites spend millions of dollars and go through so much torture by oiling, frying, and baking themselves in the sun and even buying things like 'Man-Tan' to make themselves darker? Why is it we say someone looks sick when he's pale and looks healthy when there's some color in his face? What is a healthy complexion?

After this, the dialogue took several turns. The teacher pointed out that standards of beauty change not only from country to country, but also from epoch to epoch. The girls mentioned the fact that they liked a certain teacher because he was a "sharp" dresser, and the teacher pointed out that when he was in school he used to think it was sharp to wear a zoot suit, but that if he wore it now he'd be laughed off the streets—times had changed the idea of what was "sharp."

This is merely one sample of the type of direct confrontation that is too often *avoided* by most teachers when, actually, the opportunity for such a discussion often arises within the classroom. Such a discussion might have numerous ramifications. It could have taken such directions as: a scientific discussion of what skin color is—"What could you tell your child if he were very, very dark that would make him feel good about his color?"; "How does anyone—white or black—resolve the idea that he or she may not be beautiful or handsome?"; or a discussion of the fact that features, as well as skin color, enter into the standards for beauty and that many, many whites have what most people would consider to be quite ugly features.

The most significant thing about these classroom discussions is not the profundity of the comments, but rather, the direct confrontation of these topics. Color is something which *can* be talked about, and talked about openly and freely. The child must realize this, and it is the teacher's job to set the example to help him realize this. This type of direct confrontation is not, however, good for *all* teachers. Only those teachers who have a mutually respectful relationship with their pupils should attempt to discuss seriously problems of such emotional complexity.

Since mere exposure to a variety of people does not automatically lead to a constructive learning experience for the child, different strategies should be considered.

However, for successful use of strategies, the teacher must have clearly in his mind the concepts he wishes the pupils to connect with their feelings, and must condense but not oversimplify them.

One such concept is that human color varies along a scale, that there are degrees of difference, and that these actually *unite* people on the same scale rather than divide them into two sharply separated categories of black and white. Another concept is that physical characteristics should not be confused with social characteristics since the two have little to do with each other. The corollary to this concept is that minority group identity is incidental to the individual's quality as a person.

An important concept to make clear is that we learn our attitudes from those around us and are not born with them—our likes and dislikes depend on our teachers—and that words, by their use in context, reflect personal values. In addition, a variety of people makes all of them more interesting and attractive because of their differences. The goal of the teacher must be to show that accurate perception and verbalization are inseparably linked with racial and social sophistication, and to challenge the concept of Negro inferiority as something basic, inherent, and immutable.

The child must be able to improve his self-concept by realizing that he is a worthwhile portion of humanity. He must learn the facts about race and thus see racial reality in a broad social context. As Goodman states:

> The white child will not have to use the help he gets for purposes of defending his own ego and his respect and admiration for the We-group. The Negro child will have to use the help he gets *primarily* for such purposes. The white child's problem is to avoid an inflated and hence unrealistic sense of worth he has *because* he is white. The Negro child's problem is to avoid a deflated and hence equally unrealistic sense of worth *because* he is a Negro.[9]

The teacher must help the child understand how much of his behavior and experience has been culturally induced rather than biologically determined. Too many underpriviledged children really feel that their condition of life is something for which they and their parents are entirely responsible. They do not see that racial discrimination is actually *man made* or that it is malleable.

DISCRIMINATION AND THE NEGRO PUPIL

Discrimination itself can be a focal point for teaching the interrelationships between society and the child's condition of life. The authors, as teachers, have conducted classroom programs

[9]Mary Ellen Goodman, *Race Awareness in Young Children*, New York, Collier Books, 1964, p. 240.

to discuss discrimination but have observed that most materials and approaches developed have attempted to deal with helping only white children become less prejudiced. Certain successful approaches have been developed, and there is a great deal of useful material available to the interested teacher. But very little material has been focused on the Negro child. How does the teacher deal with a socially oppressed group?

A definite attention- and response-getting device is to ask disadvantaged Negro children if they have ever experienced discrimination. Our pupils cited incident after incident they considered discriminatory. Many of these experiences had the characteristics of a discriminatory situation, but others were questionable. It was obvious sometimes that the pupils used "prejudice" as a weapon and as a way to "get at" a teacher.

During a summer in a demonstration school, we observed a trainee meeting with her class for the second time. She had told us that her first day had been a horrible experience; the pupils had leveled their tirades directly at her and had accused her of being prejudiced against Negroes. She was, consequently, extremely upset. As we watched, the class resumed its discussion of the preceding day—listing incident after incident of how they had been discriminated against. Some told of how policemen had stopped fights and made only the Negroes leave; others told of being expelled from movie theatres whenever there was a commotion. They said they were looked down upon by whites when walking down a street. The discussion increased in intensity, and one child said, "Well, it's about time they made the white people slaves. Let them get a taste of what it's like!" Another called out, "I'll tell you one thing. They'll never have a colored president! Nobody would vote for him!"

The trainee tried to handle this emotional discussion as best she could, but she was obviously embarrassed and uncomfortable. As a white person, she was, she felt, receiving the brunt of the attack on whites by the Negro children. We learned from talking to her after class that she had taken it very personally. She had been extremely defensive and couldn't understand why the pupils were "taking it out" on her. It was pointed out that the pupils didn't even know her, so how could they possibly know how she really felt. They had simply been pouring out some of their very real concerns; any trainee who happened to be in the room at the time would have heard the same thing. In fact, this particular class had done the same thing to other teachers the day before. The problem here was to build from these pupils' feelings a constructive way to interpret, analyze, and learn.

One of the authors went before the class and told the children he knew they had been talking about their feelings concerning Negroes and whites and wondered if they had any questions. One of the more belligerent girls said, with teeth clenched and eyes narrowed, "How come some teachers stare me down every time they see me? It makes me feel they don't like me!" She was told, "I think I know just how you felt, because I feel that way right now. You're staring me down, and it makes me feel that you don't like me! Now maybe I can ask you, why are *you* staring *me* down?" This turnabout completely surprised the girl, who thought for a few seconds and then broke into a very delightful smile. It was the first time the author had seen her smile during summer school.

Another boy complained that every time he walked into the candy store and just stood for a few minutes, the white owner asked him to leave; this, he claimed, was an obvious example of discrimination. The author asked the boy to come to the front of the class. "Look," he said, "you are a department store manager, and I'm a kid. I want you to stand over here and watch me when I come into your store." The author sauntered in and began to look through the imaginary counters. He picked up imaginary items, handled them, and put them back; meanwhile glancing over his shoulder at the manager. After a few minutes, Sam (the pupil who was the "manager") was asked, "Well, what do you think? Are you going to let me stay in your store?" "No," Sam said. "You'll have to leave. It sure looks like you're going to take something." "Tell us the truth, Sam, is that the way you look when you go into a store?" The class laughed and so did Sam. He didn't even bother to answer and went back to his seat.

Observation of such episodes has shown that:

1. The more defensive the teacher, the less useful the learning experience.
2. The school's program must allow discussions of this kind, and a creative venting of hostility must be dealt with frankly, openly, and as objectively as possible: i.e., is this really evidence of discrimination?
3. One way to view hostile feelings from more than one perspective, is through *role reversal.*

The school should not deny discrimination but must show its dramatic influence on the lives of the children. However, perspective must be maintained to determine when discrimination really is present, when other forces are involved, and to what extent the pupils *themselves* are discriminatory. Children must be taught to see the causal forces which influence their position in society and where and how they can change it. They must see the crucial roles education and their own involvement play in attempts to break the historical cycle of discrimination.

CHAPTER 12

THE CHALLENGE

We have entered into an age in which education has officially been declared the key to America's defense and social renewal, both nationally and internationally. This age has been officially ushered in by the accelerated passage of Federal legislation related to education, starting with the National Defense Education Act of 1958, and extending through the War on Poverty. The conditions put forth by the U.S. Office of Education and the Office of Economic Opportunity in making educational funds available, however, imply that the purpose of the money is educational *reform*. As evidence of this governmental perspective, the consultants who are brought in to draft the guidelines for Federal fund use, and to review the proposals soliciting Federal funds are selected because they are *disposed to change and reform*. Those hired to administer the funds are also those who reflect a change philosophy. Increasingly, the criteria for funding reflect innovation and change, and an orientation toward developing the new rather than toward strengthening the old. Thus, governmental involvement has led to what Francis Keppel calls "The Necessary Revolution in American Education." Frank Bowles of the Ford Foundation puts it this way:

> The signing in November, 1965 of the Higher Education Bill marked the completion of a remarkable two-year cycle of legislation on American education. Historians may write of this cycle as the opening phase of an educational revolution; certainly it has been a powerful, purposeful reshaping of our educational institutions.[1]

Education has been *told*, not asked, to lead the march toward the "Great Society." This directive offers unprecedented opportunities to the educator, who for decades has been severely limited in his attempts to provide quality education for all. The first effects of this recent governmental funding, however, have simply been to make money available to the educator. The proposition has been: Here is some money. We are making it available to you. How do you want to use it?

[1]F. Bowles, speech to 21st Annual Conference on Higher Education, sponsored by the Association for Higher Education, Chicago, March 14, 1966.

Bob Adelman, Center for Urban Education

THE CHALLENGE

Herein lies the challenge to educators. If the funding agencies view this period as an opportunity to reform education, while the educator uses this period to add to an outdated system, millions of vital dollars will be spent for naught. In other words, there is a paradoxical danger here: While education desperately needs these funds, making money available to education at this time is analogous to making water available to farmers after a drought. It is desperately welcome, yet, at the same time, the need to provide equality of opportunity to the poor literally forces a "quick" usage of money.

The educator has responded to the government's mandates for faster educational change but that is much of the current problem—he has *responded,* not led. He has acted *after* rather than before the fact.

As in the past, the educator has been forced to *reflect* the wants of society. Education has always reflected the wants of society. Education has always reflected the existing social order, and has consequently lagged far behind that social order. Yet, what society thinks it wants may not be what it needs, and schools should be granted sufficient scope to *alter* society itself. The situation is now quite different from what it has been; now the educator is being asked to lead in terms of society's *needs,* not its wants. Society now *expects* education to assume a much more critical leadership role in the decades to come.

This places the educator at a crossroads. While the old road made him the follower, the new road calls for leadership. The old road rendered the educator impotent—he has witnessed inequality of opportunity, he has witnessed the decay of urban schools, and he has watched a system of education develop which promotes a caste system. His inability to act when confronted with these and other issues has been seen by some as a default in leadership. Yet, as Kenneth Clark points out:

> Such a default in leadership by professional educators can only reduce their total influence in the community at large. . . . Yet in matters of health, the medical profession submits to the fears and anxieties of the uninformed or to the pressures of vested interests. Can educational leadership

> consider the educational health of a community to be less important? . . . If educators respond merely to pressure, whether it is *against* integration, like the Parents and Taxpayers groups, or *for* it, as in the case of the civil rights boycotts, they have abdicated their right to decision on the basis of their knowledge and insight as educators. . . . This is a passive rather than a dynamic, socially responsible role. . . . It is the responsibility of strong leadership to represent the common good—not only because it is right, but because the despair of the weak in the end threatens the stability of the whole.[2]

If the educator is to fulfill his new role of leadership he must develop a new orientation. This may mean giving up the comforts of a familiar system; it may mean giving up certain vested interests. But, even if he is willing to go this far, in what *direction* shall he lead society?

The challenge of diversity

In whatever direction the new educational system may go, it must be founded on the existing facts insofar as they may be acertained. A most important fact to be considered is that this is a nation built from a variety of cultures; it is, historically and currently, a culturally diverse nation. Historically speaking, it is a land composed first of a variety of culturally different American Indian tribes which even today are not culturally integrated into modern American life. It is a land composed of the various and culturally different European settlers who, loosely speaking, established the cultural basis of the nation, such as it exists today. It is a land of African Negroes who were imported as slaves by these settlers and who not only brought with them their African culture, but also developed their own distinct cultural system in the midst of the European culture. It is a land populated by those who came in the later immigration waves and their descendants: The Chinese, the Japanese, the

[2]K. B. Clark, *Dark Ghetto,* New York, Harper & Row, 1965, p. 152.

Germans, Swedes, Italians, Irish, the European Jews, the Puerto Ricans. Each of these diverse cultural groups and their descendants bring to bear on the nation their own ways of doing things and, more importantly, their own ways of looking at things. Each group's frame of reference allows the members to understand some things more readily than others, and to be confounded entirely by still others. In short, America, the "Melting Pot," is a land of cultural diversity.

Another extremely important fact for the new educational process to consider is that this is a land of *individual* diversity. Every person is a distinct and unique individual with different potentials, interests, talents, and aptitudes. This is, of course, true in any nation or in any human group, but it is a far more relevant factor in this culturally diverse country than perhaps anywhere else, for the diversity of cultural influences and the cross pollination that come to bear on the shaping of each individual merely accentuate the differences that are innate to each person. Significantly, the historical evolution of this nation has always placed emphasis on this individualism, and even today, in the midst of salient mass conformity, we pay animated lip service to the virtues of the "rugged individual."

MEETING THE FACTS OF DIVERSITY

It must be fairly clear at this point that one basic objective of the new educational system is necessarily to accommodate the cultural and individual diversity that exists in the population, and to do so realistically. The classroom, the school, and the educational system as a whole must be so oriented as to permit of a wide array of instructional approaches, and of sufficient flexibility in these approaches, that individual differences in developed abilities and developable potentials can be met. This of course means that individual and cultural differences must first be assessed realistically. By way of an obvious illustration, if in a given classroom 60 percent of the children speak English and 40 percent do not, it would be quite unrealistic to assume that the 40 percent do or will eventually understand English under present practices. However, it is possible to have all the children taught in two languages, thereby having both groups profit. Such a bilingual program is being implemented in a Miami, Florida school.

The first cry may be, "That is impossible!"; yet, far from impossible, the kind of flexible and efficient process that such an accommodation would require would actually serve to meet a host of individual needs other than those based on mere linguistic differences. Indeed, the new educational system must be geared to meeting diversity in far more areas than language.

To teach pupils from rural Appalachia to read with books and materials based on affluent and white suburbia is tantamount to teaching our mainstream pupils elementary social-studies concepts in fluent French; to teach science concepts to pupils in city slums in the same way they would be taught to middle-class children who have been accustomed to expensive scientific toys is just as futile; and to expect children raised in a highly idiomatic and slang-ridden vernacular to adjust immediately to articulated formal English is to expect them to understand Greek without any prior experience with Greek. And finally, to teach all pupils as though they had identical frames of reference is to exclude from the educational process all those who do not have the assumed frame of reference. The school in modern society must deal effectively with *existing* diversity.

DEVELOPING DIVERSITY

If meeting the realities of a diverse population is a fundamental necessity in view of the facts, capitalizing on diversity and deliberately encouraging it is another highly desirable objective of educational organization. As Keniston puts it in *The Uncommitted,* "Human diversity and variety must not only be tolerated, but rejoiced in, applauded and encouraged."[3] The ideals of democracy, private enterprise, individual success and achieve-

[3]K. Keniston, *The Uncommited,* New York, Harcourt, Brace & World, 1965, p. 443.

ment, the right to own property, the right to privacy, and individual freedom are all based on an individualistic philosophy; more important, they cannot prevail without individualism. And individualism cannot endure without diversity.

To cultivate an individual person's uniqueness, to encourage him to be himself and the best self that he can be, is to cultivate diversity in the population at large. Conversely, to insist that an individual person learn this particular fact, in this particular fashion, and according to this particular way of seeing things is to encourage him to be like all the others on whom these precepts are successfully imposed. Further:

> . . . Social diversity has a double connection to individual fulfillment: not only is a diverse society a precondition for human wholeness, it is its consequence—the kind of society whole men and women choose to live in. Those who are inwardly torn, unsure of their psychic coherence and fearful of inner fragmentation, are naturally distrustful of all that is alien and strange. Those whose sense of inner unity is tenuous are easily threatened by others who remind them of that part of themselves they seek to suppress. Our "one-hundred-percent Americans" are those whose own Americanism is felt to be most tenuous; the bigoted and the prejudiced cannot live with the full gamut of their own feelings. And conversely, those who can still sense their shared humanity with others of different or opposite talents and commitments are those who are sure of their own intactness. The goals of human fulfillment and social diversity require each other.[4]

There is yet another virtue to diversity in the population: We know that survival depends on the ability to adapt successfully to a changing environment; this is as true for an organization of organisms as it is for an individual organism. In the human world, the environment includes ideas; as new ideas and new knowledge become part of the environment, old ones become obsolescent or at least require reevaluation for their relevance and validity in the changing human environment. Conformity in

[4] *Ibid.*

a society, however, produces a sameness and rigidity which resists adaptation to a changing environment. Rigidity of attitudes and customs soon leads to stagnation and decay, and to the disintegration of the society. By contrast, diversity encourages adaptation, and cross-cultural pollination among the members of a human society maintains that society in strong and flexible condition to meet new circumstances as they arise. New and original ideas will always be mandatory to the survival of a nation in a changing human environment, and they cannot come from a society in which mass conformity has been highly developed.

Significantly, and perhaps fortunately for us, the recent educational failures with the various disadvantaged segments of our society have been an integral part of our ever-changing human environment. Because of these failures, we have begun to recognize the unique frames of reference that exist among our diversified population, frames of reference in which lie the potential for new ideas which will revitalize the society itself. As Riessman states:

> . . . my concern for building on the strengths of the disadvantaged child is not simply so that he can be more efficiently brought into the mainstream of American life; rather I want also to have him bring into this mainstream some of his characteristics: his style, his pep, his vitality, his demand that the school not be boring and dull, his rich feeling for metaphor and colorful language. . . . the Negro people, have made an enormous contribution to the mainstream of American life through their articulate non-compromising demands for integration "now." These people have brought a new morality to American life as a whole. To the extent that we are beginning to move toward integration through law and practice, we are beginning to hold our heads up high and feel again like democratic, ethical, human Americans. This is what one minority disadvantaged group has given us. . . . In education, . . . the mainstream of American life can profit from what the various groups among the poor can bring to the school system both in terms of the demands made upon the system that it be peppier, livelier, more vital, more down-to-earth, more real and in the style

> and interests brought to the school. This style will enable the school to become far less bookish and will enable it to utilize a great variety of styles—an action style, a physical style, a visual style—far more than the over-utilized and over-emphasized reading-lecture styles traditionally in vogue.[5]

Thus, diversity as an objective of the new educational system may be viewed from two perspectives. On the one hand, cultural and individual differences are an *existing fact* in our society, and if our educational system is to provide for the entire society which supports it, it must be prepared to deal with this fact. This means that the educational system must be flexible and adaptable enough to serve realistically a wide range of needs, individual and cultural. On the other hand, the *cultivation* of diversity in our society through the encouragement of individual uniqueness not only acts as a safeguard of our political integrity as a democratic nation, but also leads to human fulfillment, the consequences of which are numerous, but which can be summed up as both personal and societal health. Cultural and individual differences should stand as basic attributes of the products turned out at the end of the educational process. This is perhaps a more difficult objective in a mass-production society where even our educational products are mass produced; nevertheless, a carefully organized, highly coordinated new educational process which is flexible enough to meet the facts of existing diversity should have little difficulty in achieving this aim as well.

Toward a career-oriented educational process

One way of dealing with the diversity that exists in our society is paradoxically to identify what the diverse cultures and individuals have in *common*; that is, the cultivation of diversity does not imply that the schools have different purposes for different groups.

All cultures require economic sustenance in their environ-

[5]F. Riessman, "It's Time for a Moon-Shot in Education," presented at conference on "Training the Non-Professional," sponsored by Scientific Resources Incorporated, March 15–16, 1967, Washington, D.C., p. 6.

ment, for example, and this means that their constituent members must have the abilities necessary to fill the labor demands extant in the society. All individuals require, in addition to economic sustenance, the fulfillment of themselves through productive activities which are meaningful to themselves and to others in their group. To achieve this fulfillment, individuals must not only have developed skills and abilities, but these skills and abilities must emerge from a genuine interest and ability *intrinsic* to each *unique* individual. Thus, one goal of the educational system is to fulfill simultaneously the vocational needs of each individual and the labor needs of the society as a whole, without violating the cultural integrity of the societal subgroup. Toward this end, the new educational system must be geared to encouraging a *work career* among all of its pupils, yet be flexible enough to accommodate the wide variety of work careers implied by a diverse population in a society with diverse labor needs.

Another need common to all cultures is to produce and to raise children who will perpetuate the culture within the environment without violating its integrity or that of a larger society on which it may depend. Individuals need to produce and to raise children who are whole, fulfilled individuals in their own right and who can contribute to the society's growth and healthy continuance. For this difficult *parental career*, individuals need emotional and intellectual preparation. It should be the school's goal to educate its pupils for this parental career, and in such a way that individual, cultural, and the larger societal needs are met.

This leads to a broader and more encompassing need common to all individuals and cultures, and to the society as a whole: the need for, or to be, fully participating citizens of the community. As already mentioned, if the United States is to maintain its integrity as a nation among nations, it must rely on the constructive contributions of a diverse population. While a diverse citizenry also implies *conflicting* points of view, it is the *harmonious* interaction of these very opposing ideas which will maintain the nation's vitality. It is out of this harmonious interaction of opposing views that higher, broader, and more workable ideas are synthesized. Thus, it is the school's responsibility to devote its efforts toward providing all of its products with a viable *citizen career.*

In order to meet this need for a citizen career, as well as those for work or parental careers, the educational system must orient itself toward preparing all of its pupils for a career *in self-development.* A vital nation is built from vital institutions, organizations, and other societal subgroups; and these are, in turn, built from vital individuals. Yet, a vital individual does not exist solely and primarily for the society, but, rather, for *himself,* and only if his personal and individual needs are met to the fullest satisfaction of his organic, emotional and intellectual health, is he likely to be oriented positively toward his larger community. But one of the primary needs of the individual is to *participate* in the fulfillment of his *own* needs, and to be fully active in his own adaptation to his changing environment. Therefore, the school must aid its pupils in the art of self-fulfillment and self-development, so that each individual can assume more and more of the responsibilities for the satisfaction of his physical, emotional, and intellectual needs. The educational product who can do so will automatically contribute constructively to the larger society.

These four career orientations—a work career, a parental career, a citizen career, and a career in self-development—represent the essential needs common to every individual in every culture and subculture, and to the societal totality of a diverse population. Unless it be the school, there exists no social institution which can fulfill each and all of these individual and societal needs at once; yet, without such an institution to develop these career orientations, individuals will not be able to function integrally for the mutual benefit of themselves and society. In rising to the challenge of diversity, then, the school must keep these four common needs firmly in mind.

THE WORK CAREER

Every culture produces its wide range of individual talents which potentially will meet its own wide range of needs; that is, each culture will produce its doctors, its artists, its craftsmen, it food producers, and so on. The difficulty which has existed in our culturally diverse society is that, through the deprivation imposed upon certain subcultures by our mainstream educational process, too many cultural minority groups have had to rely on mainstream doctors, lawyers, scientists, artists, and the like, while they supply in unbalanced proportion the skilled and unskilled labor force. This is because the educational system—in assuming an innately low intellectual ability for these people *en masse*—has met the need for career development among these constituents of the population by instituting nonacademic vocational schools which emphasize training in the manual arts at the expense of the liberal arts. Vocational education has substituted sheer job-skill training for genuine career development.

There is a vast difference between these two orientations: One implies a mere technical mastery of a specific task, while the other implies a broad set of attitudes and skills required to comprehend the role of employment in a highly industrialized and technological society, and an understanding of the changing world of work. As Marvin Feldman of the Ford Foundation explains:

> . . . there is little place for vocational education divorced from general education or liberal education; liberal education is *not* an education if it does *not* help the individual understand the role of occupations and careers and does *not* stimulate the individual to find *his* talents to develop his competence so that *he* can make a contribution in our work force.[6]

Moreover, in processing all elementary-school children as though they had the same cultural and individual backgrounds, interests, and potentialities, the unique creativity of those children who lie outside of this frame of reference goes undeveloped. By the time these children reach the age where work careers begin to take on some personal meaning, they are not equipped

[6]M. J. Feldman, "Remarks to the Comprehensive School Improvement Conference," sponsored by The Ford Foundation, Fort Lauderdale, Fla., January 6, 1966, p. 6.

with a true understanding of the wide expanse of choices available to them, or with the attitudes and skills necessary to make a truly meaningful choice. Children from city slums may select from among such careers as plumbing, electrical repair and maintenance, auto mechanics, and the like, rather than from such as architectural planning, engineering, and technical design.

On the other hand, although the middle-class-oriented school has overlooked it, the mainstream culture produces its share of truly talented plumbers and auto mechanics along with its brilliant engineers and scientists. Yet to the middle- or upper-class child, only a long academic experience with the liberal arts, followed by specialized training in the theory and practice of the chosen profession, are available. If he can't succeed in this direction, he is considered an individual failure; any feelings of personal fulfillment and satisfaction such an individual might achieve from some intellectually less ambitious career is overlooked, viewed with suspicion, or even negated by his own culture. Worse, if sufficient numbers of mainstream educational products fail to fulfill the high academic standards required of higher educational courses, the academic standards are all too likely to be lowered insidiously, so that the level of *top* skills and abilities in the society—including those required in the planning and teaching of top-level university courses—is likely to become more and more mediocre.

In other words, the basic aptitudes required to be an assembly worker, a plumber or electrician, a secretary or clerical worker, a merchant, a physician or psychiatrist, a teacher, or a social worker are not *naturally* centered more densely in one culture or socioemonomic level than another, as the present division of labor would indicate, but rather cut across all socioeconomic groups. It is the school's responsibility both to the individual and to society as a whole to tap the true potential that lies hidden in the nation, and to do so in the earliest grades, as well as in the secondary schools, colleges, and universities.

The inclusion of employment orientation in the curriculum at *all* levels in the educational process would give the learner a continuously reinforcing exposure to, and increasingly elaborate development in, the realities of the world of work, including the broader and more relevant economic significance of this world of employment. As Dewey stated:

> The continually increasing importance of economic factors in contemporary life makes it the more needed that education should reveal their scientific content and their social value. For in schools, occupations are not carried on for pecuniary gain but for their own content. Freed from extraneous associations and from the pressure of wage-earning, they supply modes of experience which are intrinsically valuable; they are truly liberalizing in quality.[7]

While this orientation in economics as an integral part of the preparation for a work career implies a stress on cognitive learning, it should be noted that vocational education cannot take place without due emphasis on physical reality and concrete experience with this physical reality. Firsthand experience is central to the vocational-education sequence—nay, to all education—and must be provided integrally with intellectual learning. Children are vigorously industrious by nature; beginning perhaps with mud pies, they are continuously "making things," and enjoying the very activity of this. For some reason, by the time they are ready to join the world of work, any connection between the sheer enjoyment of *doing* and the earning of a livable wage has been lost, to say nothing of the value to others in the social setting of the *products* of doing. The school has failed to capitalize on the natural industriousness of children as a vehicle for introducing economic and employment concepts.

To capitalize fully on the "learning by doing" idea, the school would provide its children with the necessary connections between doing, contributing, and earning—and truly enjoying the entire process—and, at the same time, would be providing the necessary cognitive, attitudinal, and skill learning required for any finally chosen work career. As Dewey put it many years ago:

> The problem of the educator is to engage pupils in these activities in such ways that while manual skill and technical

[7]J. Dewey, *Democracy and Education*, New York, Macmillan, 1961, p. 200.

> efficiency are gained and immediate satisfaction found in the work, together with preparation for later usefulness, these things shall be subordinated to *education*—that is, to intellectual results and the forming of a socialized disposition.[8]

In other words, in the process of firsthand interaction with physical reality, the learner would acquire the necessary cognitive information about the concepts, tools, and materials which will be involved in his specific work, and the mechanical skills necessary for implementing these concepts, tools, and materials. He would also begin to develop a conceptual understanding of the self-social-economic context in which his activities play so important a role.

THE PARENT CAREER

As evidence is compiled in the behavioral sciences, it becomes increasingly clear that the parent has the critical role in child growth and development, and that this role has its most crucial influence before the child reaches school age. We now know that mental illness, neurosis, and a good deal of psychosis can usually be traced to early family influences. But, as important as this parental role is in developing our future citizens, where does one learn to be an effective parent? Where does one learn all the intellectual understanding of the intricacies of child development and parenthood, and—more important by far—the emotional requisites for parenthood?

The answer is simple: The basic emotional requisites for parenthood are provided by the individual's own parents' emotional influence upon him early in his own life; they are further developed by the behavioral models for parenthood his parents provide in rearing him, and, as such models, they begin to shape the child's implicit *cognitive* understanding of child rearing also. As the growing child becomes aware of the parents of his peers, his understanding of parent behavior is further shaped—as far as it goes. By the time he reaches high school, he has received

[8] *Ibid.*, pp. 196–197.

no formal guidance in his explicit understanding of parenthood—his own future role or that of his own parents in dealing with him; yet the role he will some day play has already largely been determined. In high school, he will perhaps attend a course in personal hygiene, in which he will learn some of the biological mechanics of conception, gestation, and birth, and the sociological and social consequences of premarital relations. In a family planning or similar course, he may learn some of the mechanics of formula preparation, bottle warming, diapering, and how to recognize the symptoms of typical physiological disorders common among infants. He is told that a baby needs "love," but nowhere throughout his school career is he told *what* love *is*, nor is he helped to develop in himself the *ability* to love. If he goes on to college courses in psychology, he is somewhat better prepared for parenthood *intellectually*, but it is not likely that this academic learning will have much effect on his *emotional* adequacy for parenthood.

Consequently, the individual who finds himself faced with the many complex responsibilities of parenthood must make do as best he can with such potluck preparation as he has acquired during his life. If he has been physically hurt in the name of parental "love," he may express his own understanding of love in the same fashion upon his child; if he has been punished unfairly, he may not question the fairness of punishing his own child on any given occasion; if unreasonable demands were made upon him, he may assume that all such demands he makes on his own child are reasonable; and so forth. Clearly, the much-cherished word *love* can become the justification for a parent to release upon his undeserving child a great deal of unrecognized hostility that may be pent up in the parent as a result of his own inadequate upbringing. The result: another unprepared parent when this child matures.

It becomes increasingly obvious that if we are to survive as a healthy nation of healthy individuals, we can no longer leave to chance the development of parental skills and abilities; yet the conventional education process is not equipped to deal with this aspect of education. As indicated earlier, the conventional process is geared to the very specific goal of intellectual mastery of subject matter in a narrowly defined curriculum. To append to this conventional process more intellectually oriented courses in parenthood for high-school pupils is useless, and only makes an already highly ineffective and unwieldy educational system more ineffective and unwieldy. Instead, the basic educational system must be revised to integrate the emotional and intellectual education of future parents from the *outset* of the educational process. Beginning, perhaps, in preschool classes—where play-oriented activities are an ideal context for beginning education in parenthood—through the middle and upper grades—where older children can help with younger pupils—to junior and senior high-school classes in the biological, emotional, and social realities of marriage, childbirth, and child development, the school can do much toward building a population of good parents. But, throughout this sequence, instruction and guidance must be consistent and geared to the individual realities of each pupil.

THE CITIZEN CAREER

In a society predicated upon rule by the people, the role of citizen is of utmost importance. We pride ourselves in the fact that our leaders, including our highest government officials, come from the ranks of ordinary citizens. If financial means are important to election *campaigns*, an individual's personal wealth or lack of it is no obstacle to *winning* in an election. We have had in our Presidency a Roman Catholic, a Midwestern small-town haberdasher, and a military general. Even Negroes have taken a few seats in Congress and other governmental positions of prestige. And we, the people, put our ordinary fellow citizens in these posts.

These citizens—the elected and the voters—are processed by our educational system. How well are they prepared to lead the country if elected? How well are they prepared to assess the candidates up for election? Do these citizens truly understand the issues at stake? Are they fully equipped to *think out for themselves* the consequences of this or that political measure? Do they act only in their own best interests and for those who happen to agree with them, or have they carefully considered opposing views in the interests of the larger society?

Throughout their formal education, our citizens have been indocrinated with the names, places, and dates important to history, and with the standard textbook interpretations of these facts. They "cover the curriculum" as set by the conventional process until they leave the process, at whatever level that may be. But have they been taught to think creatively and for themselves, or do they rather adopt the "thinking" of their own ingroup?

The conventional educational process has always officially accepted the goal of producing critically thinking citizens, but, in assuming that a learner who has mastered academic content—and who, through a process of "studying about," has covered the required subject matter—would be a critical thinker, it has fallen far short of this goal. Serious questions can be raised concerning the true thinking ability among our mass-educated citizenry, especially when one considers the low percentage of eligible citizens who actually vote; and, among those who do vote, how few seem to understand the full implications of their choices. Yet even if citizens were fully capable of thinking out these choices, mere thought is not sufficient in today's world; thought must be translated into action.

In accepting the intellectual assimilation of facts as the criterion for good citizenship, the school does little to prepare its products for social action. In addition, the narrowly circumscribed social-studies curriculum in the early grades, as well as the limited course availabilities at the secondary-school level, are highly inadequate to understanding the many intellectual and behavioral principles underlying good citizenship. The Civil-Rights protest and other mass demonstrations—particularly on our college and high-school campuses—are testimony to the need young people have to participate, and to learn *how* to participate, in the adult world. More and more students are finding the traditional school curriculum irrelevant to the outstanding social issues of the day. Real citizenship training must recognize the need young people have for acquiring the skills which will enable them to influence constructively our social institutions so that these institutions can confront public issues more effectively.

Here again, it is not a question of appending more subject matter to an outmoded system; it is rather a question of reorganizing the educational process to accommodate training in citizenship integrally with training for a work career and for parenthood. The teaching of skills needed for constructive social action must begin with the preschool and continue throughout the educational process. These skills, in essence, follow a similar procedure to the scientific method:

1. The ability to define clearly the objectives of social action
2. The ability to evaluate the existing situation, to identify obstacles to the goal, and to identify the available resources for overcoming these obstacles
3. The ability to analyze and to generate alternative measures for action, and to predict the various outcomes of each alternative
4. The ability to select the most valuable of these alternatives and to test them through social action
5. The ability to evaluate the tested procedure and to revise plans, thus beginning the cycle again

To develop these abilities, the preschool class might well be thought of as a political entity, and, as the grades progress, the children would be allowed more and more to participate in decisionmaking and activity projects which are related to real issues in their lives. All of this would take place under the guidance rather than the strict rule of the teacher, who should provide the behavioral model for democratic social action. The activity projects would take the emphasis off using reading, writing, and listening activities as ends in themselves, and these traditional school activities would become subordinate tools through which students may learn to deal more effectively with real issues.

A CAREER IN SELF-DEVELOPMENT

The basic questions faced by every individual are, Who am I? Where am I going? How do I get there? What role will I play, and how will it be received by others? The answers provided by the conventional educational system are "You are white (or should be), clean and neat and good (or should be); you speak very good English (or should). If you are not these things—oh well, we'll do the best we can until, poor deprived creature, you finally drop out." And, "You are going to grow up to be gainfully employed and have a nice house in the suburbs with a washing machine and the rest; be a good voting citizen, a loyal husband or wife, and a loving parent—but *only* if you learn what *we* tell you to learn, the way we want you to learn it. If you don't; oh well, you can't say we didn't try." The result for the lower socio-economic groups and for the dropouts is a lack of the intellectual and emotional skills necessary to further self-development, and frequently a blatant disrespect for the books and extension courses available to the private individual.

The orientation, attitudes, concepts, and skills required to enable the individual to continue his own development after he has left the formal educational system can be initiated early in his formal training. A good part of self-development lies in the development of self-awareness and understanding, which leads to a heightened awareness and empathetic understanding of others. For this, significant emphasis on the effective domain needs to be integrated into the curriculum.

During the past 50 years or so, great gains have been made in the behavioral sciences in understanding personality and emotional behavior. While courses imparting this information do exist at the college level, we have yet to institute this subject matter in the primary and secondary schools. In ever-increasing numbers, books are published on these subjects, aimed at the general reading market, and psychological counseling and therapy is in increasing demand. Why cannot this content be made available to all learners at an early enough age to have its fullest beneficial effects? If human potential is truly to be cultivated, many of the tools and content areas of the behavioral sciences must find their way into the school as an agency for human development. New content areas in what Huxley called the "non-verbal humanities" need to be developed and taught in a concrete, experiential, and personally meaningful way. The curriculum at the Esalen Institute at Big Sur, California, is suggestive of content areas: "Emotional Expression," "Sensory Training," "Inner Imagery," "Visual Process Training," "Sound Exploration," "Expressive Physical Movement," "Creativity Training," "Encounter Groups," "Meditation," and "Two-person Encounter" are some of the courses given.

Surely this sort of subject matter is likely to meet more *universal* human needs than say, science, higher math, literature and poetry, art, industrial-arts courses, and foreign languages; yet the first eight years of a child's formal education is spent in indoctrinating him *beyond* his basic needs in these areas. Where genuine interest and talent in science, math, literature, and art evidences itself, the emphasis on these subjects is certainly merited. But not all children have the same talents and interests, and—while every child should be literate, articulate, and able to compute mathematically in practical everyday situations—it hardly seems necessary to expose *all* children to an *equal* amount of instruction in all of these areas.

In meeting the challenge of diversity, the school should consider arranging units so that basic instruction and practice in reading, writing, and mathematics is provided as only a part of the current instruction in other subjects, thus freeing a part of the school day for a curriculum in emotional development. For example, common personal concerns of the pupils can become a part of the school subject matter. A series of units which provide the children with skills for assessing the criteria by which they judge themselves and others in their environment should be a natural part of the school's total program. In other words, the school should provide normal opportunities by which children can learn all the steps involved in finding out who they are.

In preparing pupils for a career in self-development, as well as for the three other careers, the school would do much to make the educational process congruent with its stated aims. Yet many educators, already overburdened with a rapidly proliferating academic curriculum, may object to the addition of these new responsibilities. It should be pointed out in this regard that, as curriculum objectives, these four careers offer a more workable framework for integrating instructional programing than does the presently fragmented approach to content learning. In other words, by restructuring the academic curriculum to meet these four objectives, a far more efficient educational process can result.

The three-part school program

Clearly, if it is to meet its new challenge, education must consider such a self-restructuring, and it must encourage its schools to assume a new pattern of relating both to pupils and to learning generally. This new pattern need not replace or discard traditional subject-matter objectives, but rather, include them as important tools toward achieving these four career orientations among the pupils. The relationship of intellectual skills and concepts traditionally imparted by the school to the skills and concepts in the affective and behavioral realms may be clarified if one visualizes a school with three curriculum arenas, each of which occupies its own portion of the normal school day.

The first of these arenas would encompass typically academic content. The reading, writing, and mathematical skills, as well as the factual and conceptual information required for pupils to acquire a basic understanding of the world, would be imparted for one part of the school day. The basis of the skills of "learning to learn," of convergent and divergent thinking and problem solving, and similar process skills would also be established in this arena. These learning outcomes would be acquired primarily through self-instruction on the part of the learners, and most of the current availabilities in individualized instruction—programed learning, learning laboratories, multimedia kits, and other devices—would be utilized during this portion of each day.

The second arena, or curricular mode, would focus upon the individual talents, interests, and innate abilities of the learners. For example, if a child showed a particular interest or ability in music, this arena would provide the opportunities for him to expand his musical talents and skills. A certain portion of the school day would thus be devoted to helping children to explore and to discover their *own* interests and talents, and then to developing these personal potentials.

During these periods, children would be offered a wide range of activities—for example, creative writing, art, dramatics, film-making, science project laboratories, etc.—and each child would be free to choose the activity he most wanted to attend. During the activity period, the child would be assisted by a counselor to recognize his responses to his experiences, and to evaluate his satisfaction or dissatisfaction with the experiences. In no case would these activities be highly prestructured, but rather, the structure and direction of a child's specific project would emerge from the child himself, with the counselor acting as catalyst. For example, a child who is personally interested in science would be encouraged to pursue any experiment of his own invention, or to work on a research project of his own design. Similarly, a child who enjoys writing would be encouraged to write—in his own words—a story, poem, or play around a theme of his own choosing. Thus, the content of learning in this curricular arena would be drawn from the child himself, rather than fed from the school to the child as would occur in the first curricular arena.

While the first and second arenas concentrate on the individual pupil, the third would center on group interaction, participation, and inquiry. Two main curricular objectives would be emphasized during this part of the school day:

1. An awareness, understanding, and ability to deal effectively with common personal concerns (needs for power, social connectedness, and self-identity) would be developed among the pupils.

2. An awareness, understanding, and ability to act upon contemporary societal issues (e.g., those concerned with citizenship) would be developed among the pupils.

This third arena would attempt to develop each pupil's intra- and interpersonal relationships; that is, his relationships with himself and with others in his social environment. During this part of the school day, each child would learn to identify, articulate, and evaluate his feelings, concerns, and opinions, and to compare and contrast these with the feelings, concerns, and opinions of others in his group. In other words, this curricular arena would be devoted to activities through which an *affective* curriculum can be pursued.

With greater self-understanding and awareness, a greater sense of connectedness with others is established, and this connectedness finds expression through constructive participation in relevant social issues, thus contributing to the pupils' sense of worth and power. This third arena would provide each child with the skills necessary for his own self-development career, as well as for his career as a citizen.

While each of these curricular arenas would provide necessary learning outcomes for all four careers, each arena would focus on a particular *set* of skills, attitudes, and information. In other words, each arena would not stand alone as an isolated entity, but would overlap and interlock with each of the others. For example, in order to complete a given project in the third arena, the pupils may need certain skills or information which can be acquired from the first arena; or, the project may lead to a related and parallel project—for example, the creation and presentation of a play on the subject—to be engaged in within the second curricular arena. Thus, without the resources provided in each of the other arenas, any one arena becomes too narrowly focused to accomplish all educational objectives. As Bruce Joyce explains:

> Each of these curricular modes can be adapted to perform unique and important functions in elementary education.

> Blended, they can offer a common general education, the development of personal talent, and the humanizing effects of cooperative inquiry into critical issues.[9]

A school program so arranged would be geared to meeting the common needs of all children without sacrificing individuality or cultural diversity. Moreover, it would foster the kind of meaningful mental framework that is conducive to the learning of academic subject matter and, because this learning would be personally meaningful to the pupils, the ability to transfer ideas and principles acquired in one context to another context would be engendered in the school's products. In other words, by dividing the school schedule into such segments as these three, rather than according to subject-matter disciplines; and by orienting all instruction toward preparation for these four universal careers, rather than toward subject-matter learning *per se*, the educational process would be significantly more efficient in accomplishing its long-expressed aims. Indeed, only through such reorganization and reorientation can educators hope to meet America's need for the human resources which will revitalize and perpetuate the country as a healthy and self-renewing nation.

This time of national crisis is a time for new leadership, and a time when needed and effective changes in our social institutions have the best chances of being implemented and sustained. The crisis of the disadvantaged has provided educators with a unique and epoch-making opportunity for effecting true and penetrating reform; what will they do with this opportunity? Will they use it to perpetuate the unwieldy, ineffective, and deteriorating status quo? Will they adopt a policy of "wait and see," reacting only *after* the fact to societal demands? Or will they seize this opportunity to assume the roles of initiators, revising education to become the instrument of societal reconstruction and renewal, of individual and societal health, and of human progress?

This is the challenge of the disadvantaged to education.

[9]B. R. Joyce, "Restructuring Elementary Education: A Multiple Learnings Systems Approach," New York, Teachers College, Columbia University, 1966, p. 4.

INDEX

68 69 70 7 6 5 4 3 2